GAMING THE STAGE

THEATER: THEORY/TEXT/PERFORMANCE
Series Editors: David Krasner, Rebecca Schneider, and Harvey Young
Founding Editor: Enoch Brater

Recent Titles:

Gaming the Stage

PLAYABLE MEDIA AND THE RISE OF ENGLISH COMMERCIAL THEATER

Gina Bloom

UNIVERSITY OF MICHIGAN PRESS

Ann Arbor

Published in the United States of America by the
University of Michigan Press
Manufactured in the United States of America
Printed on acid-free paper

A CIP catalog record for this book is available from the British Library.

Library of Congress Cataloging-in-Publication data has been applied for.

ISBN 978-0-472-07381-8 (hardcover : alk. paper)
ISBN 978-0-472-05381-0 (paper: alk. paper)
ISBN 978-0-472-12391-9 (e-book)
ISBN 978-0-472-90108-1 (Open Access ebook edition)
http://dx.doi.org//10.3998/mpub.9831118

Digital materials related to this title can be found on
www.fulcrum.org at doi.org/10.3998/mpub.9831118

For Max

Contents

Illustrations following page 22

Acknowledgments

In game development and in the theater, collaboration is invaluable. Nothing gets made without a team. That is true of this book as well. Although it has my name on the cover, it is the product of many minds, hands, and hearts. I am pleased to share the credit with those who have worked and played alongside me as this book came to fruition.

This project in its current form began at the University of California, Davis, where I have been lucky to find incredible colleagues in both early modern studies and game studies. Fran Dolan has been an especially attentive mentor and friend, supporting my scholarship and my career in too many ways to count. I am indebted to her and to Margie Ferguson for their feedback on earlier versions of many of my chapters, as well as to other writing group members over the years: Seeta Chaganti, Stephanie Elsky, Ari Friedlander, Noah Guynn, and Claire Waters. My thanks also to Molly McCarthy, whose feedback on grant proposals also pushed the project in useful directions, and to Lee Emrich, who provided superb editorial assistance on several article versions of my chapters. Sarah McCullough organized an early writing group on games, where I received excellent feedback from her, Joe Dumit, Susan Kaiser, and Colin Milburn. Colin has been a vital interlocutor for me throughout the book's development, and I cannot thank him enough for helping me articulate my contribution to game and media studies and for generously reading the entire manuscript to offer feedback at crucial junctures. Many of my ideas about games were shaped by my engagement with the ModLab Colin founded and particularly through conversations with Stephanie Boluk, Patrick LeMieux, Tim Lenoir, Michael Neff, and Amanda Phillips; graduate students Evan Lauteria, Joseph Nguyen, and Emma Waldron; and dozens of undergraduate interns who work on *Play the Knave*. I would highlight especially my fruitful collaboration with graduate students Evan Buswell and Nick Toothman, the architects of *Play the Knave*, and Sawyer Kemp, whose observations about vicarious spectatorship at installations of the game helped me figure out how to situate *Play the Knave* in relation to my book's larger argument about gaming and spectatorship. The influence of this collaboration is most evident in my book's Epilogue, which draws on the article the four of us cowrote, "'A Whole Theatre of Others': Amateur Acting and Immersive Spectatorship in the Digital Shakespeare Game *Play the Knave*." *Shakespeare Quarterly*, special issue on "#Bard," ed. Douglas Lanier, 67.4 (2016): 408–30.

Portions of several of my other chapters appeared as articles, and although these sections have been significantly reframed for the book, the editors who worked with me on those publications shaped my larger arguments and methods. Valerie Traub has been a constant source of guidance and friendship for over twenty years and remains one of my most trusted readers. Part of Chapter 4 was published as "Time to Cheat: Chess and *The Tempest*'s Performative History of Dynastic Marriage" in her edited collection, *The Oxford Handbook of Shakespeare and Embodiment: Gender, Sexuality, Race* (Oxford: Oxford University Press, 2016). Henry Turner, a wonderful editor and friend, worked with me on "Games," an essay that incorporates parts of my Introduction and short sections from Chapters 2 and 3; it was published in his collection *Early Modern Theatricality* (Oxford University Press, 2013). A larger section of Chapter 3 was published as "'My Feet See Better Than My Eyes': Spatial Mastery and the Game of Masculinity in *Arden of Faversham*'s Amphitheatre" in *Theatre Survey* 53.1 (2012): 5–28, where it benefited from the feedback of Catherine Cole, Leo Cabranes-Grant, and anonymous readers. My thanks to Oxford and Cambridge University Presses for permission to reprint sections of these essays.

In order to write a book as interdisciplinary as this one, I relied on feedback from scholars at diverse venues. I am thankful for invitations to present versions of my chapters at the Technology and Society Lecture Series at the Tandon School of Engineering, New York University; the "Theatricality" conference at Rutgers; the Columbia Shakespeare Seminar at Columbia University; the Medieval-Renaissance Workshop at the University of Pennsylvania; the Medieval and Early Modern Studies Institute at George Washington University; the "Attending to Early Modern Women" conference; and the "Phenomenal Performances: Getting a Feeling for Shakespeare's Theater" conference at Northwestern University. I also benefited greatly from feedback offered by fellow participants in various working groups at the American Society for Theatre Research and audiences who attended my talks at conferences organized by Performance Studies International, the Modern Language Association, and the Renaissance Society of America. Many of the chapters in this book began as seminar papers for the Shakespeare Association of America, which consistently has provided a home for my scholarship, no matter where I choose to range. Of the many individuals not yet cited above who engaged with my work at these venues—with tough questions, useful suggestions, and supportive words—I am especially mindful of Amanda Bailey, Tom Bishop, Andrew Bozio, Katie Brokaw, Pam Brown, Rebecca Bushnell, Tom Cartelli, Jeff Doty, Don Hedrick, Jean Howard, Nathan Kelber, Natasha Korda, Genevieve Love, Rebecca Lemon, Jeremy Lopez, Steve Luber, Jeff Masten, Richard Preiss, Nova Myhill, Steve Mullaney, Katherine Rowe, Richard Schoch, Mike Sell, Laurie Shannon, Jerry Singerman, P. A. Skantze, Bruce Smith, Andrew Sofer, Jonathan Sofer, Lyn Tribble, Elliott Visconsi, Jen Waldron, Wendy Wall, Mike Witmore, and Bill Worthen. Several SAA colleagues deserve special mention. Feedback from Erika Lin early in the project helped crystalize my thinking about games and theater. My most heartfelt thanks go to Ellen MacKay, who brought her usual brilliance to a reading of the whole manuscript. I have learned a great deal also through collaborative writing with Anston Bosman and Will West—who will see our collective brain reflected in Chapter 4—and with Susan Bennett, with whom I have enjoyed a fruitful dialogue about performance studies and early modern drama.

A number of institutions and organizations provided critical support. The project transformed completely during my academic year fellowship from the American Council for Learned Societies. Thanks to short-term fellowships from the Newberry Library and the Huntington Library, I was able to gather key archival materials. I also made much use of the collections held by the Folger Library, the British Library, and the British Museum, and I thank the staff for their assistance. Additional funding for research came from the UC Davis Interdisciplinary Frontiers for the Humanities and Arts and the Academic Senate Committee on Research. I was grateful also to receive a Faculty Development grant and a Publication Assistance grant from the Humanities, Arts, and Cultural Studies division and the Office of Research. For helping to arrange this funding, I thank departmental chairs John Marx, Liz Miller, and Scott Simmon as well as Deans Jessie Ann Owens and Susan Kaiser. In addition, the UCD Library provided a TOME grant to support open access publishing of the book. My research on *Play the Knave* was made possible through my involvement with the IMMERSe Research Network for Video Game Immersion, led by Neil Randall and supported by the Social Sciences and Humanities Research Council of Canada, as well as through a digital humanities grant I received from the University of California Humanities Research Initiative.

LeAnn Fields at the University of Michigan Press intuitively understood this project from the moment I shared it with her. I am grateful to her for believing so strongly in this book and for efficiently shepherding the manuscript through the publication process. My thanks as well to Jenny Geyer and Marcia LaBrenz for their attention to detail, and to the press's outside readers, who provided thoughtful feedback on the manuscript.

This book has been a long time in the making, and my friends and family have encouraged me along at every stage. My life in Davis has been enriched through friendships with many. In addition to colleagues mentioned above, I thank Beth Freeman, Claire Goldstein, Tobias Menely, and Margaret Rhonda, for providing stimulating company and sound advice. To Barbara Nichols I owe my health in body and spirit. Although I am the worst long-distance correspondent ever, somehow Alexis Boylan, Jill Garrett, Brandon Fogel, and Lara Trubowitz have put up with me for years and years, and it helps to know that I can always rely on them. Also far but never more than a phone call away are my siblings, Karen Porat, Ronette Throne, and Joel Bloom, who were my first playmates and remain bedrocks of support. I'm grateful as well to Ann and Tooey Miller, who love me like I am their own daughter and have nurtured my creativity by whisking me away to incredible places. Foremost among my supporters are my parents, Louis Bloom and Bernice Schmitz, who have always made sure I know how proud they are of me. Both sacrificed a lot to give me the unbelievable education that serves me to this day, and they ought to take much more credit than they do for my achievements.

My greatest debt of all is to Flagg Miller, who has done far more than his fair share these last years to make it possible for me to finish this book. Well before I started this project, our motto was "in play we trust." And so it remains.

This book is dedicated to my son, Max, who always wants more time to play and reminds me that I should, too. I am inspired every day by his creativity, passion, and love of words.

Gaming the Stage

For about the past fifteen years, game makers have been meeting annually to participate in Game Chef, a competition that challenges designers to create in one week a nondigital game that fits an assigned theme. The selected themes have tended to be broad enough to appeal to a range of interested participants, but in 2011, for the first and thus far only time in its history, Game Chef oriented its theme around a particular literary figure: William Shakespeare.[1] The choice hardly alienated game makers with its specificity and high-culture reference: game entries topped the numbers from the year before. Why would Shakespeare be such an attractive theme for game designers today? Sure, Shakespeare is an iconic literary figure with plenty of cultural capital. But I submit that Shakespeare is fitting inspiration for game designers not only because of the literary content of the plays and the biographical fame of the author, but because of the theatrical context in which those plays were first and continue to be performed. Theater is a good model for games because it is one of the earliest media technologies for interactive play.

The overlap between games and theatrical plays was a foregone conclusion for premodern people. Medieval writers used the term *ludus* for both games and plays.[2] And the earliest commercial theaters of Shakespeare's era, known as "playhouses," were built right next to gaming establishments; some of these theaters even doubled as blood sport venues.[3] This tight historical linkage between games and theatrical plays has been forgotten over the past half millennium, however. Game Chef aside, theater is no longer an obvious or even likely reference point for most gamers and theorists of gaming, despite the formative impact of work by such scholars as Janet Murray.[4] Moreover, although many theater and performance scholars and practitioners have followed Richard Schechner's view of performance as gamelike, they tend to treat conventional dramatic plays primarily as scripts for theatrical performance and to assume that only avant-garde performances can be conceptualized as games.[5]

As we have entered a moment in history when games are more pervasive than ever, while theatrical plays tend to be relegated to the status of elite entertainment, it is vital that we ask: What do theatrical plays and games have in common, for their producers and their spectators? And what can we learn about gaming and about theater by uncovering the links between these media forms? Recent developments in digital gaming make these questions particularly timely and urgent. The emergence of performing arts games like *Dance Dance Revolution* and *Guitar Hero* and the popularity of full-body gaming platforms like the Nintendo Wii and the Microsoft Kinect (best known for its use with Xbox systems) signal a return to traditional theatrical concepts in gaming. These games mandate that players become embodied performers, treat the game space as a kind of stage, and even encourage spectators to cluster around and watch gameplay as if it were a performance for an audience.[6] Although the content of most of these games is dance or music, not theatrical drama, the gaming done via Xbox and Nintendo's Wii systems is fundamentally theatrical in design and effect.[7] To understand this gaming technology and its social uses fully, we need to overcome what Jussi Parikka calls the "strategic amnesia of digital culture"[8] and look more closely at a historical moment when theater and games were decidedly interdependent media technologies: the sixteenth and seventeenth centuries, or the "early modern" period. My book turns to this moment in history to argue for games as theatrical media and theater as an interactive gaming technology.

Few scholars of games have explored the early modern period, even as scholars of media have advocated for studying contemporary media in relation to technologies of the preindustrial age.[9] Yet the fifteenth through seventeenth centuries are highly significant to the history of games, as they are to the history of theater, and thus to theorizing the relationship between these media forms. This period of gaming and theater history is especially important in the case of England, for it was during the late sixteenth and early seventeenth centuries that commercial theater first emerged in England, turning playgoing into a commercial activity that vied for customers in London's "new leisure market."[10] Entertainment seekers with limited resources of money and time had a wide range of entertainment possibilities from which to choose in the fast-growing metropolis of London, and among their options were attending plays and visiting drinking establishments to wager on games like cards, backgammon, and chess. These options were not as different as they might first appear, for the new commercial theaters that emerged in the last quarter of the sixteenth century turned playgoing into something of a gamble: patrons had to pay *before* seeing the play. Londoners had for centuries been wagering their money on games, in and out of drinking establishments, but the idea of paying before seeing a play was a novel concept.

My book investigates how the pervasive gaming culture of early modern London eased the transition to a commercial theater and, in turn, how this history of commercial theater speaks back to pervasive gaming culture today. The shift from noncommercial theatrical performance to theater-for-pay presented challenges for producers of theater and for audiences, who were not used to treating plays as commodities. Purpose-built theaters restricted audience members' physical interactions with actors and objects onstage, offering a presumably less participatory form of theatergoing than had been available before and elsewhere. For the theater to compete in London's leisure market, it had to convince theater spectators, however, that a less physically interactive theatrical experience could still *feel* like interactive play. I maintain that producers of theater made this argument by modeling theater on its ludic competition, which, because it involved spectators betting on games they watched, already had successful ways of engaging nonplayer participants. The commercial theater, in other words, was fashioned as a gaming apparatus for its consumers, whose spectatorship was participatory, albeit in ways that might be missed at first glance. Indeed, the participatory nature of spectatorship in these theaters opens up very different ways of thinking about "interactivity," in theater and in games.

Interactivity has been misunderstood and undertheorized in both theater and game studies partly because both fields tend to approach interactivity as an affordance of digital media. The assumption that the rhetoric of interactivity is derived from digital culture has been a useful starting point for important critiques of the commercialism of a range of contemporary "interactive" performance experiences: from "immersive theater" (such as Punchdrunk's *Sleep No More*, a long-running adaptation of *Macbeth* that, at the time of this writing, has become a veritable theatrical theme park in New York City, complete with its own restaurant, merchandise, and repeat customers) to experiments with "original practices" at more traditional theaters, like the rebuilt Shakespeare's Globe on London's South Bank. Indeed, heritage Shakespeare institutions regularly tout the value of "interactivity" to build their customer bases: from the "immersive journey" called "Life, Love & Legacy" that the Shakespeare Birthplace Trust launched in 2009 to replace its earlier exhibits; to the Elizabethan-style theaters that even the Royal Shakespeare Company has embraced; to practices like shared lighting that facilitate audience–actor interaction in spaces like Shakespeare's Globe or the reconstructed Blackfriars Theatre in Virginia.[11]

Scholars have drawn attention to the commercial logic driving these very different projects by emphasizing the digital rhetoric that underpins their conceptions of interactivity. Shakespeare scholar Kate Rumbold maintains that values of "interactivity, participation, and creativity" are drawn from the "positive discourse of the Internet," and its commercial intent.[12] Theater and performance scholar William B. Worthen argues that when "terms like 'interactive' and 'immersive' migrate to the theater," they remain moored to "the vision of the user-as-commodified-by-interaction that structures the conceptual and financial economy of the digital medium."[13] As important as these critiques are, their emphasis on interactivity as a *digital* phenomenon is at best limiting and, at worst, misleading.

I submit that the rhetoric of interactivity so pervasive in the marketing of contemporary theaters and institutions today is borrowed less from digital culture than from gaming culture. This distinction matters. Once we recognize how the discourse of interactivity is indebted to gaming culture, we can trace a much longer history to the commodification of interactivity, identify deeper causes for this phenomenon, and, crucially, explore the means by which audiences/users might resist being conscripted by the productions with which they interact. Experiments with making drama more "interactive" today satisfy not simply a desire to reproduce digital experiences, but to make theater more pleasurable by making it more playable. To explain this desire, we need more than a well-developed theory of user interactions with digital interfaces. We need to know how and why playable theater is more pleasurable for its audience-users. Although the answer to this question can and has begun to be explored through analysis of contemporary immersive performances, there are benefits to focusing analysis on the early modern theater.[14] Produced at a time before digital games, early modern playable theater can be analyzed without the baggage of digital culture.

I would go even further to suggest that bracketing the digital age is essential to achieving a fuller understanding of interactivity in games and theater, because digital games, by design, limit robust forms of interaction between gamer and machine. It is for this reason that the game studies scholars Stephanie Boluk and Patrick LeMieux question whether videogames are games at all. They point out that the videogame is a closed system to be executed by the user through interaction with the computer interface.[15] Where is the play in that? In the interaction between gamer and digital game, who is using whom?—a question that has become all the more urgent as big companies like Google and Facebook as well as gaming companies retrieve information about users through their online interactions with digital systems. A related set of questions have arisen around contemporary immersive theater, which aims, in philosopher Jacques Rancière's words, to "emancipate" the spectator by physically transforming theatrical spaces and/or blurring the lines between performers and spectators. Rancière argues that experiments to make theater more interactive and increase the agency of spectators often miss the mark when they manipulate theatrical spaces to eradicate the separation between actors and spectators: "by placing the spectators on the stage and the performers in the auditorium; by abolishing the difference between the two; by transferring the performance to other sites; by identifying it with taking possession of the street, the town or life."[16] However enriching these experiments with more participatory performance have been, they have not emancipated the spectator but left in place the power dynamics of performance, wherein actors create and audiences consume, and where spectators, like their digital counterparts in online systems, are put to work to create theatrical engagements.

Like Rancière, I question whether the only or best way to turn passive, consuming spectators into active, participatory ones is by changing the mechanics of spectator–actor interactions—or, to put this in digital gaming terms, to change the interface. We can start to see other forms of spectators' active participation in theater when we put gaming at the center of our theories of interactivity. As is true in gaming, interactivity in theater is not simply a matter of users physically manipulating an interface. As it is, in both immersive performance and digital games, such interactions are more rhetoric than reality, since these systems must control carefully the kinds of interaction possible, thereby setting rules for what can and cannot be altered. Thus, following Boluk and LeMieux, I would argue that real interactivity comes from the audience-users' ability and encouragement to play *with* the objects and narratives presented via the interface. In videogames, such ludic interaction can come in the form of *modding* (game modification), *griefing* (online, in-game harassment), *cheating* (exploiting bugs, codes, or special hardware), and a variety of forms of *metagaming*—practices that can enable gamers to sidestep the constrictive and co-opting logics of the digital objects with which they engage. It is the ethos of play that makes true interactivity possible, and this is as much the case in theater as it is in games. Interactivity emerges in the theater when audiences don't simply consume, but *play*. To be sure, whether audiences choose to play is another matter—codes of socialization in the theater may prescribe and even punish spectators who play too much or in unsanctioned ways. This is true in the world of videogames as well. But unlike in the case of videogames, where the codes that structure the interface are invisible to most users, in theater and in nondigital games, the option for audience-users to play, to really play, is available. By focusing on theater as an interactive game, and on spectators as potential players of theater, we can begin to see the ways theater spectators can manipulate rules and technologies for their own enjoyment. My book explores how early modern theaters, even as they appeared to restrict physical forms of interaction, encouraged their audiences to play with, around, and through the dramas presented onstage. The theater was "playable media"—a term my title borrows from game studies scholar Noah Wardrip-Fruin, who employs it, as I do, to highlight the crucial role of audience-users in defining what counts as a game.[17]

My evidence of early modern theater as playable media comes largely from dramatic texts, and, as such, I follow Friedrich Kittler—a founding figure in the field of media archaeology—in arguing for literature as a crucial archive for media studies.[18] Though overlooked by most scholars of media and games, plays offer much for our understanding of games as media, not simply because games often employ dramatic narratives, but because the cognitive and emotional experiences of gameplay and of theatrical spectatorship are similar.[19] Dramas, I maintain, are forms *of* play; they are ways of gaming. The ethos of interactive gaming permeates early modern drama, but the mechanisms and ideological effects of this gaming context can most clearly be seen when we focus on a fascinating topos in the plays: scenes of staged gameplay.[20] At climactic moments in a number of plays, characters partake in what I will call, following early modern terminology, *sitting pastimes:* for instance, the backgammon match that provides the occasion for murder in the anonymous *Arden of Faversham;* the card game through which a husband tests his wife's infidelity in Thomas Heywood's *A Woman Killed with Kindness;* and the chess game characters play when Prospero reveals his political scheme in Shakespeare's *The Tempest.*[21] Although game structures are at the heart of the early modern commercial theater enterprise and could be analyzed at multiple moments in any number of plays, I hone in on these cameo appearances of games onstage because they foreground so elegantly how plays engage spectators by cuing their desire to play.

Gaming the Stage argues that staged game scenes trigger spectators' cognitive and emotional involvement not in spite but *because* of their withholding of information about and physical participation in the game in progress. On the one hand, staged games foreground the commercial audience's passivity, for when sitting pastimes were presented onstage, theater spectators—used to playing and betting on sitting pastimes in more intimate gaming spaces—couldn't follow gaming action directly. On the other hand, gaming scenes take advantage of spectators' competency as *vicarious* players to invite alternative forms of interactive engagement. By preventing spectators from knowing through sight or touch, these scenes encourage audiences to *know by feeling*. The scenes show particularly clearly how all dramas are games of information and how theaters of all kinds can be set up to be game spaces: sites of engagement among audience members as well as between audiences and actors and/or characters, dramatic plots, stage objects, and theater buildings. These dramas thus offer useful evidence not only for macrohistories of theater spectatorship and microhistories of particular sitting pastimes, but also for the study of games more generally. As these dramas pause to represent the act of gameplay, they help us to understand better how players of any interactive game at any time come to know by feeling.

This notion of knowing by feeling informs my book's methodology, wherein I use insights from gaming to study dramatic literature. If early modern plays are games, then we have to read them differently, studying them in much the way we might other games from the past. But therein lies a dilemma. Unable to see or touch the games of the past directly, we have access only to their traces. In this, the modern historian of games finds common ground with the critic of early modern drama, as well as with spectators in a conventional theater: the past is like a theater stage, and we cannot get close enough to touch or see its gaming experiences. However, the character dialogue on which theater spectators rely to follow a game staged beyond their direct view is also a resource to the historian of games, provided we read these traces differently than we would other literary texts. Rather than treat the language of gaming primarily as an interesting feature of a play's mise-en-scène or as literary symbol, I approach this language as evidence of gameplay.[22] For instance, when in Henry Porter's *The Two Angry Women of Abington*, Mistress Goursey asks her backgammon opponent, Mistress Barnes, "Where stands your man now?," going on to say that "It stands between the points" (1.123; 124), the play's editor reminds us that "points" refers not only to the long triangles on which the game pieces stand but also to the laces that attach a man's doublet to his hose.[23] From this perspective, Mistress Goursey uses backgammon terminology as a metaphor, hinting that Mistress Barnes doesn't know the whereabouts of her husband. This double-entendre somehow confirms for Mistress Barnes her suspicion that her husband is having an affair with Mistress Goursey, a suspicion the play has trouble explaining. What happens, though, if we take even more seriously the gaming context for this scene, reading its gaming imagery in more literal terms? From the perspective of an actual backgammon match, Mistress Goursey is calling attention to Mistress Barnes's sloppy and perhaps fraudulent playing: Mistress Goursey cannot tell where Mistress Barnes has placed her playing piece, her "man"—it is between two points instead of directly on one—which could enable Mistress Barnes to cheat when she takes her next turn, as she can choose to interpret her piece's placement retroactively, after she sees what dice number she rolls next. From this perspective, Mistress Barnes's otherwise inexplicable dislike of Mistress Goursey might be understood as a defensive reaction—accused of false play at backgammon, Mistress Barnes deflects the charge, accusing Mistress Goursey of false play in marriage. The game is both symptom and cause of the women's otherwise fairly nonsensical social conflict.

I examine the significance of this scene in more detail in Chapter 3 and, for now, wish only to underscore what is lost if the scene's language is analyzed on purely symbolic levels—which, however fascinating, are not sufficient for understanding it, particularly in performance. Consider that the theater audience, positioned at a distance from the onstage game table, cannot see the board and thus cannot be certain of precisely what fuels the characters' disagreement. Does Mistress Barnes misplace her game piece in an attempt to cheat? Is Mistress Goursey baiting Mistress Barnes, or vice versa? Spectators, who cannot get close enough to the board to see what is transpiring in the game, thus experience the backgammon game in ways that differ considerably from the game's onstage players. In fact, as I discuss further in Chapter 3, the scene aligns its audience with the *husbands* of the gaming women, who, though onstage, are positioned too far from the game board to follow the ludic action, leaving them almost tragically oblivious to their wives' mounting disagreement. Their lack of full information about the degree and cause of their wives' fury is a central motivator for the drama's plot.

Porter pulls theater spectators into the social drama of the scene by inviting their vicarious participation in the drama of the backgammon game itself, which, though it is scripted, can feel like an actual match to audience members familiar with backgammon. Theater and performance scholar Stanton Garner describes "actuality" as the "currency of ludic exchange," arguing, for instance, that quasi-darkness in a theater draws on the sensual experience of actual darkness.[24] Although audience members are fully aware that theatrical darkness is fictional, their knowledge of what actual darkness feels like "infuses" their experience of theatrical darkness.[25] In a similar way, I argue, audience members' past experiences playing, watching, and betting on backgammon matches infuses their spectatorship of Porter's scripted game. The result is that audiences, though literally held at a distance from the game board—which they cannot see, let alone touch— are able to *feel* as if they are interacting intimately with the fictionalized game onstage. Some degree of the cognitive processing and emotional rush they have felt while playing or betting on a backgammon match can transfer to their experience of this scene such that they may feel they have a stake in the women's argument even if, in actuality, they do not.

As my brief reading of *Two Angry Women* begins to illustrate, scenes of gaming urge a shift to a mode of reading and analysis that we might describe as less *semiotic* than *phenomenological*, attending not only to what games mean but also to how it feels to play them or even watch them played by others.[26] In order to read dramas as scripts for gameplay, I analyze scenes of gaming through a method sometimes used in videogame studies: play as research.[27] That is, to understand how it felt to play and watch others play the games staged in drama, I not only consult early modern rule books and material objects related to these games, but consider what it feels like to me to play these games today. This methodology is especially suitable for study of early modern games because this was the period when the material objects and rules for ancient sitting pastimes changed, taking on the forms they continue to have today. For instance, tarot cards morphed into the fifty-two-card deck, and the Queen came to be the most powerful figure on the chessboard. Changes like these impacted what it felt like to play these games and, subsequently, the social and political implications of that experience. Rather than telling the history of games as a story primarily of change, though, *Gaming the Stage* emphasizes continuities in gameplay.[28] Approaching the past as on a continuum with the present, not as a radical break from it, opens up a somewhat different role for the literary and theater historian. Our personal experiences of gameplay, instead of needing to be set aside because they are merely "subjective" knowledge, become useful, even crucial, supplements to the archival study of early modern materials related to gaming, a methodological approach I explicate further in Chapter 1. Games are not something we simply read about, but something we and early moderns alike *do* with and through our bodies and our embodied minds.

Readers willing to engage in this more participatory form of reading are better able to discover, I argue, the participatory forms of spectatorship enjoyed by early modern audiences. Like spectators of games, spectators of theater could become players, actively involved in producing the phenomena before them. We can say much the same thing about scholars. Indeed, as I discuss further in Chapter 1, games help us to see what might be gained by thinking of the literary and theater historian less as an archaeologist than as a spectator of the past: not a spectator who sits back and watches, but the kind of participatory or "emancipated" spectator who creates through the act of watching. The historian, in other words, is a gamer who engages her body and embodied mind in the act of playing with the past.

INTERACTIVE PLAY IN THE COMMERCIAL THEATER

Encouraging audiences to feel as if they were active participants in the fictions staged before them was vital for London's first commercial theaters, which had to introduce their audiences to a relatively new way of consuming drama. To be sure, traditional entertainments with a theatrical dimension had flourished for centuries before—and continued to compete throughout the period with—the plays staged in the first commercial theaters. But there were important differences between the commercial stage and its predecessors/competitors. In the first place, commercial theaters demanded that audiences pay money up front, before a performance, an innovation with a number of consequences for how those performances were experienced.[29] And second, though theater's defenders often presented the goal of plays to be moral instruction, in truth the commercial theater's goal was predominantly and openly pure entertainment. Other kinds of theater, including religious drama, educational plays, and court performances, had very different goals and involved different systems of economic exchange. Street entertainments perhaps came closest to the commercial theater in their aims: a secular performance put on for the public purely for entertainment purposes. But these performances would have been more informal in nature, and audiences paid only if they enjoyed the performance and/or felt that it deserved their support; as continues to be the case today, the performers would send a hat around to collect contributions at the conclusion of the show. In contrast, the professional theaters developing in London in the late sixteenth century were commercial enterprises, open to anyone willing to pay the admission price. Once inside purpose-built amphitheaters or converted hall theaters, audience members, used to close involvement and even physical contact with performers, were held at a physical distance. To be sure, the thrust stage promoted some exchange between actors and audiences, and the hall theaters even allowed audiences to pay extra to sit onstage. But many other features of commercial theaters—such as the raised stage height, the admission cost structure (with more expensive seats further from and higher above the stage in amphitheaters), and the construction of a backstage area hidden from audience view—separated theatergoers from onstage action, helping to define spectators as consumers.

From our perspective today, where commercial theater of this kind is widely available and, at least in the Western world, the norm, it is easy to underestimate the effects and implications of this commodification of performance.[30] Scholar of early modern theater and culture Michael Bristol maintains that audiences in early modern London, already familiar with the workings of a commodity culture and its "more passive habits of cultural consumption," were prepared for the transition to a commercial theater.[31] But, I would submit, insofar as audiences were not as accustomed to viewing *plays* in this way, the transition would not have been easy. Audiences needed to learn *how* to approach theater as a commodity. It is no wonder that the commercial theater drew on traditional forms of entertainment, such as festive performances, inviting audiences to take a more participatory role in plays.[32] To be sure, when commercial theaters appropriated these more familiar forms of entertainment, they offered audiences a way to invest emotionally and cognitively in an otherwise alienating commercial production. But I maintain that the goal was not, as others have suggested, to produce in the theater the kind of communal affiliation found elsewhere; it was to teach audience members their proper place as consumers. After all, audiences appear to have taken great pleasure in disrupting and even destroying the plays they ostensibly paid to see, creating a somewhat unsustainable form of entertainment.[33] No-holds-barred forms of participation may have kept (at least some of) the audience laughing, but if commercial theaters hoped to convince their audiences that plays were a valuable commodity in and of themselves, they needed to channel spectators' desires for participation. Producers of commercial theater needed to bridge festive performance practices with the emerging idea of theater as commodity. They needed to make audiences *feel* like participants without allowing for actual physical interaction with the elements of the production (actors, stage, script, etc.).

Conceiving of plays as games helps shed light on how the commercial theater accomplished this balancing act. Although others have explored ludic elements in early modern drama, their approaches have limited applicability for explaining how theaters engaged audiences in theatergoing, particularly in a commercial context. Many prior studies approach games and play as broad categories that, in most cases, reflect on the nature of pretense in drama, instead of looking at specific game types in relation to theater. This approach risks not only flattening important differences among games but also overemphasizing pretense as the key competency exercised by participants in gameplay and theater, when, in fact, both call for a broader range of skills.[34] Those studies that do attend to particular games tend to focus on spectacle-driven games or sports, such as bear-baiting, wrestling, traditional festive performance, and fencing, all of which were either performed in venues not unlike theaters or at least shared theater's fundamental modalities: one or more performers (human or animal actors) engage in spectacular actions for the benefit of spectators.[35]

Gaming the Stage follows the example of these latter studies in its focus on a narrower set of games, an approach that enables me to explore how the formal structure of a game provokes and helps develop particular competencies in a game's players and spectators—and, by extension, theater audiences. However, my focus on unspectacular pastimes reveals a deeper perspective on theater's relationship to gaming. In their usual venues (e.g., parlors and taverns), games such as cards, backgammon, and chess were played by seated participants around a table, with spectators betting on the action. When these games were staged in theaters, however, audiences could not participate as spectators in the ways to which they were accustomed. Unlike wrestling, fencing, or other more spectacle-driven entertainments, sitting pastimes draw attention to the differences between theater and other forms of commercial entertainment. There were sound economic and ideological reasons for the theater to underscore differences between itself and its competitors in the leisure market. Consumers had only so much time and money to spend on entertainment, so the theater needed to demonstrate the "relative entertainment value" of their product.[36] Another factor was the need to combat the rhetoric of antitheatrical religious zealots, who strategically collapsed theater and games to argue that all pleasures were the same, no matter their form. The staging of unspectacular sitting pastimes precisely helped to underscore the formal *differences* among games and between games and theater. Rather than simply exploit the game–theater overlap, then, scenes of gaming defamiliarized and put pressure on analogies built upon it. They called upon audiences not simply to exercise their gaming competencies but to repurpose and adapt them. They invited audiences to approach the play as a different *kind* of game, one that audiences would, nevertheless, be equipped to play.

Scenes of sitting pastimes underscore effectively how the commercial theater's efforts to limit spectators' physical and visual access to the stage, instead of undermining interactivity, could stimulate audiences to discover alternative forms of engagement. John Sutton's work in cognitive philosophy of sport suggests that spectators who have embodied experience of a game may feel they are playing even if only watching it.[37] Similarly, staged board and table games invited theater spectators to draw on their familiarity with these games and to play them vicariously from the sidelines, becoming invested cognitively and emotionally in much the way they would if betting on these games in a tavern or parlor. But because these were betting games, they also helped audiences retain some distance from the object of spectatorship and treat the performance, like a game, as a commodity. Through the staging of these games, the theater could take advantage of its patrons' expertise with and interests in competing forms of recreation in order to build a theatrical form that was new but *felt* familiar. Staged games, in effect, conjoined the participatory and the commercial, offering spectators a way to interact more intensively with commodified theater and, in effect, turning spectator consumption into a mode of production. From this perspective, the staged game scene might best be understood as a "metagame," as that term is defined by Boluk and LeMieux—not simply games about games, but practices that "anchor[ ] a game in time and space."[38] If in contemporary videogame culture the metagame uncovers the often hidden and constraining commercial logic of the videogame industry, then metagames in early modern drama, as they situate sitting pastimes in the historical and material context of the early modern theater, expose the commercial logic of these early playhouses, making audiences as well as modern scholars aware of the emerging and yet unwritten constraints of theatergoing.

In tracing the ways the early theater commodified interactivity, *Gaming the Stage* offers something of a prehistory not only to interactive games but also to contemporary immersive theater. Some have suggested that the genre of immersive theater emerged in the second half of the twentieth century when directors explicitly began to blur and even reverse the lines between actors and audiences, turning the audience into an empowered community.[39] Such practices have a long history, however, going back well into the medieval period. In England religious cycle plays had theater audiences walk from one performance site to another hundreds of years before avant-garde directors used the promenade theater technique, to take one example. Such spectator mobility and related forms of audience interaction with the performance certainly were more contained in early modern theaters, but they were not eradicated so much as they were sublimated and redirected. Early modern plays may not, like contemporary immersive theater, have invited their audiences to become physically part of the performance, even if Francis Beaumont's *Knight of the Burning Pestle* (1607)—in which several actors pretend to be audience members, directing play action and sending their apprentice onstage to take on a part—suggests audiences may have or would have liked to invite themselves.[40] But staged gaming scenes exemplify theater producers' broader efforts to make their plays as cognitively and emotionally immersive as possible. Even if held at a physical distance from the action, audiences could feel like participants in it. Staged games help us to see how early modern commercial theaters attempted to commodify interactivity, much as today's digital games do.

SOCIAL AND THEATRICAL INFORMATION GAMES

To understand how theatrical dramas functioned for audience-users as playable media, it is useful to conceive of plays in much the way some have conceived of games: as systems of information. Modern game designer and scholar Celia Pearce theorizes four kinds of information that players have or pursue: information known by all the players, or to only one player, or to the game only (i.e., to no players), or generated randomly (e.g., by dice).[41] The kind(s) of information used in a game and the ways in and extent to which that information changes over the course of a match determines the degree of chance and, thus, level of risk involved, features that distinguish games from each other. For example, chess can be identified as a game of *perfect information*, as it is played on a game board seen by both players and their spectators equally at all times. Because there are no elements of chance internal to the game, chess is less risky than a game involving cards, for instance. Cards are designed for use in games of *imperfect information*, as information is hidden and revealed to players during the course of a match. Card games are riskier than chess because some of the information hidden is left entirely to chance, due to the shuffling of the deck and the randomness of dealing.

Given how crucial the circulation of information is to board and table games—both for players and for spectators betting on the action—it is not surprising that when these games are staged in early modern drama, they almost always appear at key moments where information is at stake within a plotline. In fact, games tend to appear onstage when a character is or is alleged to be hiding something. Through games, characters in plays practice, discover, or hide duplicity in their social relationships. Of note is that the relationships established, negotiated, and tested in and through scenes of onstage gaming in early modern drama are almost without exception those of same- and cross-sex friendship, romantic courtship, and marriage. The emphasis of these game scenes on intimate relationships makes sense, since relatively compact and/or private parlor-like settings where sitting pastimes would be played are conducive to explorations of social and sexual alliances.[42] As well, games are opportunities for social bonding; as is true today, when friends, romantic partners, or spouses play together, they do so because they enjoy each other's company—or wish to show that they do.

Early modern dramas use gaming to investigate codes of social intimacy, and as such they reveal broad ideological implications of interactive play: in particular, they call attention to friendship, courtship, and marriage as games of risk. In this, the plays counter other early modern writings that tend to mythologize these relationships as, we might say, games of perfect information: relationships involving less risk because participants know all they need to know about each other. The plays, however, emphasize quite the opposite, instead critiquing idealistic views of friendship, courtship, and marriage. This becomes particularly clear when actual games are staged as part of a play's plot. For instance, as I discuss in Chapter 2, the card game scene in *A Woman Killed with Kindness* underscores the play's critique of a humanist model of ideal male friendship, suggesting that even ideal male friendship is, like cards, a game of imperfect information, where intimacy is produced by each participant/friend revealing information that the other does not know.

Anthropologists and social theorists have studied the ways, in particular, men in many cultures use games to negotiate social ties and to assert social dominance over other men as well as women; but early modern drama proves a particularly fruitful archive through which to explore the complex intersections among gender, social status, and gaming.[43] The plays foreground the extent to which, in the largely patriarchal culture of early modern England, men of higher status had the most at stake in idealistic models of friendship, courtship, and marriage and, consequently, were under greater pressure to negotiate the risks inherent in these social games of imperfect information. Again, the gaming scenes in the plays distill and exaggerate these issues. I find that games offer a testing ground for characters' achievement of *patriarchal masculinity*, a concept I draw from the work of historian Alexandra Shepard. Shepard identifies "patriarchal manhood" and "anti-patriarchal manhood" as two different social codes that were available to early modern men: while some men pursued or exercised their patriarchal privileges through the demonstration of qualities such as "[s]trength, thrift, industry, self-sufficiency, honesty, authority, autonomy, self-government, moderation, reason, wisdom, and wit," others, who could not gain access to patriarchal privileges on account of their lower status or younger age, developed a counter-code of conduct, embracing "prodigality, transience, violence, bravado, and debauchery" as signs of their manhood.[44] Shepard's work is useful because its definition of manhood takes into account class and age, thereby helping to explain the different ways that male privilege and hierarchy were exercised in early modern England. But sitting pastimes, which in early modern England were as available and popular among women as they were among men, complicate Shepard's findings in important ways. For one thing, scenes of gaming foreground *women's* pursuit of patriarchal masculinity, reminding us that some women—perhaps because of their higher status, more advanced age, or particular social circumstances (e.g., widowhood)—subscribed to codes of patriarchal masculinity. As is demonstrated in Chapter 2's reading of *Gammer Gurton's Needle* and Chapter 3's reading of *Two Angry Women*, games provide a means through which some female characters pursue patriarchal masculinity and its privileges.

My focus on games also enables me to highlight a subtle but illuminating distinction between Shepard's two codes of masculinity: that they involve very different levels of risk. Most of the qualities of patriarchal masculinity that Shepard identifies—particularly thrift, industry, self-sufficiency, honesty, autonomy, self-government, moderation, and reason—minimize an individual's risk in terms of personal comportment and economic and social interaction with others. By contrast, the prodigality, transience, violence, bravado, and debauchery that mark antipatriarchal masculinity are significantly riskier forms of social and economic engagement. In focusing on the tolerance of risk endemic to different codes of masculinity, *Gaming the Stage* shifts attention away from the individual and toward the social constitution of gender, demonstrating how patriarchal masculinity was achieved not simply through an individual's exercise of virtuous behaviors but through active competition with others over sparse resources. Because the terms of that competition were unpredictable, the plays often end up highlighting an inevitable tension: although the model of ideal patriarchal masculinity emphasizes surety, the pursuit of it necessitates risk.

My treatment of intimate social relationships as risky games of imperfect information puts pressure also on certain critical understandings of friendship, courtship, and marriage, emphasizing their *epistemological* rather than primarily their *affective* registers. That is, intimacy in these relationships is a function not only of individuals' emotional bonds but also of what they feel they know or don't know about each other. The implications of this difference are especially evident when we think about a matter like cheating—so often a source of conflict in the dramas, as it is in games.[45] If friendship, courtship, and marriage are approached predominantly as affective bonds, then cheating is an ethical affront and a sign of betrayal of the bond. But if these relationships are thought about as games of information, cheating constitutes a manipulation of an inherent imbalance in knowledge between parties. The gaming context helps us think about cheating not simply as a destructive violation of trust that undoes a relationship, but as an opportunity to assess and sometimes, I argue, even strengthen the bond between two people. Consider that in games, the line between violating rules and exercising strategy is constantly negotiated; as games evolve, actions once considered violations of the rules can be integrated into the game to produce new and more pleasurable versions of old games. For instance, medieval chess rules prohibited the Queen piece from moving more than one space at a time; but by the sixteenth century, the Queen could be moved in any direction as many spaces as the player wished. An action that once constituted violation of the rules became one of the more interesting new rules of the game.

Arguably, what distinguishes cheating from this sort of productive breaking and changing of the rules is simply that cheats usually conceal their violations. But early modern dramas and many gaming contexts today (e.g., the phenomenon of griefers, discussed in Chapters 2 and 4) highlight the actions of cheats. In fact, just as in early modern paintings depicting gameplay (see, for instance, images of cardplay in Figures 13–15), theatrical game scenes almost always center on cheating. As game scenes raise questions about and lay bare the violations of game rules, they use cheating to comment on the role of information in social relationships. Imbalances in information, though they create the conditions for cheating, also can create the conditions for intimacy. In games and in intimate social relationships, the deceit that can undermine a game is difficult to separate from the deceit that makes the game pleasurable to play.

Viewing friendship, courtship, and marriage as relationships grounded in contest need not lead to an entirely cynical view of intimacy.[46] Even in competitive games, contest and cooperation are dialectical partners. Like game participants, friends, lovers, and spouses in early modern plays often agree to take up contestatory positions, and antagonism sometimes is portrayed as a source of their pleasure. Consider, for instance, *The Tempest*'s closing chess match, which I discuss in Chapter 4. The play represents the marriage of Miranda and Ferdinand as a comedic triumph not despite but because of Miranda's questioning and acceptance of Ferdinand's alleged cheating. Miranda demonstrates a gamer attitude that may not please her father—who, I argue, arranges Miranda's marriage as if it is a game of perfect information over which he has total control—but is represented as pleasurable for Miranda and Ferdinand. *The Tempest* and other plays suggest that in games and in intimate social relationships, little is gained by minimizing risk; the greater the risk, the greater the reward.

Miranda's acceptance of marriage as a game of imperfect information—and the possible foul play that can ensue as a result—models a different perspective on social intimacy as well as a different view of theatrical intimacy. I argue that theater—like friendship, courtship, and marriage—can be envisioned as a game of imperfect information played between its producers (dramatists, actors, etc.) and audiences. Theater, as Andrew Sofer argues, may be defined by what it hides from its audiences.[47] And part of the pleasure of theater comes from the audience's willing participation in this state of unknowing. As characters in a drama navigate imperfect information in their fictional social relationships, they engage theater audiences in another, related game of imperfect information.[48] Dramas inspire hermeneutic work on the part of audiences, but they can make that work feel, to audiences, like play. In the playable media form that is theater, as in other games, risk can be a site of pleasure and the ludic currency through which to establish intimacy with other theater participants. Even if in the early commercial theater, actors were professionals instead of friends and neighbors, even if the theater reinforced spatially the difference between those actors and the audience, and, yes, even if spectators had to pay in order to watch, the theater used gaming structures to offer itself up as a site of social bonding between its producers and consumers.

Conceiving of theater as an information game played between its producers and audiences gets us out of a stalemate in the current study of early modern audiences and the question of how much power spectators had. Few doubt that early modern audiences in commercial theaters—either rowdy by nature, spurred on to be demanding as a result of their newly sovereign position as paying customers, or simply radically individuated in terms of interests and identities—needed to be managed, to have their attentions directed toward the play on offer. But how successfully playwrights, actors, and theater entrepreneurs achieved this management has been a source of much debate. Could theater's producers count on and evoke a mostly unanimous or dominant response to the play from all audience members? Some scholars maintain that whatever the challenges audiences presented, including ignoring the play completely, producers of plays found effective techniques to shape audience attention, response, and pleasure.[49] Others emphasize audiences' resistance to being controlled by the fiction onstage, the actors presenting it, and/or the theatrical space itself. In my own earlier book, *Voice in Motion*, I argued that early modern plays presented audiences as capable of resisting even the most potent and persuasive sounds coming from the stage, and maintained that the ability of audience members to refuse to hear put greater pressure on theater's producers to make audiences into their partners.[50] Other scholars posit an even greater disjunction between theater's producers and audiences in order to allow more power for the latter.[51]

Past discussions of spectatorship view theater's producers and audiences as engaged in either a partnership—in which neither party is a winner or loser—or a competition, whose outcome is a source of debate. But must partnership necessarily be opposed to competition? Approaching theatrical plays as games troubles this binary and reorients the debate about the power of spectators. In games we find a partnership around and through competition, an *agreement* to battle for temporary superiority over another. Competition in games is not a sign of destruction or enmity— though, of course, some matches may end that way. Rather, in games like cards, backgammon, and chess, competition and the display of enmity are essential to ludic engagement. They are the fictional terms by which people enter into a partnership with each other, if only for a few hours. As early modern theater producers made a bid to audiences to approach dramatic plays as games, they presented the commercial theater as a cooperative space where competition between producers and receivers was all part of the fun. Staged games made room for the audience's participatory energies not, as others have suggested, by insisting on the play only as a mimetic representation—an object consumed and enjoyed at a safe aesthetic distance[52]—but by presenting the play as an opportunity *for* play.

GAME PLAN

Chapter 1 of this book provides a foundation for what follows by surveying archival evidence about early modern sitting pastimes at the same time as it critically investigates archival history as a method for studying games. On the one hand, the chapter provides the kind of thick description of early modern parlor games that currently exists only for early modern festive recreations and sports by examining gaming objects (game boards, chess pieces, printed playing cards) as well as rule books and prescriptive literature on gaming. On the other hand, the chapter explores the limits of tradi-

tional archival evidence for a history of gaming. Surviving game objects
and published rules provide scripts for theoretical play scenarios, but they
do not capture easily how games work and change in practice. The chapter
proposes that early modern drama, and particularly the gaming scenes in
these dramas, are crucial kinetic supplements to other, comparatively more
static gaming evidence. Plays enact the *performance* of games.

Chapters 2, 3, and 4 illustrate this argument, each by investigating the
experience of playing a particular game: cards, backgammon (often called
by its more generic term, "tables"), and chess, respectively. The particular
games I have selected and the order in which the book's chapters examine
them bears further explanation. The choice of these games is partly a function of my methodology of play as research. In comparison to games like
merels (or Nine Men's Morris) and Game of the Goose—both board games
that were extremely popular in the sixteenth and seventeenth centuries but
that are known today only by the greatest of game history enthusiasts—
cards, backgammon, and chess remain extremely popular and widely
played today. And as I discuss further in Chapter 1, the rules and materials
of play for these games have changed very little since the sixteenth and
seventeenth centuries, thereby making it easier to draw on our familiarity
with these games when analyzing their appearance in dramatic literature.
Chess, for instance, is so widely represented in Anglo-American culture
(not to mention throughout the world) that just about everyone has a sense
of what it feels like to play the game even if not everyone actually sits down
to play it.

However, I also group these games together because they have historically been associated closely with each other. In one of the earliest pieces of
evidence about the playing of sitting pastimes in England, cards, backgammon, and chess are mentioned as the three games that are played during
the Christmas season at a noblewoman's house.[53] Many writers name this
trio of games as distinctive because they are worth playing despite involving no physical exertion. Sir William Forrest's "The Poesye of Princylye
Practice," presented to King Henry VIII's son, describes "tables, chesse, or
cardis" as "syttynge [sitting] pastymes" fit for sovereigns in the evenings
after dinner, but not for daytime and not for lower classes, who should get
more exercise and open air.[54] (*Pace* Forrest and his classist reservations, all
three games appear to have been quite popular among all sorts of English
people during the sixteenth and seventeenth centuries.) Thomas Elyot, in
The Boke Named the Governour (1531) groups them together as the three
games involving no physical exercise that are still worthwhile to play, distinguishing them from dice, which he advocates under no circumstances.[55]

And Francis Willughby's seventeenth-century manuscript "Book of Games," which categorizes forms of play, opens by dividing "plaies" into several categories: one having to do with what is exercised (wit or body) and the other to do with degree of chance/fortune involved. In the first category, chess, tables, and cards are the only three games mentioned by name under games that "exercise the wit." Willughby even goes so far as to limit the term "game" to sitting pastimes, naming these three as his key examples: "The word Game is most properly used for Cards, tables, /Chests &c, not for games of exercise."[56]

Although many early modern writers group the three games together, they also draw attention to a key difference among them, particularly the degree to which they involve chance or fortune. Willughby writes that chess differs from cards and tables in that it involves no chance, whereas cards and tables involve both "art & skill." Cards and backgammon belong in a category with other games of fortune (like "Inne & In, Crosse & Pile, One & Thirtie"), but also differ from these entirely chance-based games because cards involve some skill.[57] One especially intriguing treatment of cards, backgammon, and chess as a self-contained group whose members can be distinguished in terms of the degree of chance involved in each is the dialogue about games in John Florio's *Second Fruits* (1591). In the dialogue the characters Samuel and Antonio decide to play a game as their postdinner recreation because the weather prevents them from taking a walk. They first turn to cards, then backgammon, and finally to chess.[58] Notably, the games are ordered from greater to lesser degree of chance and, relatedly, imperfect information involved, a factor that also influences the amount of bickering the men do as they play. The more imperfect information in the game, the more likely the men are to accuse each other of cheating. Chapters 2–4 of my book follow Florio's organization—moving from cards to backgammon to chess—in an effort to understand how the formal properties of different games, and especially the extent to which they rely on imperfect information, provoke different experiences of play for direct participants and for spectators who play vicariously.

My book's investigations of theater as playable media come full circle in the Epilogue, which examines theatrical content and form in contemporary digital games in order to think about how theater informs game design today, and vice versa. The chapter examines "mimetic interface" platforms,[59] and particularly Microsoft's Kinect, arguing that one of the distinguishing features of these platforms is their theatrical affordances and particularly the way they expand the experience of gaming beyond the players and toward their spectators, who are encouraged to play vicariously. I argue that

Kinect's design is deeply indebted to theatrical concepts and promotes theatrical forms of engagement—as becomes evident in Microsoft's marketing of the gaming peripheral. But I also maintain that the commercially released software made for Kinect has rarely realized this potential because most software designers have yet to figure out how to harness the cognitive and emotional investments of game audiences. That potential is evinced in a game that I have been involved in developing at the University of California, Davis, ModLab: *Play the Knave*, a game for Kinect that is about theatrical performance of Shakespeare. *Play the Knave* actualizes the potential of Kinect as a theatrical platform that encourages vicarious spectator play. Drawing on my own experience designing *Play the Knave* and observing its use in numerous public and educational installations, I demonstrate how motion capture gaming rediscovers the link between gaming and theater that was so crucial to the commercial theater's success in the early modern period. As today's theaters fight to attract audiences in a leisure economy where games reign supreme, I consider how digital games can help contemporary gamers build *theatrical* competencies much in the way early modern dramas once did.

Figure 1. Games board (1581–1600). Made in Germany (probably Augsburg). Ebony and bone. Courtesy of the Victoria and Albert Museum.

Figure 2. Game board and pieces (1650–1747). Made in England, Netherlands, or Eger. Courtesy of the Victoria and Albert Museum.

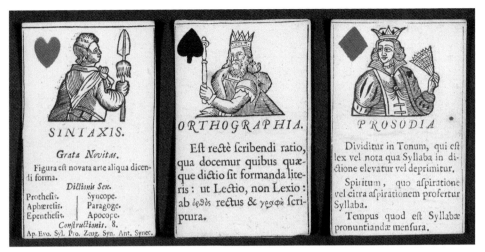

Figure 3. Joseph Moxon, *The Use of the Astronomical Playing-Cards* (1676). © The Trustees of the British Museum.

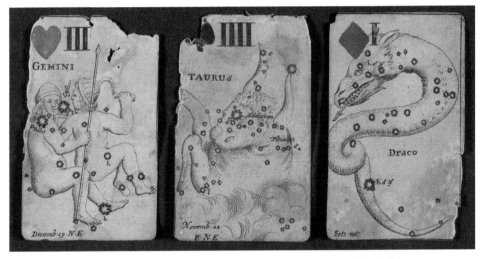

Figure 4. *Grammatical Cards* (London, 1676). © The Trustees of the British Museum.

Facing page:

Figure 5. (*top*) *Royal and Ecclesiastical Gamers* (c. 1609), by Thomas Cockson. Private Collection/Bridgeman Images.

Figure 6. (*bottom*) Francis Barlow, "Popish Plot," part of pack of fifty-two playing cards depicting four "popish" plots: the Spanish Armada, Dr Parry's Plot, the Gunpowder Plot, and the Popish Plot (London, 1679). Courtesy of the Victoria and Albert Museum.

4 · 3 · 2 · 1

Si tuta in gloria Rome. · Et fortis et fidus. · Cor unum via una. · Da Cæsari. · Cinge gladium. · Pro bello pax.

Nudus in mundum. · Deus. 4 · Fratres in unum. · 2 · Videbitis nos Deus. · 1

The Plot first hatcht at Rome by the Pope and Cardinalls.

Sr. E.B. Godfree takeing Dr. Oates his depositions.

Dr. Oates discovereth Gauan in the Lobby.

Coleman giveth a guiny to Incourage the 4 Ruffians.

Dr. Oates receives letters from ye Fathers to carry beyond Sea.

Coleman drawn to his execution.

Coleman examin'd in Newgate by severall Lords.

Coleman writeing a declaration and letters to la Chese.

The Seizing severall Conspirators.

Mr. Langhom. deliuering out commissions for severall Office.

Knave

The Irish Ruffians going for Windsor.

Mr. Everard imprison'd in the Tower.

Dr. Oates discovereth ye Plot to ye King and Councell.

Figure 7. From a complete pack of playing cards, by Augustine Ryther (London, 1590). © The Trustees of the British Museum.

Figure 8. Robert Morden, *Nottingham Sh.* and *Suffolk* (London, 1676). Folger Library call nps. ART 265507 and ART 265508, respectively. By permission of the Folger Shakespeare Library.

Figure 9. From *Geographical Cards* (London: F. H. van Hove, 1675). © The Trustees of the British Museum.

Figure 10. Print; playing card. From the incomplete pack of Henry Winstanley's *Geographical Cards of the World* (London; 1675–6). © The Trustees of the British Museum.

Figure 11. Frontispiece to Charles Cotton, *The Compleat Gamester* (London, 1674). By permission of the Huntington Library.

Figure 12. *Four Gentlemen of High Rank Playing Primero* by Master of the Countess of Warwick (c. 1567–9). The Right Hon. Earl of Derby/Bridgeman Images.

Figure 13. *Cardsharps in an Interior* (1656) by Aelbert Jansz. van der Schoor. Private collection. Photo © Rafael Valls Gallery, London, UK/Bridgeman Images.

Figure 14. *The Cardsharps* (c. 1595) by Michelangelo Merisi Caravaggio. Kimbell Art Museum, Fort Worth, Texas, USA/Bridgeman Images.

Figure 15. *The Cheat with the Ace of Clubs* by Georges de la Tour. Kimbell Art Museum, Fort Worth, Texas, USA/Bridgeman Images.

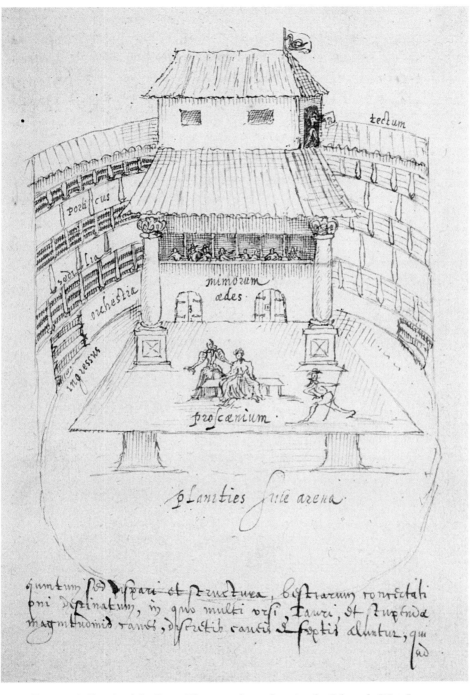

Figure 16. Sketch of the Swan Theatre, after a drawing by Johan de Witt. In Aernout van Buchell, *Adversaria*, Universiteitsbibliotheek Utrecht, Ms. 842 (7 E 3), fol. 132r (c. 1592–1621). Courtesy of Universiteitsbibliotheek Utrecht Special Collections.

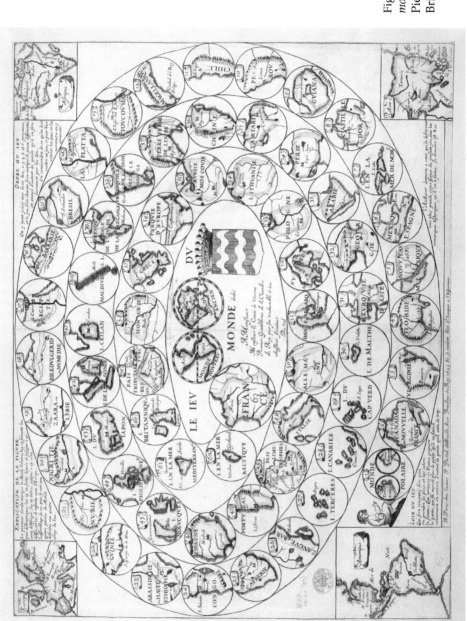

Figure 17. *Le Jeu du monde* (Paris, 1645) by Pierre du Val. © The British Library Board.

Figure 18. Frontispiece to *Arden of Faversham*, 1633 quarto edition. Courtesy of the Huntington Library.

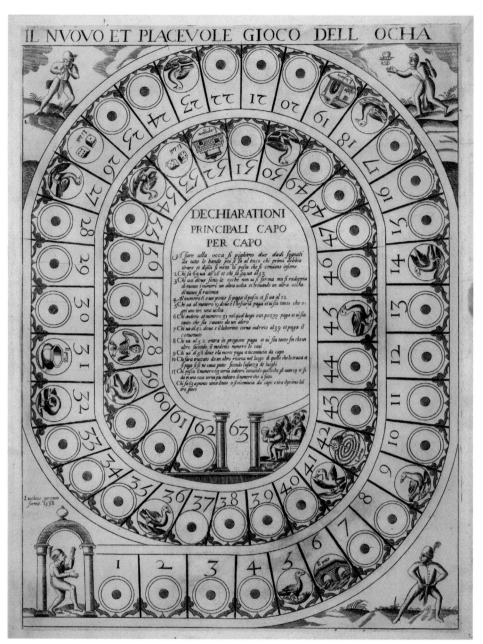

Figure 19. "Il nuovo et piacevole gioco dell ocha" (Game of the Goose). Italian, 1598. © The Trustees of the British Museum.

Figure 20. *Filosofia cortesana de Alonso de Barros* (Italian, 1588). © The Trustees of the British Museum.

Figure 21. Cirque de Soleil dancers perform physical marvels while the audience, in white ponchos, watches. Microsoft launch of Kinect at Electronic Entertainment Expo (E3), Galen Center in Los Angeles (2010). Screenshot from Playbox Games, "Speciale E3—World Premiere of Kinect," *YouTube*, 7 June 2013, https://www.youtube.com/watch?v=Uzr--8xvvF0.

Figure 22. Top left of the screenshot shows actors playing audience members who watch the show from a couch suspended from the arena ceiling. Microsoft launch of Kinect at Electronic Entertainment Expo (E3), Galen Center in Los Angeles (2010). Playbox Games, "Speciale E3—World Premiere of Kinect," *YouTube*, 7 June 2013, https://www.youtube.com/watch?v=Uzr--8xvvF0.

Figure 23. The top third of this screenshot shows the stage, a framed living room in which the members of a family play (or play vicariously) Kinect games. Below the boulder with the Xbox insignia are the Cirque de Soleil natives vicariously playing as they watch the family, while all around and behind them is the E3 audience in their white ponchos. Microsoft launch of Kinect at Electronic Entertainment Expo (E3), Galen Center in Los Angeles (2010). Playbox Games, "Speciale E3—World Premiere of Kinect," *YouTube*, 7 June 2013, https://www.youtube.com/watch?v=Uzr--8xvvF0.

Figure 24. Members of the sixth-grade class at the Epstein School (Atlanta, GA) during an installation of *Play the Knave*, 4 April 2017. Photo by Gina Bloom.

Figure 25. Users of *Play the Knave* in the University of Iowa Libraries. The game was installed in the Main Library Learning Commons on 7 September 2016, coinciding with the UI Libraries' exhibition of the First Folio as part of the Folger Shakespeare Library's national tour, *First Folio! The Book That Gave Us Shakespeare*. Photo courtesy of the University of Iowa Libraries.

ONE | Gaming History

As I argued in the Introduction, there are sound historical and theoretical reasons to study cards, backgammon, and chess as a largely self-contained group, and a material history of these games, taken as a group, is long overdue. Although there are useful studies of each of these games alone, there has been no attempt to historicize them as a collectivity.[1] Certainly there are advantages to having independent accounts of the games, given the many ways they are distinctive from each other in terms of production process and reception history. Also, as I demonstrate in the forthcoming chapters, each game creates a unique experience of play for gamers and spectators, engaging and depending on different playing competencies. That said, any attempt to understand these games in their particularities must be grounded in an understanding of their overall game genre, the *sitting pastime*. This chapter aims in part to provide a material history of sitting pastimes in the early modern period in much the way scholars have for festive recreations and sports. The chapter synthesizes vast archival research on sitting pastimes that I and others have done: when, where, and by whom were these games played; what materials were used to play them; what were the social, political, and religious attitudes toward them. However, even as I present this archival evidence, I want to think critically about what it means to write a history of games, objects that present obstacles for traditional historicist approaches for much the reason theater has done so. Like early performances, games of the past become available to historians through their material traces. In the case of games, we have, for instance, material objects of play (gaming pieces, boards, etc.); books about game rules; pro- and antigaming treatises; court records that mention gaming activity; and legal statutes that govern when and where play is allowable and what can be played. Although I use all of these records in this chapter, I also underscore throughout my analysis the limitations of these materials as evidence. Archival records of playable media do not account in any straightforward way for the fact that games are meant for and transformed through play. The challenge of telling a history of games, like one of theatrical performance, is figuring out how to account for embodied practice.

This chapter lays out two key methodologies through which *Gaming the Stage* as a whole attempts to meet that challenge. One, as this chapter points to the insufficiencies of the evidence usually used in histories of sitting pastimes, it explains why the rest of this book relies so much on close readings of dramatic texts. I treat dramatic texts not as scripts for or transcripts of theatrical performance, a textual record of what went on during performance of a play, but as supplements to the kind of evidence usually considered in histories of gaming.[2] In particular, scenes of gameplay in drama, regardless of whether they represent accurately how these scenes were staged, are valuable evidence for a history of sitting pastimes because they put games into action, showing through fictional representation what happens to a game when players engage with it. These scenes are, in effect, fictional laboratories for a historical study of gameplay. In addition to laying the groundwork for the book's valuation of dramatic texts for a history of games, this chapter also begins to set up my particular approach to close readings of these dramas. Part of what I hope to show is just how much about the history of gaming we *don't* know. Doing a history of games, indeed of any ephemeral object and embodied practice, is, we might say, a lot like playing a game of imperfect information. The past holds information that modern scholars want to know, and the aim of historical research is to provoke, compel, or coax the past into revealing what is currently hidden from us. Since the advent of New Historicism especially, historicist scholarship often takes the form of fact-finding missions, where history is the result of accumulation—the more data, the better the history—as well as a process of sorting and organizing what has been accumulated. But this sort of model of history making has its limitations, and these are especially clear when one is working with games and with theater. Both can be studied through their historical remains, but because both were created and transformed through embodied *play*, they also resist conventional historiography, which tends toward reification of timelines for events: this happened on this date. As tempting as it is to collect historical facts about games as a way to reconstruct their histories, collecting isn't sufficient.

If historicist scholarship is a game of imperfect information, then, as I've argued elsewhere, our methods of historiography might be productively informed by one of the key methods scholars use in the field of game studies: playing as a mode of research.[3] Reading about a game's rules is enlightening, but even more so when combined with *phenomenological* engagement with the object of analysis; that is, rather than just read about the games, we can learn much about them by engaging our own bodies in the act of playing them. Although this method has been defined primarily for research on modern videogames, it applies just as well to the study of analog games, including the analog games of the distant past. This method of knowing through play calls not only for a more ludic sensibility than tends to be found in history writing, but also involves questioning assumptions about the past's strangeness. Just as we must revise earlier views of gaming as a "magic circle"—where players enter a space geographically, temporally, psychologically, and psychically cut off from mundane life, subjecting themselves to a set of artificial rules[4]—so, too, we cannot see the past as a magic circle isolated from our own contemporary practices and perspectives.[5] Studying the past involves not only playing with our objects of analysis, but understanding the "metagame" we play when we do this.[6] By taking seriously the metagame as an essential and, indeed, innate part of the activity of playing with history, we not only become more aware of methodology and how it shapes the meaning of information uncovered about the past, but we recognize the ways our own historical moment, our own contexts for engagement with history, shape our understanding of the past. We need to *game* history in order to provide a history of gaming.

MATERIAL OBJECTS AND PRACTICES OF PLAY

What do we know (or think we know) about the history of sitting pastimes in England? Historical accounts of cards, backgammon, and chess generally agree that sitting pastimes, like so many objects of pleasure available to the early modern English, were an import from the Continent, where they had been introduced through cultural interactions (military and economic) with the Arab world. Historians regularly debate the origins of particular games—with a certain degree of national pride bound up in the question of initial inventor—but there is some consensus. Cards probably came to Europe from Egypt, where they were primarily used as part of fortune-telling tarot games; they migrated to Spain, then quickly to Italy, Germany, and France. In fifteenth-century France the tarot card deck was significantly altered to become the smaller fifty-two-card pack with which we play today. Historians point to the fifteenth century as the time when the English picked up the habit of playing cards, among many other things, from the French.[7]

Like playing cards, tables—what we generally call backgammon (the name of just one type of tables game)—is generally argued to have come to Europe, via Italy or Spain, from the Arab world, where a related game called *nard* was played in the early tenth century. Early European representations of the game show it played by four to seven gamers on a range of differently shaped boards, including circles and heptagons.[8] Although popular in the fifteenth century, tables is said to have been overshadowed briefly by chess until experiencing a resurgence in the early seventeenth century, when its rules and board underwent a transformation. The game that resulted was called backgammon in England (tric-trac in France, gammon in Scotland, *tavole reale* in Italy, *Puff* in Germany), and is identical to the game by that name that we play today.[9]

Like tables, chess was also originally played on a larger board and with four players, each commanding an "army" allied with one other player's army; as in tables, dice determined which piece would move.[10] A two-player version of the game, without dice, is described in Persia as Shatranj in the early seventh century, and the game spread throughout the Arab world from there. Like backgammon and cards, chess likely came to Europe via Crusaders, first appearing in Spain and Italy before coming to England. The version of the game most Europeans and Americans play today dates to the end of the fifteenth century, however, when the rules of European chess changed to feature increased movement of the Queen piece (which, under the new rules, could move as far as the player wishes in any direction instead of one space at a time); the pawn's initial move of two spaces; and the Bishop's unrestricted diagonal movement. The new rules, which sped up the game significantly, quickly became adopted throughout Europe. And by the beginning of the seventeenth century, "chess had all the characteristics of modern world chess: professional players, international competitions, team competitions, glorified star players, blindfolded players who amazed both nonplayers and experts alike, chess books with detailed analyses of playing systems, collections of games and interested public."[11]

Although scholars almost never historicize these sitting pastimes alongside each other, their histories show that cards, backgammon, and chess intersect and mirror each other in terms of how they came to Europe and what happened when they arrived. In all three cases, moreover, the games are said to have undergone changes from the fifteenth through seventeenth centuries, establishing the forms and rules with which we still play today. The story told of these games sounds quite familiar. It is a story of Renaissance Europe's absorption, modernization, and transformation of Eastern objects and practices, emphasizing Western "improvement."

The Western colonialist ideology of this historical account could use a book of its own, but let us bracket it so that we can consider the evidence on which it is based. In part, this evidence is surviving gaming materials, sometimes a tricky source of evidence since gaming objects are meant to be handled, compromising their capacity to survive over time. Gaming pieces are easily misplaced and lost. Surviving gaming objects tend to be made of precious materials, including especially ebony and ivory, indicating that when gaming objects are preserved, it is because of their value *beyond* gaming.[12] Somewhat less ephemeral than gaming objects are game boards, more substantial in size and cost, and a number of the boards used for chess and tables survive from the fourteenth century onward.[13] These materials offer evidence of the close relationships among the three sitting pastimes, particularly chess and backgammon. Mobile boards existed as part of special hinged game boxes (Figures 1 and 2). Many have chess on one face and sometimes the game of merels (or Nine Men's Morris) on the other; opening the box and laying it flat reveals a backgammon board on the inside, with spaces to store the pieces for each game.[14]

Playing cards, though less durable because made of paper instead of heartier materials, present different obstacles to preservation. Many sets of cards persist, though, as part of print collections, for cards were a product of the printing press and, indeed, often sold alongside books. The production process was similar to that used for illustrations in books. Card illustrations were engraved onto wood blocks used for printing, with multiple cards placed together on a single sheet. Prints were then colored in by hand, the sheets cut, and the individual cards mounted onto pasteboard, defined in one seventeenth-century manuscript on gaming as "3 or 4 peices [*sic*] of white paper pasted togather and made verie smooth."[15] Many playing cards have survived in uncut sheets at various stages of the production process, as well as in the form of cut and mounted cards.[16] Cards also survive because, before the tradition of printing designs on the backs of playing cards began, the backs were blank and could be used as scratch paper.[17] Playing cards were also treated as useful printing waste, and bookmakers occasionally repurposed printed sheets of playing cards as bindings for other books.[18]

Surviving evidence of playing objects from the early modern period reveals several interesting things and obscures some others. Notably, we find that the objects used for sitting pastimes have been altered very little, if at all, over the past four hundred years of their European history. Although some of the materials used to construct these objects have changed, their basic design has remained the same since the early modern period. The English still play with a fifty-two-card deck like that used by their early modern ancestors: the same numbering system (pips one through ten and court cards Jack, Queen, and King) and symbols for suits. Chess and tables boards have kept the same number of spaces and visual design (alternating black and white spaces for chess, oblong triangles for each point in backgammon), and the basic design of the pieces used on both boards have not changed much either. One can even still purchase hinged gaming boxes with backgammon or checkers on one side and chess on the other. This appears to confirm the significance of the sixteenth and seventeenth centuries for modern game studies, a field that tends to look to the mid- to late twentieth century (the advent of popular games like *Dungeons & Dragons* and the beginnings of videogames) as its modern point of origin. Surviving material objects of gaming rework game studies periodization to point to these earlier centuries as a vital moment in gaming history.

There's something deeply comforting about a narrative like this for a historicist project like mine. Anytime a scholarly study defines a particular set of years, decades, or centuries for investigation, the inevitable question is, Why that period for that project? Past histories of sitting pastimes answer that question very neatly for me. Insofar as many gaming objects for these pastimes were standardized to take their modern shapes and designs in the fifteenth through seventeenth centuries, we can confidently label this the *early* modern period of gaming. But I cite this historical narrative about games less to bolster the historicist credibility of my own study than to foreground the methodology I espouse. If gaming materials shape the experience of play, something game studies scholars have emphasized especially in the past decade through their focus on technologies of gaming and platform studies, then there is much to be gained through the discovery that moderns share with early moderns a substantial similarity in our experience of cards, backgammon, and chess games. We play cards with a deck containing four suits, thirteen cards in each. When we play backgammon, we have the same number of spaces and counters to consider. When we think about which chess piece to move, our options are precisely those that were available to the early modern player. To be sure, plenty of historical and cultural differences separate modern players from their early modern counterparts, creating all sorts of differences in how we play. But the risks of sounding like a technological determinist or an irresponsible ahistoricist are outweighed by the benefits of recognizing historical continuities. I would submit that we can know *something* of what it felt like for early moderns to play or watch others play these games because we use essentially the same gaming materials they did.

ATTITUDES TOWARD GAMEPLAY

Of course, games are more than their material parts, and the experience of gameplay is also shaped by how the activity of gaming is perceived within a particular culture. There are social, political, and religious differences be-tween early modern England and contemporary Anglo-American culture in terms of attitudes toward gaming, though the differences might be argu-ably more of degree than kind. This section looks closely at the evidence on which scholars have relied most often to understand early modern English attitudes toward gaming: legal statutes, conduct books, and religio-moral treatises. One of my aims, as mentioned above, is to underscore continu-ities between early modern and contemporary perspectives. But I also want to use game studies methodologies—particularly attention to the formal properties of specific games—to intervene in the historical narrative that tends to be told about early modern attitudes toward gaming. Instead of examining how early moderns treated the broad category of "pastimes" (the strategy pursued by most prior scholars of early modern games), I hone in on sitting pastimes as a specific subset of games in order to reveal how legal, moral, and religious questions about games and gameplay in-dexed a whole set of epistemological concerns about the flow and control of information—a concern of political and religious authorities at the time. Instead of approaching games as yet another locus of cultural production that catalyzed political and religious tensions in the early modern period, I focus on what the formal dimensions of these particular games meant in the early modern politico-religious climate. This helps us see *why* games emerged as a source of so much controversy in the period.

Despite plenty of complaints in the early modern period about game-play, the activity had its defenders, especially among writers of conduct books, who often presented games as useful for social improvement or education. Gerolamo Cardano's book on probability in gaming, *Liber de ludo aleae* (written in the mid-sixteenth century though published posthu-mously almost a century later), explains that games such as cards and backgammon are "a means of gaining friendship, and many have risen from obscurity because of the friendship of princes formed in play."[19] That certainly would have been the case for men wishing to form friendships with King James I, who was known to take much pleasure in sitting pas-times. The king recommends "carts [i.e. cards] or tables" to his son in *Basi-likon Dōron: His Majesties Instructions to His Dearest Sonne, Henry the Prince* (1603), supporting the playing of these games especially during times of "foule and stormie weather" when outdoor sports are inconvenient or on the rare occasion that the king has nothing else to do.[20] James Cleland's conduct book *The Institution of a Young Noble Man* (1607) explicitly cites King James's support for cards and tables, going further to argue that knowledge of these games is crucial to a nobleman's social identity: it is a "great simplicite and rusticitie in a Noble man to be ignorant of anie of them, when he commeth in companie."[21] Many other seventeenth-century conduct book writers concur. Nicholas Faret's handbook for social climbing, *The Honest Man; or, The Art to Please in Court* (1632), maintains that gentlemen will benefit from learning not just the usually recommended recreations, such as dancing, tennis, wrestling, hunting, shooting, and music, but also other "sports which are not so simply honest, but they many times prove profitable." These games involving chance—including "games at Hazard"—are mostly beneficial for the social connections they help make possible and sustain: "great men" play them, and if one wants to "grow familiar in their companies," one should know how to recreate in the way great men do.[22]

The emphasis of many of these treatises on the training of gentlemen can seem somewhat alienating to modern readers, who no longer view cards, backgammon, and chess as elite pursuits.[23] However, even in the early modern period sitting pastimes were hardly considered the province of nobility alone, and plenty of early modern authors maintain that the benefits of play are available to anyone, regardless of social status. Their comments on the value of gameplay, combined with the emergence in the period of games with educational content, uncannily anticipate the twenty-first-century movement of so-called "games for education" or "edutainment." A manuscript at the British Library (dating most likely to the sixteenth century) on artificial memory concludes with information about how the lessons therein can be applied to chess and cards, suggesting the degree to which these games were thought to offer a forum for improving mental dexterity.[24] Many early modern writers tout chess as capable of strengthening what early moderns called the "wit," articulating the very logic about chess that has led English and American elementary schools today to include chess boards in the classroom and to sponsor chess clubs. Thomas Elyot's *Boke Named the Governour* (1531) commends chess over other "games wherin is no bodily exercise" because it is a "ryght subtile engine, wherby the wit is made more sharpe, and remembrance quickened."[25] Pedro Damiano's influential book on chess, which was published in England as *The Pleasaunt and Wittie Playe of the Cheasts* (1562), lauds chess for the ways it "breadeth in player[s] a certaine studye, pollicie, wit, forcast, memorie, with other properties, to make men circumspect."[26]

These early modern defenses of games resonate with current rhetoric around games for learning and the ever-expanding industry of edutainment. In a keynote address at the 2014 Games in Education Symposium, Lee Sheldon, the author of *The Multiplayer Classroom*—a book that teaches teachers how to deliver educational content through games—advised teachers interested in educational games to find "'balanced' games" that occupy, in the words one attendee who blogged about the talk, "a middle ground where learning and fun intersect."[27] As they advocate for learning through gameplay, experts like Sheldon are careful to put to rest concerns that gaming is otherwise a waste of time. Games are beneficial when they occupy that "middle ground" state of both learning and fun, but not sliding too far into the latter. A similar anxiety about the unproductiveness of play gets articulated by early moderns, and early game makers used similar strategies to address that concern: they created games with educational potential.

The new wave in educational gaming is, in fact, a very old wave. Beginning in the early sixteenth and especially in the latter half of the seventeenth century, educational cards that offered, in the words of one publisher, "Pleasure and Profit" appear to have been all the rage, with dozens of different sorts of packs aiming to teach everything from grammar and geography to astronomy and history. Some of these games appear to have been designed explicitly for classroom use. For instance, *Grammatica figurata; or, Grammar as a Card Game* (1509), created by German humanist Matthias Ringmann and one of the earliest examples of educational playing cards, gives each of the eight parts of speech a figure: Priest is noun, Vicar is pronoun, King is verb, Queen is adverb, Monk is participle, Churchwarden is preposition, Fool is interjection, and Cupbearer is conjunction.[28] The teacher likely facilitated play-based learning through the *colloquiorum* technique employed by grammar schools. For instance, he might call out for a verb, and the player discards that card if he has it. (For a much later set of grammatical playing cards, see Figure 4.) Another early German advocate of pedagogical playing cards was Thomas Murner, a Franciscan monk, who wrote a letter in 1502 about how he created a game of cards to help him memorize Justinian.[29] In 1507 Murner published *Chartiludium logicae*, cards to be used for instruction in the art of reasoning. The deck has sixteen suits, each of which corresponds to a particular method of reasoning, such as "The Exception," "The Supposition," and so on.[30] Though, like Ringmann's deck, Murner's is quite different from the typical fifty-two-card deck, where there are only four suits, it is clearly designed to align on some level with regular playing cards in that it comprises fifty-two cards total. Among the most famous educational cards were the set of four card decks created by French academician Jean Desmarests in collaboration with renowned Florentine engraver Stefano della Bella, for the explicit purpose of educating the young French King Louis XIV on mythical figures, famous kings and queens in French history, and geography—with individual packs on each of those four topics.[31] Although designed for the young king, the cards were intended to be distributed to a general public, as is evinced by Desmarests receiving a patent in 1644 for a monopoly on sales of the decks.

The English also rode the wave of educational card decks. In the British Library's archives is part of the table of contents from a volume called *The Boke of the New Cardys* (1530), which advocates for cards to be used in learning a variety of grammar school subjects, including spelling, reading, and mathematics. The book offers lessons on each subject and then a set of games to help students test their knowledge.[32] Although we do not have remaining examples of it, there are records showing that William Maxwell published sometime before 1615 *Jamesanna; or, A Pythagorical play at cards, representing the excellency and utility of Union and Concord, with the incommodities of Division and Discorde.*[33] The great majority of surviving English decks of educational cards date from the middle to the end of the seventeenth century. As I discuss further below, the subjects of these cards ranged widely, from history and geography to astronomy and mythology. Many of these decks seem geared toward users outside of formal institutions of learning. For instance, a set of astronomical playing cards that Joseph Moxon printed and claims to have sold at his "Shop at the Sign of the Atlas" in London has each of the four suits correspond to one of the four seasons that affect where constellations appear in the sky (Figure 3).[34] Other decks were explicitly directed to young students. Among these are F. Jackson's *Schollers Practicall Cards . . . containing instructions by means of cards how to spell, write, cipher, and cast accounts . . . rules of calculation etc.* (1656) and a deck of grammar cards published by John Seller. The British Museum holds a cut set of the latter, their front card advertising "These *Cards* Are Ingeniously Contrived for the Comprising the general Rules of Lillie's Grammar, in the four principal Parts thereof, *viz. Orthographia, Prosodia, Etymologia,* and *Syntaxis*" (Figure 4).[35]

The purveyors of educational cards position them as the ideal form of recreation, defining recreation not simply as a break from work but as a way to occupy oneself productively *during* a break from work. The case is made in interesting terms in the prefatory material for the grammar cards when they were sold in the form of a codex. Presumably these could be read in codex form, just like any other grammar book, or cut and mounted by the purchaser to be used as playing cards, and therein they evince in their material form the overlapping worlds of work and play in early modern edutainment. In an address to the reader/buyer, T. B. puts some pressure on the difference between these activities. He points out that it is impossible to be engaged in serious study all the time; people need a respite. But he notes that if this downtime is not carefully managed and directed, people risk falling into idleness. "[T]he mind then doth necessarily require some *medium* betwixt Idleness and Labour," the aim of recreation being to "comforteth, and frameth the mind a new to weighty exercise."[36] Recreation is meant as a productive break *from* labor in order to return *to* labor, with the mind refreshed and energized, but not dulled. T. B.'s use of the term "medium" points in two different directions, both of which resonate with proponents of the modern "games for education" movement. Where medium means "intermediary" or "channel of expression,"[37] T. B. urges buyers to think of cards as objects for delivering learning *through* games. Where medium means "a middle quality, degree, or condition," cards provide a middle condition between idleness and labor, allowing the user to occupy a state that is neither of these extremes. In this, T. B. forestalls the kind of critique of games Robert Burton articulates in his recommendation in *Anatomy of Melancholy* (1621) that scholars avoid chess because it overworks their already overworked brains, a claim King James I also made about chess. Burton argues that when scholars take a break between sessions of work, they should occupy that intermediary time with vigorous exercise of the body so as to expel the melancholic humors of their sedentary daily lives, something chess cannot do because, as a seated game that taxes the mind, it is too much like study.[38] In contrast to Burton, T. B. maintains that at least these particular cards can be recreational despite being both sedentary and mentally challenging because the work can be fun. T. B. asks, "what can be more delightful than to recollect (without any labour) the rudiments of so necessary an Art as Grammar is." Learning grammar, he suggests, can feel like play. "What Recreation can be more profitable to a Student, or lover of good Letters than that which bring his mind those Rules whereby he is enabled to speak Congruously and Elegantly, and that *per jocum* without hindring him from his more necessary and grave studies."[39]

Educational games, then as now, attempted to counter cultural concerns about gaming as a sign of idleness and of unproductivity. Although today's antigaming rhetoric carries similarly moralistic overtones—and is sometimes countered with similar techniques of designing games that allow people to work productively while they play[40]—these were even more pronounced in early modern English discussions of gaming, a consequence of particularly widespread religious rhetoric about idleness as a sinful spiritual state. Additionally, in a society where church and state were more deeply and unquestioningly imbricated—where the king was expected to be both leader of the commonwealth and leader of the church—religious arguments about gaming were expressed through political policies. In this politico-religious climate, sitting pastimes raised unique theological and moral problems.[41]

The lawfulness of sitting pastimes was debated vigorously throughout Europe during the medieval and early modern periods, and a great number of prohibitions against gaming tell a story of the state's significant investments in controlling the who, what, when, where, and how of gameplay. In the mid-thirteenth century, Louis IX forbade his court officials and all subjects from playing tables, and there were repeated French prohibitions against gaming (1254, 1319, and 1369), as well as a 1397 prohibition against laborers playing cards on working days. The Spanish prohibited cards in their antigaming regulations of 1332 and 1387.[42] More leniency for cards can be found in a German prohibition from the early 1380s, which exempts cards—along with bowls, horse racing, and shooting with crossbows—from gaming restrictions as long as bets are no more than one groat. However, in 1397 we find a statute against cards in the "Red Book" of Ulm.[43] Regulations against sitting pastimes become more extensive throughout the fifteenth century, perhaps as interest in the games was spreading. In fifteenth-century France, Nuremberg and Augsburg (these two cities being key centers of card making, as was Ulm), there were bans against playing tables and cards, accompanied by public burnings of the objects used for these games. Regulations during this time seem most concerned with the gambling associated with sitting pastimes. A French law from 1430 allows card play as long as participants play for pins, not money; in 1496 England, cards were also permitted as long as players wagered only meat and drink, though in 1503, playing for any stake was considered unlawful.[44] Tables was restricted more than other sitting pastimes. Even when chess was accepted by ecclesiastical canons, tables was still considered unlawful until the end of the fifteenth century, when its players were finally given some reprieve throughout much of Europe on the condition that they did not play for big stakes and that they were of a high enough status; apprentices and university students were still prohibited from tables.[45]

In England, a series of laws about gameplay evinced a similar consensus that games were acceptable under particular circumstances of play. In 1541–2, when England's Henry VIII issued his famous statute requiring the king's subjects aged 7–60 to practice longbow, he also laid out several key policies regarding sitting pastimes. He banned common houses where games such as cards and tables were played unless these establishments advertised clearly, on "placards" placed outside the venue, which games were available there. The statute also restricted the playing of various games, including tables and cards, by "husbandmen, artificers, craftsmen, serving men, apprentices and labourers" to Christmastime and insisted the games be played in a master's house or presence. That said, men of a certain status/income (£100 per year) could license their servants to play on their own.[46] But this by no means suggested widespread acceptance of sitting pastimes. Edward Hall's *The Triumphant Reigne of King Henry VIII* (c. 1548) describes a proclamation from 1526 made against "all unlawfull games accordyng to the statutes made in this behalf, and Commissions awarded into every shire for the execucon of the same, so that in all places *Tables, Dice, Cards and Bowles were taken and burnt.*"[47] And in 1559 one of Queen Elizabeth's injunctions in the first year of her reign prohibited clergy from spending their evenings at games like dice, cards, or tables.[48]

The Elizabethan Canons of 1571 were the last injunctions against tables in England,[49] and there appears to be a shift in the late sixteenth and early seventeenth century toward greater tolerance and even support for sitting pastimes. Instead of outright bans, we find more efforts to regulate these pastimes through taxation. Perhaps governments realized that if they couldn't stop gaming, they could at least make some money off of the popular activity—a strategy that persists today in, for example, state-sponsored lotteries. Moral concerns about gambling were arguably always really about economics, since gambling led to loss of money.[50] In the case of cards, the bulk of which came into England from France, most regulations involved taxes on imports and exports.[51] Proclamations tell a story about the gradual acceptance of games by legal authorities, but from a game studies perspective, what is interesting about this story is the way it highlights games as not part of a "magic circle," separated from daily affairs, but as an emerging big business in which the state was (literally) well invested. The circulation of money in gaming created a microeconomy largely beyond the purview of the state and local authorities, so it is no wonder that legal proclamations allowing for gameplay repeatedly articulate the condition that gamers bet only small sums or less valuable objects, like pins.

Proclamations also offer evidence of how the state involved itself even more directly in the gaming economy. Throughout the seventeenth century, the English government supported the country's fledgling card-making business—much as it bolstered other English manufacturers of luxury commodities— to help it compete with foreign imports. Toward the end of Queen Elizabeth I's reign, she granted Edward Darcy a patent to make cards in England.[52] King James I took up the cause in 1615, issuing a proclamation to redress the concerns of English card makers who claimed that imported cards were still stifling their business. He addresses the problem by appointing one Sir Richard Cognisby (the card makers' choice) to be in charge of "viewing, searching, sealing and allowing" all playing cards, assessing a 5s. tax on imported cards.[53] King Charles I continues this mission to create a more robust English card-making business. In 1628 Charles incorporates the Mistery of Makers of Playing Cards of the City of London, granting it the exclusive right to supervise the trade of cards in and around London. The company agreed to make enough playing cards to meet demand throughout the kingdom and to sell the cards "at as Cheap and low rates and prices" as imported foreign cards. The charter gives card makers extensive control over their trade, mandating that playing cards may only be made by Freemen of the Company, that is, those who have served out their seven-year apprenticeship, and also that cards would have to be sealed by the company's Receiver (at a fee of 2s. per pack plus 1s. to the Receiver) with the seal showing the identity of the maker.[54] Even these actions failed to stem the tide of imports, as evinced by several subsequent regulations. Charles I's *Proclamation Concerning Playing-Cards and Dice* in 1638 mandates that all cards made abroad and imported had to be sealed in London and put into new bindings and covers. Parliament itself got involved with the cause in 1643, responding to complaints by "severall Poore *Cardmakers* of *London*, who having beene bred up in their Trades of Making Playing-Cards, are likely to perish with their Families" because of the many imported cards that continued to find their way into England and Wales. Parliament addressed the problem by ordering the seizure of foreign cards and prosecution of offenders responsible for them, since this is contrary to the "Lawes and statutes of this Realme."[55] King Charles II followed up with a proclamation in 1684 that, once again, forbids the importation of foreign playing cards, ordering them to be seized and destroyed. These proclamations demonstrate the English state's persistent interests in games as big business, not so different from the current American gaming culture, where states support the building of casinos through arguments that the revenues from them will support state programs, including public schooling.

Arguably somewhat less familiar to us in our modern era of pervasive gaming are early modern religio-moral critiques of gameplay. In contrast to today's ethical arguments that focus heavily on the narrative and symbolic aspects of a game (e.g., whether violent games prompt violent action by players), early modern moral authorities expressed most concern about the circumstances of play, particularly about when was an appropriate time to engage in pastimes, sitting or other. For laborers, holidays and Sabbath provided the only free hours possible for recreation, and thus sitting pastimes were often associated with these days.[56] Sitting pastimes had long been especially popular on Christmas. One of the earliest English references to cards, tables, and chess as a group is a late fifteenth-century letter from Margery Paston to her husband, John, describing the games that the Lady Morlee reported being played at her house on Christmas: there were "no lowde dysports; but pleyng at the tabyllys, and schesse, and *cards; sweche dysports sche gave her folkys leve to play and no odyr.*"[57] The final phrase suggests that Lady Morlee gave permission to various dependents, probably including servants, to play at these, and only these, sitting pastimes during the holiday. The tradition of sitting pastimes on Christmas continued throughout the early modern period for a range of social groups. John Stow reports that "from All-hallows evening to the day after Candlemas-day," people played "at cards for counters, nailes, and points, *in every house,* more for pastime than for gain."[58] The association of card games with Christmas was so strong that the Children of the Queen's Revels, a theater company, are reported to have performed an entire card-themed play before Queen Elizabeth at Windsor on the night of St. Stephens Day (known as Boxing Day in England): "a Comodie or Morral devised on a game of cardes." John Harrington observes that this probably satirical play "showed how foure Parasiticalle knaves robbe the foure principall vocations of the Realme, *videlicet,* the evocations of Souldiers, Scollers, Marchants, and Husbandmen."[59]

Some early modern religious figures argue that setting aside time on holy days and Sabbath for recreations was essential for keeping the peace and even for spiritual welfare. Nicholas Bownde's treatise in defense of recreating on the Sabbath maintains that recreation is natural and necessary and that if there is not some prescribed time on the Sabbath for pastimes, the people will choose games over church, a much worse predicament.[60] This position was advocated most publically and controversially by James I's famous *Book of Sports* (1618), which declared it legal for people to engage in "lawful recreations" after church on Sundays and on holy days. Charles I, again controversially, rereleased the *Book of Sports* in 1633, adding prefatory and closing remarks that present recreation as not only lawful but spiritually beneficial. The document maintains that the right to recreate is made not only on behalf of the people but "for the service of God, and for suppressing of any humors that oppose trueth."[61] Peter Heylyn's *History of the Sabbath* (1636), dedicated to Charles I, defends recreations when played after services. Heylyn gives examples of how Protestants in Geneva and England have long practiced postservice recreation, for Sabbath duties end with the morning sermon.[62] Some writers included sitting pastimes among the allowable forms of recreation on Sabbath and holi-days. Even Phillip Stubbes—infamous critic of recreations, including theater—doesn't condemn them completely. To be sure, his *Anatomie of Abuses* (1583) complains about how "especially at Christmas time there is nothyng els used but Cardes, Dice, Tables" and so forth because these games are licensed at this time; he remarks that people ought to do "holier" things at such a holy time. But Stubbes also writes that if participants are not playing for money or gain and if the games are played between Christians as "private recreations, after some oppression of studie, to drive awaie fantasies" then these games are acceptable.[63]

The sentiment was by no means universally shared, however, especially as tensions between Puritans and royalists intensified. The Sabbath and holidays may have been the only free time available for gameplay, but they were precisely the times that religious authorities wished to protect for spiritual duties, their version of "recreation." Antitheatricalist William Prynne's *The Lord's Day, the Sabbath Day* (1636) associates those who play games on the Sabbath, even after services have concluded, with papists. A poem he cites in his treatise describes how papists play after morning services, and this leads them into complete mayhem such that they have forgotten all that is learned in the morning and are unable to stop their sport to return to spiritual duties in the evening. Sitting pastimes, however sedate, are among the recreations that cause problems. The poem describes a "sort there is that doe not love abroad to roame, / But for to passe their time at Carts or Tables still at home."[64] Even this seemingly quiet and contained occupation turns raucous, for no matter the game, consumption of alcohol accompanies it: "[t]he God of wine doth never want in all their sports and play," so every Sabbath ends up with "some drunken Fray," the men unable to return to church for evensong.

Games become one fulcrum for escalating tensions over the course of the seventeenth century between Protestant reformers and royalists, and in terms of the debate about the timing of recreation, sitting pastimes were not much different from other ludic activities prior historians have discussed. However, in terms of the debate about allowable forms of play, sitting pastimes raised unique concerns. For although certain sins, such as idleness, were considered risks in any form of recreation, sitting pastimes carried their own, somewhat particular risks because of the ways information circulates in these games. In particular, an essential component of sitting pastimes is the extent to which they rely on chance, information that is unknown to any of the players. Because of their integration of this kind of information, the games raise a set of epistemological questions whose religious and spiritual implications went far beyond what constitutes a worthy use of one's time.

For religious authorities from the period, the extent to which games involve chance was often the critical factor in determining whether a game was allowable.[65] Indeed, authorities largely exempted chess from their criticism of sitting pastimes. Although medieval canon lawyers and theologians had debated whether chess play was sinful, they ultimately concluded that as a game of skill, chess could be distinguished from games involving some chance, like cards and backgammon, and thus was legal and ethical as long as players avoided the pitfalls that often accompanied gaming, such as pride and covetousness. In fact, medieval writers regularly use chess as an allegory for moralistic lessons—the most famous of these being Jacobus de Cessolis's late thirteenth-century book *De ludo scachorum*, one of the first printed books in England.[66] When Thomas Elyot advocates for chess in the fifteenth century, he maintains that the game is especially "commendable" if players have read such moralizations and can keep them in mind as they play. The conditions for accepting chess also explain why dice, solely a game of chance, was almost universally condemned. Backgammon and cards, however, were considered "mixt" games, involving some chance and some skill, and there was, thus, little consensus about them. Even Elyot, who generally favors sitting pastimes, is ambivalent on the point. In his chapter "Of other exercises, whiche if they be moderately used, be to every astate of man expedient," he begins with a long condemnation of dice, and then writes that "Playinge at cardes and tables is some what more tollerable, onely for as moch as therin wytte [wit] is more used, and lesse truste is in fortune, all be it therin is neyther laudable study nor exercise." He goes on to suggest that it is possible, much as he argues for chess, for virtuous men to use cards and tables to create games with a virtuous fictional narrative attached, such as "devising a bataile, or contentio[n] between vertue and vice," and in these cases cards and tables offer "moch solace and also study commodiouse."[67]

For many religious writers, however, backgammon and even more so cards were problematic whatever the nature of the game played with them, because they involved more chance. Well-known antitheatricalist John Northbrook, like Thomas Wilcox and Richard Rice, is tolerant of tables but excoriates card play because it doesn't require skill: "Playing at Tables is farre more tollerable (although in all respectes not allowable than dyce and cardes are), for that it leaneth partlye to chaunce, and partly to industrie of the mynde. For although they cast indeed by chaunce, yet the castes are governed by industrie and witte."[68] And Samuel Bird, who allows for games within moderation, distinguishes between games that are primarily about "looking on" (hunting, hawking, stage plays) and games "wherein men are the chiefe dooers" (dancing, tennis, etc.)."[69] Although he allows for a variety of these games in moderation, he rebukes cards along with dice, arguing that they are inextricably linked with gambling.

Early modern theologians often refer to the issue of chance in their decrees regarding which games are and are not lawful, but what is at stake in the concept of chance? A game studies approach helps reveal that what is really at issue in these debates is the question of who/what has control over information in a game. From a theistic perspective in which God knows and determines all, there isn't really such a thing as chance or luck. God knows certain information, and the casting of lots was considered a way to figure out what God knows. This is why lots were historically used to adjudicate all sorts of important questions. For early critics of chance-based games, using lots for pleasure—to adjudicate matters that are mundane and trivial—is a waste of God's time. As William Perkins puts it in his condemnation of "lusory lots," it is sinful to "referre unto Gode the determination of things of [the] moment."[70] Similarly, Jean Taffin's *The Amendment of Life* (1595) maintains that cards (again, like dice) are problematic because we "applie the lot and consequently Gods providence to our vaine and frivolous pleasures."[71] Certain games could, however, escape moral and religious condemnation if they involved more "honest industrie of the minde,"[72] letting men's wits, not God, decide the outcome.

Tables and cards present problems for religious commentators because they involve both perfect and imperfect information. The complicated nature of "mixt" games is discussed influentially in James Balmford's *A Short and Plaine Dialogue Concerning the Unlawfulnes of Playing at Cards or Tables, or Any Other Game Consisting in Chance* (1593), which, as the title indicates, condemns both cards and tables for precisely the opposite reason that Perkins allows them. Written as a dialogue between a professor and a preacher, the treatise begins with the professor character saying that he understands why dice are unlawful, but would like the preacher's opinion on cards and tables. The preacher responds that since these games "somewhat depend upon chance," they are "some what evill," exemplifying his overall point that "Lots are not to bee used in sport."[73] Although cards and tables demand some exercise of the wit, they still involve chance (the dice in tables and the shuffling and cutting in cards), thereby problematically "making God an umpire."[74] Balmford significantly expands on his arguments in *A Modest Reply to Certaine Answeres, which Mr. Gataker B.D. in his Treatise of the Nature, & use of Lotts, giveth to Arguments in a Dialogue concerning the Unlaw-*

fulnes of Games consisting in Chance (1623), wherein he refutes Thomas Gataker's influential arguments in support of games of chance.

Gataker recognizes that there is always some human industry involved, even in games that seem to comprise chance alone. He explains that although it is true that lots are used to determine which cards each player has, in "assigning each of them his chance," chance is not all. There is "arte and skil beside that to be imployed by them for the managing of their game, and for the working upon that which casualty hath cast on them."[75] But Gataker's pro-gaming argument goes further than prior treatises in that rather than arguing for particular recreations by questioning the extent to which they involve chance versus skill, he queries the foundational logic that informs antigaming writers. He theorizes a partnership between God and humans, in life and in games, maintaining that people use "Arte and industrie" to manage events even if God's providence is ultimately guiding such events.[76] Gataker simply has to accept these games because not doing so, he suggests, would end up leading to heretical conclusions. If we accept the notion that lots are the providence of God, he writes, then the fact that men can cast lots whenever they wish would mean that they have the power to make God work for them, at their pleasure. This, he says, is "absurd," and that God has more important things to do than worry about the games humans play with cards or even with dice.[77] God may know all, but it is ridiculous to ask what he knows about the outcome of a game.

Gataker, John Downe, and some other religious writers sidestep the tricky spiritual implications of lusory lots, instead shifting their focus to the ethics of gaming to argue that what matters most is the "disposition" of the gamester, not the particular game being played. Writes Downe, "although I allow the *Games* themselves, notwithstanding the Lot used in them: yet I condemne and detest . . . those foule enormities wherewith they are abused."[78] Jeremy Taylor, like Gataker, argues that cards and dice are not unlawful in themselves because chance is a feature of all human affairs; we can hardly condemn games on account of their integration of chance. He maintains that as long as the games can be separated from crimes and dangers, they can be used alongside other "innocent recreations and divertisements."[79] The key is that players should always use reason to make sure they don't venture more than they can afford. And Perkins, even as he draws a line at games of hazard where there is no skill at all involved, goes on to say that playing chance-based games is acceptable if the stakes are small and players' intentions are good and lawful.[80]

The insistence on small stakes helped ensure that gamers did not become destitute as a result of playing, a condition that had economic as well as spiritual implications. Perkins and others recognized that gaming was, as many argue today, an addictive habit. Gamers who found themselves losing repeatedly could be driven to commit spiritual sins (cursing God or cheating) and criminal acts (stealing). Writers describe the gamester as unable to stop playing out of a belief that good luck will persist or bad luck will change, resulting in a win. Richard Brathwaite warns, recalling the debate discussed above about the definition of recreation: "*Hope* and *feare* make his [the gamester's] recreation an affliction. Hee ha's no time to refresh his mind, being equally divided betwixt *hope* of gaine, and *feare* of losse."[81] When gaming becomes a habit—more about winning money instead of gaining pleasure—it is no longer a defendable pursuit, becoming instead an affliction. Moral commentators frequently cite stories of men who put everything on the line for the game, and thus lose everything they have.[82] Warning against this fate, Richard Crimsal's ballad advises young men to "forsake lewd company[,] cards, dice, and queanes [prostitutes]" and gives the first-person account of one John Hadland, who spent all his money on these engagements and now has nothing, having lost all his money and his friends.[83] Some commentators warn against sitting pastimes not because they are inherently evil, but because they set off a chain reaction of immoral and criminal activity. Roger Ascham's *Toxophilus* (1545), a treatise advocating for archery, condemns cards (along with dice) for encouraging idleness, blasphemy, and dishonesty. Ascham goes on to write that men who choose these games instead of healthy pastimes like archery fall into a downward spiral of loss: "first, he loseth his goods, he loseth his time, he loseth quickness of wit, and all good lust to other things; he loseth honest company, he loseth his good name and estimation, and at last, if he leave it not, loseth God and heaven and all; and, instead of these things, winneth at length either hanging or hell."[84] A century later, John Philpot describes the "seven constant Hand-maides" to unlawful gaming, which also spiral down from bad to worse: lying, swearing, adultery, beggary, and ultimately, damnation.[85] Losing at games was storied to result in not only social and personal, but also spiritual degradation. A common immediate response to loss, writers point out, is swearing, which leads gamesters to commit the sin of blasphemy. Brathwaite teases that the gamester "remembers God more in *Oaths* than in *Orisons*."[86]

Ironically, it is Gataker's logic that the outcome of games is controlled by men, and not God, that partly motivates sins around gaming. Even when only small amounts of money are at stake, gaming was seen to sow discord and lead to violence as players debate the rules to sway the outcome of a game in their favor. Bird offers several card game scenarios to illustrate the dangers of this metagaming: "At Mawe, if the ace of hearts be turned up, when he that is to make, maketh this for it, then doth a mervailous controversie arise, whether he that turneth it up should win the set, or he that winneth five tricks: then must wagers be laide."[87] The rules of games vary so much, and players familiar with variations can use this knowledge to their own advantage, arguing for the version of the rules that would best support their case for winning. Debate about those rules could spell the end of friendship, as Bird warns through a story about a card game gone awry when there was a disagreement about "whether the trumpe that was turned up at the last, should be a voide card, or no." This mundane question led two men who had been "dailie companions" into an argument that drove them apart for "a quarter of a yeare after."[88] Quarrels, writers point out, often began because of accusations of foul play, which, they maintain, is rampant because gamesters do whatever they can to ensure a win. In effect, it is the belief that a player can change the outcome of a game that leads to the use of skillful argumentation, as well as cheating and crime.

Games were dangerous because they materialized through play weighty theological issues of the day. Indeed, as I discuss further in the next chapter, some Protestant preachers took advantage of the material analogy of games to help their parishioners think about faith as itself a game of imperfect information. For many others in this theistic society, however, gameplay touched a vein. The act of playing games arguably led users to espouse beliefs in atheistic concepts like luck; put pressure on theological arguments about the role God plays in human affairs; and resulted in righteous men behaving wickedly. In their writings about sitting pastimes, moral and religious authorities recognize, as do state officials who legislate against gaming for other reasons, that games cannot exist in a space outside of social, political, economic, and spiritual life, but rather are shaped by and impinge on it. It is their profound understanding of the game as metagame that informs their efforts to manage recreational activity.

THE POLITICS OF GAMEPLAY

Arguably, part of what drives these larger cultural debates about recreation is a recognition that games compete effectively for people's attention, creating allegiances that are beyond and can supplant those of state and religion. One way that political and religious authorities attempted to recapture public attention was by legislating or moralizing against games, as we've seen, but another was to appropriate games to serve political and religious aims. Chapter 2 discusses in more detail the religious appropriation of gaming motifs in relation to cards, but here I focus on political appropriations. In the early modern period, games were frequently used as a platform for conveying political arguments and as a medium for propaganda, particularly during the English Civil War and Interregnum. One obvious reason for this is that, as discussed above, recreation was a hot-button political issue of the day, with James I and Charles I issuing decrees in support of gameplay as a way to assert their monarchic power vis-à-vis Parliament. But another reason is because the narrative content and formal features of games—particularly the ways they schematize information—made them well suited to political themes and arguments. And insofar as games encourage players to focus on the rules of play rather than what those rules might mean, games have the capacity to slip ideological content to players without their necessarily recognizing indoctrination. That said, such indoctrination is limited in its effectiveness due to the variable ways that players engage with games. Players manipulate gaming materials in all sorts of ways that game designers cannot predict, and even when players follow game rules closely, the unfolding of a particular match can often complicate or even undermine the ways game objects present politically loaded information.

All three of the sitting pastimes on which I focus have been used to communicate or comment on religious and/or political ideas, and their formal features help to explain why. Chess, used as a political allegory arguably since the game's invention, stages a battle between two kingdoms, with capturing the enemy's King as the condition for victory. Others have discussed extensively how chess was used as a political allegory in the medieval and early modern periods, something I address further in Chapter 4, and so at this point I would highlight only a few interesting details that are pertinent for the discussion at hand.[89] One is that chess's narrative elements, particularly the characters represented by gaming objects, address especially well the politics of the Interregnum, when England had executed its monarch and was governed by Parliament: the game presents figures from both the court and the populace, the pawns. What is more, the inclusion of Bishop figures in chess offers rich ground for politico-religious commentary. One pro-Parliament treatise allegorizes the English Civil War as a conflict between two sides of a chessboard, the White side as Parliament and the Black side as the royal army. It warns that if the King doesn't "put the residue of His blacke *Bishops* into the same bag where their fellowes are," then the game will just "continue in full force and vigor."[90]

Even backgammon, which has blank counters with no obvious allegorical meaning, makes its way into political commentary. Arguably this is because as it stages two sides playing a game of imperfect information, it raises questions about whether opponents can be trusted to play fairly. One particular anti-Catholic engraving was reused on a number occasions, the names of the players changed to suit the particular political context. The Dutch version (c. 1598) depicts three Protestant gentlemen from the Netherlands playing backgammon and cards, against three monks, while the pope and a cardinal try to steal the winnings. A later British reissue of the cartoon (c. 1609) substitutes the reigning kings of England, France, and Denmark for the Dutch gentleman (Figure 5). This version was reprinted and updated in 1626, presumably to coincide with the coronation of King Charles I.[91] In the reissued versions, King Charles plays tables against a monk who hides his face while a dog urinates on his foot. In the middle of the plate sits Henry IV of France playing his trump card in a game against a monk, whose highest card, we can see, is a knave—the name of the card as well as a colloquial term for a crooked or untrustworthy man. First produced at a moment when the French and English were negotiating a peace between Spain and the Dutch Republic, the print underscores these sitting pastimes as dramas of imperfect information to suggest—much like the anonymous pamphlet cited above allegorizing cards—that in the game of world politics, Catholics cannot be trusted.

The sitting pastime that appears to have worked particularly effectively to convey political propaganda was cards. Political issues, figures, and events often are allegorized through the theme of playing cards. Sometimes the allegory is a minor part of the text. For instance, the anonymous political pamphlet *Tom Tell Troath; or, A Free Discourse Touching the Manners of the Tyme. Directed to His Majestie by Way of Humble Advertisement* (1622) at one point compares King James I's conflicts with the Spanish—the same subject allegorized in Thomas Middleton's play *A Game at Chess*—to a card game of Maw, reputed to have been one of James's favorite games. The author describes how the king is criticized in taverns for having played badly at the game of international politics: "Ever, in the very gaming Ordinaries where men have scarce leisure to say grace yet they take a tyme to censure your Majesties actions and that in their oulde schoole Termes. They say you have lost the fairest game at Maw that ever King had for want of making the best advantage of the five finger and playing the other helpes in time." The "five finger" is the ace of trumps, and according to the rules of Maw, whoever has the ace of trumps has the right to "rob the pack," which means the chance to exchange some cards in one's hand for ones that have not been dealt out, thereby improving one's hand.[92] The intimation is that James had the advantage in the political game but failed to use it effectively and at the right time such that he lost his advantage and thus the game. The pamphlet goes on to tell James that his options are now limited because in the new political matchup, he must play against a known cheater, the Spanish, and the only remedy for the situation—as would be true in any tavern game where the opponent is suspected of cheating—is to quarrel. In this case, confrontation is especially risky because the opponent uses tricks in his fighting as well: "hee you played withall hath ever been knowne for the greatest cheater in Christendome. In fine, there is noe way to recover your losses and vindicate your honour but with fighting with him that hath cozened you. At which honest downe righte play you will be hard enough for him with all his Trickes." Playing cards were used again as analogy c. 1630 in a pamphlet, now lost, that apparently took the form of a pack of cards. Published by the Habsburgs, it attacks Protestant Bohemia and especially Frederick V of the Palatinate, King James I's son-in-law.[93]

Perhaps because card play was espoused by royalists and criticized by many Puritans, a number of writers use card-playing imagery to reflect on the tumultuous tensions of the Interregnum. One royalist pamphlet, entitled *The Bloody Game at Cards. As It Was Played Betwixt the King of Hearts and the Rest of His Suite, against the Residue of the Pack of Cards. Wherein Is Discovered Where Faire Play; Was Plaid and Where There Was Fowle* (1642), compares the civil war to a game of cards, with the monarch as the King of Hearts and the commoners as pip cards who do not play by the rules. Even the title page keeps the political allegory afloat with the publication details listed thus: "Shuffled at London, Cut at Westminster, Dealt at Yorke, and Plaid in the open field, by the Citty-clubs, and the country Spade-men, Rich-Diamond men and Loyall Hearted men." Cards prove especially fruitful for allegories about royalist politics because of the deck's honor cards: a King and a Queen as well as a Knave, the perfect figure for the political imposter qua villain. What is more, the hierarchy of suits in the deck—with hearts at the top and clubs at the bottom—provides royalist writers especially an easy metaphor for the topsy-turvy politics of the Interregnum. A royalist treatise by Edmund Gayton, called *Chartæ Scriptæ; or, A New Game at Cards Call'd Play by the Booke* (1645) figures Charles I as the King of Hearts; the King of Diamonds is England's two eyes that had been "sparkling" until now; the Queen of Spades is the Queen of Spain.[94] Cromwell, though not named specifically, is clearly the person referenced in the description of the King of Clubs: "This is the worst of Kings, beware of him, / No King indeed, but a meere popular *Pim*." It goes on to describe how he incites the people: "he perswades to tumults the rude Club. / When swarmres of was-pes, and hornets buzze: Then fly. / No honour in a Crowd for Majesty."[95] Perhaps the most interesting of the political satires, especially in light of my project's emphasis on theater, is the faux drama *Shuffling, Cutting, and Dealing, in a Game at Pickquet* (1659), a satire of Cromwell's government in the form of a dramatic dialogue among a group of men ostensibly playing the card game Piquet. Their commentary on the game is double-entendre for their political positions and actions.[96]

In addition to being a thematic trope in political writings, cards were also themselves a medium for political commentary, and a number of themed decks were published in the late seventeenth century on topics including the Spanish Armada, the Presbyterian Plot, the Popish Plot, and the Rump Parliament.[97] Such decks employ the systematic structure of card decks for organizing and presenting views on highly politicized historical events. For instance, one deck links four historically distinct events as part of a larger argument about the dangers of Catholics to Reformation England—the four suits rendering, respectively, the Spanish Armada, William Parry's Plot to assassinate Queen Elizabeth, the Gunpowder Plot, and the Popish Plot (Figure 6). With their template of suits and numbers, card decks are able to organize information into easily digestible chunks, whose relationship to each other could be presented without being explicitly argued. The convenience of the card deck template is well evinced in the case of nationalistic geography-themed decks. The earliest deck of English map cards about which we know was a 1590 collaboration between playing card maker William Bowes and well-known maker of scientific instruments and engraver Augustine Ryther: a fifty-two-card deck depicting the counties of England and Wales (Figure 7). Each card offers a map of a county and some additional verbal information about it, and the deck as a whole is organized into the usual playing card template of four suits of thirteen cards each, each suit corresponding to a particular geographical area. A portrait of Elizabeth I graces a cover card for the deck, which also includes a map offering a birds-eye view of London and several chorographic cards describing England and London.[98]

Publishers of geography decks pick up on the games-for-learning rhetoric discussed above in relation to grammar-themed decks: the cards provide a way to learn ostensibly ideologically neutral "Universal" information "easily, pleasantly and familiarly."[99] But, of course, there is nothing "Universal" about the geographical information presented, just as there is nothing purely objective about the story the Spanish Armada deck tells about that particular historical event. Geography decks convey loaded arguments about space, borders, and citizenship, although their game format delivers these arguments in less overt ways than do many political pamphlets. A pack of cards that maps English and Welsh counties, for instance, uses the schematics of cards to depict counties as belonging not only to regions but to the nation as a whole (Figure 8). Although individual cards present counties as self-contained localities, each with their unique characteristics, all affiliate with/belong to greater regions, the suits. Local as well as regional differences (including, notably, differences between Wales and England), moreover, are subsumed by a sense that all counties and regions belong to the greater deck that is (here, literally) presided over by England's monarch on the deck cover.

In Pierre du Val's set of playing cards depicting all the countries of the world, the schematic organization of card decks does similar work, but on a global scale. Created in France, the cards present a distinctively French perspective on the information they present. As was commonly done in geographical card sets, the world is separated into four suits: Europe is hearts, Africa spades, Asia diamonds, and the Americas clubs. The association of a continent or part of the world with a certain suit is loaded with symbolic meaning that du Val, to some extent, encourages his users to investigate, even if he does not spell out the details.[100] Nevertheless, that meaning is fairly easy to ascertain. Hearts is the highest-valued suit in many games and thus an unsurprising choice for the continent to which du Val's France belongs. Clubs, often the lowest-valued suit, is associated with what the French would have considered to be the uncivilized lands of the Americas, while Asia, renowned for its treasures, is designated by diamonds, and Africa, historically raided for manual laborers, is designated by spades. The organizing principles endemic to playing cards help to imbue relative value to the countries within each part of the world, too. In du Val's deck, the King card for the Europe suit is Le Roy de France, and the Queen is Italy, whereas Britain occupies the measly spot of pip three, while its other Protestant allies, Denmark and Norway, are relegated to the absolute lowest pip two position. By contrast, in a roughly contemporaneous English version of world geography cards, the King of the Europe suit is the British Isles, complete with a portrait of Charles II, and Catholic Italy is demoted to pip four. France is represented at pip eight, still below Protestant Germany at ten, and the deck reinforces British control over lands in the New World by having a portrait of Queen Elizabeth on the card for the American colonies (Figure 9).[101] Another English geographical card deck, presumed to have been published in the third quarter of the seventeenth century by Henry Winstanley, keeps England as the King of Hearts (Figure

10), offering the precious Queen spot to England's German allies, while literalizing the English derogatory view of the Italians by having them assigned to the Knave card. What's more, the deck doesn't bother to represent France at all.[102]

The meaning of card decks seems fairly straightforward when we look closely enough at their symbolic systems, but it is important to note that geographical cards are not simply a set of texts to be read, their symbolism decoded; they were objects to be used in play, and that play could complicate their symbolic meaning and political arguments. Any sense that the cards are meant only for display, not play, is belied by their prefatory material. In the English geography deck, the introductory card, "The Explanation of These Cards," encourages the deck's use in gaming by underscoring the correspondence between these and regular playing cards: "the use of these cards are the same with the Common Cards in all respects useing the Numbers in these instead of the spots on the Other." And another preliminary card in the pack explains that the cards are "plaine and ready for the playing all our English Games, as any of ye Common Cards."[103] If the cards were used in games, the experience of playing with them could significantly complicate ideological and political arguments the decks make through their schematization of information. For instance, although world geography decks use the valuation schema of a deck to assert the superiority of some nations over others, these valuations are destabilized during gameplay. The English card deck that assigns Britain to the King of Hearts demotes the Turks (who must be hearts because they are also in Europe, the part of the world represented by the hearts suit) to the lowest-valued pip card, two. But during games of cards involving trumps, pip two could be just as powerful as a King from another suit, for if hearts is the trump suit, the Turk card can capture any card of any value in the other suits. In a game using these English geographical cards where the trump suit is clubs, the Chileans, presumably subjugated symbolically through their position as pip three in the low clubs suit, can handily capture Britain, whose King status provides no stable or natural superiority when a game is under way.

SPECTATORSHIP, PERFORMANCE, AND HISTORY

I have been suggesting that early modern materials of gaming are flexible symbolic systems whose meaning changes during the act of gameplay. The relationship between games and gameplay is, thus, much like that between dramatic plays and performance. Both games and dramatic plays use scripts—the rule book and playscript, respectively—that are purportedly designed to authorize and define the actions of the objects (game pieces or actors) during performance. However, the relationship between scripts and theatrical performance is rarely straightforward in practice, for theatrical performance is authorized by a range of conventions and material practices that exist independently of any particular script.[104] The same is true for games. Although this presents complications for studying the history of games, much as it has for studying the history of theatrical performance, some of the methods that have been used successfully to approach the latter prove fruitful, I suggest, for approaching the former.

The complex relationship between rule books and game practice is evinced by the terminology early moderns use to describe these aspects of gaming. Arthur Saul's book on chess emphasizes a difference between the "lawes" of the game (what you are allowed and not allowed to do—what we would call rules) and what early modern writers termed the "rules" (how one navigates the game's laws during gameplay). Saul writes about chess "That there is no Rule for this game" because everyone plays it differently—and therein lies the pleasure. In fact, if gamers play by one preset rule and do not take into account how their opponents play, adjusting strategy accordingly, they will lose.[105] Modern gamers no longer use the term "laws"; "rules" has come to mean the same thing, and a third term, "strategy," is now used to describe what early moderns called "rules." When and how did the early modern term "rules" lose its association with strategy to refer, instead, to another script for play?

This shift in terminology arguably indexes changes in gaming practice during the early modern period, which resulted in part from the growth of the printing industry. Consider that before the printing press was used to publish gaming manuals, information about how to play sitting pastimes could be circulated only orally and in manuscripts. In the medieval period, such information was generally held and spread by clergy in monasteries and then outward to universities and schools.[106] As literacy grew, players appear to have created their own instructional writings via manuscripts, essentially producing crib sheets for their own or others' quick reference before or during play. Pasted into a commonplace book held by the British Library is a sheet entitled *The Groome-porters lawes at Mawe, to be observed in fulfilling the due orders of the game* (c. 1597), which lays out in several numbered points the method for playing the card game Maw. The practical function of these writings is evinced by their prose: dry and unembellished, with laws often numbered, perhaps to aid memory.[107] Perhaps the most comprehensive of these manuscripts is Francis Willughby's book of games (written in the seventeenth century, though not published until the twentieth), which offers a fairly detailed overview of cards, tables, and chess. By the end of the seventeenth century, however, as handbooks on many subjects were being published in print, so, too, were a number of books, or sections of books, devoted to instruction in sitting pastimes. These made it possible for communities of players to publicize their play strategies more extensively, and the result, arguably, is that strategies became so well known that they essentially operated as rules of play.

To be sure, the interest in writing up gameplay strategies was not solely a print phenomenon. A manuscript commonplace book at the Folger Library (c. 1650–70) contains a crib sheet for tables inside its back cover, presumably so that it could be accessed easily during a match. Entitling the sheet "Trickes with the Tables," the author scratches out a series of numbers between one and six, probably representing some sort of dicing scheme, and offers a brief comment on a strategy for how "to bring a man from the other tables."[108] And many seventeenth-century books containing chess strategies remained only in manuscript, because players using them wanted to protect their play secrets.[109] Yet print made it possible to circulate these strategies among much wider groups of players, and authors and printers capitalized on this new reading market. A posthumous reprinting of Saul's book indicates that readers were hungry for books that would give them not only basic guidelines for play, but also possible strategies or "rules" as well. The first two parts of the book contain most of the same material from the first edition and in the same order, but the information is divided into two clearly distinguished sections: one concerned with introducing the pieces and how the game is set up (laws); the other covering strategies for winning at chess.[110]

Similar efforts to elucidate strategies can be found in the range of publications focused on chess gambits—opening moves that could operate as formulas for victory or at least advantage. When Francis Beale translates *The Royal Game of Chess-Play* (1656), a collection of gambits used by the famed player Gioachino Greco, his dedicatory letter to Montague, Earl of Lindsey, explains that part of the point of his book is to enable those who are "but small Proficients" at chess "to take a greater delight" in "this Pastime," while also helping experienced players like the Earl. Again, the book's organization recognizes the two distinct aims of game instruction. For beginners there is the "very plaine" set of "Instructions" that are already in print. A separate section of "*Gambetts*" offers players some understanding of the "rule" or strategies of play, providing ninety-four gambits that show exactly which moves would lead to a victory if performed just so by both sides. Beale affirms the importance of this section by reciting the old adage that chess has laws but no rule of play: "The consideration, that to finde out a certaine Rule for this Princely *Game of Chesse*, is generally . . . esteemed to be impossible, was the first cause that invited me to publish these *Gambetts*, which doe, in a very great measure, supply the defect of such an advantage."[111] Ironically, in spelling out these gambits so clearly, making it possible for anyone to follow them, the book may well turn rules into laws. In fact, they tell so much about how to play well that Beale asks for the protection of the Earl: he fears that those who have already seen these gambits, which have been circulating in manuscript, will be angry that he is making them available to the masses through print; players who once had a monopoly on strategy risk losing their advantage if their opponents know what is at stake in a particular opening move.

When John Cotgrave publishes his description of games for gentlemen in his *Wits Interpreter* (1655), the distinction between rules and laws has all but dissolved. Cotgrave ends his description of the card game Gleek with a caveat that he has done his best to give a full account, but "if by accident, any other difficulties not here mentioned arise in play, they may easilie be resolved out of these Rules here set down, examining them by the Rules of Reason."[112] Here, the terms *rules* and *laws* are blurred or perhaps interchangeable, as if the discussion of strategy has become so widespread and expected that the rules are now virtually like laws. When Cotton publishes his thorough game instruction manual almost twenty years later (reprinting much from Cotgrave), he cautions against taking rules for laws, maintaining any set strategy will compromise the player's game. Nevertheless, the emphasis of his text is on strategy. Although the book includes a short, straightforward list of the "Laws of Chess," the bulk of it is devoted to describing particular moves that will help the player gain advantage. In fact, Cotton does not even bother to lay out the laws of the "commonly known" card games Ruff, Honours, and Whist, describing only strategies for winning at these games and advice on how to spot cheaters.[113]

Given their extensive discussions of strategy, these gaming instruction books would appear to offer historians valuable evidence not only about how games were supposed to be played, but how they *were* played. Yet Cotton's dual investments in describing strategy and cheating schemes offers a subtle warning not only to the gamer but to the historian of games who takes these descriptions as hard and fast evidence of gameplay. Once there was no clear distinction between laws and rules because the circulation of gaming manuals meant that everyone was well versed in strategies, then players were bound to find new ways to game the system, to manipulate the laws via new, less widely known strategies and/or through cheating. The distinction between cheating and using novel strategies is less obvious than it may seem at first glance. Some of my readers might insist that in strategy, one attempts to win the game by working within the laws, whereas in cheating one wins by violating those laws. But as scholars in game studies have shown, games are defined as much by efforts to violate regulations as to follow them.[114]

The history of games substantiates this claim, as we can see how game objects and "laws" evolved as a response to and prophylactic against cheating. Cheating, that is, has driven the development of games. Willughby's gaming book explains, for instance, that the dicing box players use to throw the dice in tables is there to prevent "cogging"—the use of "sleight of hand or anie trick" to roll a particular number on the dice.[115] As I discuss further in Chapter 4, the "touch rule" in chess developed to prevent sleight-of-hand manipulation of chess pieces. And the stipulation in card games that someone besides the dealer cuts the deck before it is dealt is meant to help prevent the dealer from arranging cards to benefit his or her hand, something I address further in Chapter 2. Early modern writings about sitting pastimes, including nonmoralizing and quasi-scientific accounts as well as texts affirming the usefulness of gaming, almost always address cheating and imply its inevitability in these games, even in the best of circumstances. In the same sentence that Cleland advocates for noble men to learn cards and tables, he submits that learning to play well will help gentlemen avoid being cheated by fellow players: "yea I would wish you to bee so perfit in them al, that you maie not be deceived, or cousened at play."[116] Mentions of methods of cheating appear frequently and often seamlessly alongside dry game descriptions. Randle Holme's section on cards, written in the early to mid-seventeenth century (published in 1688), provides long lists of well-known games, terminology used by gamesters, and "general laws of card playing," concluding with a section on "Names given to false and ch[e]ating cards," which, though it contains only three items (far fewer than the entries in other sections), appears to be essential enough for inclusion.[117] Willughby's manuscript, which is uninterested in the morality of gaming, still provides a list of five "Waies of Cheating" with the dice in tables[118]:

1. Playing with severall pare of false dice. . . . Dice are false when one side is heavier then the other, the die allwaies resting on the heaviest side

2. Wetting a side of the die, with spittle, sweat, earwaxe &c. which makes it rest on that side.

3. Slurring, which is a trick to make the die slide & not tumble over.
4. Throwing the dice just one upon another; the undermost will never change the side it is thrown upon.
5.

He leaves the fifth point unwritten, suggesting he is planning to fill in more kinds of cheating, perhaps when he witnesses them or remembers them. Whatever his intention, the still-to-be-written point intimates that there are so many ways of cheating that any list is bound to be incomplete. Cardano, who, like Willughby, is far more interested in intellectualizing than moralizing sitting pastimes, represents card fraud as so inevitable that good players must be proactive in defending themselves against cheaters. Cardano describes an "art" to handling one's cards so that they cannot be seen by opponents: in Primero "it is customary to uncover the cards from the back and from above as little as possible so that kibitzers [spectators who may be colluding with one's opponent] cannot see anything; a great part of the art appears to consist in this, and players boast about their skill in this respect."[119] In other words, players should expect opponents to cheat and so develop skills to limit repercussions for their game. Cardano goes even further to complicate the distinction between fraud and strategy, between "cheats" and "prudent" players. His description of techniques for "recognition of the cards" struggles to articulate the difference between strategy and cheating. Of cheating, he writes:

in its worst form it consists of using marked cards, and in another form it is more excusable, namely, when the cards are put in a special order and it is necessary to remember this order. Such players are accustomed, when they know where the desired card is, to keep it on the bottom and to deal out others, which chance alone would not call for, until they get the suppressed card for themselves. But the other players in the first-mentioned class carry out very dangerous frauds which are worthy of death, as in fact the latter is also, but it is more concealed. Those, however, who know merely by close attention what cards they are to expect are not usually called cheats, but are reckoned to be prudent men.[120]

Cardano presents a continuum between "prudent men" who pay "close attention" to the cards and "dangerous frauds" who use marked cards, with an imprecise middle ground occupied by those who use creative dealing to keep a certain card for themselves. Although the latter two kinds of action would seem like obvious forms of cheating, Cardano does not lump them together, offended much more by those who use marked cards, a practice he thinks deserves the punishment of death. Even more interesting, when he describes the players who "know merely by close attention what cards they are to expect," he intimates that even this sort of action, what we call the strategy of card reading, produces some disagreement regarding its lawfulness. In saying that players who do this are "not usually called cheats," Cardano implies that on the rare occasion they might be.

Even moralizations of sitting pastimes tread a fine line as their expressions of outrage about cheating end up providing readers guidelines for employing cheating successfully in their own play. Gilbert Walker's *Mihil Mumchance, His Discoverie of the Art of Cheating in False Dyce Play, and Other Unlawfull Games* (1597) observes the inevitability of cheating in dice and cards—"there is no game though it be never so laudable, yet is it abused by Cheating companions"[121]—and announces that his aim is to disclose all the tricks of cheaters so that his reader will be able to spot them in others. However, he cannot help but worry that his readers will apply what they have learned: "Therefore I purpose to let you understand some part of the sleights & falshoods that are commonlie practised at Dice and Cardes: opening and revealing the thinge, not so that I would learne you to put them in use, but to discribe and lay open the wicked snares, and hookes that are laid to picke Gentlemens purses."[122] Writing three quarters of a century later, Cotton grapples with the same paradox. He insists that he writes his comprehensive description of games not to make new Gamesters, "but to inform all in part how to avoid being cheated by them."[123]

Texts that describe methods of cheating offer interesting evidence about the performance of early modern sitting pastimes, substantiating an intriguing intersection between games and theater: that these games were social and communal events often played before spectators. The accomplices of cheaters could easily masquerade as game spectators, explain several writers. Walker tells of one gamester who had a woman sit close enough to see the cards of his opponent and use the guise of sewing to communicate the contents of the opponent's cards: "by the swift and slow drawing of her needle, give a token to the Cheator what was the Cosens game."[124] Cardano goes into significant detail about the dangers of playing before a crowd, whether its members are intent on foul play or not:

you can scarcely avoid folly if they are against you, or else injustice
if they are for you. They can injure you in many ways: for example,
by giving your opponent open advice and information, which is

twofold evil, since it not only helps their side but also provokes you
to anger and disturbs you; . . . Others will annoy you by their disorderly talk, even without giving definite information. Some will pur-
posely consult you on serious business; some will even be so impu-
dent as to provoke you to anger by quarreling with you; other will
make fun of you in order to make you angry; others, more modest
than these, will indicate to your opponent by foot or by hand that
the decision he has made is not the right one; others again, a little
farther off, will do this with a nod, perhaps with no other purpose, it
may be, than to help him by filling your mind with suspicion. Still
others will state falsely how the die has fallen; other again will worry
you by accusing *you* of such things.[125]

Successful players need to do more than manage their own game; they
must also tune out the hubbub of the crowd around them, without being
negligent in watching for those who might conspire with an opponent in a
foul play scheme.

The likelihood of facing the sorts of distractions Cardano describes
would have been high in the case of sitting pastimes. Games of cards, tables, and chess, especially in public settings like taverns, typically had
spectators present. Their sport was not only to enjoy a good match, but also
to make money off of its outcome. In the five illustrated scenes of gameplay
that grace the frontispiece to Cotton's *The Compleat Gamester* (cards, backgammon, hazard/dice, cockfighting, and billiards), the only scene that
doesn't include spectators is billiards (Figure 11). Chess may have been
even more of a spectator pastime in the early modern period than it has
become in the modern age of competitive tournaments. Chess problem collections (which date from the mid-thirteenth century and onward) were
partly about encouraging new or more sophisticated ways for spectators to
gamble on a game in play. The problemist could invite onlookers to bet on
the likely outcome of a particular position demonstrated on the board;
problemists knew the outcome, and so could be quite canny. Indeed, Richard Eales argues that some problems in early collections "were made deliberately unsound" so that problemists could cheat unaware gamblers. Additionally, exhibition matches not so different from those staged today
occurred throughout the mid-sixteenth through the seventeenth century,
as Italian chess players traveling to find patrons played before noblemen
and at court. (One of these players, Gioachino Greco, toured England in
1622 and 1623.)[126] The translator of Damiano presumes there will be specta-

tors at chess matches and warns players, "talke not with any other stand-inge by" lest the player become distracted and lose the game.[127]

Turning sitting pastimes into spectator sports may have encouraged cheating, but it also and, indeed, simultaneously appears to have encour-aged game development. Perhaps the most interesting example of this comes not from gaming manuals but from fictional representations of games. Chess historians, in fact, credit one particular chess poem, Marco Girolamo Vida's *Scacchia ludus,* for helping spread knowledge of modern chess rules throughout Europe in the fifteenth and sixteenth centuries. Es-pecially notable about Vida's poem is that Vida revises a mythical tale of chess's beginnings, giving it a theatricalized setting, where spectatorship and cheating play a crucial part. In the poem Jupiter introduces the game of chess to all the gods and then, after describing the pieces and how they move, calls upon Apollo and Mercury to play a match before the other gods. Cardano's description cited above of the dangers that ensue as spectators take sides is illustrated well, as Venus and Mars battle each other indirectly through their support of different players, Venus backing Apollo and Mars backing Mercury.[128] The poem's readers act as audience to the fictional game itself, as well as to the metagame played by the spectating gods.

Much as a staging of chess spectatorship enabled Vida's readers to learn chess by watching the metagame, so, I would suggest, theatrical stagings of sitting pastimes have pedagogical value for modern scholars interested in writing a history of these games. Spectacles of characters gaming the game, as the rest of my book shows, complement the kinds of evidence most often used in gaming histories. Although I have drawn on the latter evidence to produce the kind of thick description of sitting pastimes that scholars have provided for early modern festive recreations and sports, I have also at-tempted to show its limitations. One limitation of the document-based his-tories of games that most historians employ is that these imply that certain ideas can be dated to the time a text about them is written, and this conve-niently supports efforts to produce overarching historical narratives about sitting pastimes—even my own. Consider, for instance, my claim that as legal authorities became more permissive (and even supportive) of sitting pastimes in the late sixteenth century, religio-moral critiques of these pas-times increased. Such a conclusion certainly can be supported by printed documents (fewer royal proclamations against gaming and more published sermons condemning it), but it is also true that royal proclamations are merely one piece of evidence representing official views on games. Local regulations, whether written down or not, may have continued to be as harsh as ever, possibly even explaining the need for intervention from more permissive royal authorities. Indeed, in his *Book of Sports*, James I claims that he feels compelled to write his declaration because his progresses through the kingdom have revealed the harshness of local regulations against games on Sabbath and Holy Days. Even then, it is difficult to ascertain with certainty whether local regulations relaxed in response to James's declaration. These sorts of limitation would confront any historian on any subject, but games are particularly resistant to overarching narratives of historical change. For example, consider my claim that the period of investigation for my study can accurately be called the *early* modern period of gaming insofar as this is the time that the rules of backgammon and chess change to become those rules we use today, and the gaming materials currently used for backgammon and cards standardize at this time as well. Such a claim neatly validates my book's focus on gaming in sixteenth- and early seventeenth-century drama. And although it can be substantiated for the most part, it arguably oversimplifies a more complicated story about how games change over time. It is not possible to date with certainty when changes to a particular game occur, for a game may undergo changes in patterns of play well before those changes are captured in a written document, and certainly well before that document would be published. For instance, changes that defined the "new" chess evolved slowly over the late Middle Ages, not in one fell swoop.[129] Even with the advent of print, knowledge about games, then as today, is circulated orally as much if not more so than through written documents. Although game objects and writings about games can be archived, gameplay is an embodied practice that typical archives cannot capture easily, if at all. As the early modern distinction between rules and laws underscores, guidelines for gameplay and the material setup of a game in no way dictate how a particular match would be played. Surviving game objects and published rules provide the plot for theoretical play scenarios, but they do not indicate how games work and change in practice, or how the practice of gameplay affects the objects and rules of a game.

With that in mind, let us return to the analogy with which this section began, an analogy that proves useful for historicizing games: game rules are to gameplay as dramatic texts are to theatrical plays. Consider that, contrary to the assumptions of many in and out of drama studies, the dramatic script does not necessarily exist prior to and thus authorize performance.[130] As William B. Worthen argues, the "force" of performance comes, for instance, from other sources, including the many conventions of theatrical institutions themselves.[131] We can say much the same about game rules. When a group sits down to a game of cards, their match is less simply a reiteration of the game's rules than it is a citation of the conventions of gameplay—in this case, shuffling, dealing, revealing, bluffing, table talk, and so forth. The analogy to dramatic performance can help us think differently about the gaming objects and written gaming regulations that we find in archives. If we resist presuming that these texts are scripts that authorize, we can better attend to them as texts in their own right, subject to the "practices, economics and rhetoric of print" that Worthen argues give *dramatic* texts their performative force.[132] A telling example is Beale's translation of Greco's *The Royall Game of Chesse-Play*, which presents itself as a chess instruction manual and includes an elementary introduction to the game taken from Saul's *Famous Game of Chesse-Play*. If treated as a script for gameplay, the text is a fairly straightforward, even dry account of how to play chess. But if we use the methods of book history to think about how the text operated *as* a book, a more complex story emerges, showing the ways the Greco–Beale book uses chess as a rhetorical weapon against Cromwell. Eales observes that not only is Charles I featured as a crowned monarch on the book's frontispiece, but many of those involved in the publication, including the writers of prefatory poems (one of whom was Richard Lovelace) and the book's printer had well-known royalist sympathies.[133]

Just as it makes sense to study *The Royall Game of Chesse-Play* as a *book*, it also makes sense to study the game it describes as a *game*. Even if Greco–Beale's rules present one script for how to play that game, this script is hardly the authorizing one. Indeed, just as the print history of early modern drama offers evidence that performances shaped the scripts of early modern plays in all sorts of ways, so the "laws" of a game and even the design of gaming objects evolve in response to gameplay scenarios. As we have already seen, game objects might have been developed or redesigned in response to newly discovered ways of cheating, such as the case of dicing cups used for tables. Alternatively, the games and their laws might be transformed to create more pleasurable gameplay, the most significant example of which may be the development of "new chess," which significantly sped up the play time of a game that many found tedious. The point is that if there was a relationship between the rule books/gaming objects and gameplay (and, as in the case of theatrical performance, there wasn't always a relationship), then the relationship worked in both directions simultaneously. Rule books and objects attempted to script gameplay as a practice as much as they were sculpted and transformed by it.

How, then, can we produce a history of sitting pastimes in the early modern period that accounts for gameplay as a practice? One way is to supplement our studies of the archive with attention to repertoires of embodied actions associated with gaming that have been handed down from the past to the present as games have been taught by one generation to the next.[134] Our methods here are not that different from the methods we might use to study the traces of performances past.[135] Instead of thinking of rule books and gaming objects as static traces of these games of the past—as so many histories of sitting pastimes have done—we can view them as prompts for future reenactment, a reenactment in which scholars themselves can and, I would suggest, must engage. For it is by putting these objects into play that their fuller histories can be uncovered. A consequence of such an approach is that we might take more seriously the practices of reenactment groups like the Society for Creative Anachronism, an active site of research on medieval and sixteenth-century sitting pastimes. Perhaps most SCA participants reenact games to relive the past "as it was," but that need not be the sole or even an essential objective of these practices. Enacting a game might, in fact, lead the player to discover problems in the ways the game is represented in texts, leading to new questions about archival "sources." At the very least, playing medieval and early modern games enables participants to investigate with their bodies how certain games feel in play, helping to explain, for example, why Primero was associated with politics in Elizabethan England, as some early modern writers suggest. Playing Primero might help us understand how the game encourages, in John Hall's phrase, "*a dexterous kinde of rashness.*"[136] What is it about the rules of Primero and how they shape use of the cards that rewards a player who can make rash decisions with dexterity? As this example underscores, I do not mean to suggest that the archive—with its written documents and material objects of gaming—serves no purpose or is necessarily in tension with an embodied repertoire of actions. For certainly the texts of gaming, such as books about regulations and strategy, inform today as much as they did four hundred years ago. The archive is essential to reenactment practices. My point, rather, is that a robust history of gaming must put repertoires of ludic action into conversation with game scripts, whether these are gaming objects, books of laws, or manuscripts regarding strategy.

Live reenactment such as that conducted by the SCA is not the only way to enact archival materials, however. In the chapters that follow, I suggest that scenes of gaming within drama are optimal resources as well. Dramas stage a conversation between the repertoire and the archive. Particularly when they enact game*play*, dramas highlight the archive's aliveness and performativity. This (re)enactment is all the more interesting when we consider that the plays were performed live before spectators, much like the games sometimes represented in them. The archive and the repertoire of gaming come together in the embodied action of theatrical performance both onstage and in the theater more broadly. It should not go without saying that they also come together through the efforts of me, the embodied historian of literature and games. The historian is less a discoverer than a maker of evidence, collecting and connecting scraps of information about the past from a host of different realms of knowledge.[137] And one key source of that knowledge is the critic's own body. What we discover about the past through archival work is necessarily shaped not only by our training and personal or political investments but also by our own perceptive practices.[138] What we find in the archives is partly a function of how we look at what we find. To explore how game scenes worked onstage and to understand what they taught their audiences about theatergoing, I refer often in the chapters that follow to what it feels like to play these games, feelings I can report because I've had them myself during play or because my familiarity with the games enables me to imagine what it feels like to play them. Just as game scenes in drama invited their on- and offstage spectators a chance to play along, so they make possible, and indeed call out for, a ludic mode of engagement from modern readers. Perhaps, then, we might think of historians not only as makers, but as gamers, who play with the material they find in archives. Like all gamers, historians do not simply follow the rules that govern these materials and their uses, but create the rules in the process of play. So let's play. Cards, anyone?

| Cards

Imperfect Information and Male Friendship

When Frankford, the cuckolded husband in Thomas Heywood's *A Woman Killed with Kindness*, suspects his wife Anne of adultery, he chooses to test her fidelity by sitting down to a game of cards with her and her lover, Wendoll. Readers who take note of the scene have observed its emphasis on domestic detail and its intriguing use of card terms as double-entendres.[1] For instance, the name of the game played, Vide Ruff, puns on Anne's clothing, a symbol of her body and sexuality, and Wendoll's knave card puns on his deceitfulness—*knave* being both the honor card we call the Jack as well as a term for a ne'er-do-well. But Vide Ruff is more than simply a symbol in this scene; it is the name of a particular card game whose rules and conventions of play structure the drama of the scene. Why does it matter *to the game* that Wendoll draws a knave from the deck? What are the implications of Frankford seeking proof of the sexual liaison through a card game rather than, say, a game of chess or, for that matter, through spying or intercepting a letter? Knowledge of card games and the rules of Vide Ruff in particular shed light on these questions, and their answers matter not only for this game scene but for the play as a whole and especially for its commentary on playable media. As *A Woman Killed with Kindness* tells its story about friendship and adultery, it probes the problem of information in social relationships as well as in the theater, itself a kind of social contract between producer and receivers. Conventions of play invite theater audiences—like game players—to manage information in particular ways. In its staging of Vide Ruff, Heywood's play focalizes on the ways theater is a game of information.

As noted in the Introduction, modern game designer Celia Pearce argues that all games are systems of information, and she theorizes four kinds of information that players have or pursue. There is information known by all the players (e.g., cards laid face-up on the table); information known to only one player (e.g., cards in a player's hand); information known to the game only (e.g., when there is a stack of cards lying face-down, for players to draw); and information generated randomly (e.g., from the shuffling of the deck).[2] In all games information crosses from one category to another as the private becomes public, and sometimes vice versa. Indeed, the *drama* of many games comes from this movement be-tween the known and the unknown. Additionally, variability in information—who knows what and how much is known—distinguishes one game from another. Thus, chess has been categorized as a game of "perfect information" because both players can see the board and its pieces at all times. Cards, by contrast, are used in games of "imperfect informa-tion," since their two-sided design conceals knowledge from players.[3] For Heywood's scene about a husband trying to find proof of his wife's adul-terous affair, a card game could not be a more ideal choice, particularly when we factor in the state of information for Heywood's theater audience: they know all about Anne and Wendoll's affair, but they are unable to see directly what cards are being played in the staged game. Card games, in fact, share much in common with theatrical performance, which similarly engages the unseen and the unknown.[4] As Andrew Sofer puts it, "theater unfolds as a dance between the withheld and the disclosed"; the "dark matter" we cannot see "frames and defines the phenomenology of theatri-cal pleasure, which both satisfies and frustrates our desire."[5] Applying the terms of gaming to Sofer's conception of theater, we might say that theater invites its spectators to play a game of imperfect information. It is perhaps not surprising then that early modern plays productively use card games to explore the circulation of theatrical knowledge—the dance of withhold-ing and disclosure. Although any number of moments in a play might be used to explore theater's information games, card game scenes are particu-larly exquisite sites for analysis, because they reveal how the plays not only meditate on the nature of theater (its ontology) but also teach spectators skills for engaging with information in the theater (its epistemology).

Cards are mentioned in about a dozen early modern English dramas and some of these include staged card games. In Christopher Marlowe's *Tamburlaine*, Part II, a card game played onstage keeps Tamburlaine's sons from battle. In William Rowley's *A New Wonder, a Woman Never Vexed*, cards seem to be played on the balcony or offstage, since there is a stage direction for "a noise above at cards" while the men play dice in 2.1. There even seems to have been a play, now lost, called *A Game of the Cards* (1582). My focus here will be on two plays, Heywood's *A Woman Killed* and Mr. S's *Gammer Gurton's Needle*, which are worth reading in tandem because both are also about friendships that become strained as their participants withhold information from each other. Although the information presumed to be hidden in the comic *Gammer* (a missing needle) may be far more trivial than the information hidden in *A Woman Killed* (adultery), the plots of both plays present hidden information as a problem for friendship. Friends who hide information cannot be trusted. I want to suggest, however, that both plays also depict friendships as constituted, like card play and theater, by the very uncertainty and imbalances in knowledge that would seem to destroy them. The plays depict social relationships in much the way sociologist Erving Goffman does in scholarship that was, notably, inspired by his fieldwork on card playing in casinos.[6] Goffman describes social relationships as "strategic interactions": interactants attempt to uncover information that they know their fellow participants are hiding and carefully manage the information they give off about themselves.[7] This interaction is less nefarious than it sounds, for the game of hiding and revealing information is, Goffman points out, a cooperative venture, one that helps reveal the character of each of the participants and solidify their social bond.[8]

My chapter uses the drama of card play to explore what is at stake for our understanding of gaming in social interaction, and vice versa. Although my aim is to shed light on the role of information in producing the social bonds crucial to gaming in any age, I suggest that in order to understand this model of social interaction and its relevance for gaming, it is useful to trace its emergence out of particular historical and cultural conditions. For the sixteenth and seventeenth centuries, one of the most influential of contexts for understanding friendship as a game of information was humanism. Renaissance humanists adapted from Cicero and other classical authors an idealistic view of true friends as sharing one mind; true friends are said to know each other so well that they become other selves, unable to hide anything from each other.[9] In effect, these writers depict friendship as a game of perfect information. The humanist model of utopian friendship would have been especially familiar to and valued by the audience for whom *Gammer Gurton's Needle* was first performed: male students at Cambridge University. It is also the model of friendship that Heywood's male characters cite and pursue in *A Woman Killed*. I argue, however, that both plays critique this idealistic humanist model of male friendship, suggesting that even ideal friendship between equals is necessarily structured, like card play and theater, by gaps in knowledge of the other. Staged card matches in plays are particularly interesting sites of reflection on friendship as an information game. These scenes—their ludic action largely hidden from the audience's direct view—engage theater audiences in a game of imperfect information. As such, they invite audiences to feel through theater the sometimes frustrating pleasures that make games and friendships worthwhile. The scenes reveal how theatrical plays, like all playable media, affirm social bonds among participants by providing a pleasurably uncomfortable space to practice navigating social relations.

IMPERFECT INFORMATION IN *GAMMER GURTON'S NEEDLE*

Before turning to the dramas, it is helpful to examine more closely the competencies card games require and teach. Card games encourage participants to derive enjoyment from a state of uncertainty, and anyone who has played cards will be familiar with the rush of emotion in the moment before hidden information is revealed—as a new hand is dealt, an opponent's card played, the top card of deck flipped over. At the same time, the process of the game, which at every turn involves the revelation of previously unknown information, provokes participants to develop their interpretive skills so that they can figure out hidden information and use it effectively before other participants do. The better participants' interpretive skills and the more vigorously invested they are in applying interpretations, the more successful they will be in decoding the ludic action and figuring out what information to divulge and when to divulge it. While there are certain cognitive skills that can help a game participant excel in interpretation—for instance, a good memory helps one recall which cards have already been played—what distinguishes mediocre from expert players is both their level of investment in deciphering the game's secrets and their knowledge of the conventions of the game, conventions that enable participants to reveal and conceal information through particular codes of play. The more one is familiar with the conventions of the game and intent on applying them, the richer one's interpretive skills and the more hidden information one can ascertain before others. In fact, the most skilled players, having rehearsed thoroughly and internalized the conventions of a particular game, may decipher a fellow player's secrets almost intuitively, with little or any deliberative cogitation.

The complex game of information that is card play and its implications for spectatorship are well illustrated in the sixteenth century painting *Four Gentlemen of High Rank Playing Primero* by Master of the Countess of Warwick, which depicts four powerful courtiers—believed to be Elizabeth I's key advisors and friends Francis Walsingham, William Cecil, Henry Carey, and Walter Raleigh—in the heat of a game of Primero (Figure 12). Each figure is poised to execute his strategy, his fingers fixed on the card he aims to play. The drama of knowing is heightened for the viewer of the painting by its flirtatious revelations and coy occlusions of the game's status: the leftmost figure shows the viewer the cards he holds and the one he will play, while the rightmost figure openly reveals some of his cards but protectively obscures others, and the two central figures hide their hands entirely. The effect is to draw the viewer vicariously into the drama of the game, offering a glimpse, but only a glimpse, into the ludic experiences of its powerful players. Like each of the figures in the painting, the viewer is invited to decipher who will win this hand without being able to draw any certain conclusions.

The drama of card play works especially well on the theater stage. For like the Primero painting, staged card games extend to spectators the epistemological experience of their represented card players. A comparison between chess and cards helps demonstrate this point. Consider the experience of watching a chess match in its common venue in the early modern period, an intimate interior like a parlor or tavern. Having all of the same basic information as the game's players, spectators in these venues are invited to play along, projecting themselves into gamers' decision-making processes: If I were in that seat, what move would I make, and what would its repercussions be? This sort of future-oriented decision-making might be said to constitute a fundamental form of engagement in chess, for players and spectators alike. When a chess game is staged in a theater, as it is at the end of *The Tempest*, however, the audience has a far different engagement with the game than do the players. As I discuss further in Chapter 4, whereas the onstage players participate in a game of perfect information, the audience, unable to see the board, experience a game of imperfect information.

Card games work differently, for even when played in an intimate space where audiences can see the card table, the game *always* remains one of imperfect information, inviting not a future-oriented mode of projection, as in chess, but a past-oriented mode of reconstruction. As new information becomes available (e.g., a player throws out a certain card), gamers and their spectators think back to the cards that have already been played (what's known as "card reading") in an effort to try to ascertain the content of cards still concealed. This experience of negotiating imperfect information extends to theatrical performances of card games, where both characters and audience grapple with partial knowledge, albeit of different degrees and kinds. Just as players cannot easily know what information their opponents hide, so audiences, positioned at a distance from the staged game, cannot easily know what cards are being played. Yet through characters' dialogue and gestures, a staged card game gives off partial information. As private information becomes public, audiences, like onstage gamers, are invited to reconstruct what is known and unknown.

The drama of imperfect information takes a distinctive form in theatrical performance, in comparison with other kinds of fiction (such as novels and films), because theater audiences cannot manipulate their medium to find out information sooner than it is revealed. Like a game, live theater unfolds at its own pace. To be sure, an audience member who has seen or read the play before the performance will know more than someone who has not. But productions of a play differ widely; even the same drama put on by the same actors with the same props can play out differently from one day to the next. Whatever their prior experience with a particular drama, audiences bring to the theater a gamer's mind-set[10]: they cannot know how this production will play out on every level (plot, actors' gestures/delivery, stage properties, costumes, etc.), but if the play is at all successful, it will encourage audiences both to relish and to seek to overcome their lack of knowledge, whether through interpretive effort or through less deliberate forms of recollection.[11]

This drama of information is managed in interesting ways in one of the earliest English comedies, *Gammer Gurton's Needle*, in which the main character, Diccon, uses the language of gaming to unravel and then reconstitute friendships between *Gammer*'s characters simply by convincing them that each friend hides information from the other. *Gammer* sets up this drama of information, tellingly, through a card game, which offers the backdrop for the opening move of Diccon's scheming, and thus of the plot as a whole.[12] Diccon has just informed the audience that he plans to "make a play" (2.2.10), a "cleanly prank" (2.2.3), out of an old countrywoman's distress at having lost her needle. He promises great pleasure to the audience if they will simply let him alone to play his game. Indeed, he wagers his life that the audience will be pleased by his ludic schemes: "If ye will mark my toys, and note, / I will give ye leave to cut my throat / If I make not good sport!" (2.2.16–18). Immediately after this speech, Diccon calls upon Dame Chat, who is engaged in a game of cards, a version of Ruff, inside her alehouse. Coming to greet him at the door, Dame Chat tells Diccon that "We be fast set at trump, man, hard by the fire; / Thou shalt set on the king if thou come a little nigher" (2.2.23–4). She invites Diccon into the home, "a little nigher" [closer] to watch the card game, promising him that he shall see a great trick, the taking of the king. When he declines, saying he does not have time to tarry and wishes only to speak to her, Dame Chat calls into the house and asks her servant to hold her cards and play in her place: "Doll, sit down and play this game, / And as thou sawest me do, see thou do even the same. / There is five trumps beside the queen" (2.2.27–29). Once alone with Dame Chat, Diccon, feigning reluctance at first, finally agrees to share with her what he claims to be a secret: that the old woman, Gammer, believes Dame Chat has stolen Gammer's precious cock.

Though it is mentioned quickly and happens offstage, the card game is the perfect ironic backdrop for Diccon's schemes, which not only spread mistruths, but rely for their effectiveness on other characters' failures to negotiate imperfect information. Diccon's lies, which create the comic business of the play, create a false network of hidden information. Diccon convinces Dame Chat to believe that Gammer is hiding, and will soon reveal, her belief that Dame Chat has stolen Gammer's cock. He then goes to Gammer and convinces her that Dame Chat is hiding Gammer's needle and is thus a false friend. The women are easily persuaded, never doubting that the other friend acts dishonestly, even though the revelations come from an untrustworthy source, a poor and starving beggar who may be motivated more by material than altruistic motives.[13] The success of Diccon's schemes rests on the presumption that any friendship, even one that has existed for years, as Dame Chat's and Gammer's seems to have done, involves interactants who hide some information from each other. Diccon exploits this state of affairs, simply adding detail and matter to this structure of friendship.

It goes without saying that Diccon is playing games with Dame Chat and Gammer, but to understand these games as more than simple fun for fun's sake, we need to think more carefully about the kind of games that Diccon favors.[14] Diccon's character repeatedly uses games of imperfect information, and specifically card play, to explain and manipulate human behavior. When the audience first meets Diccon, he tells us about the scene at Gammer's house, where "There is howling and scowling, all cast in a dump," and his only way to make sense of all this "whewling and puling" is to compare it to behavior of card players: it is "as though they had lost a trump" (1.1.11–12). Diccon alludes to the fact that people take their cards far too seriously, agonized by something so trivial. We may at this moment laugh at Diccon for such an absurd analogy—how silly to suggest that the degree of distress he describes could be attributed to the loss of a trump card—but the description turns out to be quite apt, since the distress is caused by the loss of something arguably even more trivial, a needle. And, in fact, Diccon and Mr. S.'s play take games quite seriously; like the needle, games are not trivial at all.

Diccon will use the trump game analogy again later in the play (with the same end rhyme of "dump"). When he is convincing Doctor Rat, the curate, that he has witnessed Dame Chat with the needle, he figures himself as a strategic player in a card game with Dame Chat: "I handled myself so well, / And yet the crafty quean had almost take my trump. / But or all came to an end, I set her in a dump" (4.4.10–12). The card analogy is appropriate here, as Diccon advises the gullible Doctor Rat that negotiating imperfect information requires *strategy*; though it would make sense for Doctor Rat simply to ask Dame Chat about the stolen needle, Diccon warns Rat against this course of action by figuring Dame Chat as a tactical game player, a case all the more convincing given that Dame Chat does seem to be a fan of games of trumps. Diccon persuades Rat that Dame Chat is well skilled in hiding her cards, and thus the Doctor will need his own strategy, an area in which Diccon, who claims to have already successfully matched wits with the wily Dame Chat, is prepared to assist.

After culminating in the play's most intense social interaction—a verbal and physical battle between Dame Chat and Gammer Gurton—the game of imperfect information Diccon sets into motion comes to a close with the bailiff forcing all to reveal what has been hidden. At this point, Doctor Rat, the character most humiliated by Diccon's antics, insists that the bailiff "set him fast" (5.2.234) by which he means to set Diccon in fetters. But Diccon, reminding us that he approaches social relations as games of imperfect information, twists Rat's meaning, and, taking advantage of a phrase from card playing, asks, "What, fast at cards, or fast on sleep? It is the thing I did last" (5.2.235). Diccon does not simply refuse to admit his wrongdoing; he represents the whole episode as a game of cards, and he asks the audience to do so as well.

In this heavily moralistic drama, Diccon is meant to convey the moral message not only to the villagers of Gurton within the fiction of the play but to the youth of Christ's College, Cambridge, the audience for the play's first performance.[15] There was a clear fit between these lessons and the humanist curriculum of the College, and it is not surprising that some literary scholars view the play as epitomizing humanist education. Others have argued, however, that *Gammer* mocks particular elements of humanism.[16] In particular, the play addresses the social and erotic consequences of Cambridge's all-male humanist education system, poking fun at its disavowal of women and domesticity. This mockery comes through especially clearly in the culminating moment of the play, when Diccon manages to prick Hodge's bottom with the long sought-after needle, setting up a comically sodomitical relationship between Gammer's servant and Diccon. Part of the joke here, as Wendy Wall discusses, is that Diccon and Hodge are rural, lower-class figures, and their theatrical participation in the homoerotic humanist education system makes them and the system look absurd.[17] It is not just class differences between audience and characters that render the depiction of intimacy comical in this play, but gender differences as well. For the play also encourages its elite male audience to laugh at the friendship between the women depicted in the play, which is a far cry from the sort of ideal friendship that Cambridge's students would have been reading about in their humanist tomes.

I would suggest that the play displaces onto its female and lower-class characters anxieties about the feasibility of the humanist model of ideal male friendship. As Diccon manipulates the friendship between Dame Chat and Gammer by claiming to be a perfect friend to both women, he occasionally deploys the humanist rhetoric of ideal friendship to secure the trust of the play's female characters. According to Cicero and early modern essays on friendship by humanist writers such as Francis Bacon and Michel de Montaigne, the friend is a second self who can keep no secrets from the other and who cares for his friend as if he is caring for himself, no matter the risks. Diccon swears this sort of loyalty to Gammer, claiming that when he saw Dame Chat take up the needle, "I spoke in your behalf" (2.4.37), and at some risk, given Dame Chat's reputation as a "crafty" (2.4.26), wily opponent. Later, he refers in passing to Gammer as his friend when he refuses to tell Rat about the needle-stealing incident he claims to have witnessed. Sharing secrets with one's friends is a risky endeavor: "there is many an honest man, when he such blasts hath blown / In his friends' ears, he would be loath the same by him were known" (4.2.46–7). Diccon plays the friend with all his victims, presenting himself as a noble confidant who cannot keep information from his true friends. When he expresses reluctance to share with Dame Chat his secrets about Gammer's accusations, but ultimately does so, he explains that he could not help but share this information because of his friendship with Dame Chat. As he justifies why friends cannot keep secrets, he recalls a common motif in the humanist discourse of friendship: "Because I know you are my friend, hide it I could not" (2.2.77).

To Cambridge's university audience, Diccon's claims to friendship would have already seemed comical. According to the Ciceronian ideal, ideal friendship is found solely between men, and although the classical model of ideal friendship could be taken up and adapted for female friendship, it had little traction in the representation of cross-gender alliances.[18] This was because women were seen to be incapable of, in Montaigne's words, the "conference and communication" so central to friendship, a point to which I return later.[19] Additionally (and relatedly) for Cicero and those who adapted his ideas in the early modern period, ideal friendship could flourish only between individuals of similar and high enough status, where neither participant is more economically or socially dependent than the other.[20] Hearing Diccon appeal to true friendship is thus all the more humorous to an audience familiar with humanist rhetoric, for Diccon, a beggar, is the very epitome of need. Hardly pure and unselfish, Diccon's "friendships" are motivated by his desire for bacon and ale.[21] When we add to this the fact that Diccon's baring of his soul and secrets is, in fact, the sharing of carefully manufactured lies, Diccon stands as a total mockery of the humanist ideal of friendship. A skilled con artist, Diccon presents himself to victims as playing a game of perfect information with them in order to convince them that *they* are playing a game of imperfect information with others. He convinces them to take his friendship for granted so as to refocus their attentions on a different interactant, a different game, one that they consequently try to win using information Diccon has provided. In sum, through Diccon, the play invites its predominantly male college audience to interrogate the rhetoric of ideal friendship they have been studying in their books.

To see this critique of classical male friendship play out, we must, however, attend to gaming as more than a metaphor, more than a recurring set of images in Diccon's language. For at this level—the level of linguistic representation—the play's critique of idealistic male friendship is circumscribed and limited, as it is displaced onto lower-class women and crossgender friendship. Since these relationships are always and already disqualified from meeting humanist ideals, they provide a safe and contained way to poke fun at the rhetoric of ideal friendship while leaving its core principals intact for men. But when we pay closer attention to the experience of gaming *Gammer* presents to its *theater audience*, the critique of male friendship becomes much more pronounced. *Gammer*'s audiences were not simply observers of the play; they were active participants, something the staged card game helps to reveal. The play puts pressure on the humanist rhetoric of friendship by engaging its predominantly male audience in a game of imperfect information, at social, dramatic, as well as theatrical levels.

Diccon is at the center of this theater game, for he pretends to be a perfect friend not only to the play's female characters, but also to theater spectators, ultimately revealing to them, as well, that he has been playing a game of imperfect information. Diccon's information games with theater spectators begin during the card game scene that initiates his plot. It is notable that in that scene *Gammer* makes a virtue out of the necessity that the audience cannot see the cards being played in its staged game of Ruff. Indeed, Dame Chat flaunts the cards hidden from the theater audience's view when she comes to the door of her alehouse: play *this* game, she tells Doll, pointing to the cards the audience cannot see. As if to further pique the audience's curiosity, Dame Chat's interlocutor, Doll, remains hidden from view.[22] These occlusions would have been all the more enticing because audiences at Christ's College, as was true for most college plays in the mid-sixteenth century, stood close to the stage during performances, sometimes even on it;[23] were *Gammer*'s card game played on the stage instead of off, some audience members would have been able to see Dame Chat's hand. Staging the game behind a door is thus essential for producing in audiences a state of imperfect information and an interest in overcoming that state. Audiences familiar with Ruff are drawn into vicarious engagement with the offstage card game through partial descriptions of Dame Chat's hand and her strategy: "There is five trumps beside the queen, the hindmost thou shalt find her" (2.2.29). Dame Chat shows that she has been reading the cards and perhaps is working to flush out all the trump cards, including the queen. This is a common strategy still used today by players of trumps games, like bridge: one attempts to get all the trump cards out of other players' hands so as to use one's own trumps to capture other players' high cards in other suits. The passage works on two contradictory levels. On the one hand, as a double-entendre, the passage shares with the audience privileged information about how *Gammer*'s plot will unfold: Diccon will capture five trumps (Gammer; Cock, her maid; Tib, her servant boy; Hodge; and Rat) in addition to the queen (Dame Chat herself). As double-entendre the passage presents the game as one of perfect information for the audience; they, and only they, are privy to Diccon's plans. At the level of gameplay, however, the passage offers only *partial* information, inviting the audience to play the offstage game vicariously by negotiating imperfect information in much the way Dame Chat and Doll do.

This ambivalence epitomizes Diccon's relationship with the theater audience throughout the drama. For while Diccon set up a game of imperfect information for his villagers, feigning friendship, to the audience he *seems* to be a true, ideal friend, confiding in playgoers everything there is to know about his plan. And, as we'll see similarly in the case of Heywood's *A Woman Killed*, friendship is solidified through the sport of wagering. As he divulges his plans, Diccon repeatedly bets the audience that they will enjoy the game. "Here will the sport begin, if these two [Gammer and Dame Chat] once may meet; / Their cheer, durst lay money, will prove scarcely sweet!" (2.5.1–2). Diccon invites the audience to a metagame, a wager about the game of imperfect information that Gammer and Dame Chat play, but he promises a definite win: "He that may tarry by it awhile, and that but short, / I warrant him, trust to it, he shall see all the sport" (2.5.7–8). Diccon's openness assures the audience that they will not be victims of imperfect information in the way the play's characters are. This offer of full information is echoed more broadly by the play as a whole, whose prologue reveals the entire plot, including the comic ending, where the needle is found in Hodge's pants.

However, Diccon does not divulge everything to his audience "friends," and this becomes clear at the end of the play, when the audience discovers they are, in fact, engaged in a game of imperfect information.[24] To appreciate the gamelike structure of this final scene, where Diccon discovers the needle in Hodge's pants when it pricks his buttock, we need to place into further cultural context what others have identified as the sodomitical symbolism of Diccon's pricking of Hodge.[25] Another cultural analogue for sticking a needle in someone's pants was the sixteenth-century game of "prick the belt," otherwise known as "prick the garter" or "fast and loose." In the game a piece of leather hide—such as a belt, garter, or thong—is folded and rolled up, the two ends left on the outside. The rolled-up hide is then placed edgeways on a table so that the intricate folds are visible to all. The player bets that he can stick a pin or other sharp object through an inside loop so that when the two ends of the belt are pulled apart, the belt will be either caught (fast) or free (loose). This was a well-known shell game in the sixteenth century. The swindler would manipulate the ends of the belt, creating the illusion of a fold in the belt's middle, and invite the passerby to play what seemed a sure thing.[26] The game was so widely associated with cheating that its name was and continues to be a proverbial expression for dishonest gaming, "playing fast and loose." References to con artists cheating with the game appear in several early modern dramas. Antony accuses Cleopatra of playing "at fast and loose" (*Antony and Cleopatra* 4.13.28); Costard contends, "To sell a bargain well is as cunning as fast and loose" (*Love's Labour's Lost* 3.1.92); and Falstaff alludes to the game when he tells Pistol to go off and make some money illegally with a "short knife and a th[]ong" (*Merry Wives of Windsor* 2.2.17)[27] —the latter being the very item that Hodge has used to mend the pants he wears in *Gammer*'s final scene.

Allusions to "prick the belt" at this climactic moment of the play deepen its sexual inferences; not surprisingly, the game of fast and loose, with its invitation to "prick" a phallic object through the folds of a leather hide is often a euphemism for copulation, particularly sodomitical, insofar as it is a *hide* that gets penetrated. If the final scene enacts the game of "prick the belt," its sexual significance is all the more interesting: in the con game, the swindler symbolically displays his sexual mastery at the expense of the dupe, who is exposed in this zero-sum game as sexually incompetent. Unlike the con artist, the dupe in a game of "prick the belt" fails to recognize whether the phallic object (needle or knife) has penetrated the folds of the hide. Either the dupe fails to wield the needle effectively, believing himself to have penetrated when, in fact, he has missed his target, or, if he is the guesser, he fails to recognize that the needle inserted by the swindler intentionally misses the target. This is no better. Moreover, insofar as the sham is accomplished by the con artist manipulating the ends of a leather hide, the dupe is exposed for failing to know, quite literally, which end is up. In any event the dupe is not only punished financially, but shamed sexually as well.

If Diccon is the swindler working the needle, we may be tempted, as many have been, to read Hodge as the dupe. Looked at more closely in terms of the game, though, Hodge is only a tool for play, providing the leather hide or thong to be "pricked." Who then is the real dupe? I would suggest that it is the theater audience, who threaten to be shamed by their realization that they, like the characters in *Gammer*, have been lured into a game of imperfect information, for the play has hidden from them key details about its "end."[28] The prologue ostensibly reveals to the audience that the play will close with Hodge recovering the needle in his pants when it pricks his buttock. But the prologue hides Diccon's role in the "springing of the game" (5.2.318), presenting the finding of the needle as a matter beyond human agency, "Whether it were by fortune or some other constellation" (l. 16). The audience is thus somewhat surprised, indeed duped, by the ending. This need not be a bad thing, though. If part of the pleasure of theater stems from its status as a game of imperfect information, like cards, the prologue threatens to undermine that by sharing too much, removing all suspense from the plot. Nevertheless, it is notable that the audience must lose the game to experience the theatrical pleasure; they, too, must be duped by Diccon, who here (as elsewhere) stands in for the playwright who crafts the plot. The audience does not need to be pricked in the buttocks to learn this particular lesson; they merely need to watch another hide being pricked. And like other lessons of the humanist classroom, which were driven home through the use of the schoolmaster's birch rod on the student's behind, this one is learned through a complex erotic and theatrical economy of shaming and pleasure.[29]

Others have pointed out how this gendered and erotic economy is at work in *Gammer* and, more important, what it meant to the young male Cambridge audience watching the play. The aim of my reading has been to deepen their trenchant insights by highlighting how *Gammer* uses gaming to create a phenomenology of theatergoing that rivals the classroom in its power to educate about the nature of male intimacy. Watching the needle prick Hodge's hide, the audience is both uncomfortably and pleasurably shamed by having failed to predict in full the scheme of the plot, of how the ends will be brought about, how, to use Diccon's terms, the game will be sprung. Duped by Diccon into a false confidence about their access to dramatic information, they come to learn through loss of a little dignity the joy of *not* knowing and of trying to uncover what is unknown. In certain games, as in certain dramas and, yes, certain personal relationships, that is a key site of pleasure even as it is a source of anxiety.

Notably, the play condones Diccon's actions, even though he uses cheating to convey this lesson. Leaving him unpunished for his insubordination and trickery, the play rewrites Diccon's cheating as successful gamesmanship. Indeed, the play treats Diccon's cheating in much the way Dame Chat treats the cheating of her fellow card players. When Dame Chat asks Doll to play on her behalf, she counsels: "Take heed of Sim Glover's wife—she hath an eye behind her!" (2.2.30), perhaps an allusion to the fraud scheme described in *Mihil Mumchance* (1597) and illustrated in Figure 13, Aelbert Jansz. van der Schoor's *Cardsharps in an Interior* (1656), where a mirror is placed behind the swindled opponent so that the cheater can see the opponent's cards in the mirror's reflection.[30] Dame Chat does not accuse her opponent of cheating, even though she is quite certain of this (she *hath* an eye behind her, not she *might have* an eye behind her); instead Dame Chat plays more warily, advising Doll to do the same. Alliances, whether social or theatrical, are not about revealing everything; they are about recognizing that others are playing a game of imperfect information, too, and that, to put this in Goffman's terms, one's ethical responsibility is not to call out a fellow player's strategies or even foul play, but rather to keep the interaction going, playing along one step *ahead* of one's interactants. Like Dame Chat, *Gammer*'s audience must play a game of imperfect information with a cheater whose behavior cannot be publicly exposed lest the game be disrupted completely.

The pleasures of playgoing are as complex and ambivalent as those of card games and of friendship. Playgoers risk being shamed by lack of knowledge, for committing to the play, being willing to see it through, can mean risking one's own butt, as it were, and accepting that that in the end, the play may "leave you behind" (5.2.331), as *Gammer* almost does.

Playgoing, like male friendship, even as it nurtures bonds between interactants, renders their relations precarious and risky; for theater thrives, as
does friendship, on participants' willingness to hide and seek out hidden
information.

CARDS, THEATER, AND MALE FRIENDSHIP AT
CAMBRIDGE UNIVERSITY

The students of Christ's College may have been especially amenable to a
play that used cards to convey this message, especially if the play was, like
so many other mid-sixteenth-century comedies, performed during the
Christmas season.[31] As mentioned in Chapter 1, cards were a central part of
Christmas revels, and they would have become even more closely associated with Christmas following the 1541 edict that restricted servants, apprentices, and other laborers from playing cards outside Christmastime.[32]
At some points in its history, Cambridge University explicitly forbade card
play among students, allowing fellows from Christ's and St. John's colleges
to indulge in cards only during the Christmas holiday.[33] One explicit reason for laws against card play was the concern that cards and other sitting
pastimes would promote idleness, and that recreations ought to be of a
more active sort. Yet another reason may have been that cards were the
epitome of an emerging commodity culture that was heavily critiqued by
Cambridge social reformers, who believed that such imported commodities threatened traditional social bonds and English national identity.[34]
Similar sorts of criticism of playing cards can be heard throughout England
in the early modern period. As discussed in the previous chapter, mon-
archs and governing bodies, under pressure from English card makers,
outlawed the importation of playing cards, which generally came to England from France. But their laws had little effect, and French cards continued to flood the English market. There is material evidence of these imported cards at Cambridge University: playing cards from the early 1630s
from two different decks, one of which is marked with the name of the
French card manufacturer Jean Desmarests, were found buried in a staircase at Trinity College.[35] And however much they were disparaged by legal
and moral authorities, cards continued to be played throughout the sixteenth century. Recall that Henry VIII's 1541 statute did not restrict the
card playing of higher-status groups, including noblemen and gentlemen,
and it even allowed these men to license their servants and children to play
cards within the grounds of the master's house.[36] Card playing remained

acceptable to many Cambridge leaders, too. So much so that when Protestant Reformer William Ames, a fellow at Christ's College, preached against playing cards and dice in 1610, he was pressured to resign from the university under threat of expulsion.[37]

Hardly a straightforward emblem of vice for students and fellows at Christ's College,[38] cards may even have had a decidedly positive valence, serving as symbols of spiritual self-knowledge and, of particular relevance to my subject here, Christian fellowship. At the time *Gammer* was likely performed at Cambridge, students could, through the allusion to playing cards, recall their connection to one of Cambridge's most famous preachers, Hugh Latimer, who had reemerged in the 1550s as a powerful voice of the Protestant Reformation. Latimer's rise to power two decades earlier had coincided with his having delivered his groundbreaking "Sermons on the Card" at Cambridge. The sermons had ignited major controversy in 1529, using the analogy of card playing both to demand the Bible be translated into English and to underscore the importance of Christian fellowship—the latter claim inviting the fury of Cambridge's church conservatives in that it prioritized social service over "voluntary works" like building churches, lighting candles, and going on pilgrimages. The second of Latimer's sermons was delivered directly in response to Robert Buckenham of the Dominican Friars, who, according to John Foxe's expanded *Actes and Monuments* (1583), sat right under the pulpit gritting his teeth.[39] The message of Latimer's sermons is that true devotion to Christ and spiritual salvation come through the building and maintenance of social bonds. And although Catholics and traditionalists had long associated friendship with Christianity—the Eucharist having served as a space for sworn brotherhood rituals[40]—Latimer's sermons urge parishioners to mend and create social bonds *before* coming to church, not just inside it. Even more to my purpose here, Latimer's sermons use a game of trumps to elucidate this message.

Latimer claims to be using the trumps game analogy to appeal to his audience members, who, he realizes, are about to play cards during the Christmas season. Faced undoubtedly with distracted auditors as he attempts to explain Christ's teachings, Latimer engages, instead of fighting, students' current preoccupations. He presents himself as playing a game of cards with his auditors:

> I will apply myself according to your custom at this time of Christmas: I will, as I said, declare unto you Christ's rule, but that shall be in Christ's cards. And whereas you are wont to celebrate Christmas in playing at cards, I intend, by God's grace, to deal unto you Christ's

cards, wherein you shall perceive Christ's rule. The game that we will play at shall be called the triumph, which, if it be well played at, he that dealeth shall win; the players shall likewise win; and the standers and lookers upon shall do the same; insomuch that there is no man that is willing to play at this triumph with these cards, but they shall be all winners, and no losers.

The good Christian must, like any game player or spectator, know the rules of the game, in this case "Christ's rule." Latimer then proceeds to describe the value of two of the "cards" in the deck, both of which mediate relations between friends and neighbors. One "card" cautions against giving into one's "Turks," emotions of anger that can lead to bickering with others and, in the worst circumstances, committing violence against them. The second, closely related "card" compels the good Christian to mend any broken friendships before offering oblations to God. As a pair the sermons emphasize the spiritual value of forgiving one's enemies and of not letting petty conflict get out of hand—in short, of building and nurturing social alliances. Latimer does not simply elucidate these "cards," he advises his hearers in how to use them in play:

Now I trust you wot what your card meaneth: let us see how that we can play with the same. Whensoever it shall happen you to go and make your oblation unto God, ask of yourselves this question, "Who art thou?" The answer, as you know, is, "I am a christian man." Then you must again ask unto yourself, What Christ requireth of a christian man? By and by cast down your trump, your heart, and look first of one card, then of another. The first card telleth thee, thou shalt not kill, thou shalt not be angry, thou shalt not be out of patience. This done, thou shalt look if there be any more cards to take up; and if thou look well, thou shalt see another card of the same suit, wherein thou shalt know that thou art bound to reconcile thy neighbour. Then cast thy trump upon them both, and gather them all three together, and do according to the virtue of thy cards; and surely thou shalt not lose.[41]

Latimer compares the important work of seeking spiritual self-knowledge to the taking of a trick in a game of "triumph," another name for games of trumps such as Ruff. The parishioner's game is, like any card game, about negotiating imperfect information. When coming to prayer, parishioners experience a state of uncertainty. They do not have all the information needed for spiritual salvation and must, like the Pharisees who wondered whether Saint John the Baptist was the savior they needed to worship, ask "Who are thou?" The question is central to Latimer's sermons, which use this parable and its query for information as their launching point. But, Latimer implies, if salvation is a game of imperfect information like Trumps, it can be won if players understand the value of the cards, watch what is played by others, and use their "trump" cards effectively. The analogy works on a fairly simple level here. The suit of hearts is trumps; thus to win the trick and take both of the other cards, the Christian need only look carefully at the two cards and throw down a "heart," which conveniently is both a suit in card play and the bodily organ associated with Christian faith. In effect, Latimer was suggesting that parishioners could have an intimate relationship with God by treating this relationship as one of imperfect information—a claim that would have resonated powerfully during the Reformation years, as Protestants emphasized a more direct instead of mediated connection to God.

The sermons were so controversial that Latimer came under attack after delivering them. Yet just when Latimer's Cambridge career, and perhaps more, was to be lost, King Henry VIII, having heard that Latimer supported his cause for divorce, came to the preacher's defense. His critics silenced, Latimer was soon invited to preach before Henry VIII, ultimately being promoted to Bishop of Worcester in 1535. Though Latimer's position of authority during Henry's reign waxed and waned—at the time of Henry's death, Latimer was committed to the Tower—he emerged afresh as a popular preacher in the early 1550s when Edward VI took the throne and when *Gammer* was being written and performed. Thus, when Mr. S.'s play uses the card game as an analogy for friendship, this may have had special, timely resonance for Cambridge's clerically minded student audience.

In linking Mr. S.'s play with Latimer's sermons, my goal here is not to argue that the play is a religious parable in disguise, though it may well be: certainly the play's villagers are guilty of indulging in petty conflict with friends.[42] Nor do I aim to offer further evidence for the play's anti-Catholicism.[43] For though Protestant Reformers used playing cards to spread their religious ideas—as is attested by a 1603 German deck of educational cards that teach biblical history[44] and by Luther's own use of the card game as spiritual metaphor on at least three occasions[45]—many Protestant preachers also criticized card play, and, as discussed in Chapter 1, royalist writers with more conservative religious views were just as quick to use cards as witty metaphors for their cause.[46] As well, Catholics were as eager as Protestants to find pedagogical value in card play. Rather than linking the metaphorical and practical value of playing cards to a particular moral, religious, or political perspective, I am interested in the fact that for a Cambridge student audience in particular, the game of cards was an ideal vehicle for investigating social relationships as information games. Like Latimer's sermon, *Gammer Gurton's Needle* trades on commonplace views of card playing as a vice in order to deliver its moral punch about social alliances. Playing cards may well be dangerous commodities, threatening English livelihood and corrupting good men; nevertheless, they have the potential not only to destroy social bonds, but also to create them. The play, like Latimer, shows its audiences that imperfect information about another is cause not simply for anxiety but for pleasure and even spiritual joy. Pleasure comes not from the commodity item itself, but from its employment in social relationships. Alone, a card is a card, a needle a needle—just another commodity item. When it is put into use, however, the card, like the needle, can become a vital part of the community and a mode for securing social connection.

The resultant bonds are powerful but also vulnerable, not unlike the kind of faith that Latimer preaches. For even the most rule-bound of card games is still a game of imperfect information, where some of what needs to be known is hidden. The card game, like a friendship, creates epistemological challenges and, thus, leaves interactants vulnerable to being bamboozled by wilier players, who can manipulate imbalances in knowledge to their advantage. As is elucidated in the next section's reading of *A Woman Killed with Kindness*, cheating, defined broadly, is, in fact, built into the rules of card games, as it is into friendship. And thus imbalances in information are inevitably vulnerable to exploitation. These opportunities and anxieties around interaction are undoubtedly there in any social relationship. But they are a particular source of concern for the young men who first watched *Gammer* and who are depicted in *A Woman Killed*. Insofar as their claims to masculinity were reliant on creating and maintaining homosocial alliances, friendship mattered deeply. A fraudulent friend could be a man's social and financial undoing. For early modern men in particular, then, there was a lot at stake in being able to negotiate a relationship of imperfect information.

IMPERFECT FRIENDSHIP IN *A WOMAN KILLED WITH KINDNESS*

Heywood's *A Woman Killed with Kindness* dramatizes those stakes, as it depicts the rise and fall of a friendship between two men who, tragically, love the same woman. Like *Gammer*, much of the plot of Heywood's play is concerned with hidden information, in this case about Wendoll's adulterous affair with Frankford's wife, and the question of when and how that information will come to light, and what Frankford will do when all is revealed. A pivotal scene in this drama of information is the staged card game through which Frankford hopes to test his recently acquired suspicions; he engages in a tabletop game of imperfect information in order to solve problems of imperfect information in his friendship and his marriage. I want to focus in particular on how the card game draws the play's audience into an experience of negotiating imperfect information by inviting them to play the staged card game vicariously. Although, unlike Frankford, spectators know that Wendoll and Anne have been having an affair, they, like Frankford, learn over the course of the game scene that Wendoll and Anne—who are partners in the card game against Frankford and another friend—are also cheating at cards, exploiting the differences in knowledge that motivate routine card play, and friendship too.

When Frankford first alludes to Wendoll's cheating during the card game, the accusations are subtle and the cause specious enough that Frankford seems to refer only to Wendoll's adulterous affair. Before the game begins, each character draws from the deck to determine the dealer. Though the audience cannot see and thus does not know what card Frankford draws, the fact that he wins the right to deal after Wendoll and Anne draw a Knave and Queen, respectively, indicates that Frankford draws something of higher value. As he takes the card deck, Frankford observes, "They are the grossest pair that e'er I felt" (8.170).[47] Beyond its implications as a double-entendre reference to the adulterous couple, Frankford intimates that the card deck, referred to in this period as a "pair," feels "gross," or rough, an allusion perhaps to dirty, marked cards. Charles Cotton's *The Compleat Gamester* (published in 1674) explains how cards may be marked by nicking their edges: "take a pack of Cards and open them, then take out all the Honours, that is . . . the four Aces, the four Kings, &c. then take the rest and cut a little from the edges of them all alike, by which means the Honours will be broader than the rest."[48] The honor cards in such a marked deck protrude just slightly, undoubtedly rendering the pack "gross" to the touch. That Wendoll and Anne should both draw honor cards, and ones so befitting of their promiscuous sexuality (knave and queen, a pun on "quean," are both terms of slander conveying sexual criminality),[49] is somewhat suspicious but by no means confirms dishonest play, especially since it is usually the dealer who benefits from using marked cards. At the same time, though, the conventions of card play imply that Frankford's designation as dealer leaves Anne in charge of cutting the deck and Wendoll in charge of shuffling: "Shuffle, I'll cut" (8.171), says Anne.[50] While, again, there is nothing immediately suspicious about these actions, they do, as Cotton's exposition on card sharks explains, put Anne in the position to place high honor cards strategically in the deck so as to help her partner, Wendoll—a point to which I return below.

Once the cards are shuffled, cut, and dealt, the game begins, and Frankford reports having "lost my dealing" (8.172), to which Wendoll responds, "Sir, the fault's in me. / . . . / Give me the stock" (8.173–75). More than a double-entendre in which Wendoll admits his fault in the affair, the line can be interpreted from the game's perspective as indicating that Wendoll has the ace of trumps (the most valued suit in the game) in his hand and wins the right to "ruff the stock"—or exchange any of the cards in his hand for those in the pile of four left on the table after all the other cards have been dealt. As the game proceeds and Wendoll's good luck builds, the characters refer more repeatedly to the conclusion that Wendoll is cheating. On one level, to be sure, Wendoll's double-entendres and asides concerning cheating pertain to his affair with Anne, but the scene invites audience members who attempt to play the game vicariously another interpretation of the lines: that they pertain to Wendoll's performance in the card game itself. The next game action the audience can ascertain comes from Frankford's declaration, "My mind's not on my game. / . . . / You have served me a bad trick, Master Wendoll" (8.175–77). Someone familiar with Vide Ruff will know that Frankford appears to have lost the trick he led to Wendoll, who has now led with or "served" a card that Frankford cannot beat, "a bad trick." After Wendoll responds, "Sir, you must take your lot. To end this strife, / I know I have dealt better with your wife" (8.178–79), Frankford offers the audience the first clear indication that he suspects Wendoll is cheating at cards: "Thou has dealt falsely then" (8.180). For Wendoll to be sure his card will win the trick, he must have some knowledge of Anne's hand, impossible unless they have illicitly shared information.

As the trick concludes, Frankford communicates to the audience absolute certainty about Wendoll's cheating. Anne, who is to put down her card after Frankford,[51] asks, "What's trumps?"; Wendoll answers "Hearts" and, presumably after Anne and Cranwell (Frankford's partner) play their cards, Wendoll takes the trick, "I rub" (8.182). Engaging a homonymic pun on "rub," Frankford responds in an aside,

Thou robb'st me of my soul, of her chaste love;
In thy false dealing, thou hast robbed my heart.

> Booty you play; I like a loser stand,
> Having no heart, or here, or in my hand. (8.183–86)

and then he abruptly ends the game, claiming illness.

While the lines obviously work metaphorically in a cuckoldry plot—Wendoll has stolen Frankford's one true love, his "heart"—an audience following the dramatic arc of the game can interpret them as indicating that when Wendoll wins the trick, he takes Frankford's sole trump card. Why would this confirm Frankford's suspicions of cheating? A spectator playing vicariously might reconstruct the action of the trick as follows: That Frankford loses a trump card and still loses the trick tells us that Wendoll had to have *led* with hearts. For if Wendoll had led with any other suit, Frankford's lone heart card could have trumped it. So we know that Wendoll leads with a heart and that Frankford follows with a lower-valued heart. What does Anne play? The fact that she asks the group, "What's trumps?" after Wendoll has led with hearts suggests she doesn't have any hearts in her hand. If she did, she would, by the rules of the game, have to play hearts and wouldn't have the option to play the trumps suit. That she, apparently forgetting trumps is hearts, considers playing trumps tells us that she doesn't have hearts in her hand.[52] If Anne has no hearts, and Frankford just played his last one, then Wendoll and Cranwell have the rest of the hearts from the deck between them. Cranwell's hearts, if he has them, are, however, clearly lower in value than Wendoll's. This tells us that Wendoll has all of the highest trumps in the pack and, thus, should take every or almost every remaining trick. Frankford's subsequent outburst and sudden decision to end the game has been read by critics as evidence of his uncharacteristic loss of control,[53] but from the perspective of the card game, Frankford has simply realized not only that he and Cranwell have no chance of winning because Wendoll's cards are too good, but that Wendoll most likely had to have cheated in order to achieve such a hand.

For someone familiar with Vide Ruff, the cheating scheme would be fairly self-evident in retrospect: through marked cards and some sleight-of-hand techniques, Wendoll managed to win the ace of trumps and place the next four highest heart cards at the bottom of the deck before it was dealt. Such a scenario would have given him an unbeatable hand, for the ace wins him the right to ruff the stock so that he would then hold the five top trumps. For Wendoll to have arranged the marked cards in such a way, though, especially in a hand that he did not deal, he would have to have had Anne as an accomplice, for it is she who cuts the deck before Frankford deals, strategically ensuring that these cards will be at the bottom of the deck and thus in Wendoll's stock. Frankford's furious aside, "Booty you play," is then directed to both Wendoll and Anne, who have joined in league to victimize him through false play.[54] We may be tempted to interpret this fraudulent action as yet another great double-entendre: Wendoll and Anne have cuckolded Frankford, so it is not surprising that they should extend their treachery into a card game. But cheating at cards is more than an allegory for or extension of cuckoldry; it is a metacommentary on the epistemologies of gameplay and male friendship.

Heywood's audience may be just as surprised by Wendoll's cheating as Frankford is, for spectators, too, are participants in the game Wendoll plays. To be sure, we witness Wendoll wooing Anne and thus betraying his friend, but he has until this point presented himself to Anne and the play's audience as a hapless victim of love who cheats his friend because his emotions get the better of him. When Wendoll decides to declare his affection for Anne, he appears the quintessential melancholic lover: indecisive, overly dramatic, conflicted, distracted. He delivers a heartfelt series of soliloquies about his plight, deciding that he cannot help but give in to his feelings. His confession begins like those of Shakespearean villains Richard III or Lear's Edmund when they soliloquize on their innate evilness, "I am a villain." But Wendoll quickly changes course, presenting his lack of loyalty to Frankford as a regrettable option, not an expression of inner villainy:

> I am a villain if I apprehend
> But such a thought; then, to attempt the deed—
> Slave, thou art damned without redemption.
> I'll drive away this passion with a song.
> A song! Ha, ha! A song, as if, fond man,
> Thy eyes could swim in laughter when thy soul
> Lies drenched and drowned in red tears of blood. (6.1–7)

For those who read the play as essentially a morality drama, Wendoll is a straightforward villain, but the representation of his treachery is far more complex.[55] The card game urges that Wendoll also be read, like Diccon in *Gammer Gurton's Needle*, as a skilled swindler. In retrospect, his melancholic soliloquies appear a calculated attempt to portray himself to audiences as committed to love, not cheating.

My purpose in presenting this reading of Wendoll is not to substantiate the view of him as the play's Vice figure or to trace some sort of consistency in character that would fulfill realist expectations for drama. Rather, I am interested in the play's use of the card game to reveal to the theater audience that Wendoll's character cheats, which leads spectators beyond ethics in contextualizing his foul play. By exposing Wendoll's rooking to the audience only after Frankford discovers it, and only through the game's dramatic arc, the play asks its audience to consider Wendoll's foul play less as a reflection of villainous character than as an epistemological problem. The card game insists audiences reconsider the degree to which they, like Frankford, can "know" Wendoll.[56] Significantly, Wendoll's performance of intimacy with theater spectators puts them in an analogous position to Frankford.

Other early modern plays about infidelity have the audience identify with the jealous husband, paradoxically by structuring the plot so that the audience knows about the cheating before the husband does.[57] But Heywood's card game produces a disparity between audience and characters that is the inverse of the "dramatic irony" in the play's larger plotline. Whereas the audience knows about the affair before Frankford and other characters do, in the case of the card game, the audience—who cannot see any of the cards on the staged game table—sees and thus knows less than Frankford does. If the gap in knowledge between protagonist and audience ordinarily prompts interpretive work on the part of the protagonist (the play's plot concerns his efforts to uncover the adultery), then, I would suggest, the card game shifts this interpretive work away from Frankford's character and toward the theater audience.[58] Spectators of a game they cannot see completely and whose moves are available to them only through snippets of dialogue, the audience is called upon to reconstruct the moves of the card game, negotiating imperfect information in much the way the characters onstage do. As a consequence, the audience's theatrical experience of the play doesn't map neatly onto the movement of its plot: while the plot builds toward what most would consider the climactic scene of the play—the bedroom discovery scene—the climax of theatrical engagement and participation is, in fact, the card game scene.

This has important implications for how we understand the play's treatment of male friendship and its relationship to marriage—social bonds that *A Woman Killed* invites the audience to explore through play. Many have read *A Woman Killed* as a "domestic" drama about a breakdown in a marriage, whereas others maintain it is a friendship play about male homosociality and a breakdown in kinship networks.[59] Male friendship and marriage are not mutually exclusive, however, and the card game reveals the complex intersections between them. Well before Frankford discovers his wife in bed with Wendoll, he discovers Wendoll colluding with Anne to cheat Frankford at cards. How exactly does this cheating at cards threaten Frankford's friendship with Wendoll? To answer this, we might recall again the idea that cards are used in games of imperfect information, structured around imbalances in players' knowledge. Male friendships were seen to be similarly grounded in gaps in knowledge between participants, a situation Wendoll exploits in and out of the card game.

My claim that, in operative terms, friendship is grounded in *lack* of knowledge of the other would appear to conflict with the humanist ideal of male friendship, wherein the friend is considered another self and knowledge of the other is complete and immediate. But I would suggest that this discourse of ideal friendship, even in its purest rhetorical form, recognizes imbalances of information at the heart of true friendship.[60] Toward the end of his classical essay on friendship *De amicitia*, Cicero, notably using a game analogy, warns his readers about false friends who can hoodwink even the most upstanding and self-composed of men. The danger of such a false friend is that he is "not very easily recognized, since he often assents by opposing, plays the game of disputing in a smooth, caressing way, and at length submits, and suffers himself to be outreasoned, so as to make him on whom he is practising his arts appear to have had the deeper insight. But what is more disgraceful than to be made game of?" Cicero is so repelled by the notion that friendship is a game that can be manipulated by cheaters that his essay quickly retreats from this line of thought. "But I know not how my discourse has digressed from the friendships of perfect, that is, of wise men,—wise, I mean, so far as wisdom can fall to the lot of man,—to friendships of a lighter sort. Let us then return to our original subject, and bring it to a speedy conclusion."[61] The skilled rhetorician suddenly appears to have lost control of his discourse. Momentarily stepping down from the lofty ideals he has described throughout the essay, Cicero grapples briefly with the messy mundane practice of friendship, and he is horrified by what he finds. For Cicero's ideal friendship to work, each of the interactants must know the other entirely. The deepest character of the one must be easily legible to the other. But, Cicero's digression considers, what if the other cannot be fully known? Rather than take up this question in much detail, he quickly retreats to the rhetoric of ideal friendship, wrapping up the essay before it can realize the practical implications of the ideas just introduced.

Some early modern writings on ideal male friendship take up, with less anxiety than Cicero, how even ideal friendship may be structured by games of imperfect information. They observe that friends who attain perfect knowledge of each other gain that knowledge through the act of sharing privately held information or secrets—a process, ironically, dependent on momentary imbalances in knowledge about the other. In an early French

treatise on Christian friendship—whose English translation by Thomas
Newton was published in 1586, bound, perhaps not coincidentally, with a
treatise on gaming—Calvinist theologian Lambert Daneau highlights the
centrality of such sharing to "perfect Friendship tearmed *Amicitia*" which
relies upon "the familiar conversation of friends," for it is through "familiar conversation" that "liking and affection is usually encreased, strength-
ened, and made greater."[62] In true Christian friendship the affections of
each man for the other "may not bee smoothered in secrecie, or kept un-
knowne, but be apparaunted, made open and manifested" as "the one ut-
tereth and testifieth to the other."[63] Michel de Montaigne's "On Friendship" (translated in 1603 by John Florio) posits a similar direct
correspondence between the sharing of secrets through conversation and
the growth of affection: he writes that the minds of him and his friend
"have with so fervent an affection considered of each other, and with like
affection so discovered and sounded, even to the very bottome of each others hearts and entrails, that I did not only know his, as well as mine owne,
but I would (verily) rather have trusted him concerning any matter of mine
than my selfe."[64] To be sure, the emphasis of the passage is on the men's
unity of mind, but Montaigne also alludes to the mundane means through
which this mutual knowledge has been attained: through making "discovered and sounded" information from "the very bottome of each others
hearts and entrails." Francis Bacon's essay "On Friendship" calls this act of
divulging privately held information the first "fruit" of friendship. Encouraging remedies that open the body, thereby preventing diseases caused by
blockages, he advocates the humoral healthfulness of friendship: "no re-
ceipt openeth the heart but a true friend, to whom you may impart griefs,
joys, fears, hopes, suspicions, counsels, and whatsover lieth upon the heart
to oppress it, in a kind of civil shift or confession."[65] At the center of the
humanist ideal of friendship, then, is the quite ordinary work of "confession": imparting private thoughts and feelings to someone else. Indeed, the
act of imparting or sharing, of making known what isn't known, affirms
that the relationship between two people is, in fact, a friendship. Or, to put
this another way, friendship involves actively bridging a gap in knowledge
about the other.[66] Ironically, then, if the action of friendship is the mutual
sharing of secrets, friends need not divulge everything at once; they must
have secrets in order to share them and thereby enable a performance of
friendship.

Bacon's "civil shift or confession" might also be thought of in terms of
modern sociologist Erving Goffman's "interaction ritual," a social encounter that is structured by certain (usually unwritten and underrecognized)

rules. While Goffman is not interested in friendship per se, but rather in any social interaction, his perspective helps to highlight what is at stake in the exchange of information to which Daneau, Montaigne, and Bacon allude. Goffman views social interactions as moments of "mutual monitoring" through which each interactant has the opportunity to introduce "favorable information" about him- or herself.[67] Interaction rituals are the means through which friends come to recognize each other *as* friends, if only because they use the encounter as an opportunity to, in Bacon's terms, "impart griefs, joys, fears, hopes," and so forth. But Goffman importantly points out that these interactions are games, often zero-sum games at that. Each participant strategically chooses what information to impart and when to do it. While monitoring what they communicate, interactants also attempt to uncover information about others, sometimes resorting to spying to draw out concealed secrets.[68] Hiding and withholding information from interactants, like spying, is not the mark of an unethical cheater but a necessary part of play, the assumption here being that every interaction, and the relationship that is created through it, is structured and, indeed, bolstered by gaps in knowledge about the other.

Such gaps are at the foundation of Wendoll and Frankford's relationship. When Frankford first mentions an interest in offering Wendoll "a second place" in the household and "my best regard" (4.34), he appears to know very little about the man.

> This Wendoll I have noted, and his carriage
> Hath pleased me much. By observation
> I have noted many good deserts in him:
> He's affable, and seen in many things,
> Discourses well, a good companion,
> And though of small means, yet a gentleman
> Of a good house, somewhat pressed by want. (4.26-34)

Frankford has judged Wendoll's fitness for a more intimate friendship through "observation," having "noted . . . his carriage," or conduct. And readers of the play tend to be surprised by his decision soon after to offer everything, "table and . . . purse" (4.64), to a person who seems, at this point, merely a good acquaintance. Yet Frankford has begun to decipher the information Wendoll gives out, at the very least his "carriage." And, if we consider friendship as a game of imperfect information, then part of what attracts Frankford to Wendoll is the challenge and excitement of not knowing all there is to know about this man; Wendoll has secrets yet to be revealed.[69] Most important, Wendoll presents himself as someone willing to share that information. The timing of Frankford's offer of friendship makes sense then: just after Wendoll informs Frankford of the fatal hawking wager that has led Frankford's brother-in-law, Sir Francis Acton, to take legal action against Frankford's friend Sir Charles Mountford.

Immediately after thanking Wendoll for delivering the bad news, Frankford extends his friendship:

> I thank your pains, sir. Had the news been better
> Your will was to have brought it, Master Wendoll.
> Sir Charles will find hard friends; his case is heinous,
> And will be most severely censured on.
> I am sorry for him. Sir, a word with you.
> I know you, sir, to be a gentleman
> In all things, your possibilities but mean.
> Please you to use my table and my purse,
> They are yours. (4.57–65)

The midline shift from Frankford speaking of Sir Charles's plight to extending unbounded friendship seems puzzling at first, an apparent non sequitur. But the two seemingly different topics of this speech are intertwined, the former explaining the latter. When Wendoll shares his knowledge of the wager debacle, an event in which he was deeply implicated, he appears to unburden his heart and mind to Frankford and thus act as a true friend. Indeed, Frankford's transition from praising Wendoll for sharing this news to offering Wendoll friendship comes by way of an observation that Sir Charles, by contrast, "will find hard friends." In sum, the cognitive and emotional experience of male friendship is quite similar to that of a game of cards: friends, like card players, choose to engage in a relationship where parts of the self are hidden from the other, to be divulged over the course of the relationship. By divulging unknown information, friends, like card players, demonstrate their willingness to participate in the social interaction.

But if Wendoll and Frankford's friendship is like a card game, its pleasure stemming from each participant withholding and then strategically divulging privately held information to the other, then it is also worth noting that these acts of confession serve an overall competitive scheme. At the end of the game, Goffman reminds us, one side will win, and the other will lose. Such contest, Heywood's play suggests, is as central to male friendship as it is to card games.[70] The surest evidence of that is the play's earlier hunting wager scene, another staging of recreation where suspicions of cheating threaten male friendship. Like the card game, the hunting wager apparently is an opportunity for homosocial bonding. After Frankford and Anne's wedding, the gentlemen guests gather to contemplate how they may best celebrate. Sir Francis, observing that the servants are enjoying their "rounds and jigs," asks the other men, "What shall we do?" (1.85). The answer is a falconry wager between Sir Francis and Sir Charles, to be undertaken the next day, with all the men participating by laying bets on one side or the other. At this point, there is no reason to presume that the contest will destroy male homosocial bonds, for part of the pleasure of a game, like a male friendship, stems from its competitive nature. Contemporary game designers Katie Salen and Eric Zimmerman point out that while games are competitive, they are simultaneously cooperative: "To play a game is to submit your behavior to the rules of the game, to enter into the time and space that the game demarcates," to enter what they call a "lusory attitude."[71] The problem in the case of the card game and the hawking match is that Wendoll, like many gamers, does not abide by the borders of a lusory, "magic circle." He invents his own rules, creating and moving information in ways that exceed the game's design. He thus points to the ways friendships grounded in playful contest are vulnerable, for they rely on, but cannot ensure, consensus and cooperation between the parties.

The hawking scene bears out the limitations of the terms of male friendship. When Sir Charles wins the contest, his hawk killing the bird, Sir Francis refuses to accept the outcome and calls for the other friends to judge the match for, he claims, "My hawk killed too" (3.11). What might otherwise have remained a sporting disagreement, to be settled through cooperative arbitration about who has seen what, erupts into violence and accusations of cheating, leading to Sir Charles slaying two of Sir Francis's men and the impetus for the play's subplot, which follows Sir Charles's attempts to suture his broken friendship with Sir Francis. Worth note is that, as in the later card game, Wendoll is at the center of the cheating. With a monetary wager and perhaps the promise of friendship with Sir Francis's new brother-in-law Frankford riding on Sir Francis victory, Wendoll vigorously defends Sir Francis's side, escalating the debate from "words to blows" (4.47).[72] Insofar as Wendoll will later tell Frankford that Sir Francis, in fact, *had* lost the bet—"your wife's brother, had the worst, / And lost the wager" (4.41–42)—his arguments during the match on behalf of Sir Francis can be read in retrospect as cheating. And they are enough to spur Sir Francis forward, for, picking up the momentum from Wendoll's justification, Sir Francis ups the ante of Wendoll's accusation of dishonor, accusing Sir Charles's hawk of being "a rifler" (3.27), a hawk that doesn't take its prey cleanly, grasping only feathers instead of sinking its talons into the flesh.[73]

As in the card game scene, Wendoll doesn't simply cheat; he exploits the uncertainties of information that are built into the game. As card games thrive on uncertainties about information, so hawking matches thrive on friendly bickering about which side presents the strongest case for victory. Wendoll uses this imprecision to his benefit, violating the game rules to which other players have subscribed. The results work to his benefit, for the story of the fatal duel that results proves well worth the telling. It is no wonder that Wendoll rushes to be the first to inform Frankford about what has happened. As Frankford's servant Nick reports, "It seems he comes in haste. His horse is booted / Up to the flank in mire, himself all spotted / And stained with plashing. Sure he rid in fear / Or for a wager" (4.20–23). As is so often the case in the play, Nick's instincts about Wendoll are right, for Wendoll's risky ride pays off: by arriving at Frankford's house with the news before anyone else, he manages to endear himself to Frankford and gain financially, not to mention romantically.

It is notable that Wendoll performs his cheating quite openly. Like his performance of melancholic love in his soliloquies, Wendoll's cheating during the hawking match is no secret to the theater audience, who witness Wendoll arguing for Sir Francis's hawk during the match but admitting the hawk's loss later. So, too, in the card game, Wendoll's cheating is hardly cagey. Instead of arranging the cards in such a way that he would win by a slim margin and remain unsuspected, Wendoll gives himself an impossibly strong hand, thereby announcing his cheating at cards in the same way that he uses obvious sexual double-entendres to declare his affair with Anne, who even comments that Wendoll is "too public" in his demonstration of affection for her (11.93). The theatricality of Wendoll's cheating turns him, I would suggest, into the play's most articulate commentator on gaming culture and, by consequence, male friendship. He reminds the audience that cheating is less a violation of the ludic world than an unavoidable feature of it.[74] In his public display of cheating, Wendoll resembles the "griefers" of today's online gaming world, who theatrically break the rules of games and frustrate other players. While some in the gaming world label griefers spoilsports and even terrorists (insofar as their antics can overload servers, shutting down routine gameplay and costing players time and money), many griefers maintain that they are restoring the spirit of play to a gaming world than has come to take itself too seriously.[75] Playing by their own rules, griefers underscore the extent to which games, for any player who wishes to win, are often less about following the rules than about figuring out ways to work *around* them. Such players are less cheaters than what Stephanie Boluk and Patrick LeMieux call "metagamers."[76] These players encourage a modification of Celia Pearce's definition of the kinds of information present in a game, for in addition to the information designated by the rules, information can be created and manipulated by participants themselves, who change the rules to fit better their purposes in playing.

Griefers demonstrate that cheating, rather than being understood solely in terms of ethics, has a metacommunicative function: they call attention, by refusing to conform, to the frame of the game. We might recall here anthropologist Gregory Bateson's formative definition of gameplay as a metacommunicative act. As players meditate on a game's rules (this is cheating or it isn't), they enter into a communicative mode that, Bateson argues, is essential to ludic activity.[77] Wendoll's foul play might be read similarly as a social overture, an attempt to step outside of the card game in order to call attention self-consciously to its epistemological structure and meaning. By performing his cheating openly, Wendoll initiates a metaconversation about gameplay as well as about friendship. In fact, Anne's flighty question "What's trumps?" may constitute an effort to interrupt the heated metaconversation taking place here and thereby diffuse the tensions so obviously building between Wendoll and Frankford.[78]

In depicting cheating as an unavoidable feature of card games, Heywood participates in a cultural commonplace. Early modern representations of card play (dramatic and otherwise), though they may rebuke cheats, also compulsively illuminate cheating strategies. Continental paintings depicting card games inevitably dramatize rooking. Caravaggio's famous *Cardsharps* (c. 1595) shows the rook pulling a hidden card out of his belt in response to the gestures of his accomplice, who can see the opponent's cards (Figure 14); a similar move is dramatized in *The Cheat with the Ace of Clubs* by Georges de la Tour (c. 1630–4; Figure 15). Moral and religious criticisms of playing cards similarly underscore the inevitability of cheating. Richard Rice's *Invective against Vices, Taken for Vertue* (1581) condemns card play by maintaining that the honest player is an illusion: "For marke the moste honest gamesters that will professe themselves before they enter into plaie, by their false fidelitie, that they will plaie never a Carde false, nor never an Ace wrong, and when they are once entered into plaie, there shall be packyng of Cardes, winkyng with the eyes, blaryng out the tongue, renouncyng the Trompe" and other such typical schemes.[79]

Even the earliest instruction manuals for card play, such as John Cotgrave's *Wits Interpreter* (1655) and Charles Cotton's *The Compleat Gamester* (1674), move fluidly between descriptions of games and elucidations of how to cheat at them. Immediately after explaining how, in Ruff games, one "ought to have a special eye to what cards are play'd out" so as to strategize play effectively, Cotton underscores that "[r]eneging or renouncing, that is, not following suit when you have it in your hand, is very fowl play, and he that doth it ought to forfeit one, or the Game upon a Game."[80] Cheating moves are common enough that they have names—"reneging" or "renouncing"—and predetermined punishments. Cotton moves so briskly between descriptions of games and explanations of how to cheat at them that it is difficult to distinguish where he draws the line between rule breaking and skilled play. For instance, he writes, "He that can by craft over-look his adversaries Game hath a great advantage" and goes on to describe ways partners can communicate "what Honours they have, as by the wink of one eye, or putting one finger on the nose or table."[81] Does he condemn cheats or describe good strategy here? The inevitability of cheating or the failure to spot it helps explain, perhaps, why the game Ruff developed later in the century into Whist, which initially was supposed to be played in virtual silence, thus ostensibly eliminating one avenue through which players illicitly share information, what we call "table talk." To be sure, Cotton's and others' revelations of cheating are intended to depict the underside of popular recreations, warning innocent players of the dangers that may befall them. But I am interested less in their moralizing function than in their effect. The enactment of a card game seems almost inevitably to raise the specter of cheating, so that the question becomes not whether or even why people cheat, but what sort of role cheating plays and how cheating is to be addressed during a game session.

This shift away from the ethics to the effects of cheating helps us to see that what is notable about Heywood's card game is less *that* Wendoll cheats, or even that he cheats so flagrantly, but that Frankford says nothing in response. In fact, Frankford covers up Wendoll's dishonesty, for were the match to continue, Wendoll's impossibly good hand would be revealed to all—and Frankford would have no choice but to accuse his friend of dishonorable play. By ending the game prematurely and feigning illness, Frankford prevents Wendoll's exposure. The cover-up preserves at least the illusion of Frankford's friendship with Wendoll, avoiding the kind of rupture of male homosocial community that we witness in the falcon wager scene. When Sir Charles accuses Sir Francis of foul play—the latter claims he has won when everyone knows that he hasn't—the result is tragic. Men die, Sir Charles loses everything, and it takes great sacrifice to suture the broken male bonds. Instead of denouncing Wendoll on the basis of dishonesty during a game, Frankford waits and catches Wendoll out on the charge of adultery, which affects Frankford's relationship with Anne far more gravely than his with Wendoll. In fact, as critics have noted, while Anne is harshly punished with public shaming and forgiven only on her deathbed, Wendoll escapes punishment completely.[82] Indeed, he plans to return to England when "these rumours / . . . abate," expecting to find again his "worth and parts being by some great man praised" (16.130–33). Catching someone committing adultery, as it turns out, is far less disruptive to male bonds than catching someone cheating at games. And the play ends with all the men declaring their friendships for one another and their intentions to live happily ever after.[83]

Frankford's cover-up constitutes an acceptance, however ambivalent, of cheating as part of the terms of card games and of male friendship. As we have seen, in a game of imperfect information like cards, the prospect of cheating is all the greater because information is hidden; the deceit that can undermine the game is difficult to separate from that which makes the game pleasurable to play.[84] A similar paradox inheres in the humanist view of friendship, I've suggested. If the relationship between friends, like that between card players, depends on repeated transactions of knowledge, then a good friend, like a good player, does not necessarily undermine the friendship if he withholds some information, saving it for strategic revelation later. The friendship and the game continue and, in fact, to some extent *depend* on revelation as an ongoing process in the social transaction. Significantly, revelation can exist only when there is something hidden left to be revealed. To be sure, imbalances can be exploited toward unethical ends, but the simple presence of gaps in knowledge about the other does not necessarily compromise friendship. Wendoll and Frankford both act unethically with each other when they withhold information—Wendoll by cheating and Frankford by allowing the cheating to go unchecked—and this paradoxically sustains their friendship.

WAGERING ON THEATER

In arguing that the enactment of games enables the audiences to Heywood's and Mr. S.'s plays, not to mention Latimer's sermons, a way to query early modern male friendship, I follow the work of anthropologist Clifford Geertz, who argues in his influential essay "Deep Play: Notes on the Balinese Cockfight" that games can offer a forum for, as well as a metasocial commentary on, the terms of male homosociality in a particular culture. Significantly, Geertz argues that the cultural and social force of a game comes not only from the dramatized contest (in Bali between two fighting birds, and the men to whom they belong), but from the engagement of the event's spectators. My focus on the epistemology of audience engagement takes Geertz's conclusions in a very different direction, though. For Geertz, what audiences gain through the game is "a kind of sentimental education," and, notably, Geertz turns to an analogy with the Shakespearean theater to make his point:

> If, to quote Northrop Frye again, we go to see *Macbeth* to learn what a man feels like after he has gained a kingdom and lost his soul, Balinese go to cockfights to find out what a man, usually composed, aloof, almost obsessively self-absorbed . . . feels like when, attacked . . . and driven in result to the extremes of fury, he has totally triumphed or been brought totally low."[85]

Spectators of games and of theater are drawn into the emotional plight of others, but they are also, and I'd argue, even more prominently drawn into alternative states of knowing.[86] What Heywood's play and the performance of *Gammer Gurton's Needle* at Cambridge suggest is that theatergoing and male friendship work on not only affective but epistemological registers. The drama of a game reveals cultural beliefs about masculinity and homosocial affiliation by externalizing and animating spectators' emotions, to be sure, but also by inviting audiences to negotiate imperfect information.

Although I have grouped *Gammer* and *A Woman Killed* together because both use card play to meditate on the informational game of friendship and its risks, it is worth noting not only the temporal gap between initial performances of these plays (about fifty years), but, more pertinent to my argument in this book, the differences in their performance venues. Whereas *Gammer* was a university play, staged in an indoor hall primarily as an academic exercise, *A Woman Killed* was first performed publically in a commercial amphitheater, probably the Rose.[87] Partly at stake in these differences of venue are issues of space and theatrical staging; as I have suggested, *Gammer*'s performance in a space that allowed onstage seating may explain why the play must move its card game offstage to create the same dynamics of imperfect information that *A Woman Killed* accomplishes. But the venues also differ in terms of the level of social intimacy shared by performers and their audiences. *Gammer*'s actors likely had close relationships with some if not all of their audience members, who were fellow students and staff at the university. The social history

Gammer's audiences shared with the play's performers arguably helped produce a sense of intimacy, of friendship, between *Gammer's* producers and consumers. By contrast, the audiences who first attended *A Woman Killed* were generally strangers, unknown to the actors and other producers of the play. Having bought their tickets in advance to see professional drama, the audience to *A Woman Killed* approached their experience at the theater as a commercial transaction.

One way to read the staged game in *A Woman Killed*, then, is as a reworking and suturing of the social bond between producers and consumers of theater in this commercial context. When, beginning around 1576, theaters demanded payment before the production, they likely fostered an environment of some distrust and anxiety. Theatergoing became a gamble: Would playgoers get out of the experience as much as they had put in? Interestingly, one of the earliest stories about this new system of prepayment centers on cheating. Playgoers who had put their coins in the money box before entering the theater were bamboozled by the show's producer, who ended up leaving from a side door, locking the audience in the theater and escaping with their money.[88] Although an extreme example of how the commercial theater's imbalances in information could be exploited, the incident helps explain why playwrights and actors developed numerous strategies for establishing trust. If playgoing was a gamble, then producers of theater had a stake in reminding audiences that gambling was about more than financial profit, that the game could be enjoyed on its own terms, regardless of its outcome. Theater's producers profited from convincing playgoers that the commercial transaction of theater was not necessarily a cold, imbalanced one, where the audience could be exploited by fraud. Not knowing was part of the pleasure in theater, as it is in all gambling.[89] As *A Woman Killed* revises a discourse of friendship, presenting it as a game of imperfect information, it offers its audiences a way to think of commercial theater as constituted by a more intimate relationship between producers and consumers, characterized by exchange and sharing, even if also structured by imbalances, secrets, and withholding.

For theater makers, the advantages of this approach are numerous, especially in a vibrant entertainment marketplace such as that of early modern London, where theater competed with many other leisure activities. Such activities were available in taverns and alehouses right next door to the theater, and evidence suggests that patrons may have even brought their favorite sitting pastimes into the theater with them. Farmer Chetham's commonplace book describes a gallant who "playes at Primero over the stage" possibly while the play was being performed.[90] In a commercial theater, where the paying customer is always right, there was little to prevent anyone from playing Primero "over the stage" or even on it. If audiences viewed the play as a commodity that had been purchased and could be used however the consumer wished, then Heywood and his actors may not have been able to prevent audiences from playing cards during the show. However, as I've been suggesting, they and their fellow producers of theater tried to convince playgoers that theater could be just as satisfying as a game of cards, and for many of the same reasons.

Staged card games, as they hyperfocalize on the dynamic of imperfect information, reveal particularly clearly how theaters used the ethos of gaming to sell the pleasures of commercial theatergoing. Even if theater was, to some degree, a power struggle between parties with different kinds of knowledge and competing spheres of influence, as others have argued, that competitive ethos could be reframed to present the commercial theater as a space for cooperative games of imperfect information. Scenes of card play, I have suggested, manifest particularly elegantly the ludic dimensions of the theater. Spectators who approached theater as playable media—vicariously participating in the fictional card games onstage—could more easily get drawn into the psychological and social dramas represented by the play's actors, experiencing firsthand the anxieties of imperfect information that a character like Frankford is meant to have. At the same time, these spectators could come to view imperfect information in the theater, along with concomitant disparities in knowledge among theater's participants, not solely as uncomfortable realities of a competitive theatrical economy but as the grounds for establishing a new kind of social bond, a sort of friendship, with theater's producers.

THREE

Backgammon
Space and Scopic Dominance

The anonymous *Arden of Faversham* (c. 1592) ends with a backgammon game during which the eponymous character—who has managed to preserve himself despite almost a dozen murder attempts—is finally taken out.[1] The backgammon setting is instrumental to the scene, as Arden's game opponent and antagonist Mosby cannot call out the cue to the waiting murderers "'Now I can take you'" (14.229) until he rolls a number on the dice that enables him to capture one of Arden's game pieces. Readers of the play have often been confused about the game being played in his climactic scene, mistakenly thinking it to be a game of dice or cards.[2] These games do share some common features—backgammon, for instance, involves the use of dice—but the distinctions among them are significant. If, as I have been arguing, the mechanics and gameplay experiences of particular pastimes give us insight into how England's first commercial theaters operated as playable media, then we cannot conflate backgammon with other sitting pastimes. We have to take into account the particularities of this gaming platform and the modes of interaction that it invites.

Similar to board games such as chess, the focus of Chapter 4, backgammon requires its players (usually two) to move "men" strategically across a board. In backgammon the board has been divided into twenty-four marked spaces, called "points."[3] The points are arranged to create a linear track, so that each player moves his or her men in a different direction, attempting to be the first to reach the goal—usually getting all those men to a quadrant of the board called "home" and then removing them from the board. Like chess, backgammon encourages aggressive interaction: a man left alone on a point is called a "blot" and can be captured and removed temporarily from the board, thereby delaying the player's progression toward home. But backgammon differs from chess in that how far one's men move is determined by the roll of dice. In this, backgammon resembles the game of cards, which, as discussed in the previous chapter, has been called a game of "imperfect information," because, unlike in chess—where possible moves are, at least in theory, visible to both players (who can see the board equally)—in cards certain information is structurally hidden from players.[4] The dice in backgammon produce a similar effect: they hide information, leaving it, in this case, entirely to chance. If, as I argued in the previous chapter, card games teach participants competency in negotiating imperfect information, then backgammon teaches the additional competency of mastering space in the face of aggressive opponents and unpredictable chance.

Backgammon may not be represented in dramatic literature nearly as often as dice and cards, but because of the ways backgammon depends on and builds its players' competencies in spatial navigation, dramatizations of the game onstage are fascinating case studies through which to investigate how the first commercial theaters worked more generally as game spaces. The first commercial playhouses were amphitheaters, usually round, with several tiers of seating and, as is illustrated in the only surviving drawing from the seventeenth century (Figure 16), a thrust stage that jutted out into a central yard, or pit.[5] The audience surrounded the stage on most sides, either standing around the stage in the yard or sitting in the galleries above. Theaters could be crowded and often disorderly, especially in the yard, which was standing room only and available to anyone who could afford the one pence admission price. Amphitheaters could thus prompt aggressive interaction among their socially and economically heterogeneous patrons, who competed for the best viewing spots. Entrepreneurs took financial advantage of this disorderly scene by offered patrons with economic means seats literally positioned above the fray, seats in the galleries. The most expensive of these seats—the perspective of the artist of the early drawing—looked down upon the stage and the yard, providing something close to a bird's-eye view of the action.

From our modern frame of reference, it is surprising that patrons would have paid more for seats in what they called the "two-penny galleries," but that we would call the nosebleed sections. Yet I want to argue that the seats had a unique value: they held out to patrons the fantasy of dominating through vision the tumultuous theater space and socially heterogeneous patrons and actors below them. High above the action, these patrons could abstract themselves not only physically but cognitively and emotionally from the chaos below. The economic logic of the two-penny galleries threatened to undermine the theater's operation as playable media, however. How could patrons who imagined themselves dominating the theater space through their vision engage fully in the dramatic action, playing vicariously? If actors and playwrights were invested in cultivating engaged participants, willing to play along, rather than distant observers abstracted from the ludic action, then they had a vested interested in debunking the economic logic of the two-penny gallery galleries.

Critiques of this logic come to the fore especially powerfully at moments in plays when spectators become aware of their spatial positioning in relation to the stage, particularly when they are invited to think about what it means to watch from above—as happens in a staged backgammon game, as well as an actual one. This chapter examines two of the rare early modern plays that present backgammon matches onstage: *Arden of Faversham* and Henry Porter's *The Two Angry Women of Abington*. I show that as these dramas use backgammon to take up questions of visual surveillance and the navigation of space, they offer up direct analogies to theatergoing to suggest that theatergoer pleasure and power come not from abstract, visual surveillance of—but rather, risky, engaged interaction with—the ludic world of the boards.

THEATER SPACE AND SCOPIC DOMINANCE

Contending with aggressive "opponents" and unpredictable chance was as much a part of the spatial experience of the early modern playhouse as of the game of backgammon, especially in the case of amphitheaters, where patrons probably interacted physically with one another far more than is the custom in most theaters today. Because there were no assigned seats, patrons attending the more popular plays had to compete for the best viewing spots.[6] Even when they were not full, amphitheaters were set up in such a way as to encourage, or at least by no means inhibit, physical interaction among patrons. With plays performed in full daylight, moving around was all the easier and probably quite necessary, since, unlike in the indoor theaters, playgoers did not enjoy intermissions between every act: they would have needed to move about while the play was being performed in order to buy refreshments, relieve their bladders, and socialize with friends. Such movement presumably could become disorderly. Albeit to promote his antitheatricalist agenda, religious zealot Anthony Munday captures some sense of this chaotic movement in *A Third Blast of Retrait from Plaies and Theaters* (1580), where he decries those "yong ruffins" and "harlots" who "presse to the fore-front of the scaffoldes."[7]

Navigating theater space must have been all the more troubling to patrons who considered themselves superior to ruffians and prostitutes. It is not surprising that the first commercial playhouses—which brought people from all walks of life into the same space—established tiered seating, designating certain sections of the theater for patrons with economic means. For an additional penny beyond the one-penny price of admission to the yard, patrons could sit in the covered first gallery; if they paid more, patrons could sit in the upper tiers; and for even more, they could sit in the Lord's Rooms, the balcony above the stage. Though the amphitheater was still less formal in its architecture than many theaters today, tiered seating enabled these playhouses to present themselves as more *sociofugal* than *sociopetal:* that is, differently priced seats enabled patrons to conceive of the theater as a space that set people apart and offered a more individualized theatergoing experience (sociofugal) rather than a space that brought people together and produced a more collective experience (sociopetal).[8] To be sure, compared with private venues for playgoing (such as noblemen's houses, which were invitation only), early modern commercial theaters appeared to level social distinctions, presenting plays as cultural commodities that could be enjoyed in the same way by anyone who could afford the price of admission.[9] But it was precisely because the professional theater *seemed* to flatten social differences that there was pressure on the emergent institution to mark out social distinctions among patrons, and many theaters did so by placing a premium on certain viewing spots. There is, of course, no way to know whether patrons of means always, indeed ever, chose the two-penny galleries, just as there is no reason to presume that ruffians and prostitutes always stood in the yard.[10] In a commercial theater, anyone could sit anywhere after paying the demanded price. Yet regardless of how theatergoing worked in practice, it is clear that theater entrepreneurs designated seats in the upper galleries and Lord's Rooms as more valuable than spots in the pit and the lower gallery, attempting to create social distinction through the valuation of theatrical space. The priciest seats, I would maintain, offered a qualitatively different encounter with a play, a different experience of *play*.

Part of the seeming value of these seats is that they offered spectators a way to avoid aggressive "opponents" and unpredictable chance as they navigated theatrical space. For one thing, the galleries appear to have been much less crowded than the yard; entrepreneur Philip Henslowe's records for the Rose theater indicate that the galleries were probably only half full at most performances.[11] Even when the galleries were full, it was probably easier to lay claim to a seat in them than to an unmarked standing position in the pit, and the raking of the upper galleries limited the degree to which a playgoer's views might be blocked by other patrons' heads or feathered hats, as would have been the case for those in the yard and in the lower galleries. The second generation of amphitheaters (including the Globe, the Swan, the Fortune, and probably the Rose) further decreased physical contact between patrons in the upper galleries and those in the rest of the theater by providing the former with separate entrances. Access to the lower gallery was through the yard—anyone in the pit could pay an additional penny to move to this gallery (e.g., if they desired cover from the elements or wanted to sit down)—but access to the upper galleries was gained through staircase turrets.[12] If the theater acts as a "container," creating a sense of community among those present, then it is no wonder that entrepreneurs could demand more money from those patrons eager to gain spatial distance from, and thus undermine communal bonds with, patrons they believed to be socially inferior.[13] In effect gallery seating promised (whether or not it delivered) a more "civilized" theatrical experience, claiming to eliminate some of the chance and aggression that characterized playgoing in amphitheaters.

But if theater financiers wanted to give wealthier patrons a formal space apart, why did they establish that space above and farther away from the stage? This placement is surprising given that throughout much of theater history, from the days of the ancient Greek amphitheaters to the indoor theaters of the early seventeenth century and beyond, the most privileged playgoers have been positioned closest to the stage. The bird's-eye view of the two-penny galleries has generally been associated with seats of *lowest* cost. This is still the case today. So why did entrepreneurs feel confident that patrons of means would pay *more* for the bird's-eye view in the emerging public amphitheaters? One way to make sense of this historically unusual spatial configuration is through an analogy to board games, which similarly position game participants and spectators with a bird's-eye view of the ludic action.

To understand the value—as well as the limitations—of the bird's-eye view in theaters and in board games, we might compare these playable media with a technology whose use of the bird's-eye view has been helpfully theorized: the map. French philosopher Michel de Certeau argues that the map offers the kind of pleasure one experiences when viewing the city of New York from atop an exceptionally tall building: the viewer is able "to be lifted out of the city's grasp," leaving behind "the mass that carries off and mixes up in itself any identity of authors or spectators."[14] The bird's-eye view transforms that entangling mass of the city into a "text" to be read: static, immobile, transparent, and accessible. Or, to rephrase this in the terms de Certeau uses elsewhere in *The Practice of Everyday Life*, the bird's-eye view transforms the moving, variable realm of "space" into stable, static "place."[15] De Certeau goes on to describe, however, the ways in which the daily practices of people who walk the city disturb the totalizing power that the bird's-eye viewer claims.

De Certeau's theories of the map can be productively extended to board games and theater, although only the latter has been attempted by others.[16] Yet historian of cartography P. D. A. Harvey has speculated that board games may be a form of "pre-cartography," demonstrating "a culture's disposition to replicate place in miniature" and "as viewed from above."[17] Regardless of whether we pursue the full cultural and historical implications of Harvey's conjecture, there are compelling reasons to link maps and board games in the sixteenth and seventeenth centuries. Although board games, including versions of tables, had been played in the earliest ancient societies, the rise of printing made it possible to produce game boards cheaply so that they were available to a wider range of players. The process for mass-producing game boards was similar to that used for producing maps: illustrations were printed, colored by hand, and then mounted on canvas or linen.[18] The material link between game boards and maps is perhaps most compellingly demonstrated in late seventeenth-century geographical board games such as *Le Jeu du monde* (Paris, 1645), whose board features nations of the world, as illustrated from a bird's-eye view: movement from space to space represents travel across the world (Figure 17).[19]

There are philosophical as well as material reasons to link gaming and mapping technologies. In his work on mapping, de Certeau turns briefly to an analogy with board games to underscore his distinction between "place" and "space." He compares the checkerboard to a "system of defined places" because of the way it "analyzes and classifies identities": the act of gameplay in checkers, according to de Certeau, exemplifies the sort of transgressive spatial practices that frustrate the "scopic and gnostic drive."[20] The *practice* of space "opens up clearings; it 'allows' a certain play within a system of defined places. It 'authorizes' the production of an area of free play (*Spielraum*) on a checkerboard."[21] We might say, then, that the game board is to *place* what gameplay is to *space*. That is, the game as form—with its grid lines, specified places, and conspicuous rules—is meant to discipline movement and furnish players with an intelligible plan for managing space. But the practicalities and pleasures of play necessitate less static, controlled, and abstract approaches to the board, requiring players to engage instead in dynamic, risky, and physically interactive navigations of space.

The example of board games supports but also complicates de Certeau's distinction between space and place, for gameplay, a spatial practice, can transform the seemingly fixed visual regime of the game board.[22] Gameplay, for instance, has historically altered the game board's appearance: antecedents of the game of tables—which we now call by one of its variations, "backgammon"—were played on boards shaped like spirals, circles, and crosses as well as squares. Additionally, gameplay has changed the rules of the game: over the course of its history, the game of tables has seen variations in the number of players, the amount of interaction between men on the board, and the significance of capturing blots, among other things. There is some mystery about how games adapt and change over time, but the prevailing theory is that players reshape game rules to create more pleasurable playing experiences, and those variations are then reiterated over and over until they become institutionalized as the new rules of the game. As I suggest in Chapter 4, theatrical innovation and custom take shape through a similar process of reiteration and transformation. What I would underscore here is that if the theater stage—which from the eighteenth century onward would notably be called the "boards"[23]—was like a game board, then those in the upper galleries paid not just a financial but a ludic price for the ostensible advantages of their bird's eye view. Although positioned like board game players, seeing the action from above, these patrons risked becoming too abstracted from the "boards," and thus unable to influence their action and form. Unless they abandoned their fantasies of total spatial management, what I'll call *scopic dominance,* they risked losing the opportunity to play the play.

As I argue in the next section, *Arden* uses backgammon to develop a critique of fantasies of scopic dominance, delivering that critique through a narrative of male social conflict. Before turning to my reading of the play, it is worth noting that my discussion of the bird's-eye view in board games, theater, and masculinity is less part of a project to historicize vision than it is a way to theorize the social implications of different ways of interacting with space. Indeed, as will become evident below, characters in *Arden* and in *Two Angry Women,* attempt to master space visually even without access to an actual bird's-eye view. That said, I am interested in the ways these dramas deploy the topos of board gaming to query a fantasy of scopic dominance.[24] And what is perhaps most intriguing about the plays, especially in terms of their implications for thinking about theatrical space, is that both pursue this critique by problematizing vision itself. As if rendering in material terms the epistemological issues de Certeau raises, *Arden* and *Two Angry Women* dramatize the ways a literal failure to see undermines efforts to master space. Consequently, the dramas suggest that successful gamers—whether playing directly or vicariously and whether in a backgammon match or a theater—ought not rely too much on an unstable visual regime but instead cultivate all their senses when they engage with playable media.

NAVIGATING SPACE AND PLACE IN *ARDEN OF FAVERSHAM*

The backgammon scene in *Arden* encapsulates elegantly the play's much broader and sustained use of geography and place to question an ideology of scopic dominance. *Arden*, which was based on a real murder that took place in Faversham, England, in 1551, is concerned with changing conceptions of land ownership in early modern England, dramatizing the ways a shift to a capitalist conception of land destroys the social relationships possible under a more feudalist system. Surveying and other emergent mapping practices were central to this shift, for by rendering the land in an abstract, textual form, such practices gave the landlord a fantasy of complete power and knowledge of the land and the tenants with whom he had increasingly less social contact.[25] Although the play's plot is centrally concerned with Arden's unfaithful wife, Alice, who colludes with her lover, Mosby, to have Arden murdered, the play repeatedly emphasizes Arden's status as a landowner who has benefited from emerging capitalist land practices, making many enemies in the process. The play thus serves in part as a "cautionary tale" about absentee landlords who, through surveillance technologies, treat the land primarily as a source of financial profit rather than as a paternalistic responsibility.[26] Land ownership was important, moreover, because it signaled social position, and thus *Arden* has also been read as a play about the perils of social climbing. Arden and his murderers are driven not simply by their appetite for land but by their belief that owning land will raise their social status.[27]

Indeed, the murderers' desire for "place"—in both geographic and social terms—is an overriding feature of their plot to kill Arden. Though they never manage to survey their target from that most auspicious of positions, the bird's-eye view, the murderers remain preoccupied throughout the play with surveillance and placement of Arden. One murderer, Greene, who believes Arden has unjustly taken his land, is somewhat obsessed with finding a specific locale for the murder, even though his hired guns, Black Will and Shakebag, are initially unconcerned with spatial propriety. When Black Will sees Arden for the first time after receiving the charge to commit the murder, he is eager to jump his victim immediately, but Greene holds him back. Through careful observation, Greene has learned that the

Nag's Head is Arden's "haunt" (3.38),[28] and he advises that Black Will attack Arden as he moves to this locale. Greene's murder strategy depends upon a sense of predictable, stable place, an unwise assumption. While Black Will waits in St. Paul's to capture Arden on his way to the Nag's Head, an apprentice lets down the window of his stall and, by chance, injures Black Will instead. In the flurry of activity, Arden escapes. Greene learns nothing from this experience. When he finds out how his plan went awry, he simply pursues another strategy of placing: "let us bethink us on some other place / Where Arden may be met with handsomely" (3.77–78) and again, "seeing this accident / Of meeting him in Paul's hath no success, / Let us bethink us on some other place / Whose earth may swallow up this Arden's blood" (3.107–10). The murderers may not have a bird's-eye view of their target, but they are nevertheless driven by a desire to master the spaces through which Arden moves.[29]

Greene's fixations with *emplacement*—with tracking Arden's movements in order to isolate a very specific place for the murder—make more sense when we bring the analytic of gender to bear on de Certeau's largely gender-neutral discussion of mapping.[30] Consider that the landowners who commissioned maps of their estates in hopes of dominating these spaces were predominantly men who were the heads of households. They used these maps to underscore and exercise their patriarchal power (despite having abandoned a sense of paternalistic care). Yet gender by no means guaranteed access to a position of social power, which, as *Arden* demonstrates, was not available to men such as Greene, Black Will, and Shakebag.[31] What is at stake, then, in these characters' pursuit of murder through strategies of emplacement? To answer this question, we need to think carefully about how gender and social status intersect in the early modern period, something many of *Arden*'s readers have overlooked in their debate about whether the play is predominantly a critique of the institution of marriage (and thus of early modern patriarchal systems) or of social climbing (and thus of early modern systems of social hierarchy).[32] The debate rests on a logical fallacy, for social status and gender were deeply imbricated in this period: social status helped *constitute* gender. My point here is not that *Arden*'s story of class conflict (between Arden and his male assassins) mirrors or intersects with its story of gender conflict (between Arden and his wife, Alice, or between Alice and her lover, Mosby), though that may be the case.[33] Rather, negotiations of power among men can be construed as "patriarchal," regardless of whether they involve or even have explicit implications for women.

Early modern patriarchy worked not only through the subordination of women but also through men's subordination of other males, such as youths, second sons, servants, and vagrants.[34] Some such men attempted to overcome their disenfranchisement by climbing the ranks that were supposed to be closed to them and, through marriage or commerce, working their way into positions of social and economic privilege, wherein they could exercise authority over not only women but also men of lower status. Whether or not they achieved their goals, they bought into and thus helped bolster the mythos of what historian Alexandra Shepard calls "patriarchal manhood" by conforming to the codes of the club they wished to join. Men who failed to climb the ranks in this way and reap "patriarchal dividends" had other options, Shepard argues: they could pursue a different set of codes for masculine behavior, some of which directly countered patriarchal virtues. In this latter model of "anti-patriarchal" manhood, anarchic violence could be a sign of rather than a deviation from manhood.[35]

The play's staging of backgammon operates as a material analogy for contradictions within early modern masculinity, and thereby extends Shepard's argument. *Arden* dramatizes masculinity as achieved not simply through an individual's exercise of particular qualities or behaviors, but also through a contest with other men over sparse resources; masculinity is shown to be a competitive game that some men win and others lose. Significantly, those competing for masculinity are not necessarily playing the game the same way. Whereas backgammon encourages its players to be competent simultaneously in violent conquest (removing the opponent's men from the board) and spatial mastery (thinking strategically about where the game men are placed), the game of early modern masculinity calls for a choice between these: those pursuing antipatriarchal masculinity are better served by developing competencies in violent conquest, whereas for those pursuing "patriarchal" masculinity, the focus is on spatial mastery.[36] I would suggest that Arden's assassins Greene, Black Will, and Shakebag fail at their task because they strive, unsuccessfully, to integrate these two competencies. They attempt to master Arden's movements across the landscape in their plot to murder him, a plot that they believe will ensure their social advancement and thus win them the dividends of patriarchal masculinity.[37] But to succeed at the murder, the assassins must practice a kind of anarchic violence that better befits a code of antipatriarchal masculinity.[38]

The killers' violent actions are incompatible with their desire to master what de Certeau calls a "system of defined places."[39] The play suggests that their plots fail because murder involves significant risk—as does backgammon, a game that is as much about luck as strategy. Knowing well the rules of the game and keeping track of where all the men are placed is not enough, as it might be in chess, a game with less imperfect information. Whereas skilled chess players can predict with some and often much accuracy when they will be able to capture the opponent's men, the practice of aggression in backgammon is largely unpredictable, being controlled primarily by the roll of the dice. Indeed, the drama turns Arden into something akin to a backgammon blot, also known in one early game treatise as *homo vagans,* a wandering man.[40] Arden spends much of the play wandering without protection toward his home and, like a blot, avoiding capture largely because of luck.[41] Arden's murder can be accomplished only when the killers come to terms with the risks and indeterminacy of their spatial practice, developing a style of play that given them closer access to, but paradoxically less control over, their target.

Greene hires Black Will to murder Arden because Black Will is known for approaching violence in just this way; but, ironically, when Black Will begins working with Greene, he adopts a less efficacious criminal style. Initially, Black Will exhibits the kind of rash overconfidence essential for the deed. Not only does he enjoy committing murder—as one character puts it, "My death to him [Black Will] is but a merriment. / And he will murder me to make him sport" (4.83–4)—but he doesn't need much instruction or planning, forging ahead as if on instinct. As he salivates at the prospect of carrying out the murder, Black Will compares himself to a thirsty, "forlorn traveller, / Whose lips are glued with summer's parching heat" and who wants only to "see a running brook" (3.92–4). Imagining himself as winding his way through an unknown landscape without a map, Black Will focuses on what lies directly in front of him and seeks only gustatory satisfaction; he will happily quench his thirst for murder with any live body he happens to come across. The money he will receive as compensation is just a bonus. But as Will's relationship with Greene develops, he begins to express other motivations for the murder, as if he has become subsumed by Greene's insistence on place, in both the social and geographic senses of the term. Like Greene, Black Will begins to describe the carefully plotted murder of Arden as a stepping-stone toward his own attainment of patriarchal masculinity. Black Will fantasizes about murder as an "occupation" that might win him respect and power: "Ah, that I might be set a work thus through the year and that murder would grow to an occupation that a man might without danger of law. Zounds! I warrant I should be warden of the company" (2.102–5).[42] He daydreams that the murder will elevate his economic and social status so much that he will wield power not only over Alice but over her lover as well: "Say thou seest

Mosby kneeling at my knees, / Off'ring me service for my high attempt" (3.84–85).[43] With the promise of riches and authority over other men, Will's accomplice Shakebag, too, agrees to fulfill Greene's plan, provided Greene can "give me place and opportunity" (3.101).

But the murderers' efforts at surveillance and emplacement of Arden fail again and again, and having traded in their rash overconfidence for the measured certainty characteristic of patriarchal masculinity, the murderers flounder when chance undermines their best laid schemes. For instance, after being unable to capture Arden on his way to the Nag's Head, the murderers happen upon Arden's servant, Michael, and having questioned him about Arden's whereabouts—"Where supped Master Arden?" (3.120)—they coerce Michael to take part in their conspiracy: "Thy office is but to appoint the place" (156).[44] When Michael fails to follow through on the plan, he defends himself from blame with a concocted story and then deflects the murderers' rage by giving them what they want, another *place* to do the murder: "you may front him well on Rainham Down, / A place well-fitting such a stratagem" (7.18–19). This particular place is less spatially confined than the earlier prospective murder spots have been, presenting further geographical challenges. Rainham Down was an open countryside around the town of Rainham, a place defined only in relation to other places: it was on the road from Rochester to Faversham.[45] But this plot fails because Master Cheiny and his men happen to come upon Arden and escort him out of harm's way. Rainham Down may well be a "place well-fitting" murder, but place is not enough; if Arden is like a blot or *homo vagans*, then the lucky arrival of Lord Cheiny and his "men" and their capacity to cover Arden as he wanders protect this blot from capture. And Black Will, rather than rushing onto the scene anyway and killing any man who blocks his path—the sort of behavior we would have expected from his earlier characterization—bides his time and waits for another well-chosen place and more carefully controlled circumstances.

The play thus underscores a conflict between the murderers' aggression and their pursuit of patriarchal masculinity by emphasizing tensions in their approaches to space. To be successful in capturing their man, the murders need to take more physical risks instead of fixating on placing their target; but their social-climbing agenda and their pursuit of patriarchal masculinity lead them to emphasize safe placement over risky, physical contact. One of the key ways that the play interrogates the murderers' fixations on placement, underscoring a conflict between their murderous aggression and their pursuit of patriarchal masculinity, is by literally problematizing their vision and thus frustrating what de Certeau would call their "gnostic and scopic drive."[46] The play mocks the murderers for their strategies of surveillance and emplacement by suggesting that such strategies, which abstract the murderers from their intended victim, depend too much on an unstable visual regime. In *Arden* the mythos of spatial management that de Certeau associates with the scopic drive cannot be achieved because vision, in a very material sense, is easily impaired. In one especially interesting scene, Black Will and Shakebag fail to kill Arden because a fog rises, obscuring their view of him and leaving them incapacitated by sudden blindness.

> SHAKEBAG: Oh Will, where art thou?
> BLACK WILL: Here, Shakebag, almost in hell's mouth, where I cannot see my way for smoke.
> SHAKEBAG: I pray thee speak still that we may meet by the sound, for I shall fall into some ditch or other unless my feet see better than my eyes. (12.1–6)

Shakebag and Black Will's strategies of emplacement have rendered them so reliant on visual modes of perceiving and abstract modes of interaction that they are unpracticed in engaging their other senses to navigate space and interact with their target. As it leaves them "making false footing in the dark" and attempting to follow Arden "without a guide" (12.51–2), the murderers' visual impairment is a material rendering of the blindness of those who, according to de Certeau, walk the city streets, unable to see the "urban 'text' they write" with their movements.[47] Unlike de Certeau's urban walkers, however, *Arden*'s murderers stumble unproductively in the darkness. They are so fixated on engaging their eyes that they fail to realize they might be able to "see better" with their feet.

The play reserves its most trenchant critique of the murderers' scopic and gnostic drive for the climactic murder scene itself, however, where Arden is killed while playing backgammon with Mosby. How does this murder plot differ from the previous ones? To answer that question, we must approach backgammon not simply as a literary symbol but as an actual game, and thus benefit from drawing on our own experiential knowledge of what it feels and looks like to interact with and through the space of a backgammon board. Like prior murder attempts, the backgammon murder plot places Arden: Mosby will bring him back to the house and "play a game or two at tables *here*" (14.96; my emphasis). And Black Will goes further, specifying that Alice "place Mosby . . . in a chair" and Arden "upon a stool" (14.115–16) so that Black Will, when he rushes out, can drag Arden to the ground to be killed. Whereas in previous scenes Arden has enjoyed the liberating benefits of movement, this new plot stabilizes him; he will be inside the parlor, sitting on a stool, and, most important, engaged with a board game. During the previous murder plots, Arden has been like de Certeau's urban walkers: blind to the text he writes with his movements and to his place in a/the plot, he nevertheless engages in subversive tactics that undermine his murderers, who believe themselves to have all the privileges of de Certeau's "voyeur-god."[48] The backgammon plot differs, though, in that Arden will not simply be an object of surveillance, subjected to the observation of others; as Arden plays backgammon, he will partake in a god's-eye view himself, gazing down on the game board while others gaze down on him. Occupying the position of player, rather than simply a "man" to be played, gives Arden the (false) sense of power and security his murderers possess.

The foolishness of Arden's fantasy of scopic dominance is strikingly foreshadowed in a dream he describes of having been in a deer park where preparations were afoot for a hunt. Notably, Arden reports that in his dream he occupied a bird's-eye view of the hunt, standing "upon a little rising hill / . . . whistly watching for the herd's approach" (6.8–9), only to discover that he was "the game" to be hunted (6.19). As in the hunt, Arden can be "taken" during the backgammon game because he looks down—in this case, at the board—rather than attuning himself to the social game around him. Indeed, the play cheekily suggests that were he simply to look up from the board, Arden might glimpse his murderers before they can attack. As the game begins and Black Will enters the room, Alice warns, "Take heed he see thee not," and Black Will registers concern, "I fear he will spy me as I am coming" (14.224–25). Part of the tension of the scene, then, stems from the precariousness of Black Will's scopic dominance: Arden can ruin the whole plot if he simply abandons his visual fixation on the game board.

But the most pressing tension of the scene stems from the way it materially links Arden's life to his competency at backgammon. Mosby has instructed the murderers to wait for him to utter the "watchword," "'Now I take you'" (14.100–1), before rushing out. Thus, theoretically, Arden may preserve his life if he manages to keep his blots from being captured by Mosby. Although earlier accounts of the historical crime describe Arden as having been killed while playing tables, the connection between the murder and the outcome of the game—between physical and ludic aggression—is far more prominent in the drama than in these other texts. The *Wardmote Book of Faversham* reads: "He was most shamefully murdred as is foresaid / as he was playing at Tables frendely w^t thesaid morsbye for sodeynly cam out (of a darke house adioyning to thesaid plo^r) / the foresaid Blackwyll." In the *Wardmote Book,* Black Will does not respond to a watchword that corresponds to a game move but simply comes out "sodeynly" [suddenly]. Holinshed's version of the crime story includes the watchword but suggests that Mosby ultimately uses it independent of the game context, confusing or angering Arden: "In their plaie Mosbie said thus (which seemed to be the watchword for blacke Wils comming foorth) Now maie I take you sir if I will. Take me (quoth maister Arden) which waie?"[49] In having Arden question Mosby's claim that he can take one of Arden's blots, Holinshed's account disarticulates Arden's fate from his and Mosby's performance in the actual backgammon game. By contrast, the drama goes to great lengths to connect these. In a scene that would take significantly longer to perform onstage than to read from a printed script, the murderers wait in the wings while the game is played, and they anxiously wonder if Mosby will ever manage to take one of Arden's men and speak the watchword. As the game proceeds, Black Will complains, "Can he not take him yet? What a spite is that!" (14.223). Finally, Mosby, in a climactic moment, declares that he is about to lose his final opportunity to capture a blot if he cannot cast a one on his next roll of the dice: "One ace, or else I lose the game" (14.227). The audience, like the murderers, wait with bated breath as Mosby throws the dice, turning up, Arden informs us, double aces (one on both dice).

For contemporary audiences who know anything about backgammon, as for early modern playgoers who would have been familiar with the popular game, Mosby's comment immediately conjures up a game puzzle: how might the board be set up so as to bring the match to this exciting crux? That the state of gameplay fascinated early playgoers is evinced by the famous frontispiece to *Arden*'s 1633 quarto edition, which not only represents this scene from the play but highlights the game board, angling it so as to give readers a bird's-eye view of the ludic action (Figure 18).[50] The illustration helps demonstrate the oddly ambivalent effects of this staged game scene. On the one hand it reveals this to be the climactic moment of the play, demonstrating how Mosby's report on the status of the game produces much-needed dramatic tension. Such tension kept early modern playgoers engaged in what easily could have become an anticlimactic murder scene: most theatergoers probably knew from historical accounts that the actual Arden murder happened during a tables match. The play's success depended on its ability to manufacture dramatic tension about the famous crime. On the other hand, however, and this is the point I would underscore, the illustration shows readers something that playgoers would never have seen. Like the murderers positioned on the edges of Arden's parlor, playgoers did not have visual access to the game board, whose details could not be seen from afar. The staging of the scene thus belies a mythos of scopic dominance, insisting that theatrical pleasure—the sense of climax experienced with Mosby's gesture of casting the dice—is possible only when spectators use all their senses to play along with the game, becoming involved cognitively and emotionally with its unpredictable risks and aggressive interactions.[51]

In the final section of this chapter, I discuss in more detail the integrated modes of perception that the Arden murder scene calls upon its audiences to exercise; but before I leave the murder scene itself, it is worth observing how the backgammon topos, with its critique of scopic dominance, carries the play through to its tragic end. Whereas others have read Arden's house as a successful place for the murder because, unlike the locales of previous murder attempts, it can be carefully controlled,[52] I would suggest that the play uses backgammon to reveal fixity and spatial control as mere illusions, even at the play's end. When the murderers finally manage to kill Arden, they turn out to be falsely confident about their accomplishments, for like a blot in backgammon, even when Arden is removed from the boards, he is not permanently displaced. This plot development is in keeping with the drama of backgammon as a game. Unlike earlier versions of tables, where loss of a blot could end the game, in backgammon the game continues, and the captured blot has a chance to reenter the board onto the home table of the opponent. For instance, if Player A's blot has been taken and he or she then casts a one, the captured blot enters on the first point of the opponent's table, unless the opponent, Player B, has two or more men protecting that space. From this position on the board, the reentered blot can continue to be played. In fact, if Player B has a blot standing on the point where Player A's blot reenters the board, Player A may capture Player B's man even as it sits seemingly safe on its home table.

In his seventeenth-century manuscript on gaming, Francis Willughby explains how these game rules can be manipulated strategically by a player whose opponent has brought most of his own men home and, as he bears them off the board, appears set to win the game. The underdog player can strategically allow one of his blots to be captured, sacrificing this man so that it may later have a chance of penetrating the opponent's home table and keeping the underdog's chances in the game alive. Willughby uses this gameplay scenario to provide an etymology for the game of Irish, an English version of tables that is backgammon's closest cousin.[53] Drawing on English stereotypes about the barbarism of the Irish, he writes: "An Irish man is never dead till his head bee cut of (the Irish having a custome to cut of the heads of all those they have killed), nor a game at Irish wun till the last man bee borne."[54] That is, in the game of Irish, as in backgammon, a player who seems defeated may revive his chances as long as his opponent still has men that need to be borne off the table. When Arden is captured, he, like a blot, is removed from the boards: his body is dragged offstage to an imagined field behind an abbey. But like a captured blot in a game of Irish or backgammon, Arden returns to the boards by stroke of fortune: snowfall captures the imprints of his murderers' feet so that the movement of Arden's body can be tracked by those who wish to solve the murder case. The "plot of ground" (Epilogue, l. 10) where Arden's body is found is by no means a final resting place for a character who resists placement.[55] Arden's game is not done. Not only is "his body's print" (Epilogue, l. 12) reported to have remained for years on the abbey grasses, but his body itself—or, rather, that of the actor playing him—takes up a position on the boards again, literally placed back on the stage so that Alice, confronted with it, can confess her crimes in response to Arden's telltale blood, which, "gushing forth, / Speaks as it falls" (16.5–6).

With Arden's eerie return to the boards to identify his murderers—an only slightly less spectacular move than in Holinshed, in which the murdered Arden, who has been moved to the countinghouse, suddenly gives "a great groan" and has to be murdered again[56]—*Arden* completes its dramatization of the social stakes of the parallel between gaming and theater. Like these playable media, masculinity turns out to be an aggressive contest where topping one's opponents does not guarantee lasting power over them: the competition goes on as long as the game does.[57] What is more, surveillance and emplacement of Arden undermine instead of facilitate the murderers' capacity to win this competitive game. It is through Mosby that the play best expresses this tragic paradox, linking it, significantly, to the bird's-eye view. Reveling in having "climbed the top bough of the tree / . . . to build my nest among the clouds" (8.15–16), Mosby both reflects on his successful social elevation and bemoans its impermanence. Even as he considers himself to have achieved social, spatial, and scopic dominance, he recognizes that he must now kill off his allies lest they try to supplant him and prompt his "downfall to the earth" (8.18). Rather than being emblematic of secure patriarchal masculinity, Mosby's bird's-eye view underscores the instability of place—in both social and geographic terms—and the impossibility of achieving scopic dominance. His decision to use a backgammon game with Arden as the setting for murder is the perfect culmination of his character's tragic perspective on spatial management and patriarchal masculinity. The match Mosby plays against Arden dramatizes how those who pursue patriarchal masculinity, like inhabitants of the two-penny galleries, cannot play the game successfully if they don't take the risks.

THE TWO ANGRY WOMEN OF ABINGTON AND BLIND PLAY

Whereas *Arden* dramatizes the tragic consequences of investing in scopic dominance, Henry Porter's *The Two Angry Women of Abington*, whose backgammon scene begins instead of ending the play, dramatizes a comic alternative. It has been noted that Porter's play resembles and may even burlesque a number of Elizabethan plays, but its relation to *Arden* has yet to be recognized.[58] The affinities of *Two Angry Women* and *Arden of Faversham* go well beyond the similarities of their titles, specifying key characters and the English town from which they hail. Like *Arden*, *Two Angry Women* begins with suspicions of adultery. Mistress Barnes believes (in this play wrongly) that her husband is having an affair with Mistress Goursey, the wife of his close friend and neighbor. As in *Arden*, the suspected cuckold's failure to deal effectively with the problems of his household—in this case, his failure to intervene on his wife's behalf—leads to a breakdown of social, familial, and communal bonds, and finally to aggressive action and the threat of mortal violence. The primary site of that violence is, as in *Arden*, the English countryside, where the characters range for about a third of this play. When Mistress Goursey and Mistress Barnes learn that their husbands plan to patch up the women's quarrel by marrying their offspring—Francis and Mall, respectively—to each other, the women are irate. Mistress Goursey convinces her servant, Dick Coomes, to kill Mistress Barnes, and both women pursue the young lovers through the countryside in order to prevent their elopement. What follows is a game of elaborate chase, with characters attempting to find and confront each other but failing to do so because of bad fortune—a combination of comedic timing and various cases of mistaken identity.

Most notably for my purposes, characters' aggressions in *Two Angry Women* are initially acted out through a game of backgammon, played by the wives with their husbands and the theater audience as spectators. As in *Arden* the backgammon game produces and encourages, instead of containing or channeling, participants' physical aggression toward each other. But whereas the backgammon game in *Arden* is the climax of that play, in *Two Angry Women* it is the event that sets the plot into motion. The temporal placement of the game is a function of differences in genre. As a tragedy

Arden moves toward increased aggression and finally the death of the protagonist(s), whereas *Two Angry Women*, a comedy, moves from aggression and violence toward reconciliation. As a consequence, although both plays use backgammon as an efficient topos through which to query the relationships among spectatorship, playgoing, and patriarchal masculinity, their genres drive them toward different treatment of these issues. *Two Angry Women* uses its genre of comedy to imagine a less tragic conception of spatial practice along with a more multifaceted critique of the relation between scopic dominance and patriarchal masculinity.

The backgammon game that opens the play efficiently sets up this critique, though to follow its implications for theater as playable media, we must (as in our earlier analysis in *Arden*) read references to backgammon as clues about an actual game in play, not simply a set of convenient and witty literary metaphors. The game scene immediately draws attention to what is at stake in the spatial positioning of backgammon's players and game spectators. Masters Goursey and Barnes, initially planning to play a match themselves, decide instead to become spectators to their wives' game: "Our wives shall try the quarrel 'twixt us two / And we'll look on" (1.81–83). The husbands go on to present their spectatorship as a mode of control, using vision metaphors to describe their command over their wives and the game as a whole. For the husbands, spectatorship means scopic dominance. When Mistress Barnes quips that she is certain Mistress Goursey will "play me false" (1.85), or cheat—at the game and, by inference, through adultery— Master Goursey assures her, "I'll see she shall not" (1.86). Mistress Barnes immediately challenges Master Goursey's link between seeing and social control: "Nay, sir, she will be sure you shall not see. / You of all men shall not mark her hand, / She hath such close conveyance in her play" (1.87-89). But Master Goursey restates his confidence in scopic dominance and a visual basis for his patriarchal authority, "Is she so cunning grown? Come, come let's see" (1.90).

As the husbands assume something like a bird's-eye view of the game board, their perspective echoes that of patrons in the two-penny galleries, and arguably the play critiques the latter through its mockery of the former. The husbands' viewing position turns out to have detrimental consequences, for as they become increasingly abstracted from the backgammon game their wives play, they fail to track, and thus moderate, the women's mounting aggression. Although they believe their bird's-eye view gives them scopic dominance, in fact, this viewing perspective takes them out of the drama of the game the wives play. After the women have agreed on the stakes for which they will play—which at "a pound a game" are, the husbands admit, "too much" (1.96; 98)—Masters Barnes and Goursey comment in abstract terms on the match, all the while missing its key ludic action because they don't play vicariously.[59]

> MASTER BARNES: Master Goursey, who says that gaming's bad
>   When such good angels walk 'twixt every cast?
> MASTER GOURSEY: This is not noble sport, but royal play.
> MASTER BARNES: It must be so, where royals walk so fast.
> MISTRESS BARNES: Play right, I pray.
> MISTRESS GOURSEY: Why so I do.
> MISTRESS BARNES: Where stands your man?
> MISTRESS GOURSEY: In his right place.
> MISTRESS BARNES: Good faith, I think ye play me foul an ace.
> MASTER BARNES: No, wife, she plays ye true.
> MISTRESS BARNES: Peace, husband, peace. I'll not be judged by you.
> MISTRESS GOURSEY: Husband, Master Barnes, pray both go walk.
>   We cannot play if standers-by do talk.
> MASTER GOURSEY: Well, to your game. We will not trouble ye.

[Master Barnes and Master Goursey] goes from them. (109–22)

The husbands' opening banter turns on a set of puns on the money wagered in the game and the women who wager it, "angels" and "royals" being names of coins. The banter recalls a point of tension in early modern debates about the ethics of gaming, as discussed in Chapter 1, with more permissive moralists arguing that games like tables were acceptable provided they did not involve high stakes, as this one does.[60] The husbands defend their wives' gaming by suggesting through puns that the women's natural nobility and innocence—that they are "royals" and "angels"—rescues their activity from the impropriety that would ordinarily be associated with betting coins as valuable as royals and angels. From one perspective the husbands have already failed in their claims to scopic dominance, for they misjudge their wives, who prove far from angelic in this scene and in the rest of the play. Because they are so busy out-punning each other in their own metagame, the husbands miss the ludic action that prompts Mistress Barnes's accusation of foul play. Mistress Barnes accuses Mistress Goursey of misplacing one of her men on the board, essentially moving it one space or point, an "ace," off its proper position.

The husbands have no way of knowing whom to believe because they have not been monitoring the action of the game; and one could say the same thing about any theatergoers who, like the husbands, buy into a logic of scopic dominance instead of playing vicariously. Mistress Barnes's rebuke of her husband, "I'll not be judged by you," can double as a rebuke to those theater spectators who have commandeered ostensibly superior viewing positions in the upper galleries; they, like the husbands, cannot really judge the situation effectively because, despite their "better" seats, they cannot decipher if Mistress Goursey has, in fact, cheated in the game, let alone in the marriage. The rebuke is in keeping with the dialogue that begins the play, where Masters Goursey and Barnes discourse on the pleasures of "neighbor amity" (1.5), friendship between neighbors. Their paeans to the geographical closeness of friends quickly becomes a meditation more broadly on the virtues of spatial proximity and the problems of viewing any scene from afar. That which cannot be seen well, because too far away, cannot be judged effectively. Goursey says:

> Kind sir, near-dwelling amity, indeed,
> Offers the heart's enquiry better view
> Than love that's seated in a farther soil,
> As prospectives, the nearer that they be,
> Yield better judgment to the judging eye:
> Things seen far off are lessened in the eye,
> When their true shape is seen, being hard by. (1.9–15)

From its first moments the play considers the problems of spectatorship for those "seated in a farther soil." The judgment of the latter can be compromised, the play suggests, by distance, whereas those who view the action more closely will see its "true shape."

The "judging eye[s]" of Masters Barnes and Goursey become all the more compromised when, as the stage direction above indicates, they move away from their wives' game, leaving the women to play while the men look on from an even greater distance. The husbands' choice to abstract themselves further from the game board—not only physically but also cognitively and emotionally—is emblematic of their failed patriarchal management of their households; for Mistress Barnes's contempt for Mistress Goursey has become all too evident, and leaving the women more or less alone is obviously risky. Potentially serious animosity is virtually guaranteed in this case because there is not only pride but significant money at stake in the game. Indeed, backgammon's inherently aggressive ludic action escalates tensions between the women. Mistress Barnes, perhaps by mistake or as part of a cheating strategy, leaves one of her counters, or "men," ambiguously placed on the board (between two points instead of clearly on one), leading Mistress Goursey, who needs to know where the counter is located if she wishes to capture it, to inquire, "Where stands your man now?" The pun on standing man as erect penis becomes evident when Mistress Barnes queries back, "Doth he not stand right?" and Mistress Goursey responds, "It stands between the points" (1.124), with "points" referring both to the marked spaces on a backgammon board and to the laces that join a man's doublet to his hose.[61] Mistress Barnes then accuses Mistress Goursey of using loaded dice—"methinks the dice runs much uneven, / That I throw but deuce-ace and you eleven" (1.125–26)—which would enable Mistress Goursey to move her men more quickly toward home and thus toward a win. Mistress Goursey takes offence at Mistress Barnes's far from subtle insinuation that Mistress Goursey's "game" (1.32) is not confined to tables. "I have read Aesop's fables / And know your moral's meaning well enough" (1.134–35). By the time the husbands return, casually asking, "Now now, women, who hath won the game?" (1.137), the situation is beyond repair, and the play suggests the husbands are largely to blame because of their failure as patriarchs to monitor and thus intervene in the tensions that have been building. The husbands' failures of engagement have disastrous consequence that, we might argue, could have been avoided: had they played vicariously, like good gamers, Master Goursey could have come to his wife's defense, and Master Barnes could have disputed his wife's charges of infidelity.[62] Again, the play's representation of the husbands functions simultaneously as a subtle critique of twopenny gallery theatergoers who abstract themselves from the play's dramatic action. When the husbands move away from the game board, but not off the stage (they have no stage direction to exit), they become even more firmly aligned with playgoers in the upper galleries.

When the husbands do finally attempt to intervene, they simply resume their earlier positions of scopic management over the game and their wives, and thus their efforts fall short. The husbands seem oblivious to the tenor of Mistress Barnes's accusations of infidelity. They take at face value the women's debates about foul play, presuming these pertain to the game alone. But the husbands fail to realize that their wives' argument about the game has exceeded its ludic context. Or, to put this in anthropologist Gregory Bateson's terms, the husbands misread the "frame" of the game: they believe that "this is play," when, in fact, on many levels the game has ceased to be play, aggression no longer contained within the game's ludic border.[63] The puns on foul play as adultery reach a fevered pitch with Mistress Barnes's facetious comment that if the outcome of the game depends on "the bearing"—once players get all their men home, they must cast the dice to "bear" their men from the board, the winner bearing all her men off first—then Mistress Goursey will be victorious. Punning on "bearing" as sexual performance, Mistress Barnes submits that Mistress Goursey is exceedingly skilled at bearing, even trying to "bear one man too many" (1.145), to which Mistress Goursey responds, "Better do so than bear not any" (1.146), a sly comment on Mistress Barnes's failure to retain the sexual interests of her husband. Tensions reach their zenith when Mistress Goursey, having already accused Mistress Barnes of cheating in the placement of her man, as discussed above, now mocks Mistress Barnes for her bad cheating strategy: it is because Mistress Barnes has not "kept your man in his right place" (1.159) that Mistress Goursey has been able to "hit" (1.151) or capture the man. By this point the fractures are beyond repair, and the husbands' suggestions that their wives "keep within the bounds of modesty" (1.171) only aggravate matters. As Mistress Barnes storms out, now furious with her husband for chiding her, the husbands bemoan having left their wives with any responsibility for maintaining the men's friendship: men's minds, "[h]aving the temper of true reason in them / Afford a better edge of argument / For the maintain of our familiar loves / Than the soft leaden wit of women can" (1.228–31). From the play's perspective, men who hold such points of view are doubly to blame if they have chosen not to monitor more carefully the high-stakes game of backgammon their wives play.

The backgammon game in *Two Angry Women* lasts only one scene, but the competencies of backgammon it encourages in its players and their spectators, onstage and off, remain important throughout the play. The conflicts of the backgammon board spill out into the social relationships of the players and their spectators. Ultimately all of the play's characters, even those not present at the original game, will take up the skills of backgammon: navigating space in the face of aggressive opponents and unpredictable chance. In effect, the entire play becomes a game of tables. The characters roam around the theater boards—fictionally turned into a countryside space—trying to capture others or avoid capture while the theater audience has the chance to play along, wondering, maybe even wagering, on which side will win.[64]

From the start *Two Angry Women* presents scopic dominance as an impossibility as well as a hindrance to vicarious play. When the wives try to halt their husbands' plans for Mall and Francis to marry, the latter, with the assistance of Mall's brother Phillip, escape in an attempt to elope. The wives pursue their children, and the husbands pursue their wives; even the servants take part in the chase. All of these plans go awry, however, when night falls, throwing the characters into total darkness. Used in ways reminiscent of *Arden*'s fog scene, the darkness trope is extended here, continuing for about a third of the play.[65] As in *Arden*, in *Two Angry Women* the trope of invisibility—only a trope, since early modern amphitheaters had no other light source besides the sun—speaks to both theatrical and social concerns. Through the trope of invisibility, the play queries the visual logic of patriarchal masculinity: characters pursue scopic dominance in order to attain patriarchal power that is unavailable to them by virtue of their status—and in this play, also their gender and age. And as in *Arden*, that pursuit fails repeatedly. However, *Two Angry Women* is able to go further than *Arden* to imagine a compelling alternative to this inherently tragic narrative. Alongside its scopically fixated social climbers (the two angry women, Phillip, and the servant Coomes), *Two Angry Women* dramatizes de Certeau's surprisingly powerful blind walkers through the characters of Mall and Hodge, another servant of the Gourseys. These characters do not attempt scopic dominance, but instead throw themselves into their blindness, abandoning vision so that they can engage in the messy, risky, and interactive world of (the) play. To put this in de Certeau's terms: rather than pursue a scopic regime of *placement*, Mall and Hodge revel in the pleasures and surprising power of *spatial practice*. Whereas for others, darkness—and the condition of blindness that accompanies darkness—is an impediment, to Mall and Hodge the inability to see makes for a better game.

The claims of the two angry women and Coomes on patriarchal masculinity are arguably specious by virtue of their gender and status, respectively, and the play mocks their social climbing by using darkness to expose the foolishness of their desires for scopic dominance. The drama presents Mistresses Goursey and Barnes as overly emotional women who allow their "pot quarrel" (1.179) to get out of hand, thereby disturbing the beneficial alliance of their husbands and the stability of their community. Their dangerous desire for patriarchal authority is efficiently displayed through their characters' dramatic function: blocking the comic resolution of marital concord. The two angry women spend most of the play trying to stop what almost everyone else believes to be an ideal marriage between Mall and Francis. The Gourseys' servant, Coomes, too, is presented as an overreacher. He accepts his mistress's mission to murder Mrs. Barnes in exchange for promotion in the ranks of servitude, along with "[m]oney, apparel" plus "sword and bucklers" (6.208). Even before his promotion

Coomes aspires to the part of patriarch in the Goursey family, treating Francis, his mistress's grown-up son, as if he is a child over whom Coomes has command.[66]

Coomes expresses his social superiority in part through the language of scopic dominance. He justifies his right to lecture "my young master" (8.301) Francis by figuring himself as a man with visuospatial knowledge: "I must needs say ye are a young man, and for mine own part, I have seen the world and I know what belongs to causes, and the experience that I have I thank God I have travelled for it" (8.304–7). Coomes draws on a commonplace of cartographic discourse—links among vision, travel, and knowledge—claiming that because of his more advanced age, he has had time to see the world through travel and thus is more informed than Francis about how to handle conflict resolution, "what belongs to causes." Francis and the Boy, another servant of the Gourseys, proceed to mock Coomes for claiming patriarchal authority on these grounds, questioning whether his travels are significant enough to merit such knowledge. Francis asks, "Why, how far have ye travelled for it?" and the Boy jokingly responds as if on Coomes's behalf, "From my master's house to the ale-house" (8.308–9). Coomes cannot have attained much knowledge because, they suggest, his travels have been limited in terms of geography and social context, comprising only the dependent realm of the master's house and what I have argued elsewhere to be the antipatriarchal space of the alehouse.[67] Any lessons in conflict management learned in these locales cannot be applied to the situation at hand, which is presumably well beyond Coomes's purview as a servant.

Coomes finds his social pretensions confounded even further when darkness falls, revealing the absurdity of his logic of scopic dominance. In part because Coomes equates knowledge and power with having "seen the world," he is incapable of performing authority when denied vision, experiencing instead total spatial dislocation. He and Mistress Goursey scramble to find each other in the darkness.

MISTRESS GOURSEY: Where art thou, Dick?
COOMES: Where am I, quotha? Marry, I may be where anybody will say I am, either in France or at Rome, or at Jerusalem they may say I am, for I am not able to disprove them, because I cannot tell where I am.
MISTRESS GOURSEY: O what a blindfold walk have we had, Dick
(9.74–79)

Deprived of vision yet continuing to invest in a logic of scopic dominance, Coomes imagines himself at the mercy of those who ostensibly can see: his location can be dictated to him by "anyone" who can claim to know of it. Whereas earlier he boasted of his authority as a traveler, he now fails to decipher differences among cities as distinctive as France, Rome, and Jerusalem. Coomes is utterly paralyzed by the darkness, yet nevertheless remains wedded to a visual regime that, he foolishly continues to claim, secures his authority.

The same is true of the two angry women. When Mistress Barnes finds herself lost and alone, she uses her torch as a guide. Nervous about being found by thieves, she sets the torch on a hill and then lies down nearby so that she can "look who comes, and choose my company" (13.22). But no scopic dominance results, for her enemy Mistress Goursey find the torch and attempts to take it. Although the visual regime has not served either of these characters in their pursuits of patriarchal authority—the darkness has undermined their ability to locate Mall and Francis, and to convince the couple to forgo their marriage—the women nevertheless remain committed to a link between vision and power, a point dramatized with some literalism when they engage for more than a hundred lines in a vigorous and protracted tug of war over the torch. Light, and the visual regime it emblematizes and makes possible, becomes the ultimate point of contention, as if winning the torch will secure these characters' authority over each other and over their husbands and progeny.

The play's questioning of scopic dominance extends beyond the case of characters whose pursuit of patriarchal authority appears foolish, for even Phillip, the first-born of Mr. Barnes, finds his claims to patriarchal masculinity confounded by the darkness. On account of his status and gender, Phillip may be socially superior to Coomes and the "angry women," but he is still considered a youth by early modern standards, being neither husband nor father, and thus has no de facto access to patriarchal privilege. Nevertheless, he is initially quite successful in enacting patriarchal authority over his family and friends. Though he and Francis are the same age, Phillip acts as his friend's advisor, presuming more power over Francis than Francis's own father. It is Phillip who checks Francis's raging emotions and who brokers the match between him and Mall.[68] When Phillip hears his father's idea that Mall should marry Francis, he gives it his approval: "Then, father, he shall have her! He shall, I swear" (3.302). It is Phillip, not his father, who goes to the Goursey's house to present the case, doing so successfully despite Francis's resistance to marriage.[69] Philip succeeds where Francis's own father fails.[70] Phillip is certain he can direct

Francis and Mall even in the wooing process. Indeed, commenting on Mall's wit, which has prevented other suitors from winning her hand, Phillip plans to negotiate this wooing himself, "Well, I do doubt Francis hath so much spleen / They'll ne'er agree, but I will moderate" (5.40–41). When Mall banters on and on with Francis, Phillip intervenes several times, forcefully urging, and finally simply commanding, his sister to accept Francis.

Like Coomes and the angry women, when Phillip attempts to control the people around him, he exhibits the scopic drive that is a marker of patriarchal masculinity. Phillip repeatedly directs the placement and visibility of his peers as well as his social superiors. When Mistress Barnes comes upon the wooing scene, Phillip directs Mall and Francis to "Stand aside / And closely, too, lest that you be espied" (8.159–60). It is he who chooses the coney green as the place for the young lovers to meet, instructing Francis, "let not thy mother see thee. / At the back side there is a coney green; / Stay there for me, and Mall and I will come to thee" (8.350–52). He orchestrates even the spatial positioning of his father and Master Goursey: "Stand you two hearkening near the coney green, / But sure your light in you must not be seen" (8.458–59). Moreover, in insisting that the other characters forgo torches, Phillip consigns them to darkness while they fulfill his grand plan. Everyone, even the erstwhile patriarchs of the play, put their literal blind trust in Phillip: "Come then," says his own father, "let's do as Phillip hath advised" (8.468).

The precariousness of Philip's authority is quickly revealed, though, when, like the other characters, he is deprived of light and fails to navigate space effectively without it. When Phillip enters alone in scene 10, he initially continues to play the patriarch with scopic powers but quickly finds that position untenable. His description of the darkness is paradoxical: "How like a beauteous lady masked in black / Looks that same large circumference of heaven. / The sky that was so fair three hours ago / Is in three hours become an Ethiope, / And, being angry at her beauteous change, / She will not have one of those pearlèd stars / To blab her sable metamorphesy" (10.1–7). On the one hand, Phillip represents the darkness as a visual phenomenon, something that can be seen when he "[l]ooks" at the sky. But the absurdity of the conceit—seeing depends on light, so how can one see darkness?—emerges in the next set of lines. Without stars to form an ornamental contrast, the blackness of the heavens cannot be apprehended visually: nothing is there to "blab" the transformation of "beauteous lady" to "Ethiope." Phillip then goes on to lament that his inability to see undermines his plan to arrange the marriage of Mall and Francis: "I did appoint my sister / To meet me at the coney berry [sic] below, / and Francis, too; but neither can I see. / Belike my mother happened on that place / And frayed them from it, and they both are now / Wandering about these fields. How shall I find them? / It is so dark I scarce can see my hand" (10.8–14). Without vision, Phillip cannot oversee and bring to fruition his master plan.

To be sure, Phillip presents himself elsewhere as capable of functioning without vision. When the characters finally reconvene at the end of the play, Phillip taunts Francis for failing to hunt down his "coney": "Shall it be said thou missed so plain a way / Whenas so fair a wench did for thee stay? / . . . / 'Sounds, man, and if thou hadst been blind / The coney borough thou needst must find. / I tell thee, Francis, had it been my case, / And I had been a wooer in thy place, / I would have laid my head unto the ground / And scented out my wench's way like a hound" (11.347–54). The bravado rings hollow, however, given Phillip's failures throughout the play to engage his nonvisual senses effectively to find the others. Phillip never himself engages smell in the way he maintains Francis should have, and when he reluctantly employs other senses, they tend to fail him. For instance, at the end of his soliloquy, Phillip calls out, "So ho, so ho!" (10.21) in hopes of locating his friends. His calls are answered by someone he believes to be Francis but who is, in fact, Will, the servant of Sir Raphe Smith, who has been hunting. Phillip, so dependent on a visual realm, is ill-equipped to function on an aural level. And though he, unlike many of the other confused characters, eventually discovers his various mistakes in hearing, he does so too late and is, in the end, not much better off than they are. At one point Sir Raphe, mistaking Phillip for his servant, asks, "Art thou Will, my man?" (10.109), infuriating the proud Phillip who responds, "your man! / My back, sir, scorns to wear your livery" (10.111). Phillip realizes too late that his interlocutor is his social superior and feels shamed by his "rude anger" (10.118). As this example illustrates, the darkness troubles not simply spatial but social relations, leading to significant embarrassment for the characters most invested in scopic dominance of space and social climbing. Coomes suffers this embarrassment, too, when Hodge, pretending to be Mistress Goursey, tricks Coomes into thinking he is successfully seducing his employer. "Mistress Goursey" concedes that she would kiss her servant "if I thought nobody would see" (11.64–65), and the promise of a kiss enables Hodge to lead the excited Coomes around the stage and right into a pond.

Like *Arden, Two Angry Women* explores the risks for social climbers who in their pursuit of patriarchal masculinity invest in a logic of scopic dominance; but it also goes further than *Arden* to dramatize the benefits to those who criticize and find alternatives to these pursuits, using their full senses to navigate the social games around them. Whereas the characters who aspire to patriarchal masculinity—Phillip, Coomes, and Mistresses Goursey and Barnes—stumble in the dark, Mall and Hodge, who do not directly challenge gender and status hierarchies, discover a certain freedom and pleasure in darkness. They feel their way through spaces they cannot see, engaging their other senses to compensate for lack of vision.

What accounts for this difference? The answer comes by way of a question raised by the Boy, who asks, "what difference is there between a blind man and he that cannot see?" (10.86–87). Blindness offers a useful theatrical trope through which this play, like Shakespeare's *King Lear*, reflects on the interdependent, yet at this historical moment, still distinct realms of space and place.[71] The Boy's question about the difference between a blind man and someone who cannot see highlights a tension in the play between characters paralyzed and those enabled by their lack of vision. In the case of a "blind man," "blind" is an adjective, qualifying identity; the blind man's visual impairment is permanent, and he does not presume he will be able see in the near future. Alternatively, for "he that cannot see," the absence of vision is a verb, not a qualifier of identity; this man experiences blindness only temporarily. Whereas the blind man, whose visual impairment is part of his identity, accepts his blindness as a state of being and thus finds other ways to perceive the world, "he that cannot see" approaches blindness as an obstacle, a negative—seeing is something he "cannot" now do. Consider Phillip's description of the darkness as a mask that could simply be lifted off to expose what he describes as the beautiful, lighter sky. Instead of being compelled to engage his other senses more acutely, Phillip bemoans his temporary state and become paralyzed, as he anxiously waits for it to change: "shall I stand gaping here all night till day" (10.20). Like Phillip, Coomes and most of the other characters of the play cannot see what they are accustomed to seeing. Yet rather than compensate with their other senses or cognitive capacities, Phillip and these others simply wander around in the dark calling, "So ho, so ho!" in hopes of being located by others.

By contrast, Mall and Hodge maneuver through the darkness like blind men, accepting their inability to see and, with less of the tragic horror of *Lear's* blinded Gloucester, discovering the surprising pleasures and powers of being unlocatable figures who can perceive and navigate space through nonvisual means. Mall's relative comfort with movement in the dark might be read as a reaction to her having experienced a defeat earlier in the play when attempting to claim scopic dominance. When Francis, with Phillip, comes to woo her, Mall receives the suit from atop her balcony—the only character of the play to experience that presumably most privileged of perspectives, the bird's-eye view. The apparent superiority of her spatial position certainly coincides with social power at that particular moment; Francis and Phillip have to work hard to combat Mall's superior wit and convince her to agree to the marriage. But ultimately Mall agrees to accept Francis, signaling physically her drop in power when she agrees to descend from the balcony to the ground where the male characters stand. Phillip translates this physical and social descent into a sporting analogy: he says that his sister's maidenhead "must needs fall, /And, like a well-lured hawk, she knows her call" (8.141–42).

Perhaps it is because Mall has been the object of men's games and therein witnessed the false security of the bird's-eye view—which only turns her into a hawk that must obey her male trainer—that she looks for other ways to play. Indeed, Mall goes on to show how abandoning the fantasy of scopic dominance and instead becoming one of de Certeau's blind walkers offers unexpected forms of power. When, after being directed by Phillip to meet Francis in the coney green, she finds herself alone and submerged in darkness, she expresses affinity with the animals around her. She wonders why the rabbits "run more in the night than day," concluding that it is because the darkness helps to hide them from hunters who "many a hay [trap] do set / And laugh to see them tumble in the net" (9.11–15). This condemnation of men's hunting recurs in the play, with Raphe's lady similarly condemning the sport for its cruelty. Mall's condemnation is far more trenchant, though. When she describes hunting as structured by a patriarchal scopic regime, she not only bemoans her plight, but demonstrates a strategy for escaping it: those subjected to the dominating gaze of others may undermine their spectators by remaining in the dark.

To be sure, such darkness renders Mall and the coneys blind, but that blindness is less troubling to them than to those who wish to locate and place them. And Mall recognizes that it would be better to stay in the dark herself than be preyed upon by either the warrener who controls this space or even by a predatory Francis: "How if the warrener should spy me here? / He would take me for a coney, I dare swear. / But when that Francis comes, what will he say? / 'Look, boy, there lies a coney in my way'" (9.22–25). Indeed, Francis envisions his pursuit of Mall as a coney hunt. Later, as he and his boy vainly search for Mall, the boy declares, "I have not seen a coney since I came" (9.70), and Francis later complains, "I have run through the briers for a wench, / And yet I have her not" (10.52–53). Francis is not the only character hunting Mall. Mall is prey for her mother, too, who is just as invested in controlling Mall's sexuality as are Mall's father, brother, and Francis. "I have searched in many a bush," Mistress Barnes complains, while her daughter Mall mocks, "Belike my mother took me for a thrush" (9.30–31). Unlike the characters so invested in scopic dominance and emplacement, Mall finds comfort and even pleasure in the dark. Like a coney, she seeks out a hiding place to "scape her [mother's] light" (9.43). Rather than being terrified by the darkness, Mall refigures the hunt as a children's game. As her mother tries desperately to find her, Mall begins to "play bo-peep with her behind this tree" (9.28), then switching from peekaboo to a game of chase. Mistress Barnes tells Mall to stand still, but Mall replies, "No, you would catch me, mother" (9.52) and so "I'll try how you can run" (9.56). Unconcerned that she has become the game to be hunted, Mall imagines herself as taking part in a hunting game where darkness is the prey's best defense.

Like Mall, Hodge conceives of the darkness as a space of risky and pleasurable play. Whereas Phillip complains that the ordinarily serious game of wooing has been turned into this game of blindman's bluff—"Call ye this wooing? No, 'tis Christmas sport / Of Hobman-blind. All blind, all seek to catch, / All miss" (11.323–5)—Hodge purposefully requests to play this very game, asking Master Goursey to "give me leave to play at blindman-buff with my mistress" (8.446) so that he may confound her pursuit of Francis. In the traditional game of blindman's bluff (or buff) or "Hobman-blind," usually played by children, one participant wears a hood over his or her face and is unable to see; the others scatter about, call out, and in some cases buffet the blinded player, who attempts to catch them. It is a version of this game that Hodge reenacts when he discovers Mistress Barnes. Pretending to be Coomes, he "led [Mistress Barnes] such a dance in the dark as it passes. 'Here she is,' quoth I. 'Where?' quoth she. 'Here,' quoth I" (11.24–25). Hodge is not in any way troubled by the darkness that is such a problem for the others, in part because he pursues the possibilities of play in every social interaction and is flexible about ludic rules and form: though he has planned to play blindman's bluff with Mistress Goursey, when he comes upon Mistress Barnes, he quickly recognizes how her blindness can be reframed as part of his game as well.

Like famous chess players and some videogamers who up the ante by playing blindfolded, Hodge doesn't rely on his eyes but uses all his senses and cognitive capabilities to play.[72] Indeed, he has uncanny aural and tactile perception, knowing through hearing just whose voice belongs to whom and using touch to navigate the dark with seeming ease. Unlike Coomes, who falls into a ditch because he cannot see, Hodge relishes his blind state and relies on touch to pursue Coomes so that he can "play the knave with him": "I will grope in the dark for him, or I'll poke with my staff like a blind man, to prevent a ditch" (11.31–33). Hodge treats his environ-ment less like an obstacle than an intimate partner in the game: "O, what a soft-natured thing the dirt is. How it would endure my hard treading and kiss my feet for acquaintance, and how courteous and mannerly were the clods, to make me stumble only of purpose to entreat me lie down and rest me" (11.26–30). Hodge further commissions the darkness for his pranks when he devises the "fine sport" of taking away the torches of Coomes and another servant, Nicholas, so as to "leave them to fight darkling" (11.196; 198). Like Puck's games in Shakespeare's *A Midsummer Night's Dream*, Hodge's tricks are on one level simply mischief, but they also work to un-dermine Coomes's hypermasculine posturing and its link to scopic domi-nance. Having boasted of the damage he will do to the Barnes's servant, Nicholas, Coomes declares, "thou are not so good a man as I" and chal-lenges Nicholas, "I hope thou wilt say I am a man?" (11.223; 226). Yet when Hodge steals his torch, Coomes proves to be the most pathetic of cowards. He not only gives up the fight, but lies down on the ground for fear that "the rogue might hurt me; for I cannot see to save it, and I'll hold my peace, lest my voice should bring him where I am" (11.232–34). Coomes has all the more reason to worry since Nicholas, like Hodge, imagines himself as a blind man aligned with the darkness; in response to Coomes's bragging, Nicholas warns, "What, man, ne'er crow so fast, for a blind man may kill a hare" (11.169–70).

In keeping with its comedic form, *Two Angry Women* ultimately returns Hodge to his place in the social order. So it follows for Mall, who in the end is married off to Francis. Indeed, the play repeatedly represents wooing as a game that women ultimately must lose. Phillip uses gaming imagery to describe Mall's marriage as a fait accompli: "my sister's maidenhead / Stands like a game at tennis: if the ball / Hit into the hole or hazard, fare well all" (3.327–29).[73] Yet although Mall participates formally in the come-dic closure of the play, she also surreptitiously disrupts it through ludic practice. After all the characters have sutured their broken social bonds and Phillip has bestowed upon the young couple the patriarch's wish that "the next thing now you do is for a son" (13.296), the highest-ranking patriarch onstage, Sir Raphe, invites the reconciled parties to his home for a great banquet. Just as Sir Raphe begins to unveil his generosity, Mall interrupts.

PHILLIP: I pray, Sir Raphe, what cheer shall we have?
SIR RAPHE: I'faith, country fare, mutton and veal,
   Perchance a duck or goose.
MALL: O, I am sick!

ALL: How now, Mall, what's the matter?
MALL: Father and Mother, if you needs would know,
   He named a goose, which is my stomach's foe. (13.319–21)

The dish of roasted goose quickly transforms in Mall's subsequent witty speech, the last of the play, into a metaphor for playgoers' displeasure, for the goose's characteristic hiss reminds Mall of the hiss playgoers give when critical of a theatrical production. Mall's speech functions like an epilogue. She directs her comments to theater spectators, particularly "gentlemen," asking for their applause instead of their criticism, which she equates to the aggressive hiss of the goose:

> The *Rosa solis* [a liquor] yet that makes me live
> Is favor that these gentlemen may give;
> But if they be displeased, then pleased am I
> To yield myself, a hissing death to die.
> Yet I hope here's none consents to kill,
> But kindly take the favor of good will. (13.348–53)

That Mall should speak the play's quasi-epilogue is a further indication of her agency in *Two Angry Women*, especially when we consider that Shakespeare's self-assured and cross-dressed heroine Rosalind from *As You Like It* is often believed to be the sole female character in early modern drama to be given this privileged theatrical role. Mall shares Rosalind's erotic expressiveness throughout the play, including in her quasi-epilogue, which is targeted to the gentlemen playgoers who here have the power to "kill" her with a hiss if she and her betrothed "should kiss" (13.337).

Given that there are plenty of animals known to produce a hiss, the association of critical theatergoers with the goose—an association that persists at least into the nineteenth century—is worth further thought.[74] What cultural and literary meaning did geese have in the early modern period? One of the earliest literary references to the goose appears in John Lydgate's "The Debate of the Horse, Goose, and Sheep," where the three animals compete for superiority. The poem argues, as is conventional for this genre of poetry, that although the horse would seem to be obviously superior to the other more common, less noble creatures, all three have their places and unique attributes. None is innately better than the others—just different. The antihierarchical message of the poem is elaborated in the author's choric explication of the moral, that "No man shuld of hih nor lowe degre / For no perogatiff his neihbore despise."[75] The goose remains a symbol of social equality in the early modern period as evinced by John Taylor's paean to the bird, *Taylor's Goose* (1621). Taylor repeats all of Lydgate's points of praise for the goose: its usefulness for food, medicine, bedding, war (arrows made with feathers), and writing (goose quills). And like Lydgate, Taylor cites the famous episode from Roman history where a goose saved Rome when its gaggle woke the soldiers in time to defend their city from a Gallic attack.[76] For early modern audiences, then, geese were surprising resources, underscoring the degree to which the common and unremarkable have their place in what both authors call a "profitable" society. Indeed, in Taylor's poem, the good fortune associated with geese allows for social and economic mobility. Taylor describes a town in Lincolnshire that is turned over entirely to the raising geese. "Dignity" in this town is correlated with a man's capacity to "encrease and multiply" his geese and as they "breed, / From Office unto office they [the men] proceed" from Tythingman to Headborough to Constable.[77]

The goose's association with social mobility and financial profit can perhaps best be appreciated by the bird's starring role in one of history's most popular board games, "The Royal Game of the Goose," first registered in England just a year before *Two Angry Women* was first performed and becoming so popular across Europe that the Bibliothèque Nationale in Paris has more than six hundred and fifty versions of the game.[78] The game's affinities with backgammon make it a particularly interesting place to end my reading of *Two Angry Women*. Like backgammon, Game of the Goose challenges players to move their men across space in the face of chance and aggressive opponents. The board almost always depicts a spiral with sixty-three marked spaces (Figure 19). After putting a monetary stake in the pot, players take turns casting the dice, moving their men the number of spaces cast and performing penalties (e.g., adding stakes; being sent back to an earlier space) or receiving rewards (e.g., winning stakes; advancing forward) indicated on the space on which they land. Similar to backgammon, if another player's man lands on one's spot, one has to remove one's man, placing it in this case in the space from whence one's opponent came. The goose represents prosperity in this game, for players who land on a spot marked with a goose are able to travel further on the board the number of spaces they came when they arrived there. Since the aim of the game is to get one's man to the final space called, as in backgammon, "home," the goose represents the advancement equally available to anyone who plays.

Game of the Goose is significant in gaming history because it appears to have inaugurated a tradition of themed board games, many of which invite players to imagine movement on the board as analogous to movement through real-world places. Thus, the game was an important marker in the development of narrative in gaming, the most well-known of examples today being *Monopoly* but the culmination being videogames, where part of the pleasure of play, many would argue, comes from the players' engagement in a fictional world.[79] Initial versions of Game of the Goose conjure mundane narratives, inviting players to do things they would do in their own lives: go to the alehouse for a drink, travel across a bridge, visit a well. Later versions of the game dramatize more elaborate scenarios. *Filosofia cortesana de Alonso de Barros* (Italian, 1588) depicts a shipping scene, with sea monsters, fisherman, and boats in the central home space (Figure 20). Later in the seventeenth century, the connection between these sorts of themed board games and mapping becomes more explicit. In *Le Jeu des nations principales* (Paris, 1662), each of the spaces that form the spiral of the board is a chorographic account of a nation in one part of the world; the player is a traveler who casts the dice to move progressively from the Americas to Africa to Asia and finally to Europe, landing at last in, of course, France.[80] But Game of the Goose, like its avian namesake, ultimately levels sociogeographic distinctions. Although the board's grid imposes a geographical hierarchy, with the natives of the Americas inferior to the Europeans, and the English inferior to the French, gameplay would have undermined this sequence; for like the traditional Game of the Goose, movement was not guaranteed to be linear, thereby troubling in practice any sense of progress. Game of the Goose and its descendants thus underscore what I have argued to be the case in other board games such as backgammon: the rules and game board discipline space, but the practice of gameplay necessarily creates new spatial and even social relationships.

Regardless of whether playgoers would have heard resonances of Game of the Goose in Mall's epilogue, it is significant that a character who, like Hodge, has engaged in witty gameplay throughout the drama turns to an elaborate goose metaphor when she plays what becomes a final game with the audience. Like other epilogue speakers, Mall anticipates criticism of the play in order to combat it. More specifically, she underscores in order to redirect the audience's responses to the play: she grants the audience the surprising power associated with the goose while asking them to refrain from characteristic hissing, which she translates into a misuse of their theatrical power. Perhaps most notably for my purposes, Mall's association of the audience with the socially leveling figure of the goose underscores the play's larger critique of scopic dominance, extending that critique to the theater's socially and economically privileged male patrons, "these gentlemen"—many of whom, as I have argued, were encouraged by the amphitheater architecture and pricing structure to choose viewing positions that announced their superiority.

Two Angry Women questions such assumptions, dramatizing the instability and lack of dependability of the visual regime, a problem for characters that rely on vision to shore up or pursue patriarchal masculinity. The drama also demonstrates the advantages to those like Mall and Hodge for whom blind navigations of space are a site of play, an exercise of *"Spielraum"* on de Certeau's checkerboard. Mall's epilogue extends these ideas to playgoers, offering "these gentlemen" especially a chance to reconsider the nature of their relationship to the stage and its actors. Will they engage all their sensory faculties and let themselves be lost in (the) play? Or will they retreat to their abstracted positions of supposed scopic dominance and simply hiss at what they don't like or understand? To do the latter, according to *Two Angry Women*, as well as *Arden*, renders audiences incapable of effectively playing the play.

THEATERGOERS ON THE BOARDS AND VICARIOUS PLAY

If, as I have suggested, the experience of gameplay is something like the experience of theatergoing, then what are the implications for our understanding of the relationship between playgoers and actors/action on the boards? To answer this question, it is useful to invoke the work of contemporary theorists and designers of games because some studies of interactivity in video gaming account for the multisensory and embodied aspects of gameplay. In theorizing the relationship between a gamer and the game being played, Alexander R. Galloway argues that games are not texts to be read but actions: "they exist when enacted" by players. The concept of interaction is, for Galloway, even insufficient for theorizing this relationship, for players do not simply bring an interpretation to a game; their engagement with the game brings interpretations into being, and the game "restructures itself" in response to the player's participation.[81] Digital artists and theorists Simon Penny and Diana Gromala emphasize the central role of the player's body in the enactment of a game. Penny writes, "the persuasiveness of interactivity is not in the images per se, but in the fact that bodily behavior is intertwined with the formation of representations."[82] And Gromala treats gameplay as an experience of "sensory immersion."[83] Colin Milburn has gone on to demonstrate the ways that players not only produce the game but are produced by it, their physical bodies and real worlds transformed by the virtual worlds in which they play.[84]

These ideas lead directly to an understanding of theater as playable media, though game and theater scholars have not considered theater to be so aligned with games. In fact, many game scholars and designers maintain that embodied interaction is precisely what *distinguishes* videogames from theatrical plays, particularly the plays performed in premodern theaters.[85] A key reason they discount theater is because their conception of it has been shaped by the seminal work of Brenda Laurel, who uses Aristotle's *Poetics* to support her contention that in theater, as in human–computer interfaces, a barrier exists between player and game. Subsequent game scholars and designers have been right to question Laurel, but in discounting theater as a model for the more interactive form of gameplay they describe, these theorists throw out the baby with the bathwater. Laurel's conception of the game–theater link is limited only by her presumption that theater is always illusionist. She writes, "the magic is created by both people and machines, but who, what, and where they are *do not matter* to the audience. . . . [W]hen a play is 'working,' audience members are simply not aware of the technical aspects at all." What is true for theatergoers is true for computer users, she maintains. If either group is brought into the action of the game/play, there can be only chaos.[86]

However, the kind of embodied interactivity many videogame theorists attempt to define is very much part of live theatrical performance, even the theater of Shakespeare and contemporaneous dramatists. To recognize theater as playable media, we need to extend our definition of embodiment and of embodied interactivity. Research in cognitive science suggests such an expansive definition, and some have begun to examine the significance of that research for theater spectatorship.[87] Literary scholar Bruce R. Smith contends that staged physical aggression may be viscerally *felt* by playgoers because of a phenomenon that modern cognitive scientists call "proprioceptive drift"—a phenomenon, I would add, that has been vital to the development of videogame peripherals. In laboratory experiments subjects invited to identify with a projection of their bodies could feel sensations in their own bodies when their virtual selves were stimulated. While the dominance of vision is primarily responsible for cuing this phenomenon, these experiments demonstrate the ways vision and touch are deeply integrated. Well before modern science claimed to have proven the existence and means for this sensory integration, early modern writers described it in their concept of the "common sense," a synesthetic merging of multiple senses.[88] Because of the ways early moderns thought about the senses, their theater was especially well positioned to show how playgoers' bodies could participate vicariously in the action on the "boards." Hundreds of years before videogames appeared, theater demonstrated that vision works in partnership with the other senses during the act playgoing, which, I have suggested, is an act of play.

I have shown in this chapter that one of the ways the theater subordinates vision to a partnership instead of a dominating role in playgoers' experience is by denying it, not just to characters, but to playgoers, who are thereby encouraged to engage their "common sense," much as they would in gameplay. Staged backgammon scenes are useful sites for investigating this dynamic, because, unlike dark scenes that call upon the audience to *imagine* their blindness, staged backgammon scenes make it possible for interested playgoers to undergo something that resembles proprioceptive drift. To experience viscerally the dramatic tension of a staged game, playgoers must, like spectators of an actual game of backgammon, project themselves onto the bodies and minds of the game's players, imagining and reenacting cognitively what it is like to navigate space in the face of aggressive opponents and unpredictable chance. Vision cues that projection but does not work alone, for playing backgammon—in actuality or vicariously—involves many other senses: e.g., listening to table talk, touching or imagining the texture of the board's men and the dice. The backgammon scenes in *Arden* and *Two Angry Women* underscore the significance of these other senses by denying playgoers—as well as onstage spectators like Black Will and Masters Goursey and Barnes—visual access to the game board.

What was at stake in this denial for playgoers who had chosen and paid significantly more for seats with a bird's-eye view of the stage? If the design of amphitheaters enabled patrons in the upper galleries to avoid the spatial frustrations of interactive theatergoing (the smells, sounds, and touch of groundlings, for instance), they did so at an aesthetic cost, for spectators who chose the two-penny galleries in order to abstract themselves from the ludic action below were, in effect, prioritizing their desire for scopic dominance over the opportunity to play along. *Arden* and *Two Angry Women*, through their narratives and particularly through their staging of gameplay, question that choice, as they celebrate the disorienting experience of becoming lost in and part of (the) play.

But might this message about the pleasures of playing the play have fallen on deaf ears or, as it were, blind eyes? Some may argue that those who chose to sit in the galleries didn't need to derive pleasure from the play since they came to the theater to partake in other delights, like ogling other playgoers. The two-penny galleries were far better spots for this pastime. However, if the history of professional theater is any indication, patrons of means ultimately became convinced of flaws in the economic logic of the two-penny galleries. When the Blackfriars theater and other indoor venues began to be used for professional plays in the early seventeenth century, they abandoned the amphitheater's valuation of space. Seats with the bird's-eye view came to be used for the lowest-paying patrons; the most expensive seats were those closest to the stage. Indeed, the priciest placement for spectators was in the boxes that flanked or (more likely) were behind the stage[89] and on stools located on the stage itself.

Theater historians generally assume that men—and, apparently, it was only men, not women—who chose to sit right on the boards had little interest in the play, sacrificing good viewing positions in order to become spectacles themselves.[90] But if, as I've suggested, there is a certain pleasure and even power in de Certeau's "free play (*Spielraum*)" on the board, in becoming lost in a landscape, jostling sometimes blindly and aggressively with others as one navigates space, then patrons sitting on stools and in boxes had unparalleled opportunities to play the play. Becoming almost indistinguishable from actors, spectators could feel like part of (the) play, able, almost like board gamers, to manipulate the men on the board and influence the play's rules and form.

One story of theatergoer interaction in the indoor theaters helps illustrate the benefits and the risks of allowing spectators to inhabit the boards in this way. Records from a legal case describe an altercation on the Blackfriars theater stage between two patrons, Captain Essex, who was seated in a box behind the stage, and a nobleman, Lord Thurles, who had taken a seat on the stage itself:

> This Captaine attending and accompanying my Lady of Essex in a boxe in the playhouse at the blackfryers, the said lord [Thurles] coming upon the stage, stood before them and hindred their sight. Captain Essex told his lordship they had payd for their places as well as hee, and therefore intreated him not to deprive them of the benefitt of it. Whereupon the lord [Thurles] stood up yet higher and hindred more their sight. Then Capt. Essex with his hand putt him [Thurles] a little by. The lord [Thurles] then drewe his sword and ran full butt at him [Essex], though hee missed him.[91]

The story interests me for several reasons. One, it dramatizes spatial mastery as a competency of both theatergoing and patriarchal masculinity; like

Arden and *Two Angry Women,* the story uses the problematic of vision (in this case blocked sightlines) to render in material terms the scopic drive that de Certeau describes in his work on space and social relations. Lord Thurles was a newcomer to London, eager to establish his superiority to other men.[92] Like the social climbers in *Arden* and *Two Angry Women,* he does so by attempting to dominate the space around him, which we may notice not simply because of his choice to sit on the stage with the other upstarts but also because of his choice to stand up. Perhaps Thurles stood because there were no more stools available and he was waiting for one to be free.[93] Perhaps he intentionally tried to block the view of the patrons behind him, thereby asserting his social parity with or superiority to them. Equally possible, however, is that Thurles stood to get a better view of what was happening onstage. After all, seated on a stool, a playgoer would be positioned at or below the level of the actors on the stage, and his view could easily have been blocked by them or by stage furniture.

This leads to a second interesting aspect of this story: it demonstrates the degree to which onstage seating, despite its higher price tag, did not ensure patrons a better view of the action on the boards; Thurles might have had to *stand* to see better. Field of vision would have been slightly improved for those seated in boxes behind the stage, for these would have supplied a small degree of elevation. But these sightlines were easily blocked as well. Thomas Goffe in *The Careless Shepherdess* (c. 1618–29) describes a country gentleman following a courtier and a gallant whom he expects will ultimately move to a box to hide from creditors, even if this mars their view of the stage action:

> I'le follow them, though't be into a Box.
> Though they did sit thus open on the Stage
> To shew their Cloak and Sute, yet I did think
> At last they would take sanctuary 'mongst
> The Ladies, lest some Creditor should spy them.
> 'Tis better looking o're a Ladies head
> Or through a Lettice-window, then a grate.[94]

The boxes are described here as less preferable than sitting on the stage in part because one has to look "o're [over] a Ladies head," a viewing position that bears comparison with looking through a prison grate. As Captain Essex discovered, too, if just one stool patron stood up, the view of those in the boxes could be significantly hindered. Even seats close to the stage could not guarantee an unobstructed view and full visual access to the stage. Narrowly interpreted, de Certeau's conceptualization of the scopic drive of viewers atop a tall city building seems to have little in common with the unobstructed view sought here, but I am suggesting that Captain Essex and other playgoers' desires to see all stem from a similar fantasy that it is possible to dominate a space—and the people and things in it—by having unhindered visual access to that space. Like *Arden*'s murderers, Captain Essex learned the hard way that such fantasies are impossible to maintain. Instead of fighting for visual access, the captain, like Arden's murderers, might have been better served by trying, like de Certeau's urban walkers, to "see" with his feet.

Indeed, contrary to Captain Essex's implied presumption that his seats were worth the higher cost because they offered a better view, I would suggest that part of the value of seats on or almost on the stage was that they offered patrons a chance to "see" more with their feet than their eyes. From a position close to the stage action, playgoers could feel, and perhaps even be, part of the action on the "boards." Whereas the amphitheater's two-penny galleries made it possible for more economically privileged playgoers to avoid the aggression and chance that marked the navigation of space in the theater, seats on the stage or in the boxes at Blackfriars put playgoers more directly and intimately in contact with each other and with the stage action. The indoor theaters invited patrons to descend from their positions of abstract safety in the two-penny galleries and to take up more precarious spaces on or almost on the boards. To be sure, patrons on stools or in boxes were still consumers of the play; decorum and convention moderated the extent to which they interacted with the actors and objects on the stage. That said, their positions close to the ludic action could make them feel even more like players, with all the physical risks associated with that level of interaction.

To what extent and in what ways might these playgoers have been able to shape the action on the boards they came to occupy? This would have depended in part on how actors and other theatergoers responded to on-stage patrons. In the case of the altercation between Lord Thurles and Captain Essex, there is no reason to assume that the actors onstage stopped the play. Captain Essex reportedly had time to lodge a series of complaints and even to "with his hand putt [Thurles] a little by" before swords started to fly, suggesting that the play continued unabated for at least part of the time the men were verbally and physically interacting. Perhaps other theatergoers even believed the incident to be part of the play, an alternative plotline in which actors pretended to be playgoers.

This incident also demonstrates that turning spectators into players was risky business. It was one thing to invite spectators to play along from a distance, but when paying audiences could directly participate in the action on the boards, they could hamper the success of the production. As remains true today, direct participation can work in community-based theater, where audiences and actors share the same goals and know each other; but in commercial theater, where actors essentially work for spectators, the arrangement causes all sorts of problems. Francis Beaumont's play *Knight of the Burning Pestle*, performed by a company of child actors in the Blackfriars theater c. 1607, hilariously dramatizes these problems. As the Prologue begins the play, he is interrupted by two spectators (played by actors), a grocer and his wife, who complain that the comedy the company plans to stage isn't to their liking. Repeatedly reminding the actors that the paying customer is always right, they not only demand a different play but insist that their apprentice be given the main role in it. After apologizing profusely to the other spectators, the actors comply, and the new play, with the grocer's apprentice in the starring role, gets performed, alternating scenes with the originally planned comedy. The company is shown as complying partly out of fear of the grocer, who threatens repeatedly to beat the young actors, and partly because the actors discover how lucrative the arrangement can be. The grocer offers to pay for the changes he makes to the production, and the theater company milks the situation as thoroughly as they can, extracting more and more money from the pretend spectator as the play goes on. The resulting play is a fascinating theatrical and dramatic experiment, but utter chaos. What *Knight of the Burning Pestle* shows is that when paying audience members are allowed onto the stage to become players, they may put their own needs and interests ahead of the production. They create a play that pleases them. And even if their pleasure can be monetized to the benefit of the company, the resulting play may not please other consumers who have different needs and interests. Indeed, as much as scholars love *Knight of the Burning Pestle,* the play is rarely taught and has not been performed much since the early seventeenth century, when it is reported to have been a flop.

Knight of the Burning Pestle mocks the grocer and his wife for being unable to play vicariously and for insisting on the sort of direct participation that was impractical in a commercial context. The drama underscores the important difference between spectators *feeling* like players and actually becoming them. It also suggests that the new spatial arrangement of the indoor theaters failed to fix the problems with spectatorship that the amphitheaters faced. Bringing audience members closer and even onto the stage involved them more deeply in the production, allowing them to feel like players, but the risks were not necessarily worth the benefits. Rather than allowing theatergoers to play directly, the commercial theater needed to teach them how to play vicariously, how to appreciate the boards as a game board that others manipulated, while audiences played along from a distance. It is not surprising that later commercial theaters shortened the stage's apron and set the ludic action behind a proscenium arch, ultimately banishing spectators from the stage and reasserting the lines between audience and actor. By the time this happens, though, audiences, I'd argue, are ready for it, having learned how to *feel* like players without actually becoming them. The first amphitheaters were a working experiment in how to commercialize theater as playable media, and the dramas performed in these theaters reflected elegantly on the results.

Performative History and Dynastic Marriage

Of all the sitting pastimes discussed in this book, chess is the one that may have been most frequently and certainly was most famously dramatized in the early modern theater—surprising, since it would seem the most difficult to stage. A card game, as we saw in Chapter 2, is well suited to theatrical performance because it offers theater spectators a similar perspective on the ludic action as onstage players and spectators: all have only partial access to information. Theatricalized chess, by contrast, offers radically different information to those on the stage and off. Whereas onstage players and spectators have equal visual access to the board, theater audiences cannot view the details of the board at all and so, unlike spectators of a regular chess game, they cannot play vicariously in the ways spectators of a card game might. When dramas stage chess, they capitalize on its status as a game of perfect information to solicit and sometimes frustrate theater spectators' application of their knowledge of the game. Despite, or perhaps because of, these problems, chess works in complex ways as the setting for moments of revelation and concealment in dramatic literature. The game appears in at least eight plays written by well-known dramatists such as Chapman, Fletcher, Middleton, and Shakespeare, and it is often used to highlight plots of political maneuvering or intrigue. For instance, the pivotal scene in the plot of Middleton's *Women Beware Women*, the Duke's sexual assault of Bianca, is performed "above" in the theater's balcony while Bianca's unaware mother-in-law plays chess below with the Duke's procuress. In Ford's *Love's Sacrifice*, the besotted Fernando finally confesses his illicit feelings for his Bianca during a chess game with her, while her jealous sister-in-law secretly watches.[1]

We often think of chess as a game about political strategy because of its narrative content—the pieces on the board representing kings, queens, knights, and so on—and certainly the game has long been part of the training of rulers.[2] But theatrical stagings of chess reveal that its political content is conveyed less through the symbolism of its pieces than through the gameplay experience itself. In particular, I focus in this chapter on the temporal experience of chess play, which, I argue, can be politically seditious. Early modern staged chess scenes are exquisite sites for examining how the temporality of a chess game can stimulate the political imaginations of its players, actual and vicarious. My case studies are two dramas strongly associated with seventeenth-century English politics: Shakespeare's *The Tempest* and Middleton's *A Game at Chess*, the former being the most canonical early modern example of staged chess—one of the Bard's most well-known plays—and the latter the most elaborate. *A Game at Chess* turns the theater stage into a chessboard with each of the play's characters embodying a different chess piece: White Queen, Black Bishop, and so on.

It is in part because of their associations with Jacobean politics that *The Tempest* and *A Game at Chess* beg to be singled out among the many early modern plays that dramatize chess. Both plays have been read as integrally related to their historical moment and reflective, in particular, of King James I's political policies.[3] Taken as a pair, *The Tempest* and *A Game at Chess*, both performed by the playing company The King's Men about ten years apart, function as theatrical and historical bookends in King James I's decade-long use of dynastic marriage to solve his political problems abroad, effectively offering us, through drama, a direct meditation on this particular political policy. The connection between James's policy and *The Tempest* is evident partly at the level of narrative: the play is all about Prospero's attempt to arrange a dynastic marriage for his daughter, an arrangement revealed during the play's culminating chess game. The link to James is further evinced by the play's performance history: it was performed at court in 1613 in celebration of James's daughter Elizabeth's marriage to Frederick V, the Elector of Palatine.[4] That match was meant to shore up James's Protestant alliances abroad. *A Game at Chess* has links to another historically important dynastic union, one with complex ties to that of Princess Elizabeth. In the same year that *The Tempest* was performed in celebration of Elizabeth's marriage, England welcomed a new Spanish ambassador who would for the next decade advocate a Spanish Catholic union for Elizabeth's brother Charles—a match that James hoped would fix the turmoil that had ensued after his daughter's marriage. The fuller story is worth rehearsing briefly. In the early 1620s, Catholic Imperial forces had ousted Elizabeth's husband, Frederick, from his reign as king of Bohemia and deprived him of control over the Palatinate, sending Frederick and Elizabeth into exile. James hoped that by marrying his son Charles to the Spanish Infanta, he would generate the funds and alliances to restore power to his son-in-law. In 1623, a year before Middleton's play was performed, Charles's marriage negotiations began to fall apart, however, after Charles and the Duke of Buckingham pulled off a dramatic public relations stunt: after a secret visit to Spain presumably to negotiate the marriage terms, they returned to England without a Spanish bride and were received by the anti-Spanish, anti-Catholic English populace as heroes for fending off popish incursions into English sovereignty. A few months before Middleton's play was licensed, James I, under pressure from the English populace, nullified the marriage contract between Charles and the Spanish Infanta. Middleton's play—performed in sold-out theaters for nine days straight before being shut down by court officials—has long been interpreted as a commentary on these events, especially because it ends with the chess piece characters of the White Duke and White Knight (purportedly the Duke of Buckingham and Prince Charles, respectively) appearing to defect to the Black House only to emerge as heroes as they use deception to give "check mate by discovery" (5.3.174).[5]

With their barely disguised political commentary and the Jacobean court's investment in their performances, it is no wonder that *The Tempest* and *A Game at Chess* have been ripe for "topical" historicist analysis. Readers of these plays are, for good reasons, drawn to analyzing the plays in terms of their historical context, the assumption being that political events at a particular moment in time straightforwardly influence plays that were written at that same moment. My chapter puts pressure on that assumption by focusing closely on how chess functions as the setting for these dramatic narratives about dynastic marriage. Although I am interested in the intersections between early modern drama and politics, I maintain that the plays, through their staging of chess, raise questions about whether drama should be analyzed within a precise historicopolitical context. The plays instead encourage today's historians to experience time in the way chess players do: as moving in multiple directions at once—as *polytemporal*. My discussion below suggests that chess, more intensely than games of imperfect information like cards, is structured by a recursive rhythm: the game encourages players and their spectators to switch temporal frames constantly as they draw on the history of a match to project potential outcomes of a move. Whether or not conscious of this work, players and spectators of chess games become familiar at a deeply embodied level with time's recursivity.[6] The same was true when early modern spectators watched scenes of chess play in drama; though undoubtedly aware that a staged chess game was a theatrical construct, spectators— familiar with the game from having played or bet on matches in taverns and parlors[7]—could experience a staged game much as they would a game watched elsewhere. As *The Tempest* and *A Game at Chess* invited spectators to play chess vicariously, to feel *as if* they were playing the games onstage, so, too, they invite modern historians to play differently with the past, arriving at a less linear sense of history.

I am suggesting, then, that drama offers us insight into the history of gameplay but also into how to go about *producing* a history of gameplay. Drama, in other words, is both my object of study and the inspiration for my method of analysis. In this chapter, as throughout this book, I argue that gamification enabled the early modern commercial stage to compete with more overtly interactive forms of entertainment, such as blood sports and festive games. Staged games provide particularly intriguing material examples of the gaming structures at the heart of the commercial theater enterprise. I have also suggested that the mechanisms of and the ideological effects of these gaming structures can be appreciated especially well by the critic who can draw on her own embodied knowledge of gameplay to access and reenact game scenes.[8] As such, the bodies of researchers should be more explicitly implicated in producing archival knowledge about the playable media of the past. The historian is a spectator of the past—not the kind of spectator who sits back and receives, but the vicariously playing spectator I have theorized throughout this book. Lacking total authority or total knowledge, the historian-spectator cannot be certain about what game and theater participants in the past knew or didn't know. Instead, like the spectator envisioned by avant-garde playwright Bertolt Brecht, the historian-spectator is produced in dialogue with her objects of study.[9]

It may be no coincidence that Brecht, who thought about the spectator as an historian, played chess on many occasions with philosopher Walter Benjamin, whose famous essay "On the Concept of History" begins with a story about cheating at chess. Through this story, Benjamin sets up his influential critique of the way history is conventionally told—as a linear story of progress—and offers an alternative narrative of time and, consequently, revolutionary ideas about political power. In what follows, I draw on Benjamin's and Brecht's descriptions of chess's temporality to explore how *The Tempest* and *A Game at Chess* dramatize the game. I suggest that the plays use the spectacle of cheating at chess as a way of critiquing the Jacobean state, and particularly its narrative of dynastic marriage, which was undergirded by a conventional, linear view of history. Staged chess mobilizes theatergoers to query the Jacobean state's view of dynastic marriage by engaging them in a more polytemporal experience of time. Through staged chess, theater spectators honed their skills not only in interpreting political history, but in consuming commercial theater—which, we shall see, is defined by the same polytemporal rhythm that characterizes chess play.

THE TEMPORALITY OF CHESS IN BENJAMIN AND *THE TEMPEST*

Cheating is at the center of both Shakespeare's and Middleton's stagings of chess. In the case of *The Tempest*, when Prospero draws aside the curtain to show Miranda and her betrothed playing chess, the audience witnesses only the moment in the game when Miranda accuses Ferdinand of foul play. *A Game at Chess* also ends with allegations of cheating, as the White Duke's checkmate strategy involves pretending to be "an arch-dissembler" (5.3.145) to trick the Black House into confessing their own dishonesty. To understand what is at stake for temporality, historiography, and politics in these allegations of foul play, it is useful to turn briefly to Walter Benjamin's treatment of chess in his essay "On the Concept of History." The essay opens with a story of an eighteenth-century chess automaton, a puppet in Turkish dress, that won every game played against it, though it was discovered forty years and many games later that the puppet was, in fact, operated by a "dwarf" chess master hidden in a cabinet beneath the board. Benjamin allegorizes the puppet as historical materialism and the hidden chess master as "theology," historical materialism's secret weapon, which pulls its strings, allowing it to "win all the time."[10] I want to think about the opening of Benjamin's famous essay not to offer a novel or even very detailed analysis of Benjaminian historiography—an endeavor that can and has been done more effectively by philosophers and historians dedicated to that particular task—but because Benjamin's story about chess opens up for me, as it does for him, a way of thinking about the temporality and the politics of cheating. When Benjamin figures the hidden chess master as pulling the strings of historical materialism, he sanctions cheating as a way to defeat the reigning victors of history (i.e., Fascists and Social Democrats), who, he argues, adopt a rhetoric of historical progress to maintain their power. According to Benjamin, this rhetoric, articulated by some historians and politicians alike, presumes that time moves in one direction toward inevitable improvement, thereby enabling history's victors to silence the stories of, and secure continued power over, others: "*even the dead* will not be safe from the enemy if he is victorious. And this enemy has never ceased to be victorious" (391). The only way to defeat such an indefatigable opponent, Benjamin argues, is to covertly allow "theology" to drive one's actions, violating the unfair rules of the game so that historical materialism will win it. What Benjamin means by theology might best be understood through his concept of "redemption," a future state of happiness to be achieved, paradoxically, by disrupting the fluid temporality of progress. Counterintuitively, Benjamin argues for the value of taking action toward that future during moments of stillness. He maintains that revolutionary classes at the moment of action are marked by an "awareness that they are about to make the continuum of history explode" (395); thus a proper historical materialist must hold to a view of the present as not a time of transition but a time "in which time takes a stand [einsteht] and has come to a standstill" (396).

Although Benjamin's essay does not expand on the chess analogy, an understanding of what it feels like to play chess helps explain Benjamin's and, more important for my purposes, Shakespeare's and Middleton's investments in chess as a material analogy for an alternative approach to history. Chess encourages its players and invested spectators to switch among multiple temporal frames, holding the future and past in tension as they contemplate a move in the present. This competency, though part of many games, is especially essential in chess because of its status as a game of perfect information. Although a specific chess match may be affected by factors beyond players' control (i.e., a player is having a bad day and so fails to notice an available move), the formal setup of the game is meant to ensure to the greatest extent possible that both players have the same basic facts about the game during every moment of play.[11] A comparison with cards elucidates the issues at stake for players and spectators of chess. As discussed in Chapter 2, cards, being two-sided, are designed for use in games where information is at times hidden and then divulged strategically during the course of play. Thus, card games provoke participants to develop their interpretive skills so that they can figure out hidden information and use it effectively before other participants do. Chess relies on, encourages, and teaches mastery in a different set of competencies. To be sure, there are unknowns in chess: each player works to figure out the opponent's overall strategy, which the opponent tries to keep secret for as long as possible. But because the objects of chess play (board and pieces) can be seen at all times equally by both players, as well as by spectators, there is nothing internal to the game that prevents a player from discovering and undermining the opponent's broader strategy. Because of its formal structure, chess has long been seen as a game of skill at which anyone practiced enough may flourish. In John Florio's *Second Frutes* (1591), one of the characters describes losing at chess as more shameful than losing at cards:

> In Chess-play . . . all is unskilfulnes, and carelesnes of him that looseth and providence and attentivenes of him that is the winner; so when a man is overcaught in a matter within his own power, wherein he cannot pretend any excuse or hindrance, but his owne ignorance, he cannot choose but be ashamed.[12]

As a game of perfect information, chess rewards players who have "attentiveness" and "providence": careful focus on what has happened thus far in the match combined with keen analysis of the repercussions of potential moves. These skills, entirely "within [the player's] own power," facilitate victory.

It is not just the temporal unfolding of a particular match that matters in chess; as participants assess the consequences of a move, they may also draw on memories of prior games played, watched, or read about. The relation of such memories to players' decisions in the present is so elemental and virtually peculiar to chess that the game has been at the center of cognitive research on memory and decision-making.[13] Regardless of whether we buy into the empirical methodologies of this research, its terms for theorizing the temporality of chess are worth noting in light of Benjamin's and early modern dramatists' treatments of the game. Some researchers of chess and cognition maintain that when chess masters contemplate a move, they do not methodically rehearse a series of scenarios that would follow from each possible choice; this would take far too long. Instead, they filter the information on the board through recollections of prior games—whether played, watched, or read about—which have been stored in players' minds as memory modules.[14] It is as if at each moment of the game, proficient chess players take a mental photograph of the board's configuration and unconsciously check this against images of prior play scenarios. Chess masters, many studies maintain, are not any smarter than the rest of us; they simply have stored up more memories through more frequent exposure to the game. The past shapes the present and future of a match, but it does not limit that future, since no matter how many memory modules players have stored, they cannot anticipate every eventuality.[15] Although each moment of the game bears traces of prior moments (within this and in relation to other matches), even the best of players cannot be sure of victory, for every time the pieces on the board change positions, that future is reshaped. So unpredictable is chess that mastering its algorithm has been and remains a holy grail of contemporary artificial intelligence (AI) researchers.[16] The dream of a modern-day chess automaton, a computer that can repeatedly and consistently play chess as well as a grand master, remains unfulfilled, because the full scope of the chess experience is ultimately too complex to replicate. Chess participants, even as early learners, excel at the game if they are able to perform this complicated and creative temporal juggling, projecting possible futures by looking to a/the game's continually unfolding history.

Crucially, this balancing of past and future happens in the moment between the move of one player and the move of the other. This moment is charged in any turn-taking game, but is particularly significant in a game of perfect information because the status of the game—the information that players have—depends *only* on what a player chooses to do after this pause. Once a move is made on the board, the information both players have changes: new algorithms for victory are produced, new strategies formulated, and the past of the game is brought into new relief. Perhaps this might explain on some level Benjamin's use of chess to introduce an essay on his concept of "now-time" (395), the pregnant pause of history, for in a chess game the pause between each move is full of potential for bringing about a redemptive future that will, in turn, create new understandings of the past.

Given how central cheating is to Benjamin's and early modern dramatists' representations of chess, it is useful to explore why the pause in chess play is instrumental in cheating. Here, a *phenomenological* approach (attending to the embodied, lived experiences of chess play and chess spectatorship) offers insights that a more traditional literary approach (focusing on chess primarily as a metaphor or abstract representation) can miss. Although the history of chess is full of stories of cheating, the diceless form of the game played in the early modern period—the same version played by the chess automaton in Benjamin's account and by most players today—is, in practice, exceedingly difficult to rig. Players can cheat at games of imperfect information like cards or backgammon without being easily detected because they can convert unknown into known variables by doctoring the objects of play before the game begins. For instance, a backgammon player who needs to roll a certain number at a particular moment can use loaded dice or a false dice cup. And, as I point out in my discussion in Chapter 2 of the card game in *A Woman Killed with Kindness*, cards can be marked and placed strategically in the deck so as to advantage a player at just the right time. In effect, participants in games of imperfect information like cards and backgammon cheat by exploiting the disparities in knowledge that structure these games. Since in chess there is no formal difference in participants' knowledge, cheating requires very different approaches. One way to cheat is by colluding with someone else (a spectator, one's opponent, or some other external source, such as a reference book of chess strategies), as was done by the famous chess automaton Benjamin describes. Other ways of cheating can conceivably be obvious to anyone who is paying close attention to the match: for instance, reintroducing a piece that had been captured or disobeying the rules that govern the movement of pieces. These techniques of foul play help explain the development of the *touch-move rule*—where a piece that is touched must be played if there is a legal move it can make. As Cotton explains it: "What man or Piece soever of your own you touch or lift . . . you must play it for that draught if you can."[17] The rule, still used today, helps counter any sleight-of-hand techniques by which a player might cheat through mishandling pieces on the board during a turn.

The presence of the rule highlights the degree to which cheating at chess relies on players' bodily interaction with gaming objects *during* the match itself. Although a chess player may intend on cheating well before the game begins, the actual cheating can occur and be caught only when it is the player's turn to interact with the board, that is, during the pause between the completion of the opponent's move and the enactment of the player's own.[18] It is no wonder that chess rules attend so carefully to what happens during this window of time, which, in some versions of chess, is even regulated by a clock.[19] Since at least the sixteenth century, chess rules establish that players can formally raise accusations of cheating only during the pause between moves. As one early modern writer explains, "If your adversary play a false draught, and you spy it not before you play the next draught, tis then too late to challenge him."[20] Cheating is somewhat easier to detect today because of the evolution of video recording technology, which allows one not only to replay the action, but to slow down the interval between moves.[21] By interfering in the organic temporality of the game, video technology helps underscore that cheating at chess is, in effect, a way of exploiting the pause that is structurally necessary in any turn-taking game, but that is particularly replete with possibility in a game of perfect information.

Cheating is not simply an ethical violation, then; it and, indeed, debates about it are acts with the power to change or, as Benjamin would say, to revolutionize historical processes. Game studies scholarship on cheating has suggested something similar in demonstrating how new forms of a game emerge out of creative efforts to rethink and challenge its rules.[22] Recall the discussion in Chapter 2 of "griefers," who theatrically break the rules of online games.[23] Griefers call attention, by refusing to conform, to the frame of the game. And as they interfere in the game-as-played in order to spur discussion about its rules, griefers perform what anthropologist Gregory Bateson, in his groundbreaking study of play, describes as a meta-communicative act with transformational possibilities.[24] That is, griefers cheat in order to raise awareness of how a game is being played by others, and their commentary on gameplay has the potential to change it, as well as to reflect on its social and political implications.

The Tempest makes room for this potential when, as Prospero draws aside a curtain to display Miranda and Ferdinand playing chess, the former is found to be accusing the latter of cheating.

Here Prospero discovers Ferdinand and Miranda, playing at Chess

MIRANDA: Sweet lord, you play me false.
FERDINAND: No, my dearest love,
  I would not for the world.
MIRANDA: Yes, for a score of Kingdoms you should wrangle,
  And I would call it fair play.[25]

In openly raising the specter of cheating, Miranda essentially acts the part of griefer to Prospero's game, pausing play—and pausing *the* play—to question, and possibly change, the game rules. Specifically, when she halts the chess game with her accusation of foul play, she interrupts the steady march of Prospero's plot to marry her to Ferdinand and, thus, Miranda opens up a space and a time for theater spectators to rethink Prospero's conception of dynastic marriage as inevitable historical progress.[26]

In his pursuit of not only revenge, but a long-delayed and future-oriented form of political reconstitution, Prospero in many ways resembles the historians Benjamin critiques. Others have observed the ways Prospero narrates the past in order to impose his own view on the present and thus shape the future. His most powerful and troubling weapons are his attempts to master time and to control history by framing his unethical actions in the present—from the subjugation of Caliban and Ariel to the emotional and physical manipulations of the ship's passengers—as natural evolutions of past injustices. Prospero represents himself to Miranda and theater spectators as a victim of history (of Antonio and Alonso's past mistreatment of him), but he is, in truth, more victor than victim.[27] Like the victors of history Benjamin describes, Prospero tells the stories of those he has oppressed (Caliban, Ariel, and Miranda) in his own language so as to suit his own triumphal narrative. For Prospero, history is a totality, where the past's injustices legitimate his actions of the present, which will lead to a future victory. The telos or inevitable end point of this narrative is Miranda's marriage to Ferdinand and, thus, the installation of Prospero's heir (the issue of that marriage) as a leader of Milan *and* Naples. In other words, Prospero's reconciliation plot is designed not simply to right past wrongs and return to the political state/State that existed before Prospero was ousted; it is a bid for progression beyond that state/State.[28] Through this auspicious match, Prospero hopes to control the future of Europe even from beyond the grave.[29] The chess game between Miranda and Ferdinand is a seemingly perfect image of this progression, perhaps because of the game's symbolic cachet for representing both good governance and romantic love,[30] the key variables Prospero manipulates in his plot to convince Miranda and Ferdinand that their dynastic marriage is actually a match of their own choosing.[31] But the play complicates this historical narrative and its heady determinism by revealing Prospero's crowning achievement through a moment of imperfection, a moment where the strict rules and logical progression of a chess game are overturned by Prospero's own pawns.

The scene's intriguing staging raises the stakes of Miranda's accusation of cheating. Members of the theater audience witness only the moment in the game where her allegation is leveled and debated. Even after the curtain is pulled aside to "discover" the match in progress, much would have remained unknown to the play's early modern audiences since the game board must have been placed in the alcove of the theater's hidden "discovery space,"[32] thereby denying spectators (even those that paid more for a stage stool at the Blackfriars or a balcony seat at the Globe) the bird's-eye view of the board granted to Miranda and Ferdinand. This limited perspective of the game must have been unfamiliar and perhaps uncomfortable for theatergoers familiar with chess. Chess was a spectator sport in early modern taverns and parlors, as is the case today in some cultures and venues where chess is played. As discussed in Chapter 1, in the early modern period new rules that made for faster matches encouraged a culture of betting on chess games. And since spectators often had a monetary stake in the outcome of a match, they were used to watching the board closely. Chess lends itself especially well to this sort of vicarious play because spectators have the same information as the players on whom they bet.

When staged in early modern commercial theaters, however, chess became for spectators a game of imperfect, not perfect, information, since spectators were positioned so far away from the board that they could not hope to follow its action in the ways to which they were accustomed. Had this been a staged card match, the audience's experience of it would resemble that of card games watched and bet on in any range of venues, within and outside the theater. For, as discussed in Chapter 2, wherever they are played, cards are games of imperfect information for players and spectators alike.[33] *The Tempest*'s enactment of chess draws attention to the fact that the scene divides onstage gamers from theater spectators. Spectators were theatrically prevented from exercising the chess-playing competencies they may have developed from playing or watching in other contexts. Although audiences then, like scholars today, may have been invested in ascertaining whether Ferdinand is playing honestly, what matters here is not whether Ferdinand cheats but that the play withholds an answer to that question.

By staging only the pause after the alleged cheating has taken place and by hiding the board inside a curtained-off alcove, the play explicitly renders this information unknowable not just to theater audiences but to all onstage spectators of the game, including Prospero. In effect, the scene produces a cognitive tension for on- and offstage spectators between the game of perfect information they ought to experience and the game of imperfect information provided. And as such, it underscores through the *phenomenology* of gaming a logical flaw in Prospero's political plots. Throughout *The Tempest*, Prospero's character plays something like a game of imperfect information with theater spectators and with inhabitants of and visitors to the island, restricting their access to information: for example, Prospero hides Ferdinand from his father; Ferdinand's true identity from Miranda; his own interest in the marriage of Miranda and Ferdinand from the couple; and the full scope of his plots from theater spectators. No one, not even his spritely assistant Ariel, is made fully privy to all details of Prospero's plots. Prospero presents this monopoly on information as a way to ensure victory. Many of the play's readers have followed suit in viewing the dynastic marriage of Ferdinand and Miranda as a successful political outcome for Prospero, even if his means do not justify his ends.[34] But *The Tempest*'s staged yet partially occluded chess game intimates that Prospero cannot hold all the cards, as it were; if he is playing a game of imperfect information, so are others. *Pace* the presumption that Miranda's dynastic match amounts to political progress, there is no way for anyone to know or control what will transpire when Prospero's pawn marries Naples's heir and gets promoted to queen.[35] Perhaps antagonism between Naples and Milan will persist, despite the union of their princes. Perhaps Miranda will not be the dutiful wife Ferdinand and Prospero expect, complicating domestic and national balances of power. Or perhaps Miranda will fail to produce the heir who is needed to secure the unity of Milan and Naples well into the future. In short, the peace of entire states, nations, even empires rest on a partnership whose positive outcome cannot, in fact, be guaranteed.

Through its staging of chess, *The Tempest* suggests that dynastic marriages are politically ineffective because they are (like all marriages) games, involving conflict and competition. And if marriage, as scholar Frances Dolan has suggested, is a zero-sum game, then the only way to control its outcome is by cheating, imposing a certain ending on an otherwise wholly unpredictable venture.[36] Nevertheless, even in such a rigged game, one side will likely lose. *The Tempest*'s chess scene challenges Prospero's account of dynastic marriage as a linear and teleological story, where both sides inevitably win, instead exposing such unions as games with uncertain outcomes, played by wily participants who may even refuse to follow the rules.[37]

There is more at stake here than simply underscoring Miranda's and Ferdinand's control over their marital options. For if Benjamin is right that an alternative conception of history is possible if cheaters remain undiscovered—if covert theology drives historical materialism, like the hidden chess master who pulls the strings of the chess-playing puppet—then when early performances of *The Tempest* used the stage's "discovery space" to inhibit spectatorship of the chess game, they covered up Ferdinand's alleged cheating and in effect put the "dwarf" back into the cupboard to let the revolutionary potential of this moment linger. In this way, *The Tempest*'s chess scene prompted its spectators to question the logic of dynastic marriage: the belief that the conflicts of the past can be remedied in the present through a marriage that inevitably ensures peace in the future. The performance of dynastic marriage through chess, a game that plays on and through time's recursive qualities, destabilized this sort of linear temporal logic.

A GAME AT CHESS AND POLYTEMPORAL HISTORY

It is tempting to speculate on how this lesson would have been received in 1613 when *The Tempest* was performed as part of the celebration of the dynastic marriage of King James I's daughter Elizabeth. If, as I've argued, theater spectators familiar with chess are especially well positioned to grasp the play's critique of dynastic marriage as a political solution, then to what extent was this critique available to King James's children? Unlike James's predecessor, Queen Elizabeth I, who apparently was an avid chess player, King James denounced the game as "over fond," advising his son to choose

games that are more "light" and could better distract from the serious affairs of state.[38] If Charles I or the princess Elizabeth took seriously their father's advice, perhaps they were ill-prepared to grasp the message about
dynastic marriage that *The Tempest* makes available to spectators experienced with chess play. Regardless of whether James's failures of foresight
can be attributed to his lack of exposure to chess, those failures would have
been acutely visible in the early 1620s, when Middleton's *A Game at Chess*
was first performed. After all, the dynastic union that Middleton's play ostensibly allegorizes through a chess game—between England's Prince
Charles and the Infanta of Spain—was being arranged to remedy the political problems facing James's son-in-law Frederick. The new dynastic marriage was an attempt to fix the problems that resulted from the earlier one.
The historical ironies are palpable.[39] The concept of historical irony is useful
to a reading of *The Tempest* and *A Game at Chess* insofar as it can underscore
the polytemporal terms of historiography.[40] But the concept is limiting if it
presumes a narrowly synchronic relationship between history and drama,
such that Jacobean politics are "historical context" for these plays.

Even more pervasively than *The Tempest*, *A Game at Chess* has been interpreted as a topical play that reflects and comments on a very particular
historical and political context, perhaps even directly representing a specific historical event.[41] But through its staging of chess, the play calls for a
different approach to temporality, one that puts pressure on conventional
readings of the play's relationship to its historical moment. I argued above
that for *The Tempest*'s audience members, as for players and spectators of
games of chess, time does not necessarily exist in discreet units such that
one event (a marriage of princes) shares the self-same moment as another
event (the performance of a drama). Like participants in a chess match,
theater spectators can experience the present as infused with both memories of the past and potentialities for the future, producing an experience of
recursive time and a perspective on history not as unfolding but as folding
in on itself at every turn.[42] Middleton's *A Game at Chess* invites its audiences
to experience precisely this kind of polytemporal history, and it does so
through even more theatrical means than does *The Tempest*. For unlike *The
Tempest*, which obscures its chess game, hiding the ludic action from the
theater audience's view, *A Game at Chess* turns the stage into a literal chess
game; "the boards" become a chessboard. Middleton does for staged chess
what seems possible only for games of imperfect information like cards: he
offers theater spectators a perspective on the game that they would have if
watching it played in a tavern or parlor. As such, unlike *The Tempest*, which
frustrates theater spectators' desires to see the board—and thus know

whether Ferdinand is cheating—*A Game at Chess* bares all, rendering vicarious play a real option. When the Prologue tells audiences that the actors' great hope "[i]s to play our game to avoid your check" (Prologue, l. 10), he not only pleads for the audience's appreciation of the performance, but presumes the audience to be vicarious players of the staged game. Middleton's drama is, thus, an ideal final case study for my book's argument about theater as playable media.

This is not to say that *A Game at Chess* provides spectators the exact kind of chess game they might have experienced elsewhere. Although the chess piece characters sometimes move according to chess rules and perform legible game strategies (like the "checkmate by / Discovery" [5.3.160-61] that ends the play or the Queen's Gambit that begins it), there are plenty of inconsistencies. This lack of consistency in Middleton's representation of chess play has led most readers to treat the play's chess setting as merely an allegory, with little to no relationship to actual chess play.[43] But the significance of chess is not limited to its symbolism, particularly when the drama is performed. *A Game at Chess* invites spectators to play along, not to experience a particular game in progress so much as the feeling of chess play more generally.

The Prologue intimates as much when opening the play with this somewhat cryptic promise: "What of the game called chess-play can be made / To make a stage-play shall this day be played" (ll. 1–2). According to the Prologue, the actors will not perform a chess game in the abstract but rather the game as it is *played*, "[w]hat of the game called chess-*play*." The precise meaning of "chess-play" is left unclear because of the interrogative pronoun "what," a lack of clarity that recognizes the impossibility of staging an actual chess game in exactly the ways spectators might know it: all the actors can offer, can "play," is the *part* of "chess-play" that can be made into a "stage-play." Those who have even the slightest familiarity with chess can experience through Middleton's drama something of the ethos of chess play. Using modern critical terms, we might say that the Prologue invites theater audiences to adopt a *phenomenological* approach to the chess game, presenting chess not simply as a set of symbols meant to be decoded, but as a multisensory phenomenon meant to be *felt*. Approached this way, Middleton's chess setting offers audiences a way to feel time's recursivity and thus to understand at a deeply embodied level the polytemporal terms of historiography. As Benjamin's treatment of chess shows us, there is much at stake politically in this understanding of historiography.[44]

Prior readers have failed to see how chess does political work in the play because, by approaching chess primarily as a symbol, they oversimplify the game and our understanding of its ideological effects.[45] For instance, chess (with its two opposing sides, grid lines, and set rules for movement) has been viewed as a game about absolute distinctions and clear regulations, which contrasts with politics—a "game" played best by those who work around rules and who do not blindly follow authorities.[46] Yet early modern chess was anything but rigid in practice, partly because it was a betting game, and increasingly so in this period. Its rules were constantly being debated and transformed to suit the dynamic and contentious contexts of wagering. To appreciate the political meaning of chess in Middleton's drama, we need to think in very precise terms about how the game works *in play*. I want to suggest that for Middleton, chess is less an allegory for politics than it is a material metaphor through which an audience can experience, and subsequently critique, certain political ideologies, particularly those concerning dynastic marriage.[47] As does *The Tempest*, *A Game at Chess* undermines the state's ideology of historical progress in part by setting up a tension between the experience of temporality produced by the chess game-as-played and the narrative about temporality told by characters on the stage. But whereas *The Tempest* establishes one character, Prospero, as its disparaged conventional historian, Middleton distributes this work among a range of characters with ties to the Black House.

It is not surprising that in a jingoistic play that associates the Black House with Catholicism and Spain, the Black pieces prevaricate constantly; but in light of the chess mise-en-scène, it is worthwhile noting that when pieces of the Black House play false, they tend to play false with time. Indeed, manipulations of temporality are one of the Black House's defining features from the start, with the entire play being motivated by Ignatius's claim that he is a victim of history, and of the Christian calendar in particular. In the induction frame, Ignatius—the founder of the Jesuit order—complains that the Church took too long to canonize him, and, even worse, that when they finally did, they made his saint's day February 29, the intercalary day that occurs only every four years. It is his sense of mistreatment by time that provokes Ignatius's scheme for revenge, enacted through the play proper. Ignatius awakens the allegorical character Error, who describes and then goes on to stage his dream of a chess game between Ignatius's Black House and their enemy, the White House. Much like Prospero, Ignatius frames himself as a victim of past events and presents chess as an ideal material metaphor for his plot to reclaim command over the past and, thus, secure his future place in history. "O with what longings will this breast be tossed / Until I see this great game won and lost" (Induction, ll. 77–78).

In the play proper, Ignatius's disciples and especially his "son and daughter" (l. 60)—the Black Bishop's Pawn and the Black Queen's Pawn, respectively—seem to answer their holy father's desires to dominate time. To fulfill their plot to steal the virtue of the White Queen's Pawn, they manipulate ordinary time repeatedly. Early in the play, when the White Queen's Pawn threatens to reveal the Black Bishop's Pawn as an "arch-hypocrite" (2.1.147) after he attempts to rape her, the Black House is thrown into a state of crisis until the canny Black Bishop himself develops a plan to thwart her accusations by playing false with historical facts. He directs his guilty pawn to produce fraudulent letters that make it seem as though the accused was out of the country when the rape attempt took place:

> Away, upon the wings of speed take post-horse.
> Cast thirty leagues of earth behind thee suddenly;
> Leave letters antedated with our House,
> Ten days at least from this. (2.1.180–83)

The plan is successful. When the White Queen's Pawn publically accuses her attacker, she is warned that if she does not "with all speed . . . plead distraction" (2.2.166–68), she will be taken, "play how thou canst" (2.2.178). Her examiner figures the time of the attempted rape as the linchpin of the case, thrice asking her to declare that time: "Bring forth the time of this attempt's conception" (2.2.185); "The time, Pawn?" (2.2.192); and once she gives him his answer, "Is it he [the Black Bishop's Pawn], / And that the time?" (2.2.203–204). The Black House then uses forged epistolary evidence as to her attacker's whereabouts at that named time to undermine her story.

The effort of members of the Black House to manipulate history are, undoubtedly, central to the play's anti-Catholicism, suggesting, among other things, the danger of Catholic beliefs that practicing the sacraments can change one's spiritual destiny. Post-Reformation views of providential time and the doctrine of predestination directly countered such beliefs. Much more can and has been said on the play's religious allegory, which is inextricably linked to its political allegory. But for the purposes of my chapter's interests in temporality and history, my discussion below brackets the play's commentary on religion in order to think more broadly about its commentary on historiography. Not unlike the historians Benjamin critiques (Fascists as well as overly idealistic historical materialists), who retell the past in their own words so as to suit their narratives of victorious progress, the Black House's manufactured evidence rewrites history—in this case, literally—producing an alternative narrative of historical events that will help their "business of the universal monarchy / Go[ ] forward" (1.1.243–44). And because the Black House gives proof through the written word, their version of the past is more convincing than the oral narrative of rape provided by the White Queen's Pawn. With her unmarked body her only source of evidence, her narrative of the past cannot compete in this conventional knowledge economy.

As is also the case for the historians Benjamin disparages, the Black pieces' confidence in their capacity to manipulate time is a function of their belief—and their ability to convince others—that time moves in a linear fashion. The Black Bishop's Pawn expresses this view of time elegantly when questioned about how the seduction of a white pawn could possibly help the Black House achieve its plot of world domination. When his superior expresses concern that he "cannot see[ ]" how this part of the plan would work, the Black Bishop's Pawn responds, "You may deny so / A dial's motion, 'cause you cannot see / The hand move" (1.1.292–94). Time, the pawn maintains, moves forward in one direction, and a timepiece with its hidden moving hand offers an external record of this given, even if sometimes insensible, fact. The pawn articulates here what philosopher Edmund Husserl calls "objective time." Husserl criticizes the clock for its part in debasing more immediate experiences of time, which end up being relegated to the subjective and thus ostensibly unreliable realm of feeling.[48] Husserl maintains that at the level of immediate experience, time is much thicker and layered than dials would have us believe. The clock does not reflect but actually manipulates time so that it only appears to be linear in its movement. Middleton's play offers a similar critique by having its most suspect characters, like the Black Bishop's Pawn, claim an ability to harness time's linear unfolding.

This ideology of time proves to be the greatest threat to the character of the White Queen's Pawn, who gullibly buys into it. One of the troubling flaws of the White Queen's Pawn is her lack of patience for a better future, a weakness of which the Black House takes repeated advantage, encouraging her to move more quickly toward a promised end. Indeed, the Black Bishop's Pawn is initially able to get close enough for a sexual attack because she is overly eager for his spiritual guidance and the transformation it promises. When he sees her again after their first encounter, during which he had given her a book on obedience to help her "forward well" (1.1.191), he finds her voraciously reading the book and marvels at "with what alacrity of soul / Her eye moves on the letters" (2.1.30–31). The White Queen's Pawn's speed-reading is matched by an ardent desire to show her obedience as swiftly as possible. When she sees the Black Bishop's Pawn, she addresses him, "Holy sir, / Too long I have missed you; O, your absence starves me. / Hasten for time's redemption, worthy sir, / Lay your commands as thick and fast upon me / As you can speak 'em" (2.1.31–35). Craving a spiritual awakening that will transport her from the mundane temporality of her "poor span of life" (2.1.37), the White Queen's Pawn begs for quick deliverance and agrees to do anything he, as her spiritual advisor, commands. As the black pawn lures her in, she innocently persists in her willingness to obey him, only pausing and desisting from "go[ing] rashly on" when she is "on a sudden" (2.1.58) given the command that she kiss him. As her corrupt spiritual guide urges her to "come forward" (2.1.92), the White Queen's Pawn finally holds herself back. She is, unfortunately, too late, and the only reason she manages to avoid being taken is because another character, the Black Queen's Pawn, stages a disruption.

It turns out that the Black Queen's Pawn's real motivation is not to save the virtuous White Queen's Pawn but to entrap and thus satisfy a personal revenge against the corrupt Black Bishop's Pawn. Although her motivations may differ from those of other pieces in the Black House, her means are quite similar. She, too, corrects for past injustices by claiming to have the power to control time and bring the future forward more quickly, a promise that continues to entice the White Queen's Pawn. Although initially the latter learns her lesson about speeding through time, pledging to practice "patience" (2.2.265) when unfairly punished for allegedly lying about her rape, she soon reveals, once again, a vulnerability to the Black House's rhetoric of linear, progressive time. With surprising alacrity, she believes the Black Queen's Pawn's claim to have foreseen in a magical mirror the white pawn's destiny: her marriage to a gentleman in the Black House. When the naive white pawn insists she has no interest in marriage and feels no stirrings of desire for the man she is presumably destined to wed, the Black Queen's Pawn proclaims that there is no way to change one's destiny, only to speed up its arrival: "We do not always feel our faith we live by, / Nor ever see our growth, yet both work upward" (3.1.338). The Black Queen's Pawn takes advantage of the White Queen's Pawn's impatience—"I long to see this man" (3.1.345)—and offers to satisfy her "instantly" (3.1.346).

The play pauses, however, before satisfying the White Queen's Pawn's curiosity. In Middleton's earliest manuscript version of the play, sandwiched between the Black Queen's Pawn's promise to reveal the future and her delivery on that promise is a seemingly peripheral scene in which the Black Jesting Pawn, eagerly looking for an opportunity to capture a member of the White House, is suddenly taken himself. Instead of having the chance to turn an unspecified White Pawn into his personal slave, he is taken and enslaved by another White Pawn. The Black Jesting Pawn immediately begins plotting his rebellion:

> BLACK JESTING PAWN: I shall cozen you:
>   You may chance come and find your work undone then,
>   For I'm too proud to labour; I'll starve first,
>   I tell you that beforehand.
> WHITE PAWN: I will fit you then
>   With a black whip that shall not be behind-hand. (3.2.16-20)

The Black Jesting Pawn undermines the White Pawn's certainty about a victorious future by telling him "beforehand" that he plans to be a disobedient slave.[49] The White Pawn responds by promising a punishment that will perfectly fit the Black Pawn's crime of withholding his body from labor, an aptness underscored when he echoes the form of the Black Jesting Pawn's remarks but reverses their content: where the Black Jesting Pawn began midline with "I shall cozen you" and ends with "beforehand," the White Pawn begins midline with "I will fit you" and ends with "behind-hand." The description of the White Pawn's whip as "not behind-hand" likely means it will not be late or tardy,[50] suggesting that the whip will be used as swiftly as it is needed. But the term can also mean "[i]n a state of backwardness, less advanced than others [in], ill provided or prepared,"[51] which happens to be an ironically apt description of the White Pawn himself. So busy imagining his future as master over the Black Jesting Pawn, he doesn't look behind him and is taken by a different black pawn who approaches "in the breech" (3.2.31). For the White Pawn, the future turns out to be not ahead but, literally, behind him.

The scene that began with the threat of a white master planning to whip a black slave evolves into a queer erotic comedy where one pawn is "firk[ed]" (the early modern equivalent for our modern slang term "screwed") from behind by another pawn, who is subsequently "firk[ed]" (3.2.34; 35; 35) from behind by yet another. A narrative of violent capture is transformed into one of comic and, arguably, erotic pleasure for members of the theater audience, and also for the pawns. Indeed, the pawns debate who will get the most enjoyment out of this intriguing arrangement whereby they find themselves like "three flies with one straw through their buttocks" (3.2.39):

WHITE PAWN: We three look like a birdspit, a white chick
    Between two russet woodcocks.
BLACK JESTING PAWN: I'm so glad of this.
WHITE PAWN: But you shall have small cause, for I'll firk you.
SECOND BLACK PAWN: Then I'll firk you again.
WHITE PAWN: And I'll firk him again. (3.2.32-5)

In this cross-color sexual triad, the earlier threat of White whipping Black is reinterpreted as a sadomasochistic performance of master–slave relations, one that, especially as it evolves into a kind of masochistic orgy, generates not only pain but pleasure for those involved and for those who watch.

Middleton was no stranger to dramatizing the erotics of violence, having explored the subject of masochism in much more detail in *The Nice Valour*, a play he wrote just a few years before and which has much in common with *A Game at Chess*.[52] Not only do both plays use sexuality to reflect on Jacobean court politics, but one plotline of *The Nice Valour* concerns a masochistic courtier who eagerly displays his marked flesh, enjoying, instead of being shamed by, the beatings other courtiers inflict on him.[53] *A Game at Chess* similarly uses masochism to destabilize conventional social arrangements. The firking pawns scene figures its anonymous pawns as extraneous, expendable, and unproductive in terms of chess, politics, and the larger plot of the play—so much so that the scene was cut from some published versions of the play.[54] But, if included, the scene is intriguingly disruptive in a number of ways. With their eroticization of capture, the pawns disrupt a fictional political world where being "taken" is supposed to be shameful to one's house—and, in terms of the political allegory, one's nation and religion. And with their nonreproductive sexual practices, the pawns present a comic alternative to the play's weighty issue of marriage and its promise of a productive future through the creation of heirs—the fictional and allegorical matter at hand in *A Game at Chess*. Finally, as the firking pawns put the play's central business and plot on hold, even for just a few minutes, they disrupt the progression of the play and of the Black Queen's Pawn's plot more specifically, a plot that is heavily invested in linear models of progress.

The performance of sadomasochism in the firking pawns scene, in its content and in its interstitial placement, offers a cautionary tale about the dangers of investing in a linear and teleological view of history, where a better future is always ahead. Unlike the "angel of history" Walter Benjamin describes in his aforementioned essay on historiography, the pawns in Middleton's scene do not pause to see what is behind them, and they end up screwed as a result. This lesson is made available both to the White Pawn, as he is positioned between two black pawns, and to theater spectators who watch the firking pawns scene, itself sandwiched between two parts of the Black Queen's Pawn's plot. The lesson threatens to be lost, however, on spectators (and readers) who view the scene as an interruption of the play's progression, an unproductive pause of the central narrative. And perhaps my own reader will wonder why I have spent so many pages of this chapter on such a brief and seemingly inconsequential moment in Middleton's play. But, as I argued above in relation to *The Tempest*, in a game of chess—and in *A Game at Chess*—the pause between moves is a moment of anticipation and creativity. As it holds the present, past, and future in tension, the pause makes possible a different approach to history.

Unlike readers and audiences who may enjoy the pause for itself and on its own terms, the White Queen's Pawn is impatient to get on with her story. As a consequence, she puts herself in danger of being firked once again when she is easily convinced that the rich gentleman she sees in a trick mirror—in fact, her former clerical attacker in a nobleman's disguise—is her future husband. To be sure, the pawn doesn't have much time to consider the danger, for the man appears only momentarily "like an apparition" (SD 3.3.52) before he disappears, leaving the White Queen's Pawn ravaged by desire and wanting more time to see her promised love: "O let him stay a while, a little longer!" and again "If he be mine why should he part so soon" (3.3.52; 54). Though she remains uninterested in marriage, it does not take much time for the Black Queen's Pawn to persuade her that "What we still write is blotted out by fate" (3.3.58), and that the apparition in the mirror is her certain future. The White Queen's Pawn tries half-heartedly to let fate run its course when she later encounters the man she had seen in the "mirror" and resists the temptation to bring about a meeting. In response to the Black Queen's Pawn urging to talk to the man, the White Queen's Pawn insists, "The time you see / Is not yet come!" (4.1.41–42) and, "Let time have his full course" (4.1.46). But she does not put up much of a fight when the Black Queen's Pawn aims to intervene, having articulated, once again, the Black House's seductive logic: "'tis in our power now / To bring time nearer" (4.1.42–43). The Black Queen's Pawn hastily keeps the game moving, for any delay would give her opponents a window during which to recognize her cheating. She counsels the White Queen's Pawn and the disguised Black Bishop's Pawn to consummate their fated marriage right away and not to "let time cozen you, / Protracting time, of those delicious benefits / That fate hath marked to you" (4.1.106–108).

Although the promised marriage between the White Queen's Pawn and her fated partner from a different House is not technically dynastic—she is a mere pawn—it nevertheless supports the play's political allegory concerning the thwarting of the unpopular union between England's Prince Charles and the Spanish Infanta. The White Queen's Pawn misunderstands how chess works and misplays the game, tempted by the Black House's claims that actions in the present will bring about more quickly a better future whose telos is certain. The White Queen's Pawn endangers herself when she buys into this logic.[55] At stake is the progressive, teleological perspective on time and on history that, I have been arguing, is so fundamental to the Jacobean state's rhetoric about dynastic marriage. Although *A Game at Chess* does not critique dynastic unions directly in its plot, it opens the way for such a critique through its scrutiny of the White Queen's Pawn's investments in marriage. Her beliefs in marriage as her determined end—that the man she has been shown in the mirror "lately" must be her "own for ever" (4.1.95–96)—and that this destined union ensures her a better future are represented as foolish and hazardous. What imperils the White Queen's Pawn, over and over, is the Black House's investment in teleological history, the grand plan of future world domination that, they insist, can be ascertained through present action.

A critique of this philosophy of history is best articulated by the White King, who, as he berates the Fat Bishop (a member of the Black House, who defects and subsequently returns), indicts the whole Black House for their teleological historiography:

> For thee, Black Holiness, that workst out thy death
> As the blind mole, the proper'st son of earth,
> Who in the casting his ambitious hills up
> Is often taken, and destroyed i'th' midst
> Of his advanced work, 'twere well with thee
> If like that verminous labourer, which thou imitat'st
> In hills of pride and malice, when death puts thee up
> The silent grave might prove thy bag for ever,
> No deeper pit than that. (4.5.40–48)

In comparing the Fat Bishop to a "blind mole," the White King employs an image whose use by Shakespeare in *Hamlet* captured the interests of Hegel and Karl Marx in their theorizations of history and revolution. According to scholar Margareta de Grazia, the mole—which digs its tunnels slowly and steadily for years, finally speeding up as it sees the light at the end—symbolized for Hegel "the progress of world history, its strenuous drive forward toward its end of self-determining freedom," and for Marx a more radical historical materialist praxis, where political and social change is forward-moving and breaks completely with what have been considered revolutionary models of the past.[56] De Grazia points out that the image of the mole persists in the writings of philosophers until Jacques Derrida gets rid of it, calling instead for a model of temporality that is more akin to that of Hamlet's Ghost, a "hauntological" time characterized by disjointedness and rupture.[57]

Middleton's staged chess game anticipates Derrida's derision of *Hamlet*'s mole, offering a similarly Benjaminian critique of linear, teleological historiography and an alternative model of political change. When the White King compares the Fat Bishop—and, by proxy, the entire Black House—to a mole, he uses the image to warn about the dangers of subscribing to the linear, progressive view of time that the mole represents. Whereas Hegel and Marx celebrated the mole for its forward-looking persistence and resistance to delaying in its end goal, the White King frames these qualities as evidence of sinful, short-sighted ambition. As the mole tunnels up and up, further and further, the progress it makes is toward not a better life but, ironically, the end of life; the closer the mole gets to the surface, the more easily it can be captured and thrown into the "bag" that represents, at the end of the scene and throughout this play, death.

In Middleton's heavily moralistic play, the Fat Bishop's foolishness has the potential to teach theatergoers a lesson about political power and history; but the extent to which they learn the lesson is a function of how they approach the play's chess mise-en-scène. Should they decode the symbolism of chess (a semiotic approach) or experience the overall feeling of chess play (a phenomenological approach)? The White Queen's Pawn speaks to differences between these approaches when, as she recognizes the error of her ways and berates the Black Bishop's Pawn for his insincere religiosity, she uses a theatrical analogy to condemn his deceptive clerical dress: "The world's a stage on which all parts are played; / You'd count it strange to have a devil / Presented there not in a devil's shape, / Or, wanting one, to send him out in yours (5.2.19–22).[58] As she urges him to present the part of devil accurately, she draws an analogy between audience members' competencies in theatergoing and chess play, suggesting, in effect, that semiotic approaches are as insufficient in the former as they are in the latter. The Black Bishop's Pawn's devilish character is difficult for audiences to read semiotically, for only if the parts are "fitted" can "the spectators / Know which is which. They must have cunning judgements / To find it else, for such a one as you / Is able to deceive a mighty auditory" (5.2.30–33). Yet the Black Bishop's Pawn's deceptive act is easily exposed when theatergoers set aside interpretation of his sign system—his clerical dress and accoutrements—and use all their senses to attend to the *way* in which he plays. She continues, "Nay those you have seduced, if there be any / In the assembly, when they see what manner / You play your game with me, they cannot love you" (5.2.34–36). Gesturing outward to theatergoers—the "assembly" around her—the White Queen's Pawn contrasts two sorts of spectatorial competency. Those spectators who approach the play semiotically may be seduced by the evil Black Bishop's Pawn's clerical dress, much as she was tricked by it and, later, by his gentleman's clothes. Just as his gentleman's costume covered up his true identity, so his bishop's garb hides his real character, the devil. But those spectators who attend to him not as a representation but as a chess piece in play—using their embodied experience of chess play to perceive *how* he plays the game—will easily uncover his evil and despise him for it. The distinction the White Queen's Pawn makes is one that holds in a regular game of chess, too. Because the pieces resemble noble figures as if collected for battle, the game has tended to be read in a symbolic vein. But as some "ludologists" in the field of game studies remind us, the representational qualities of a game are not always that essential to the experience of playing it.[59] While imagining oneself moving kings, queens, and bishops around a battlefield is undoubtedly interesting and enjoyable, the successful game player generally brackets that symbolic meaning, focusing not on what these pieces represent but on how they occupy the space on the board in relation to each other.

When Middleton pursues his didactic aims by inviting audiences to approach chess imagery *phenomenologically*, he adapts to drama a technique that was pervasive in medieval poetry about chess. In a number of medieval texts, the chessboard functions as a kind of organizing grid that, like other mnemonic devices, helped readers understand and remember a text's content, sometimes by requiring the reader to play along.[60] The same is true for Middleton's play, though the effects are different because reading about chess and seeing a game in action are dissimilar experiences.[61] In a theatrical performance, as in a regular chess game, chess functions not as a grid but, to quote Michel de Certeau, as "an area of free play (*Spielraum*)."[62] As in the checkerboard to which de Certeau gestures here and the backgammon board I discussed in Chapter 3, grid lines and clear rules discipline and limit players' actions, but gameplay requires much more dynamic interaction with the board. Because of the complex possibilities of chess movement and its lack of unpredictable variables like dice, the game not only prompts transgressive spatial practices, like the backgammon play discussed in Chapter 3, but temporal ones as well. The use of chess as a setting in medieval poems may discipline the time of reading, but in the theater chess opens up *play* with the temporalities of spectatorship. As I demonstrate further in the next section, when chess scenes encourage theater spectators to experience time's recursivity, they teach spectators not only about the limits of linear and teleological models of time—the very models used in state rhetoric around dynastic marriage—but also about the work of theatergoing itself. In so doing, chess scenes go on to school contemporary scholars about theater and, subsequently, how best to study its history. For like the history of games, theater's history is produced through repeated performances.

PERFORMATIVE HISTORIES

I have begun to outline some of the limitations of traditional methods of historiography, limitations that become especially clear when we attempt to construct histories of chess—indeed of all games. To be sure, games leave material traces that invite these analytic methods. A range of evidence—including, in the case of chess, early pieces, verbal and visual representations of the game, and books of chess rules and problems—can document how the game has changed over time. They can tell us, for instance, that in the early modern period the chess queen had significantly more mobility, resulting in a faster game. But, as discussed in Chapter 1, material remnants are only part of a game's history. Players bend rules and redesign gaming objects all the time to create more pleasurable gaming experiences, and variations may be reiterated over and over until they become institutionalized. In other words, the rules and objects that comprise and define a game materialize through repeated performances.[63] Chess is a particularly rich game through which to investigate the performative history of games because, as I have demonstrated, recursive temporality is so fundamental to the experience of playing and watching this particular game. During every pause between moves, players and spectators anticipate the future of a match by rehearsing its past at the same time that they recall the past (of this match and other matches) in order to envision possible moves that may lead to victory.

The polytemporality of chess urges a rethinking of some commonplace methods for studying drama as well,[64] challenging in particular the assumption of an event-based model of performance: that a theatrical performance occurs in a particular place and at a particular time. I would maintain that not all, if any, elements of a performance can be fixed spatially and temporally, however. Theatrical performances, no matter how unique each may seem, draw on—indeed are made from—a common and temporally diffuse repertoire of gestures, actions, and styles. Thus, the relation among various "instances" of performance may be defined by a logic that is not always chronological. All theater, we might say, is *inter*theatrical.[65] Certainly, one can pursue a *diachronic* analysis of a play by searching for a point of origin of a particular stylistic convention and then tracing its genealogy. And one can pursue a *synchronic* analysis by situating that convention in relation to events and discourses coterminous with it. There are other options, however. One can also focus on how a convention becomes intelligible to theater audiences through the very operation of its repetition. Accounting for the "intertheatricality" of dramatic performance can thus alter our sense of the relation between theater and history. The polytemporality of theatrical performance challenges an oft-cited truism: that performance is ephemeral and always disappearing, as the performed "event" passes into history. To the contrary, as Anston Bosman, William N. West, and I have maintained, history is constantly being made in and through theater, which "stretches the event open, such that it is simultaneously a preservation of the past and a preparation for the future."[66] For theater performers and their spectators, the present is a sedimentation of the past, but through performance, the past passes into the future, which is set before audiences as a range of possibilities, or what scholar Daniel Sack describes as "potentiality."[67]

If we follow this line of reasoning, then the staging of dynastic marriage through a chess game does not stabilize *The Tempest*'s and *A Game at Chess*'s relationships to particular moments in English history. Instead, these chess games urge early modern spectators and modern readers to treat the plays as part of a temporally and spatially diffuse network of chess matches, some "staged" in the taverns and parlors that competed with early modern theaters for customers, others staged in politically engaged dramas. Thus, *The Tempest* and *A Game at Chess* are also in dialogue with Shakespeare's *King John*, a play centrally concerned with doomed dynastic marriage and which also, perhaps not coincidentally, is the only other Shakespeare play besides *The Tempest* explicitly to use chess imagery.[68] In 2.1 of *King John*, the eponymous character and his mother, Eleanor, berate Lady Constance for trying to put forward her son, Arthur, as the rightful king of England, a

claim that King John's side disputes, arguing that Arthur is a bastard. Eleanor accuses Constance, who has the support of France, of using her son for
her own political gain, a strategy she compares to that of chess: "Thy bastard shall be king / That thou mayst be a queen and check the world"
(2.1.122–23). The women's fight over Arthur's rightful place is mirrored by
the fight between the kings of France and England over the city of Angiers,
in front of which they stand. The kings are about to ransack the city, which
will not choose a side, when the Citizen speaking for Angiers suggests a
compromise: a political marriage between King John's niece, Blanche, and
the French king's son, Louis, the Dauphin. To justify the proposal, the Citizen appeals to the commonplace view of marriage as the joining of two
souls:

> He is the half part of a blessèd man,
> Left to be finishèd by such as she;
> And she a fair divided excellence,
> Whose fullness of perfection lies in him.
> O, two such silver currents when they join
> Do glorify the banks that bound them in,
> And two such shores to two such streams made one,
> Two such controlling bounds, shall you be, Kings,
> To these two princes if you marry them. (2.1.438–46)

As husband and wife become one, so, according to the logic of dynastic
marriage, the kings and their warring nations will unite. The ideology of
two becoming one is so convincing that the kings jump at this deal, and the
marriage is solemnized within minutes.

Unlike *The Tempest* and *A Game at Chess*, which are more subtle in their
critiques of dynastic marriage, *King John* offers an explicit indictment of it,
once again through the imagery of gaming. The canny character of Philip
Faulconbridge, suspicious of the way Angier's Citizen has used the rhetoric
of ideal marriage to sell the advantages of this peace treaty, figures the
Citizen as the consummate courtier and presciently predicts the downfall
of the treaty, which depends on the word of another courtier, the completely untrustworthy French king. In his famous cynical speech about the
degeneracy of a world ruled by "commodity" (i.e., self-interested gain),
Faulconbridge describes "commodity" as a "smooth-faced gentleman"
(2.1.574) who cheats when he gambles so that he can always win and take
all from those he beats: he "wins of all, / Of kings, of beggars, old men,
young men, maids,— / Who having no external thing to lose / But the word

'maid', cheats the poor maid of that" (2.1.570–73). The reference is to King John's niece, Blanche, who will lose her maidenhood status through the political marriage. As Faulconbridge predicts, the dynastic marriage accomplishes none of the aims for which it was designed. In the very next scene, just after the wedding, the pope's legate arrives and pressures France to continue its war against England. Blanche finds herself pulled between her allegiance to her new French husband and her allegiance to England, a situation she compares to dismemberment by competing armies: "I am with both, each army hath a hand, / And in their rage, I having hold of both, / They whirl asunder and dismember me" (3.1.254–56). Recalling Eleanor's earlier ludic imagery for politics, Blanche describes her situation as a rigged game: "Whoever wins, on that side shall I lose, / Assurèd loss before the match be played" (3.1.261–62).

King John tempts the scholar to read dramatic history in a linear fashion, for as it uses game imagery, including that of chess, to undermine the logic of dynastic marriage as a political solution, it falls nicely in line with other plays discussed in this chapter. And it is tempting to try to establish a genealogy, whereby *King John* influences *The Tempest*, which in turn influences *A Game at Chess*. But such a linear story discounts the impact of the many other games of chess, real and imagined, the play's spectators had experienced. It seems more useful to approach the three dramas as part of the same performance network—a web that also includes every game of chess theater spectators had played, watched, or read about. I would resist relating this web to the concept of "intertextuality," which might imply that the process of citation is traceable, if not necessarily intentional.[69] The lines of influence or precedence among nodes in the performance network I am describing cannot be so neatly delineated, because theater, much like other gameplay, is encoded in and through bodies. Not always expressed through texts, the embodied practices that comprise theater and games are not always legible enough to be traced, even indirectly, from one point to another.[70] Indeed, members of theater audiences, like other game participants, do not themselves always know how they have developed competencies of play. They may feel the recursive temporality of a chess game, for instance, without knowing for sure how, where, when, or even whether they have experienced it before.

This is a somewhat unique aspect of theater and of games, distinguishing the temporality of these playable media from that of other media, like paintings and films. Film shares somewhat the protracted temporality of theater and games—unlike painting, film can withhold parts of a narrative from the audience, divulging that narrative as time goes on, which is partly why plays lend themselves so well to cinematic adaptation. But in other ways, the temporality of film is nothing like that of theater and games. Film separates producers and receivers temporally and spatially (the action is consumed long after and in a different place than it was produced), and because of this, film has the capacity to be reperformed in much the same way time and time again. We can appreciate this difference in media by considering how a game like chess would work when represented in each medium. When a chess game is staged in a conventional theater, the spectator doesn't have the option to zoom in on the scene[71] or to slow down or repeat it, as is the case with film; the scene cannot ever be repeated in quite the same way, for theater, like chess, is predominantly live, and thus even if performed with the same actors, props, and so forth, some slight variations occur from one performance to another. This is not to say that every performance of a play is an isolated, unique event with no connection to any other. To the contrary, as I have suggested, theatrical performances recycle earlier and anticipate later performances in manifold ways. Every gesture, costume, actor, word on the stage looks back to past and ahead to future performances. Each moment of a performance is like a pregnant pause between moves in a game of chess. Similar to spectators or players of chess, theatergoers become aware of what is happening at any moment in the play by drawing (usually unconsciously) on prior moments with which they are familiar. In effect, spectators of plays could develop theatergoing competencies in much the way they did gaming competencies: through repeated exposure to and practice with these playable media. Like players and spectators of chess, theatergoers could become more competent at theater as they became better able to engage in the recursive temporality of its form.

RECURSIVE TEMPORALITY, POLITICAL AGENCY, AND EMBODIED SKILL

At stake in theorizing this recursive temporality—a feature of chess, theater, and, to follow Benjamin, history itself—is our understanding of the political power available to spectators of The Tempest and A Game at Chess. These stakes become clearer when one considers how Benjamin's theories of history resonate with his embodied experience playing chess with dramatist Brecht, who famously used the theater to spur his audiences toward political critique and social transformation. It is well known that Brecht and Benjamin influenced each other's conceptions of historical materialism, though virtually nothing has been said about the role of chess in their political thought.[72] Yet three of the four surviving photographs of these friends show them playing chess together, which seems to have been their nightly ritual whenever they lived and worked in close proximity.[73] One of Benjamin's many mentions of playing chess with Brecht is worthy of closer attention in relation to "On the Concept of History." Several years before writing the essay, Benjamin described Brecht's idea for a new version of chess:

> So, when [Marxist theoretician Karl] Korsch comes, we ought to work out a new game with him. A game where the positions don't always remain the same; where the function of the figures changes when they have stood in the same place for a while—then they would become either more effective, or perhaps weaker. As it is now, there is no development; it stays the same for too long.[74]

Benjamin records Brecht complaining about the problem of stasis in chess and proposing a creative solution: propel the game forward by allowing the past of the pieces to impinge upon their present function. How long a piece has stood in its place will determine its options for movement. Benjamin's model of history and political agency in "On the Concept of History" proposes a similar solution to the problem of historical stasis. Criticizing the staleness of conventional historicism, its view of history as "homogeneous, empty time," Benjamin argues that political change is impossible if we associate history solely with the past. At the same time, Benjamin questions the kind of historical "development" posited by Fascists and others who envision history as a totality and the present as a transition on the way toward "progress."[75] As will Benjamin in his later essay, Brecht's experimental form of chess conceives of the relationship among past, present, and future quite differently: use the past to pressure the present so as to compel the game forward. In a similar way, Benjamin imagines that revolution will best be achieved by pausing in a "now-time" that holds the past and future in productive tension with each other. For Benjamin, as for Brecht, this pausing in now-time comprises a strategy for political action. Feminist theorist Wendy Brown summarizes Benjamin's polytemporal view of political agency especially clearly:

> In contrast with a conventional historical materialism that renders the present in terms of unfolding laws of history, Benjamin argues for the political and the philosophical value of conceiving the pres-

ent as a time in which time is still(ed). But not only still—rather it is a present in which time has come to a stop, thereby implying movement behind it. The affirmation of this temporal rush behind a still present . . . avoids presentism and ahistoricity in political thinking even as it conceptually breaks the present out of history.[76]

The value of this breaking is that we get "a present that calls to us, calls on us to respond to it."[77] It leads to a sense of political urgency that is not determined entirely, but still informed, by the past.

Brecht and Benjamin prompt further consideration of how *The Tempest* and *A Game at Chess* use chess to issue this kind of call. Through their staging of chess, the plays invite spectators to question the temporal logic that underwrites the politically "progressive" narrative of dynastic marriage, showing it to be a kind of false consciousness. They do so not simply through an abstract symbolic economy where chess is an analogy for political marriages, but by appealing to, drawing their energies from, and exploiting spectators' phenomenological experience of chess play. Whether partially hidden or fully exposed, the chess games in these dramas call upon spectators to engage their embodied knowledge of gameplay in order to make sense of the dramas and of history.

Although my chapter has focused on what it feels like to participate in a game, particularly chess, my broader aim has been to show how plays and/as games accentuate the body as a site of knowledge production and acquisition, a kind of living archive. Whether playing directly or vicariously, participants build up knowledge about a game through exposure to it. When the body operates in this way as a house of memory and a medium of (re)enactment, the information it carries and transmits can compete powerfully with official narratives about the past and future[78]—including the narrative Prospero spins to justify his plots. Thus, games and dramas, regardless of whether they take up explicit political themes, can inspire political action through their playable form. By playing or playing along, participants generate alternatives to authored/authorized texts and narratives. Gaming is an especially interesting example of how political power emerges out of embodied knowledge practices because games showcase the degree to which embodied knowledge may be produced and communicated beneath the horizon of consciousness. Work in the cognitive philosophy of sport explores how bodies that engage repeatedly in a particular routine or practice develop often unconscious "habit memory."[79] Habit memory is produced through repeated performances of an action or an experience closely related to it.[80] Through this process of rehearsal, knowledge becomes entrenched in our bodies without our even knowing it is there. Few of us can say when we first learned to play chess, for instance, but through repeated practice and by watching others play or reading about the game, many of us have developed a deep knowledge of what it feels like to play such that when we begin a match, we know generally what to do, even if we need reminding of the precise rules.

This kind of process of repeated exposure to routines and practices brings about the "enskillment" of participants in both games and theater— participants learn to master these media forms via the experience of playing them.[81] At the moment when commercial theater was emerging in London as a new form of entertainment, the skill of spectatorship had to be learned. And participants became enskilled in this "new media" not only through repeated exposure to commercial plays themselves, but also, I've been suggesting, through engaging in (other) sitting pastimes. Playing a game of chess in a tavern or watching others do so could contribute to spectators' competencies in commercial theatergoing and, perhaps, vice versa. If we think of drama as playable media, then we can see how gameplay outside the theater, instead of being only a source of competition for the commercial stage, could function in partnership with it.

I have argued, moreover, that as staged games honed theatergoing skills, they could simultaneously provoke political engagement. As *The Tempest* and *A Game at Chess* solicit and frustrate spectators' application of their experience of chess play to the dramatic narrative, the plays open up avenues for critique not only of Prospero or members of the Black House, respectively, but of current, past, and future arguments for the strategic value of dynastic marriage. Invited to repurpose their chess-playing competencies—specifically, their capacity to experience time in nonprogressive terms—early modern spectators could inhabit their present as a now-time infused by possibility. Chess scenes set up the conditions for imagining future historical outcomes that official state narratives of dynastic marriage foreclosed. It may seem too ambitious to follow Benjamin and Brecht in claiming that such scenes could inspire revolution on a broad scale; but at the very least such scenes help us to think about the early modern commercial theater as a space of political transformation not only or necessarily because of the political content of the plays, but because of their temporal form.

In a book on medieval chess literature, Jenny Adams argues that one reason the chessboard ceased serving in the early modern period as a space for negotiating political conflict was because the theater began to serve this role.[82] But if the stage took over for the chessboard, then it was because this particular stage, part of a commercial theater entertainment industry, relied on and taught many of the same competencies as chess play. As Shakespeare's and Middleton's dramas demonstrate especially well, the stage was not an incidental alternative to, but a compensatory version of, the chessboard.

| Participatory Spectators and the
Theatricality of Kinect

The strong historical connection between games and theater that I have traced throughout this book has been all but forgotten in the study and making of games today. Yet not *entirely* forgotten. Links between games and theater can be felt quite palpably in the emergence in the past decade of performing arts–themed games that turn their users into rock musicians, hip-hop dancers, and celebrity vocalists.[1] These *mimetic interface games* eschew multibutton controllers, engage players' bodies in the activity represented on the screen, and emphasize the physical space of play.[2] In the game series *Just Dance*, for instance, the user mimics an onscreen dancer, and the user's bodily movements are communicated to the game's software through a simple handheld remote — or, in the case of the Xbox 360 version, via a Kinect camera, whose motion sensors read the location of the player's joints to help the software detect player movement. Because they do not require a steep learning curve, devices complex to master, and significant investment of player time, these games and the platforms on which they are played have initiated what Jesper Juul describes as a trend toward "casual" video gaming and, thus, also a broadening of the demographic for videogames.[3]

Juul and other scholars have argued that one of the main emphases of such games is their sociality. Mimetic interface games tend to be played in groups, with users sharing the same physical or virtual space, and players usually engage socially with each other around the game in addition to interacting with the game screen itself. But these games do more than transform the game space into a social space; I'd argue they also turn it into a theatrical space. In mimetic interface games, the ludic interaction is not only between player and screen or among players, but among players, screen, and nonplaying spectators. The theatrical doesn't preclude the social; in fact, as I've argued throughout this book, theatrical transactions can be understood as social transactions. But conceiving of the sociality of these games in theatrical terms sheds new light on their design principles, their broad appeal, and the gameplay experience they produce. Mimetic interface games are different and more inclusive than many other videogames not only because of the simplification or elimination of a complex controller and the extension of the playing field into the room where gameplay occurs, but also because the games facilitate the transformation of bystanders into vicarious players. If in the early modern period, as this book has shown, the theater was a gaming platform, then in today's living rooms and public leisure venues, games are becoming theatrical platforms.

What will it mean for the future of gaming and for theater if games become, once again, a medium for theatrical production and reception? To explore the theatricality of mimetic interfaces in videogames, and particularly the ways these interfaces encourage vicarious spectator play, this Epilogue will focus on a gaming device that, in my view, has the most theatrical affordances: Microsoft Kinect. Kinect was first created for use with the Xbox 360 console and subsequently updated for the more dominant Xbox One. Microsoft also released a Software Development Kit that allows developers to create Kinect programs that can run on a Windows PC. Regardless of the console used to play them, Kinect games, I maintain, promote theatrical forms of engagement among users. Indeed, Microsoft heavily emphasized this potential in their marketing of the peripheral, particularly in their initial, much anticipated launch of Kinect in 2010. Plenty of software has been created for Kinect since that time, and yet, with few exceptions, the commercially released software made for Kinect does not manage to realize the theatrical potential of the peripheral. Although the marketing of Kinect games regularly highlights spectators watching others play, in fact the design of most Kinect games does not promote spectators' cognitive and emotional investment in vicarious play. The result is that software for Kinect has rarely taken advantage of the feature that most distinguishes Kinect from other gaming peripherals: its capacity to turn gaming into a theatrical event. To demonstrate the Kinect's theatrical affordances, I turn to a case study of a game that I have been involved in developing at the University of California, Davis's Mod-Lab: *Play the Knave*. The game's theatrical dimensions extend beyond its thematic content, Shakespearean theater, to the experience that users—both those who play directly and those who watch play—have of the game's mimetic interface. Because of the way *Play the Knave* is designed, it manages to actualize the Kinect's theatrical affordances, encouraging vicarious spectator play.

THE THEATRICAL AFFORDANCES OF THE KINECT

Whether or not theater was on the minds of Kinect's designers, it was most certainly on the minds of its promoters. When Microsoft launched its much-anticipated controller-free motion capture system for gameplay, it did so through a stunning theatrical spectacle that, notably, borrowed its conventions from immersive theater and its keynotes from Shakespeare. The 2010 event for the Electronic Entertainment Expo (E3), held in the Galen Center in Los Angeles, was a collaboration between Microsoft and Cirque du Soleil.[4] Everything about the event was rooted in techniques from contemporary immersive theater.[5] For instance, before audience members entered the arena, they were given white ponchos to wear over their own clothes, a costuming of the audience that has interesting echoes with Punchdrunk's *Sleep No More*—a site-specific immersive theater adaptation of Shakespeare's *Macbeth* that has been running in New York since 2011—where audience members are inducted into the immersive theater experience by donning white masks. Like the masks, the ponchos signal to spectators that they will be active participants in the theatrical event—they are now costumed and ready to play—but at the same time these costumes create a group identity for the audience, uniting individual spectators as part of the whole, and distinguishing their group from the show's actual, paid performers. Indeed, the costuming of the Cirque du Soleil performers was radically different from that of the audience, for the former were dressed as island inhabitants. They wore fanciful headdresses and colorful beads, their torsos in brown one-pieces so as to resemble nakedness. Their faces were painted and their bodies adorned with flowery or leafy garlands. Some played drums, and when they moved, they would crouch or walk on all fours, often erupting into "primitive" dances. As is usually the case in immersive theater, audiences entered a performance in medias res. As they took seats on bleachers or perambulated around the arena floor, they could watch Cirque du Soleil acrobats perform physical marvels (Figure 21).

For its immersive setting and narrative about a breakthrough technology that allows gamers to play without the disruptive mediation of a physical controller—as Microsoft announced, "you are the controller"—Kinect took inspiration from an imaginative topos that has been tapped by scientists and science fiction writers interested in nanotechnology: the island. History of science and game studies scholar Colin Milburn has observed that nanotechnology repeatedly takes place on islands, figured as a magical place where inhabitants play with nature to produce all sorts of wonders and where all is presided over by a figure who is (sometimes explicitly, often implicitly) the character of Prospero from Shakespeare's *The Tempest*, along with his sidekick spirit, Ariel.[6] The narrative of magic and discovery so often associated, in fiction and in science, with islands was crucial to the story Microsoft told about Kinect in the E3 show and through the video they released of the event. As spectators enter the space, they walk across and around digitally enhanced pools meant to resemble blue water, which magically appears to ripple when touched. Cirque du Soleil performers literalize their identities as islanders by occupying these pools to perform the kind of virtuoso and seemingly impossible stunts for which the company is known, while audience members congregated around the "shores" of the pools to watch and applaud these almost magical manipulations of the human body. But as is always true in immersive theater, the lines between audience and performer, between receiver and creator, are constantly blurred. Audience members seem to need no formal prompting to assume their roles in what quickly turns into a staging of the colonial encounter. Clearly amazed at the curious and incredible sights around them, the audience gawks and points at the islander performers, who respond in kind, gazing curiously at the visitors, occasionally treating them like gods to be adorned with garlands or involved in rituals/performances. And as in the imaginative island world of nanotechnology, all is presided over by a Prospero-like figure and his spritely assistant. The latter appears to direct some of the performance scenes on the arena floor, meandering around the action and gesturing with his arms as if helping to orchestrate it. But his place as assistant to the grand magician becomes evident when the lights dim and an old magician takes center stage alone, standing on a rock and waving his arms dramatically to cue the show proper.

Although clearly much of the aim of this spectacular event was to show audiences a good time and get everyone talking about Kinect, Microsoft's emphasis on audience participation and its invocation of Shakespearean drama suggest that this was not just spectacle for the sake of spectacle. One effect of the show—whether or not it was the intent—was to foreground Kinect as a theatrical technology in which spectators are as much a part of the gaming experience as players. Kinect, Microsoft's show suggests, is the kind of gaming device that welcomes spectators to play vicariously. This inclusion of the audience into the gaming experience expands upon the mission and effect of mimetic interface games, as these have been discussed by others. Technologies like Kinect target users who don't have the patience, coordination, or will to learn to operate complex controllers. Nintendo had opened up this market with the introduction of the Wii system, and with Kinect, Microsoft positioned itself as an improvement on the Wii, claiming to get rid of the object controller entirely. As media scholars Steven E. Jones and George K. Thiruvathukal observe, the Wii system's design, marketing, and distribution explicitly targeted families in particular, aiming with the simple controller and low-energy-use machine to bringing gaming into every living room, to be enjoyed by the whole family. This was a market that Nintendo, which began as a playing card company, knew well how to reach.[7] Jones and Thiruvathukal rightfully point out that Microsoft pursued the same market with the development of Kinect, which was meant to help Xbox compete head-on with the Wii in the newly discovered, or perhaps more accurately, *re*discovered domestic gaming market. But this view of mimetic gaming platforms as rediscovering "social" and "casual" gaming tells only part of the story. I would argue that Kinect, more successfully than Wii, simultaneously rediscovered the deep *theatrical* roots of social gaming, expanding the game experience beyond the players to include vicariously playing spectators.

The connection between social gaming and theatricality is explicitly taken up in the E3 show. Those who witnessed the event live or in later broadcasts have tended to focus on its spectacle, meant to amaze and immerse, much like the technology being introduced. Jones and Thiruvathukal argue that the Microsoft show perfectly encapsulated the rhetoric around Kinect as a gaming peripheral that could offer the dream of total immersion, turning "your living room into a sublime, transcendent game space, realizing the fantasy of cyberspace or the holodeck."[8] To be sure, parts of the show seem to suggest this sort of total immersion model of gaming. The show's central narrative tells the story of a time-traveling boy, who stands in for the evolution of gaming controllers. The white adolescent actor, dressed in safari clothes, enters the arena on the back of an elephant, while the announcer intones:

> Since the dawn of time, humanity's long journey has lead us to countless discoveries. Objects along our path have projected our way forward, but the ever-more sophisticated inventions introduced ever-more complex languages for humans to master in order to communicate with machines. With each leap forward for civilization, more people were left behind. But our quest has now taken us to a completely new horizon. History is about to be re-written. This time, human beings will be at the center and the machine will be the one that adapts. After five million years of evolution, might the next

step—the next object—be the absence of an object? Is it possible that the future of humanity is humanity itself?[9]

After dismounting, the boy enacts this narrative by slowly climbing up a series of boulders on the stage, pausing on each to pull out of his bag the next generation of game controller and play a short game on the giant screen before him. When he arrives at the top rock, he begins to reach into the bag again for another controller (what looks like a Wiimote), but then hesitates and decide to confront the screen with no controller at all. As he stands atop what is now a giant lit-up logo for Xbox, he goes on to showcase dramatically how he can control an avatar with his own bodily movements.[10] The screen then drops to reveal the set for a living room, complete with a happy, modern, white nuclear family (mom, dad, son, daughter). They beckon the traveler enthusiastically, and he crosses over the threshold of the set, moving from his natural, primitive setting among the islanders to immerse himself in the family's living room game space, where he and they play some games for Kinect together.

Although the show presents its gamer characters as immersed, it hardly seems to emphasize a myth of total immersion or sublime transcendence. In fact, the show uses the presence of spectators—fictional and actual—to complicate this myth and to question not only how but *where* immersion in gaming happens. Despite the magical marvels around them, the E3 audience was constantly reminded of the conditions of their immersion, of their status *as* an audience, and of their complex and blurred relationship to the gamers represented onstage. That reminder is literally held over their heads when they enter the performance venue. Dangling high above them during the preshow entertainment is a living room couch, upon which is seated another modern, white nuclear family—mom, dad, and preadolescent son (Figure 22). Like the actual audience in the arena, the family gawks and points at the wonders below during the preshow entertainment. Thereafter, they continue to operate as audience stand-ins or models.

The son character, in particular, serves as a bridge between the performers, the audience, and the technology on display. When the Prospero-like figure waves his arms to begin the show proper, he cues a procession of natives, who parade into the space, moving through the audience, but stopping at the now-lowered couch to pick up the boy who waits excitedly holding a green ball. A group of natives hoists him above their heads and carries him toward the stage. As they set him down, he throws the ball out into the audience, and then is helped onto a boulder onstage by the "Ariel" character. Both watch as the ball gets thrown about in the audience for a few moments, finally landing in the hands of a young, white woman (not one of the hired performers) who looks to be a professional in her early thirties—hardly the demographic for the Xbox of the past. Ball in hand, she is shepherded by natives onto the boulder next to the boy, her audience poncho removed to create a parallel and bond between her and the young actor from the couch. And as "Prospero" stands above on a rock, his arms outstretched to show he is still directing the magical event/ritual, the natives offer their dance to the young woman, who stands self-consciously but solidly with "Ariel" and the modern boy from the couch. The symbolism is clear: the boy who had been a fictional audience member on the couch represents the gamer demographic of the past while the young woman from the actual audience represents the market Kinect aims to capture with their new technology. Notably, both are personations of a theater audience. Featured here in its diversity, the audience is fictionally and literally being welcomed *into* the technology. Indeed, as the woman holds the green ball—a simplified version of the Xbox icon—Microsoft intimates that with Kinect, it is putting the Xbox into the hands of theater audiences, in all their gender and age diversity.

The significance of the audience was more than symbolic in the E3 show, which went on to display explicitly the role of participatory spectatorship in the Kinect gaming experience. The central part of the show involved the onstage family playing a series of new Kinect games on their large television. Although on one occasion, a member of the family played alone in the room, the rest of the time, gamers played before an onstage audience. It was clear that although certain games were targeted toward a particular demographic represented by the family—Dad sword-fights, Mom does yoga—the rest of the family were to be active spectators for all the games. The fictional family and their friends cheered on the players, turning to each other occasionally to indicate approval or surprise. Onstage spectators also mimicked the game players' actions, leaning forward and sideways and jumping up when the game seemed to call for those bodily actions. The husband and children even meditated peacefully on the floor while mom tried out the yoga game. To be sure, Microsoft was presenting the Kinect as a *social* gaming apparatus, one well suited to family gaming; but the concept of sociality doesn't fully describe the phenomenon on display in this show and in other Kinect advertising, which repeatedly represents gameplay as enjoyable for gamers as well as for those who watch them from the couch.[11] The point is not only that Kinect's technology is so simple that anyone in the family can use it, or even that Kinect brings the whole family together. It is that Kinect games are not only fun to play but fun to watch. If they create connection/Kinection within social groups, they do so by drawing spectators cognitively and emotionally into gameplay.

Although later advertisements will draw on this point as well, it gets made clearly and spectacularly in the E3 show, which represents vicarious play by spectators onstage as well as in the arena at large. While the family plays and watches games inside the framed stage, the natives from Cirque du Soleil remain below on the rocks, excitedly observing the ludic action and notably making movements with their bodies that show they are responding to the game much as the players do. When mom steers during a driving game, her family stands around her in front of the screen as if in the same car, mirroring her responsive gestures to the game—but so too do the native dancers below. Their vicarious play is even more remarkable in light of their distance from the gaming scene. Fictionally, they inhabit some faraway island where no one has ever seen videogames; but literally, they also stand far away from the screen, spatially aligned with the audience in the arena (Figure 23).

Perhaps even more interesting in light of my argument in Chapter 3 about the bird's-eye view in the early modern theater, the fictional family on the couch suspended from the arena ceiling also shows signs of vicarious play. Although the couch boy—who had been bodysurfed away when the show proper began—appears to have been lost somewhere inside the gaming world onstage, his fictional parents stay on the couch for the rest of the show, fully engaged in the ludic action far below them. Whether or not members of the venue audience noticed them, Microsoft didn't want them forgotten. The video Microsoft made of the launch event repeatedly cuts to shots of the suspended spectator family to show their reactions and their continued investment in the games.[12] Microsoft's video gives the couch family as well as home viewers a bird's-eye view of the staged games below, but shows that their distance need not preclude their active engagement. The suspended couch spectators, about as far above and away from the stage as one can imagine, are just as invested cognitively and emotionally as those who are right onstage playing physically. The couch family models the spectator behavior that, I would argue, Microsoft was trying to craft and inspire with its Kinect technology. If Wii encouraged moms, dads, girls, and others not usually recognized as part of the gaming demographic to come into the living room and play, then Kinect was taking things a step further, offering a gameplay experience for literally everyone, even those who don't want to engage physically. It doesn't get any more inclusive than that.

Microsoft's inclusion of spectators gets driven home in the culminating moments of the show, when the stage clears and yet another fictional boy—the boy who has been part of the gaming family onstage—mounts a giant ball insignia for Xbox. As he waves his arms, echoing the earlier gestures of the Prospero-like figure who began the show, the audience's white ponchos are turned into screens to reflect the arena's green, blue, and red lighting. With his gestures, the boy appears to direct both the surging music and the audience-created light show below him, directing, that is, the event's spectators. In a final symbolic moment, then, Microsoft underscores the way spectators are being orchestrated by this new gaming technology and its players. Whether they want to or not, the audience, simply by watching, has been actively inculcated into gameplay.

SPECTATORS AS PLAYERS, PLAYERS AS SPECTATORS

The technology for Kinect may be novel, but its design principles and marketing strategy hark back four hundred years to the beginnings of commercial theater. The Kinect usefully showcases the argument that I've been making throughout this book about the early modern theater as playable media designed to encourage spectators' vicarious gaming. That idea is writ large in the show Microsoft staged to announce Kinect, but it is also an idea that appears to have driven the very design of Kinect and similar gaming peripherals. Mimetic interface games retheatricalize gaming by harnessing human movement, putting bodily gestures at the center of the gaming experience. It isn't at all surprising that Wii and Xbox consoles helped usher in a slew of games about the performing arts. There is arguably a natural connection between these gaming platforms and the performing arts: both encourage creative expression through bodily movement and, I have suggested, both refigure play as a kind of performance for an audience that plays along. However, the theatrical potential of Kinect remains unfulfilled largely because the designers of games for it have not recognized what theater entrepreneurs in the early modern period knew well: that spectators are an untapped market for gameplay. Peripherals like the Wiimote and the Kinect have tremendous theatrical potential, but the commercial software that has been created for them takes little advantage of the hardware's theatrical affordances.

A case in point are the music games *Rock Band* and *Guitar Hero*, which invite their users to be rock stars. The controllers in these games are shaped like musical instruments, which users manipulate to play a selected song. The game screen presents musical notation, and users are supposed to press a corresponding button on their controllers as if they are playing the required note on an instrument. When players are successful, the game's speakers emit the musical note that is part of the prerecorded song. As ethnomusicologist Kiri Miller puts it in her fascinating account of user experience, players "reconstitute a recorded song by adding performance," essentially "put[ing] the performance back into recorded music, reanimating it with their physical engagement and adrenaline."[13] Miller observes that *Rock Band* and *Guitar Hero* are "deeply theatrical, by design" and tend to bring out the performer in everyone. Even players motivated by scoring points put on a show, knowing full well that gesturing like glam rock musicians will not contribute directly to the outcome of their game.[14] Performance matters to everyone who plays. In this way, the games are "stitching recorded musical sound and performing bodies back together."[15] But what precisely is the audience's role in this performance?

Miller recognizes the presence of audience members in certain gaming contexts, but though she is fundamentally interested in the performance qualities associated with these games, she only rarely interviews audiences or theorizes their forms of participation. This is not a failure of her study, but rather a natural repercussion of the games at the center of it. In discussing the most theatrical contexts for gameplay—public bar nights where *Rock Band* is played by groups of patrons, much like karaoke— Miller observes:

> The game nights brought out rock-star physicality in some performers, but it's worth remembering that apart from the occasional singer who turned to face the crowd in the rest of the bar, virtually all players had their backs to the audience—an audience that was only occasionally paying attention in any case. While playing in public still had the power to inspire some performance anxiety and adrenaline, bandmates were mostly playing for each other and themselves.[16]

In other words, in its most theatrical playing contexts, *Rock Band* is more of a social outlet for players than it is a theatrical event in which spectators participate. This is arguably true for all of the commercial games that have thus far been produced for the Kinect. None has realized its theatrical potential because, although game designers are incredibly skilled at getting users to feel like the avatar performers they mime, no one has figured out how to harness the spectator investment Kinect-based games are arguably capable of generating.

There are a number of reasons for this, though paramount among them is what we might call the *schizospectatorship* of mimetic interface games: the presence of multiple but incompatible audiences during gameplay. My term is inspired by composer R. Murray Schafer's concept of *schizophonia*, the division between played and heard music that emerges with the invention of technologies for playing recorded music. *Guitar Hero* and *Rock Band* may, through performance, reconcile the schizophonia of the digital age, as Miller maintains, but they fail to reconcile its schizospectatorship. In commercially produced mimetic interface games, the live, human audience that watches gameplay from the sidelines is associated with but clearly separated from, and superseded by, the digital audience that is built into the game's software. Motion capture games, including *Guitar Hero* and *Rock Band*, prioritize the digital, prerecorded audience over the ambient one, thereby depleting the ambient audience's agency and sense of investment in the game. This is a consequence of their design, not of the circumstances of their use. Dance, singing, and musical instrument games code "correct" performance right into the software, challenging players to achieve it through their gameplay. Through scoring and through visual and aural representations of an onscreen audience, the games tell players when they have performed well. Even if in social scenes of play, users may ignore digital feedback, playing for their own pleasure or sometimes charged by the pressure of an audience's eyes and ears, the screen constantly reminds players and their ambient audiences that the ultimate arbiter of performance quality is the machine. And because they cast the machine as the ultimate authority, these games stop short of fulfilling the theatrical potential that Microsoft imagined and portrayed when it introduced Kinect.

But the strong historical links between gaming and theater that Microsoft tapped into through Kinect can be fulfilled. My evidence is *Play the Knave*, a Kinect-enabled game I co-created with colleagues and students at the University of California Davis's Modlab.[17] The game invites players to design and star in a Shakespeare production. After selecting their dramatic text and a particular scene from it, or writing their own script, users choose a theater stage for their production (3D background), costumed actors to take on the character roles in the scene (avatars), and background music (sound design). Once the screen has transformed to reflect these production choices, between one and four users enact the scene, karaoke style. They are invited to recite the scrolling lines, using their bodies to move their avatars onscreen (Figures 24 and 25).[18] Unlike commercially produced Kinect games, where digital avatars are models for players to follow, *Play the Knave* allows users to control their avatars directly; instead of the player mimicking the avatar, the avatar mimics the player. The scene (onscreen action and the player's voice) can be recorded and the video produced then downloaded by the user to be watched, edited, and/or shared. Future plans include developing a server to facilitate even more extensive forms of collaborative production, including allowing players to share and edit each other's scripts. Additionally, a user might record the part of one character in a scene, upload that to the server, and then have a friend or stranger download that scene to play the other character in it.

There is certainly much that could be said about how Shakespearean drama and theatrical performance are presented in *Play the Knave*, a concern I have begun to address elsewhere.[19] But given *Gaming the Stage*'s larger interests in theorizing and historicizing spectatorship, I focus in this Epilogue on the impact of *Play the Knave*'s design on audiences and especially on the game's capacity to make spectators feel like players. For the past several years, I have been working with graduate students and undergraduate interns to research how audiences respond when *Play the Knave* is installed in theaters, public spaces, and classrooms, the longest-term installation having been at the Stratford Festival in Ontario for three months in the summer of 2015.[20] One of the findings from research at over two dozen installations is that spectators of *Play the Knave* play vicariously. Even though players face the screen and turn their back on spectators, as is the case in other Kinect games, audiences remain actively invested in what is happening in the game space. They watch both the screen and the players intently, taking pictures and video of both. They laugh when players do funny things. They mime actions they want players to do. They call out suggestions, correct players' pronunciation of Shakespeare's lines, and encourage the players to alter their movements. Sometimes, they collaborate to make performances of other players better. For instance, when a player is particularly nervous about speaking Shakespeare's lines, a member of the audience sometimes volunteers to speak the lines from outside the playing space, freeing the player up just to gesture. And, of course, spectators laugh when players do funny things, and they usually applaud at the end of a session of gameplay.[21] In short, they do all the things that Microsoft dramatized audiences doing with Kinect in the E3 show, and more.

This engagement, or rather this *production*, of active spectators who play along vicariously is an outgrowth of *Play the Knave*'s design and specifically its ability to reconcile the schizospectatorship that is found in other Kinect games. To be sure, there are all sorts of tensions that the game recognizes and perpetuates through the copresence of digital technology and ambient, physical bodies in space. But because *Play the Knave* doesn't prioritize the digital spectator, it makes lots more room for the ambient one. The most obvious way this is facilitated is through the absence of a scoring mechanism within the game. The game's software simply does not judge the players. There is some prerecorded audience applause that automatically plays when users finish a scene, but this digital audience response is canned, with approval in no way connected to a player's actual performance. Many beta testers have asked for some sort of scoring mechanism, sometimes claiming that *Play the Knave* doesn't feel like a game without that. Setting aside their overly narrow definition of what constitutes a game—a definition that has been thoughtfully problematized by theorists of games and challenged by independent game designers[22]—it's worth noting the effect of denying players a machine-generated score. Because the machine does not give players feedback on their performance, they either judge it for themselves or seek judgment from other human observers in the ambient space: their playing partners or spectators. And these other audiences are empowered to give such feedback because their views are in no way superseded by the authority of the machine. In *Play the Knave*, the job of evaluating player performance is outsourced to the live, physical audience in the room, just as is true in actual theater.

Another reason *Play the Knave* encourages engaged spectatorship is because the game's design allows for a certain degree of glitchiness in the avatars, which results in a theatrical disjunction between the player and avatar. These glitches appear because *Play the Knave* gives users extensive control over the movements of their avatars. Unlike in most motion-sensing dance games, where the avatars move regardless of what the player does, in our game the player animates the avatar. The trade-off for giving more creative freedom to players is that that they sometimes misunderstand, forget, or ignore that they are working with a digital object, expecting the screen to work like a mirror. And so they make gestures that do not map effectively onto the avatars, which players then perceive as glitchy.[23] This trade-off is undoubtedly the practical reason commercial gaming software for Kinect does not allow players to control their avatars more fully; the resulting animation is unpredictable and can provoke discomfort and even revulsion in users, what is known as the *uncanny valley* effect. Kinect's ability to read and render accurately the complex motions of the performer's body is limited in part by its motion capture technique, which, especially when involving a single camera, generates significantly weaker data than that of more elaborate and costly motion capture systems; the latter are able to reflect back many more subtleties of performers' movements by using multiple cameras and by having users wear expensive gear and/or body suits.[24]

Serious artists interested in using motion capture technology in performance tend toward these more complex systems and away from the single-camera Kinect setup and, subsequently, there has been little research on the theatricality of Kinect, despite scholars' interest in how the uncanny valley produced by motion capture performance affects understandings of a performer's embodiment and selfhood.[25] I want to suggest, however, that these technological "limitations" are, in fact, key to Kinect's theatrical affordances. Glitches in the animation help to transform a session of *Play the Knave* into a theatrical event. When the avatars move in ways users don't expect, the game underscores the extent to which the avatars, though largely controlled by the players, are separate entities whose movements are governed, ultimately, by the machine. Players, their full immersion interrupted, come to feel like spectators of their avatars. This is quite an odd sensation. Users describe feeling simultaneously like player/producer *and* spectator/receiver of their own digital performance. A repercussion of turning players into spectators is that they become even more firmly aligned with the actual spectators in the gaming room. No one has total control over the avatar. And when spectators see players made into spectators, the latter are better able to imagine themselves as players.

In using a Shakespeare theater game to drive home my book's argument about the connection between games and theater, I do not mean to suggest that this connection is specific to early modern drama, plays, and theatrical culture. For although *Play the Knave* is certainly *about* Shakespearean performance (in terms of content and theme, it is a game about putting on a play), I hope to have shown that its theatricality is less a function of its subject matter than of its design—a design made possible because of the theatrical affordances of Kinect itself. The significance of that technology can be appreciated by comparing *Play the Knave* to other games about Shakespeare, as I have done elsewhere in a study of a range of other games thematically concerned with Shakespeare's life, drama, and theater.[26] *Play the Knave* is useful because it showcases how spectators can come to feel like players, regardless of whether they physically participate in the core gaming experience at hand. Ludic interaction can take many forms. This kind of inclusion of spectators, I have argued, has a long history and has served theater's development. To be sure, the current landscape for gaming and for theater is very different than it was in the sixteenth and seventeenth centuries. Today, commercial theater doesn't compete quite as directly with games as it once did. A Venn diagram of consumers of videogames and of theater probably wouldn't show a sizable overlap between these forms of entertainment, or at least not to the degree there was in early modern London. But just as building gaming concepts into theater was a boon for early modern dramatists, performers, and audiences, so building theatrical concepts into gaming has been a boon for the gaming industry today. Kinect, which was an instant success when it was released, proves that today's gamers are keen to perform and to watch others perform. They are keen to become theater participants. If anyone is uncertain about perpetuating the theatricality of mimetic interface games, it appears to be the developers of gaming platforms and of software for those platforms. Indeed, in October of 2017, Microsoft announced that it would no longer manufacture the Kinect camera, opting to invest in technologies like the HoloLens that mediate the player's digital world through headsets and glasses.[27] Kinect's inventor Alex Kipman may eschew the VR label to call Microsoft's new line of products "Mixed Reality," but this technology has much more in common with traditional VR than it does with Kinect.[28]

Scholars of theater, performance, and media have elegantly defended VR technologies, reminding us that the body doesn't disappear during the VR experience, as is often assumed. VR can offer the player a quite intense and, media scholar Mark Hansen argues, even privileged perspective on embodiment.[29] But if VR is opening up new worlds for game players, it is simultaneously closing down older worlds for game spectators. VR may, in effect, evince the antitheatricality of our age. The next generation of gaming peripherals may have the power to return players to a deeper understanding of their embodiment, but this technology also threatens to cut players off from the ambient space their bodies inhabit during gameplay, a space that can include other bodies. VR headsets require the player to be blind and often deaf to their ambient audience so that they can be "immersed" more fully in the game world they wish to enter. As a result, it's hard to take any pleasure in watching someone else play a VR game, except perhaps to laugh as the player stumbles around the ambient game space, trying not to bash into walls. More sophisticated gaming devices may please hard-core gamers who demand ever better graphics and less lag between their movements and the machine's responses—in short, greater immersion in the gameplay experience. But if the history of games and theater is any indication, detheatricalizing games risks alienating a sizable market: the spectators who take comfort and quite a bit of pleasure in playing vicariously. Their capacity to do that is largely a function of their ability to share with players the same virtual *and* ambient space.

When it introduced Kinect, Microsoft asked us to imagine a world where humans were at the center of interactive gaming. That world already exists. It is called theater. And for centuries, everyone has played. As Microsoft contemplates the future of playable media technology, here's hoping they remember that sometimes the most innovative ideas are those that catch up with the past.

Notes

INTRODUCTION

1. Themes in other years are much broader and more obviously inspired by the larger field of gaming: "Simulationist" (2003), "Fantasy" (2004), "Historical" (2005), "Time" (2007), and more recently "Technology" (2016) and "Borders" (2017). The 2011 assigned theme was "Avon Calling," a reference to Stratford-upon-Avon, the birthplace of Shakespeare.

2. Medievalists have debated the extent to which games and dramatic plays could be clearly distinguished from one another before the sixteenth century. See especially Glending Olson, "Plays as Play: A Medieval Ethical Theory of Performance and the Intellectual Context of the *Tretise of Miraclis Pleyinge*," *Viator: Medieval and Renaissance Studies* 26 (1995): 195–221; V. A. Kolve, *The Play Called "Corpus Christi"* (Stanford, CA: Stanford University Press, 1966), esp. chap. 2; Lawrence M. Clopper, *Drama, Play, and Game: English Festive Culture in the Medieval and Early Modern Period* (Chicago: University of Chicago Press, 2001). I am suggesting that this overlap extends, albeit in some different ways, beyond the medieval period. Historians of early modern theater have examined the ways other forms of recreation were implicated in theatrical production, with some, such as Glynn Wickham, even arguing that early modern plays were treated less as literature than as game.

3. Andrew Gurr, "Bears and Players: Philip Henslowe's Double Acts," *Shakespeare Bulletin* 22.4 (2004): 31–41; Jason Scott-Warren, "When Theaters Were Bear-Gardens; or, What's at Stake in the Comedy of Humors," *Shakespeare Quarterly* 54.1 (2003): 63–82; John R. Ford, "Changeable Taffeta: Re-dressing the Bears in *Twelfth Night*," in *Inside Shakespeare: Essays on the Blackfriars Stage*, ed. Paul Menzer (Selinsgrove, PA: Susquehana University Press: 2006), 174–91.

4. E.g., Janet H. Murray, *Hamlet on the Holodeck: The Future of Narrative in Cyberspace*, 2nd printing (Cambridge, MA: MIT Press, 1999).

5. See especially "Drama, Script, Theater, and Performance," reprinted in Richard Schechner, *Performance Theory*, rev. ed. (London: Routledge, 2003).

6. For an interesting analysis of how *Guitar Hero* encourages participatory performance by its players, see Kiri Miller, *Playing Along: Digital Games, YouTube, and Virtual Performance* (Oxford: Oxford University Press, 2012).

7. Among the titles currently available are dance games like *Just Dance*, *Dance Central*, and *Dance Dance Revolution*; singing games like *Disney Sing It*, *SingStar*, and *Karaoke Revolution*; and musical instrument games like *Guitar*

Hero, Rock Band, and *Rocksmith.* The only motion capture game that uses theatrical plays and performance for content is *Play the Knave,* a project from the University of California, Davis, ModLab and for which I am the director. It is discussed further in the present book's Epilogue.

8. Jussi Parikka, *What Is Media Archaeology?* (Cambridge: Polity Press, 2012), 13.

9. The exception in game studies is recent work on the long history of military games. See, for instance, Philipp von Hilgers, *War Games: A History of War on Paper,* trans. Ross Benjamin (Cambridge, MA: MIT Press, 2012); Nina B. Huntemann and Matthew Thomas Payne, eds., *Joystick Soldiers: The Politics of Play in Military Video Games* (New York: Routledge, 2010). I aim to show, however, that earlier games are pertinent to study of a wide range of contemporary games, beyond those with links to the military. On the relevance of preindustrial media to our understanding of contemporary media, see especially Siegfried Zielinski, *Deep Time of the Media: Toward an Archaeology of Hearing and Seeing by Technical Means,* trans. Gloria Custance (Cambridge, MA: MIT Press, 2006); Jussi Parikka, *A Geology of Media* (Minneapolis: University of Minnesota Press, 2015). Other scholars have also made strong cases for the importance of providing longer histories of media, though they do not go back quite as far as Zielinski's and Parikka's books. Key works include media histories such Lisa Gitelman, *Always Already New: Media, History, and the Data of Culture* (Cambridge, MA: MIT Press, 2006); and Lisa Gitelman and Geoffrey B. Pingree, eds., *New Media, 1740–1915* (Cambridge, MA: MIT Press, 2003), as well as media archaeologies such as Erkki Huhtamo and Jussi Parikka, *Media Archaeology: Approaches, Applications, and Implications* (Berkeley: University of California Press, 2011); Parikka, *What Is Media Archaeology?*; and Erkki Huhtamo, *Illusions in Motion: Media Archaeology of the Moving Panorama and Related Spectacles* (Cambridge, MA: MIT Press, 2013).

10. Michael D. Bristol, *Big-Time Shakespeare* (London: Routledge, 1996), 40. See also Steven Mullaney, *The Place of the Stage: License, Play, and Power in Renaissance England* (Chicago: University of Chicago Press, 1988); Douglas Bruster, *Drama and Market in the Age of Shakespeare* (Cambridge: Cambridge University Press, 1992); Donald Hedrick, "Real Entertainment: Sportification, Coercion, and Carceral Theater," in *Thunder at a Playhouse: Essaying Shakespeare and the Early Modern Stage,* ed. Peter Kanelos and Matt Kozusko (Selinsgrove, PA: Susquehanna University Press, 2010), 50–66. On the relationship between theater and the emerging London market economy, see also Jean-Christophe Agnew, *Worlds Apart: The Market and the Theater in Anglo-American Thought, 1550–1750* (Cambridge: Cambridge University Press, 1986).

11. The rhetoric of interactivity and its indebtedness to digital culture has been discussed in each of these examples, respectively, by Kate Rumbold, "From 'Access' to 'Creativity': Shakespeare Institutions, New Media, and the Language of Cultural Value," *Shakespeare Quarterly* 61.3 (2010): 313–36; W. B. Worthen, "Interactive, Immersive, Original Shakespeare," *Shakespeare Bulletin* 35.3 (2017): 407–24; Joe Falocco, *Reimagining Shakespeare's Playhouse: Early Modern Staging Conventions in the Twentieth Century* (Cambridge: D. S. Brewer, 2010). See also Christie Carson, "Democratising the Audience?," in *Shakespeare's Globe:*

A Theatrical Experiment, ed. Christie Carson and Farah Karim-Cooper (Cambridge: Cambridge University Press, 2008), 115–26, and Christie Carson, "Technology as a Bridge to Audience Participation?," in *Performance and Technology: Practices of Virtual Embodiment and Interactivity*, ed. Susan Broadhurst and Josephine Machon (New York: Palgrave Macmillan, 2011), 181–93, which argue that Shakespeare's Globe Theatre, in contrast to more established and well-funded London theaters such as the RSC, has successfully embraced "the new digital aesthetic which demands at least a sense of democracy and fuller individual participation" ("Democratizing," 121).

12. Rumbold, "From 'Access' to 'Creativity,'" 314.

13. Worthen, "Interactive, Immersive, Original Shakespeare," 414.

14. Important works on contemporary immersive theater include Josephine Machon, *Immersive Theatres: Intimacy and Immediacy in Contemporary Performance* (Basingstoke, UK: Palgrave Macmillan, 2013); and Gareth White, *Audience Participation in Theatre: Aesthetics of the Invitation* (New York: Palgrave Macmillan, 2013).

15. Stephanie Boluk and Patrick LeMieux, *Metagaming: Playing, Competing, Spectating, Cheating, Trading, Making, and Breaking Videogames* (Minneapolis: University of Minnesota Press, 2017). Available at https://manifold.umn.edu/read/c5926868-00c4-45f8-8e91-45cfd9140a87/section/84dabaa3-647e-4b18-8c8a-ba61cbf48fe3#cvi (accessed 19 December 2017).

16. Jacques Rancière, *The Emancipated Spectator*, trans. Gregory Elliott (London: Verso, 2011), 15.

17. Noah Wardrip-Fruin, "Playable Media and Textual Instruments" (2005), http://www.dichtung-digital.de/2005/1/Wardrip-Fruin/index.htm (accessed 19 December 2017).

18. Friedrich A. Kittler, *Discourse Networks 1800/1900*, trans. Michael Metteer, with Chris Cullens (Stanford, CA: Stanford University Press, 1990); and Friedrich A. Kittler, *Gramophone, Film, Typewriter*, trans. Geoffrey Winthrop-Young and Michael Wutz (Stanford, CA: Stanford University Press, 1999). Kittler's work has been foundational for the emerging field of media archaeology even as his insights about literary texts as archives have generally been abandoned.

19. The two most prominent attempts to use theater and drama to theorize digital media are Brenda Laurel, *Computers as Theatre* (Reading, MA: Addison–Wesley, 1993) and Murray, *Hamlet on the Holodeck*. Both books emphasize drama's narrative elements, however, and do not attend to the phenomenological experience of theater. This emphasis on narrative has been criticized by many scholars in game studies, consequently convincing many such scholars that theater is an insufficient model for games. My book rescues theater from this charge by putting dramatic narratives into dialogue with theatrical form.

20. My method is akin to that described in Erkki Huhtamo, "Dismantling the Fairy Engine: Media Archaeology as Topos Study," in *Media Archaeology: Approaches, Applications, and Implications*, ed. Erkki Huhtamo and Jussi Parikka (Berkeley: University of California Press, 2011), 27–47.

21. Sitting pastimes are mentioned in at least three dozen plays from the period, with just over half of these presenting an actual game onstage. Games of cards, chess, and especially dice are prominent also in Restoration drama

and can be found, of course, in plenty of modern drama as well. The term "sitting pastimes" is used, for instance, in the third book of King James I, *Basilikon Dōron; or, His Majesties Instructions To His Dearest Sonne, Henry the Prince* (London, 1603), which refers to dice, cards, tables, and chess as "sitting house pastimes" (122). See also Sir William Forrest's "The Poesye of Princylye Practice," which describes "tables, chesse, or cardis" as "syttynge pastymes." Cited in E. S. Taylor, *The History of Playing Cards, with Anecdotes of Their Use in Conjuring, Fortune-Telling, and Card-Sharping* [1865] (Rutland, VT: Charles E. Tuttle, 1973), 292. Throughout this book, when citing early modern texts, I have modernized i/j and u/v but otherwise retained early spelling.

22. The few critics who have examined scenes of gaming in early modern plays have tended to overlook this performance perspective, analyzing games for their symbolic meaning. The most comprehensive studies of sitting pastimes in early modern drama are Joseph T. McCullen Jr., "The Use of Parlor and Tavern Games in Elizabethan and Early Stuart Drama," *Modern Language Quarterly* 14.1 (1953): 7–14; and Delmar E. Solem, "Some Elizabethan Game Scenes," *Educational Theatre Journal* 6.1 (1954): 15–21. Others, focused on specific plays, are discussed in the chapters that follow.

23. Marianne Brish Evett, ed., *Henry Porter's Two Angry Women of Abington: A Critical Edition* (New York: Garland, 1980), 1.124n.

24. Stanton B. Garner, Jr., *Bodied Spaces: Phenomenology and Performance in Contemporary Drama* (Ithaca: Cornell University Press, 1994), 40–3, esp. 41.

25. Ibid., 41.

26. A useful touchstone for this approach is Bruce R. Smith's method of historical phenomenology, which reminds us that "[i]ncluded in the situatedness of the observer . . . are the *feelings* of the observer in the face of what he or she sees" (13). Historical phenomenology not only opens up different sorts of questions but calls for different methods of critical analysis as it urges scholars not only to historically contextualize but also *"inhabit the evidence"* (37; his emphasis). See Bruce R. Smith, *Phenomenal Shakespeare* (Chichester, UK: Wiley–Blackwell, 2010). For a trenchant application of historical phenomenology to the study of spectator affect in the early modern theater, see Allison P. Hobgood, *Passionate Playgoing in Early Modern England* (Cambridge: Cambridge University Press, 2014).

27. On play as research, see Espen Aarseth, "Playing Research: Methodological Approaches to Game Analysis" (paper presented at the Game Approaches / Spil-veje: Papers for spilforskning.dk Conference, 28–9 August 2003); Eric Zimmerman argues for playing as a mode of research during the game design process in Eric Zimmerman, "Play as Research: The Interactive Design Process," Final Draft, 8 July 2003, http://static1.squarespace.com/static/579b8aa26b8f5b8f49605c96/t/59921253cd39c3da5bd27a6f/1502745178453/Iterative_Design.pdf (accessed 18 October 2016).

28. I am influenced here by Smith's view in *Phenomenal Shakespeare* of the present and the early modern past "not as separate compartments but as relative points along a continuum" (36).

29. For interesting discussions of the implications of prepayment in the commercial theater, see Hedrick, "Real Entertainment"; and Richard Preiss, "Interi-

ority," in *Early Modern Theatricality*, ed. Henry S. Turner (Oxford: Oxford University Press, 2013), 47–70.

30. Michael D. Bristol, "Theater and Popular Culture," in *A New History of Early English Drama*, ed. John D. Cox and David Scott Kastan (New York: Columbia University Press, 1997), 231–48, argues that early modern audiences were well prepared for this "transformation of otherwise familiar performance practices into merchandise" through their exposure to London's flourishing commodity culture, which, like the commercial theater, enabled consumers to obtain "desired goods or amenities outside the complex networks of reciprocal obligation that prevail in a traditional community" (247). The argument is further elucidated in Bristol, *Big-Time Shakespeare*, esp. 30–41. While I concur that professional theaters aimed to turn plays into commodities, I doubt that the transition was as easy as Bristol implies.

31. Bristol, "Theater and Popular Culture," 248.

32. Erika T. Lin, "Popular Festivity and the Early Modern Stage: The Case of *George a Greene*," *Theatre Journal* 61.2 (2009): 271–97. On festive culture and drama, see, in addition to Lin, C. L. Barber, *Shakespeare's Festive Comedies* (Princeton, NJ: Princeton University Press, 1959); Robert Weimann, *Shakespeare and the Popular Tradition in the Theater: Studies in the Social Dimension of Dramatic Form and Function*, ed. Robert Schwartz (Baltimore: Johns Hopkins University Press, 1978); François Laroque, *Shakespeare's Festive World: Elizabethan Seasonal Entertainment and the Professional Stage*, trans. Janet Lloyd (Cambridge: Cambridge University Press, 1991); Naomi Conn Liebler, *Shakespeare's Festive Tragedy: The Ritual Foundations of Genre* (New York: Routledge, 1995); Michael D. Bristol, "Shamelessness in Arden: Early Modern Theater and the Obsolescence of Popular Theatricality," in *Print, Manuscript, Performance: The Changing Relations of the Media in Early Modern England*, ed. Arthur F. Marotti and Michael D. Bristol (Columbus: Ohio State University Press, 2000), 279–306. Further references are below. On gambling and drama, see Linda Woodbridge, "'He Beats Thee 'Gainst the Odds': Gambling, Risk Management, and *Antony and Cleopatra*," in *Antony and Cleopatra: New Critical Essays*, ed. Sara Munson Deats (New York: Routledge, 2004), 193–211; and Hedrick, "Real Entertainment." For an especially thorough treatment of gambling in French culture, with several chapters pertaining to plays, see Thomas M. Kavanagh, *Dice, Cards, Wheels: A Different History of French Culture* (Philadelphia: University of Pennsylvania Press, 2005).

33. Richard Preiss, *Clowning and Authorship in Early Modern Theatre* (Cambridge: Cambridge University Press, 2014). Preiss claims this meant plays were not commodities. I would maintain, though, that the *experience* of destroying something could itself be commodified entertainment, as it certainly has become in many modern entertainments, such as shooting games.

34. These studies are usually overreliant on theories of play by Johan Huizinga, *Homo Ludens: A Study of the Play-Element in Culture* (Boston: Beacon Press, 1950) and by Roger Caillois, *Man, Play and Games*, trans. Meyer Barash (Urbana: University of Illinois Press, 2001). Examples of studies that approach play broadly include Louis A. Montrose, "'Sport by Sport O'erthrown': *Love's Labour's Lost* and the Politics of Play," *Texas Studies in Literature and Language* 18.4

(1977): 528–52; Marianne L. Novy, "Patriarchy and Play in *The Taming of the Shrew*," *English Literary Renaissance* 9.2 (1979): 264–80; Anna K. Nardo, *The Ludic Self in Seventeenth-century English Literature* (Albany: SUNY Press, 1991), esp. chap. 2; Alessandro Arcangeli, *Recreation in the Renaissance: Attitudes toward Leisure and Pastimes in European Culture, c. 1425–1675* (New York: Palgrave Macmillan, 2003); and Alba Floreale, *Game and Gaming Metaphor: Proteus and the Gamester Masks in Seventeenth-Century Conduct Books and the Comedy of Manners* (Rome: Bulzoni, 2004). A more nuanced version of this broad approach can be found in Tom Bishop, "Shakespeare's Theater Games," *Journal of Medieval and Early Modern Studies* 40.1 (2010): 65–88. Although Bishop includes a wide range of games under the broad rubric of "play," he also provides a complex definition of game-playing competencies to include, in addition to pretense, "competitive cooperation" (73) and "improvisational interplay" (74).

35. In addition to work on festive performance by Lin, Bristol, Weimann, and others cited above, see Cynthia Marshall, "Wrestling as Play and Game in *As You Like It*," *Studies in English Literature, 1500–1900* 33.2 (1993): 265–87; Jennifer A. Low, *Manhood and the Duel: Masculinity in Early Modern Drama and Culture* (New York: Palgrave Macmillan, 2003); Edward Berry, *Shakespeare and the Hunt: A Cultural and Social Study* (Cambridge: Cambridge University Press, 2001); and Gregory M. Colón Semenza, *Sport, Politics, and Literature in the English Renaissance* (Newark: University of Delaware Press, 2003). On bear-baiting, see Gurr, Scott-Warren, and Ford. Among the exceptions are essays on chess and its uses in Shakespeare's *The Tempest* and Middleton's *Women Beware Women* and *A Game at Chess*, as well as McCullen's and Solem's surveys of parlor games in early modern drama, which do not provide much in the way of analysis.

36. Hedrick, "Real Entertainment," 56.

37. John Sutton, "Batting, Habit and Memory: The Embodied Mind and the Nature of Skill," *Sport in Society: Cultures, Commerce, Media, Politics* 10.5 (2007): 763–86.

38. Boluk and LeMieux, *Metagaming*, esp. Introduction.

39. Susan Bennett, *Theatre Audiences: A Theory of Production and Reception* (New York: Routledge, 1990); Erika Fischer-Lichte, *The Transformative Power of Performance: A New Aesthetics*, trans. Saskya Iris Jain (London: Routledge, 2008); Machon, *Immersive Theatres*. Machon's comprehensive study of immersive theater briefly notes that "participatory practice has existed in religious festivals and ceremonial pageants for centuries" (28), but her discussion of the origins of immersive theater begins with modernism. In general, performance studies scholars tend to overlook early drama to theorize interactive performance through more "gamelike" modern drama or by abandoning drama completely to focus on performance rituals and the theatricality of everyday life. The short memory of performance studies is particularly evinced in work on performance and media. Books such as Sarah Bay-Cheng, Jennifer Parker-Starbuck, and David Z. Saltz, *Performance and Media: Taxonomies for a Changing Field* (Ann Arbor: University of Michigan Press, 2015) theorize media almost entirely through contemporary digital culture. Although Steve Dixon, *Digital Performance: A History of New Media in Theater, Dance, Performance Art, and Installation* (Cambridge,

MA: MIT Press, 2007) and Chris Salter, *Entangled: Technology and the Transformation of Performance* (Cambridge, MA: MIT Press, 2010) provide longer histories of performance and media, they focus primarily on post-nineteenth-century performance practices. *Gaming the Stage* aims to open up the field of media and performance to a wider set of voices, setting a precedent for contributions to this field by other scholars working on traditional theater in pre- or nondigital cultures.

40. The extent to which playgoers competed with the play, making spectacles of themselves, has been discussed especially in relation to stool-sitters — patrons of indoor theaters who paid for seats directly on the stage. For interesting discussions of this phenomenon in Caroline theaters, see Tiffany Stern, "Taking Part: Actors and Audience on the Stage at Blackfriars," in *Inside Shakespeare: Essays on the Blackfriars Stage*, ed. Paul Menzer (Selinsgrove, PA: Susquehanna University Press, 2006); and Nova Myhill, "Taking the Stage: Spectators as Spectacle in the Caroline Private Theaters," in *Imagining the Audience in Early Modern Drama, 1558–1642*, ed. Jennifer A. Low and Nova Myhill (New York: Palgrave Macmillan, 2011), 37–54. Myhill argues that Caroline playwrights use their inductions to make stool-sitters more conscious of their spectatorship practices, directing their attention back to the play.

41. Celia Pearce, *The Interactive Book: A Guide to the Interactive Revolution* (Indianapolis: Macmillan Technical, 1997), esp. 422–3. For an overview of games as information systems, see Katie Salen and Eric Zimmerman, *Rules of Play: Game Design Fundamentals* (Cambridge, MA: MIT Press, 2004), esp. 203–11.

42. That said, one is hard-pressed to call even the parlor of an early modern household private insofar as servants moved in and out of these spaces. See Lena Cowen Orlin, *Private Matters and Public Culture in Post-Reformation England* (Ithaca, NY: Cornell University Press, 1994).

43. The foundational study is Clifford Geertz, "Deep Play: Notes on the Balinese Cockfight," in *The Interpretation of Cultures* (New York: Basic Books, 1972). Notably, even Geertz turns to Shakespeare's plays to illustrate his argument about how men negotiate social relations through the Balinese cockfight.

44. Alexandra Shepard, *Meanings of Manhood in Early Modern England* (Oxford: Oxford University Press, 2003), esp. 247–8.

45. For a thorough theorization of cheating in games — in relation to videogames — see Mia Consalvo, *Cheating: Gaining Advantage in Videogames* (Cambridge, MA: MIT Press, 2007).

46. On early modern as well as modern treatments of marriage as a contest, see Frances E. Dolan, *Marriage and Violence: The Early Modern Legacy* (Philadelphia: University of Pennsylvania Press, 2008).

47. Andrew Sofer, *Dark Matter: Invisibility in Drama, Theater, and Performance* (Ann Arbor: University of Michigan Press, 2013), 62.

48. Lorna Hutson argues along similar lines that early modern plays dramatize characters engaging in "false inference" to make audiences "aware of the contingency of fictional characters' access to knowledge about one another," subsequently prompting more intense imaginative and inferential work on the part of audiences. Lorna Hutson, *The Invention of Suspicion: Law and Mimesis in Shakespeare and Renaissance Drama* (Oxford: Oxford University Press, 2007), 314. I fol-

low Hutson in maintaining that rather than being a "'crisis of representation'" (309), as other critics have maintained, the audience's inability to gather information brought "new liveliness and power to the fictions" (2) of the early modern commercial stage. Paul Menzer makes a related argument about the production of character, arguing that "early modern theatrical performance ultimately casts doubt upon 'outwardness' and requires the spectator to believe in what he or she *cannot* see." Paul Menzer, "The Actor's Inhibition: Early Modern Acting and the Rhetoric of Restraint," *Renaissance Drama* 35 (2006): 83–111, esp. 106.

49. Jeremy Lopez argues that individual audience members were more similar than they were different, bringing to the theater a self-reflexive mode of spectatorship that plays could "rely on and manipulate." Jeremy Lopez, *Theatrical Convention and Audience Response in Early Modern Drama* (Cambridge: Cambridge University Press, 2003), 14. Along similar lines, Anthony B. Dawson and Paul Yachnin, *The Culture of Playgoing in Shakespeare's England: A Collaborative Debate* (Cambridge: Cambridge University Press, 2001)—though they disagree about whether early modern audience members gelled as a communal group or maintained their sense of individuality—share the view that plays and/or their actors managed their distracted audience members to refocus their attentions on the play. Paul Menzer, in his "Crowd Control," expands on Dawson's interests in unified audiences, maintaining that commercial theaters were highly successful in domesticating audiences by converting individuals into a "crowd," a "complacent audience" that was primed and ready to be transported by the play. Paul Menzer, "Crowd Control," in *Imagining the Audience in Early Modern Drama, 1558–1642*, ed. Jennifer A. Low and Nova Myhill (New York: Palgrave Macmillan, 2011), 19–36, at 24. See also earlier scholarship on audience response, such as Jean E. Howard, *Shakespeare's Art of Orchestration: Stage Technique and Audience Response* (Urbana: University of Illinois Press, 1984); Ralph Berry, *Shakespeare and the Awareness of the Audience* (London: Macmillan, 1985); and Phyllis Rackin, "The Role of Audience in Shakespeare's *Richard II*," *Shakespeare Quarterly* 36.3 (1985): 262–81.

50. Gina Bloom, *Voice in Motion: Staging Gender, Shaping Sound in Early Modern England* (Philadelphia: University of Pennsylvania Press, 2007). See also Allison Deutermann, *Listening for Theatrical Form in Early Modern England* (Edinburgh: Edinburgh University Press, 2016), which considers the ways dramas encouraged audiences to be discriminating listeners, arguing that this kind of resistant audition came to be a marker of social distinction and was associated especially with the genre of tragedy. Low and Myhill, in the introduction to their collection, reach a similar conclusion about the audience as a "vital partner in the production of meaning" (10) by underscoring differences among audience members and their interpretive power. Hobgood, *Passionate Playgoing*, also argues for greater spectator agency through a focus on spectator affect, concluding that "emotively palpable and powerful" playgoers attended "not as disciplined receivers," but as "potent and productive co-creators of the drama they attended" (28).

51. Charles Whitney, *Early Responses to Renaissance Drama* (Cambridge: Cambridge University Press, 2006) points out that audience members, individuated in their responses to the theater, made of the plays what they wanted, and their

written responses evince perspectives that don't necessarily align with the re-sponses actors, playwrights, or theater entrepreneurs hoped they would have. Richard Preiss goes even further, making the case for audiences' "unilateral seizure of control over the stage" (*Clowning and Authorship*, 37), often with the aim of destroying the play being staged for them. Preiss's view of audiences inverts Menzer's, but it is predicated on the same conception of theater as, in effect, combat, where audiences face off against actors, playwrights, and the-ater managers. As Preiss puts it, the "relation between theatre and audience is not 'partnership,' but competition" (27). See also Meredith Anne Skura, *Shake-speare the Actor and the Purposes of Playing* (Chicago: Chicago University Press, 1993); Paul Yachnin, *Stage-Wrights: Shakespeare, Jonson, Middleton, and the Mak-ing of Theatrical Value* (Philadelphia: University of Pennsylvania Press, 1997).

52. Preiss argues that neutralizing overentitled audiences—whose agency threatened the emergence of the play as an aesthetic and economic object—could not be done within the "mimetic field of the play" and thus it was left to the *platea* figure of the clown to manage and reinforce the line between produc-ers and consumers (81). However, game scenes, I argue, evince an effort on the part of theater's producers to manage the audience's participatory energies through the play itself. On the *platea* and its association with nonillusionistic performances in which an actor appeals to the world beyond the fictional play, see Weimann, *Shakespeare and the Popular Tradition*. The argument is extended in Robert Weimann, *Author's Pen and Actor's Voice: Playing and Writing in Shake-speare's Theatre*, ed. Helen Higbee and William West (Cambridge: Cambridge University Press, 2000).

53. A letter dated 4 December 1484 describes a Christmas party at Lady Mor-lee's home where "sche seyd that ther wer non dysyngs, ner harpyng, ner lu-tyng, ner syngyn, ner non lowde dysports, but pleying at the tabyllys, and schesse and cardes; sweche dysports sche gave her folkys leve to play and non odyr." Cited in W. Gurney Benham, *Playing Cards: History of the Pack and Expla-nations of Its Many Secrets* (London: Ward, Lock & Co., 1931), 25. Richard Eales, *Chess: The History of a Game* (Glasgow: Hardinge Simpole, 1985), 55, dates the letter to 1459.

54. Cited in Taylor, *History of Playing Cards, with Anecdotes*, 292.

55. Thomas Elyot, *The Boke Named the Governour* (London, 1537 [1531]).

56. David Cram, Jeffrey L. Forgeng, and Dorothy Johnston, eds., *Francis Wil-lughby's Book of Games: A Seventeenth-Century Treatise on Sports, Games and Pas-times* (Burlington, VT: Ashgate, 2003), 93.

57. Ibid.

58. John Florio, *Florios Second Frutes* (London, 1591), 65–79.

59. The term is from Jesper Juul, *A Casual Revolution: Reinventing Video Games and Their Players* (Cambridge, MA: MIT Press, 2010).

CHAPTER 1. GAMING HISTORY

1. Key histories of cards include Catherine Perry Hargrave, *A History of Playing Cards and a Bibliography of Cards and Gaming*, reprint ed. (New York:

Dover, 1966); Detlef Hoffmann, *The Playing Card: An Illustrated History*, trans. C. S. V. Salt, with Sylvia Mann (Greenwich, CT: New York Graphic Society Ltd., 1973); Taylor, *History of Playing Cards, with Anecdotes*; David Parlett, *The Oxford Guide to Card Games* (Oxford: Oxford University Press, 1990). For histories of backgammon/tables, see H. J. R. Murray, *A History of Board-Games Other than Chess* (Oxford: Clarendon Press, 1951); David Parlett, *The Oxford History of Board Games* (Oxford: Oxford University Press, 1999). For histories of chess, see H. J. R. Murray, *A History of Chess* (London: Oxford at the Clarendon Press, 1962); Eales, *Chess*.

2. For a useful critique of the idea that play texts are transcripts of performance, see W. B. Worthen, *Shakespeare and the Authority of Performance* (Cambridge: Cambridge University Press, 1997); and W. B. Worthen, *Shakespeare Performance Studies* (Cambridge: Cambridge University Press, 2014).

3. Gina Bloom, "The Historicist as Gamer," in *Shakespeare in Our Time: A Shakespeare Association of America Collection*, ed. Dympna Callaghan and Suzanne Gossett (London: Bloomsbury, 2016), 223–8.

4. The "magic circle" view of gaming was first articulated by Huizinga, *Homo Ludens*, but it was popularized in game studies by Salen and Zimmerman, *Rules of Play*. See also the concept of a "lusory attitude" advanced in Bernard Suits, *The Grasshopper: Games, Life, and Utopia* (Toronto: University of Toronto Press, 1978), esp. chap. 3.

5. Whether or not appearing under the sexy labels of presentism, historical phenomenology, or unhistoricism, much scholarship has begun to emphasize continuities between past and present and the ways our current, modern concerns inform the way we study the past. The concept of gaming can help to make sense of these purportedly different movements.

6. Getting beyond the ideology of the magic circle, game studies scholars Boluk and LeMieux (*Metagaming*) call attention to the metagame, which they argue to be crucial to gameplay, indeed constitutive of it in the case of videogames. Metagames comprise the range of practices gamers employ to improve their odds of winning, essentially ways of gaming the system.

7. Taylor, *History of Playing Cards, with Anecdotes*, supplies extensive evidence that the English learned of playing cards from the French. Among the earliest evidence of cards in England is a quarto book dating from 1490–1500, whose cover was partly constructed out of old playing cards in the French style. In addition, unlike the Italians and Spanish, whose four suits were Cups, Money, Swords, and Sticks, the English used the four suits found on French cards: Coeur, Carreau, Pique, and Trèfle, rendered in English as Hearts, Diamonds, Spades, and Clubs. French card makers, particularly from Rouen, supplied cards and card making know-how to the English well into the seventeenth century. Walter Morley Fletcher, "On Some Old Playing Cards Found in Trinity College," *Proceedings of the Cambridge Antiquarian Society* 11.3 (1907): 454–64, provides a detailed history of Rouen's centrality to card making and distribution in England. See also Benham, *Playing Cards*, who cites early records from the Worshipful Company of Makers of Playing Cards fining several members for employing "foreigners and strangers" (63),

whom most historians agree were card makers from France and particularly from Rouen.

8. The earliest European description of tables appears in King Alfonso X's *Libro de los Juegos* (*Book of Games*), a lavishly illustrated thirteenth-century book describing the games of chess, dice, and tables. Illustrations and a translation of the text available at http://historicgames.com/alphonso/ (accessed 29 August 2014).

9. R. C. Bell, *Board and Table Games from Many Civilizations* (London: Oxford University Press, 1960), 43.

10. This version of the game originated in India and was known as *chaturanga*.

11. Roswin Finkenzeller, Wilhelm Ziehr, and Emil M. Bührer, *Chess: A Celebration of 2,000 Years* (New York: Arcade/Little, Brown, 1990), 29.

12. Among the earliest European chess pieces are the Lewis chessmen, approximately seventy of which are owned by the British Museum, which purchased them after they were found on the Isle of Lewis in the nineteenth century. They originated most likely in twelfth-century Iceland and are made of walrus tusk. A number of chess pieces produced in thirteenth-century Europe were made of ivory. Francis Willughby's manuscript on gaming describes chess tables made of black ebony, with white squares made of ivory or bone. It also describes the triangles or "points" on the backgammon board, half white and half red, "made of red brasil" (i.e., brazilwood). The manuscript is printed in Cram et al., eds., *Willughby's Book of Games*.

13. Some of the earliest medieval chessboards were engraved into standing tables to be used solely for gaming; similar gaming tables were produced throughout the early modern period for use in noble households.

14. The V&A museum in London has numerous examples, many of which are made with ornate designs and expensive materials; as the museum catalog points out, there were probably much cheaper versions that simply haven't survived. Willughby describes them in great detail in his manuscript, where he also gives a thorough and precise description of the object: opened up, the board is about 22 in. long, 13 in. broad, and almost 2 in. thick, with one side (inside) for tables and one side for chess. He also describes how the ledge on the tables side is higher so as to "keepe the dice from flying out and the table men from slipping of" (Cram et al., eds., *Willughby's Book of Games*, 110).

15. Ibid., 128. There was a close relationship between card makers and pasteboard makers. In fact, when the Worshipful Company of Makers of Playing Cards was incorporated in 1628, they set down in their bylaws that all pasteboard makers had to report to the company regularly regarding the kind of paper they were making into pasteboard and had to pay 2d. per ream to the Company or suffer fairly significant penalties (40s. per month) for noncompliance (Benham, *Playing Cards*, 61). Interestingly this was the same amount that card makers were fined if discovered for the third time to be producing false cards — which says something about how much control card makers could exercise over pasteboard makers.

16. In one case in England, some early seventeenth-century cards were dis-

covered under an old staircase that was excavated in Cambridge's Trinity College. See Fletcher, "Old Playing Cards."

17. For example, four vocal parts for a song appear on the backs of cards dated to the early seventeenth century (Hoffmann, *Playing Card,* 9).

18. Ibid., 12–13.

19. Gerolamo Cardano, "The Book on Games of Chance," trans. Sydney Henry Gould, in Øystein Ore, *Cardano: The Gambling Scholar* (Princeton: Princeton University Press, 1953), 181–242, at 188.

20. James I, *Basilikon Dōron,* 124.

21. James Cleland, *Hērō-paideia; or, The Institution of a Young Noble Man* (Oxford, 1607), 227. Cleland cites James I directly in advocating against chess for noblemen because it "is an overwise and philosophicall follie" that rather than "free mens heades for a time from passionat thoughts of their affaires, it doeth on the contrarie fil & trouble mens braines" with schemes of how to play well (230).

22. Nicolas Faret, *The Honest Man; or, The Art to Please in Court,* trans. Edward Grimeston (London, 1632), 42, 44.

23. Chess might still carry more of an air of elitism than do cards and backgammon, but it is played widely by people from a range of social classes. Many American city parks have standing chess tables available for passersby. The popularity of chess among less privileged groups was represented in an episode of the popular television show *The Wire,* which shows members of an inner city gang playing chess while they wait for drug customers.

24. "De memoria et reminiscencia naturali et artificiosa" (British Library, Royal 12 B. XX, article 3).

25. Elyot, *Boke Named the Governour,* bk. 1, sect. 26.

26. Pedro Damiano da Odemia, *The Pleasaunt and Wittie Playe of the Cheasts Renewed with Instructions Both to Learne It Easely, and to Play It Well,* trans. William Ward (1562), A1v. The title page misattributes the translation to James Rowbothum.

27. Matthew Farber, "Games in Education: Teacher Takeaways," *Edutopia* (9 October 2014), http://www.edutopia.org/blog/games-in-education-teacher-takeaways-matthew-farber (accessed 11 October 2015). *Edutopia* offers a useful and comprehensive overview of approaches to game-based learning at http://www.edutopia.org/game-based-learning-resources (accessed 11 October 2015).

28. My description and discussion of the game is indebted to Jean-Claude Margolin and Diana Wormuth, "Mathias Ringmann's *Grammatica figurata; or, Grammar as a Card Game,*" *Yale French Studies* 47 (1972): 33–46.

29. Cited in Hoffmann, *Playing Card,* 38.

30. Taylor, *History of Playing Cards, with Anecdotes,* 189.

31. The decks, in various states of production, are all held by the British Museum and comprise *Le Jeu des fables ou de la métamorphose,* depicting mythical figures; *Le Jeu des rois de France* or *Le Jeu de l'histoire de France,* showing the various French kings and ending with Louis XIV; *Le Jeu des reynes renommées,* concerned with queens and other renowned women, from all times and all places; and *Le Jeu de la géographie.* For descriptions, see William Hughes Willshire, *A*

Descriptive Catalogue of Playing and Other Cards in the British Museum (London: Trustees of the British Museum, 1876), 127.

32. Anon., *The Boke of the New Cardys* (London, 1530).

33. Mentioned as an item in the catalog of works that is prefixed to William Maxwell, *Admirable and Notable Prophecies* (London, 1615), as is noted in William Andrew Chatto, *Facts and Speculations on the Origin and History of Playing Cards* (London: John Russell Smith, 1848), 139 n. 3.

34. Joseph Moxon, *The Use of the Astronomical Playing-Cards Teaching Any Ordinary Capacity by Them* (London, 1676).

35. *Grammatical Cards* (London, 1676). The deck is described in Willshire, *Descriptive Catalogue*, 235, sect. E. 175.

36. Ibid., sigs. A2v, A3r. The codex version is catalogued as E. 174. Descartes helped produce a set of geometrical playing cards that were probably sold alongside his book *Of the Geometrical Playing Cards* (published from his manuscript copy in 1697).

37. "medium, n.," II.4.a, OED Online, June 2017 (Oxford University Press), http://www.oed.com/view/Entry/115772?redirectedFrom=medium (accessed 27 December 2017).

38. Burton pronounces chess to be "fit for idle Gentlewomen, Souldiers in Garrison, and Courtiers that have nought but love matters to busie themselves about," but not for scholars, as it is "too troublesome for some mens braines, too full of anxiety, all out as bad as study." Robert Burton (as Democritus Junior), *Anatomy of Melancholy*, 5th ed. (Oxford, 1638 [1621]), 272–3 (part. 2, sect. 2, memb. 4). In *Basilikon Dōron* James discourages his son from playing chess because, unlike other games that "free mens heads for a time, from the fashious thoughts on their affaires; it by the contrary filleth and troubleth mens heads with as many fashious toyes of the playe, as before it was filled with thoughts on his affaires" (125).

39. *Grammatical Cards*, sig. A3v.

40. For an excellent discussion of current videogames that enable people to contribute to scientific research on nanotechnology while they play, see Colin Milburn, *Mondo Nano: Fun and Games in the World of Digital Matter* (Durham, NC: Duke University Press, 2015).

41. Leah S. Marcus, *The Politics of Mirth: Jonson, Herrick, Milton, Marvell and the Defense of Old Holiday Pastimes* (Chicago: University of Chicago Press, 1986) lays out carefully these political and religious debates about holiday pastimes, examining how seventeenth-century poets participated in them. These debates look a bit different, however, when approached through the narrower lens of sitting pastimes.

42. Taylor, *History of Playing Cards, with Anecdotes*, 217, 43.

43. Ibid., 217, 218.

44. Ibid., 219, 220.

45. Murray, *Board-Games Other than Chess*, 119.

46. Benham, *Playing Cards*, 26; Taylor, *History of Playing Cards, with Anecdotes*, 220–1.

47. Ibid., 25.

48. Taylor, *History of Playing Cards, with Anecdotes,* 222.

49. See Murray, *Board-Games Other than Chess,* 119.

50. Joyce Goggin, "A History of Otherness: Tarot and Playing Cards from Early Modern Europe," *Journal for the Academic Study of Magic* 1.1 (2003): 45–74, writes, "taxation strategies have been devised and revised to funnel gaming losses back into the greater economy, as a means of inducing irresponsible individuals to increase general and personal wealth rather dissipating it" (61).

51. In 1581, Henri III of France imposed a duty on cards for export, and a royal edict the following year heavily taxed cards exported from Rouen. These regulations caused many Rouen card makers to move their businesses to England so they could avoid the tax, which, even when reduced following protests, was still eight deniers a pack for England. On English taxes on imports, see Taylor, *History of Playing Cards, with Anecdotes,* 226. On French taxes on exports, see Fletcher, "Old Playing Cards," 460.

52. Fletcher, "Old Playing Cards," 459.

53. James I, . . . *Makers of Playing Cards within Our Realme of England* (1615), 1–2.

54. Benham, *Playing Cards,* 57–8, quote at 58.

55. Parliament of England and Wales, *Committee Appointed by Parliament for the Navy and Customes Ypon the Humble Complaints of Severall Poore Cardmakers of London* (London, 1643).

56. Benham notes that in the records of Archdeacons' Visitations in England in the late sixteenth century, there are hundreds of cases mentioned of card play on Sundays. He finds evidence of groups of men (between two and eight players) getting into trouble for playing cards, tables, and other games when they should have been at services (*Playing Cards,* 27).

57. Cited in Taylor, *History of Playing Cards, with Anecdotes,* 102.

58. Ibid., 103; my emphasis.

59. Cited in Chatto, *Facts and Speculations,* 122.

60. Nicholas Bownde, *Sabbathum Veteris et Noui Testamenti; or, The True Doctrine of the Sabbath* (London, 1606).

61. King Charles I, *The Kings Majesties Declaration to His Subjects Concerning Lawfull Sports to Be Used* (London, 1633), 15.

62. Peter Heylyn, *The History of the Sabbath* (London, 1636), bk. 2: 192.

63. Phillip Stubbes, *The Anatomie of Abuses* (London: 1583), sigs. D2v–D3r.

64. William Prynne, with Henry Burton, *The Lord's Day, the Sabbath Day* (London, 1636), 59.

65. For an excellent study of French attitudes toward chance (medieval through modern) as these were expressed via various discourses on gambling, see Kavanagh, *Dice, Cards, Wheels.*

66. Cessolis, *Game and Playe of Chesse,* was printed by William Caxton.

67. Elyot, *Boke Named the Governour,* bk. 1, sect. 26.

68. John Northbrooke, *A Treatise Wherein Dicing, Dauncing, Vaine Playes or Enterluds with Other Idle Pastimes [&]c. Commonly Used on the Sabboth Day, Are Reproved* (London, 1577), 111. Richard Rice, *An Invective against Vices, Taken for*

Vertue (London, 1581) groups cards together with dice and bowling, presenting them as equally destructive to men's souls. Thomas Wilcox, *A Glasse for Gamesters: And Namelie for Suche as Delight in Cards & Dise* (London, 1581) condemns cards alongside dice as unlawful because they are "games of chau[n]ce or fortune (as we call it)" (sig. B6v). To those who maintain that they need these games to refresh themselves, he counters that this indicates the games are providing too much pleasure and suggests that those desiring refreshment play chess instead.

69. Samuel Bird, *A Friendlie Communication or Dialogue between Paule and Demas Wherein Is Disputed How We Are to Use the Pleasures of This Life* (London, 1580), sig. D3v.

70. William Perkins, *The Whole Treatise of the Cases of Conscience* (1606), cited in Thomas Wood, "The Seventeenth Century English Casuists on Betting and Gambling," *Church Quarterly Review* 149, no. 298 (1950): 159–74, at 167.

71. Jean Taffin, *The Amendment of Life* (London, 1595), 250–1.

72. Lambert Daneau, *True and Christian Friendshippe . . . Together Also with a Right Excellent Invectiue of the Same Author, Against the Wicked Exercise of Diceplay, and other Prophane Gaming.* Trans. Thomas Newton (London, 1586), sig. F4r. Daneau includes cards among condemned games only when they are used for games of hazard. Dudley Fenner, *A Short and Profitable Treatise of Lawfull and Unlawfull Recreations, and of the Right Use and Abuse of Those That Are Lawfull* (London, 1590) is more restrictive, allowing the "exercise of wit, honest ridles" (sig. A5r), but condemning cards along with dice because they involve recreating with lots, which is God's exclusive domain.

73. James Balmford, *A Short and Plaine Dialogue Concerning the Unlawfulnes of Playing at Cards or Tables, or Any Other Game Consisting in Chance* (London, 1593), sig. A4v.

74. Ibid., sigs. A6v–A7r.

75. Thomas Gataker, *A Just Defence of Certaine Passages in a former Treatise Concerning the Nature and Use of Lots* (London, 1619), 121.

76. Ibid., 143. John Downe's *Treatise in Defense of Lots* (published posthumously in a 1633 collection) also sidesteps kibitzing about particular games and boldly states that "*Lots* both *Mixt* and *Meer* are lawfull even in the lightest matters: and consequently that *cards* and *dice*, and *tables*, and all other *Games* of the like nature, are lawfull, and may be used for recreation." John Downe, *Certaine Treatises of the Late Reverend and Learned Divine, Mr John Downe . . . Published at the Instance of His Friends* (Oxford, 1633), 3.

77. Gataker, *A Just Defence,* 146.

78. Downe, *Treatise in Defense of Lots,* 51.

79. Cited in Wood, "Seventeenth Century English Casuists," 162.

80. Ibid., 167.

81. Richard Brathwaite, *Whimzies; or, A New Cast of Characters* (London, 1631), 50.

82. The Nicholas Breton poem "Farewell to Town" describes a young man who bids "farewell to all gallant games / Primero and Imperial" (names of card games) after having been reduced to poverty. Nicholas Breton, *The Workes of a Young Wyt, Trust up with a Fardell of Pretie Fancies, Profitable to Young Poetes,*

Prejudicial to No Man, And Pleasaunt to Every Man, to Passe Away Idle Tyme Withall (London, 1577), sig. 12r.

83. Richard Crimsal, *John Hadlands Advice; or, A Warning for All Young Men that Have Meanes Advising Them to Forsake Lewd Company Cards, Dice, and Queanes, to the Tune of the Bonny Bonny Broome* (London, 1635).

84. Roger Ascham, *Toxophilus*, ed. Peter E. Medine, Medieval and Renaissance Texts and Studies 244 (Tempe: Arizona Center for Medieval and Renaissance Studies, 2002), 67.

85. John Philpot, *A Prospective-Glasse for Gamesters; or, A Short Treatise Against Gaming* (London, 1646), 2.

86. Brathwaite, *Whimzies*, 48.

87. Bird, *Friendlie Communication*, sig. G5r.

88. Ibid., sigs. G5r–v.

89. The key medieval study is Jenny Adams, *Power Play: The Literature and Politics of Chess in the Late Middle Ages* (Philadelphia: University of Pennsylvania Press, 2006). Much of the work on early modern English political allegories of chess focuses on Middleton's play and is discussed in detail in Chapter 4 of the present book.

90. William Cartwright, *The Game at Chesse: A Metaphoricall Discourse Shewing the Present Estate of This Kingdome* (1643), 8.

91. The engraver was Thomas Cockson. An extensive description can be found in Frederick G. Stephens and E. Hawkins, comps., *Catalogue of Prints and Drawings in the British Museum, Division 1: Political and Personal Satires*, vol. 1. (1320–1689) (London: Chiswick Press, 1870), 42–4.

92. Parlett, *Oxford Guide to Card Games,* gives a useful overview of the rules of Maw and observes, citing *The Groom-Porter's Laws at Mawe*, that the "five-finger" and rob the pack conventions were in operation in the late sixteenth and seventeenth centuries (189). The passage from *Tom Tell Troath* (here and below) is quoted in Chatto, *Facts and Speculations*, 126–7.

93. Hoffmann, *Playing Card*, 43.

94. Edward Gayton, *Chartæ Scriptæ; or, A New Game at Cards Call'd Play by the Booke* (London, 1645), sig. B1v.

95. Ibid., sig. B2v. Another interesting political pamphlet of the 1640s, although not quite as extensive in its use of the card analogy, is George Wither, *Prosopopoeia Britannicus: Britan's Genius, or Good-Angel, Personated; Reasoning and Advising, Touching the Games Now Playing, and the Adventures Now at Hazard in these Islands* (London, 1648).

96. Henry Neville, *Shuffling, Cutting, and Dealing in a Game at Pickquet* ([London], 1659). Even after the Restoration the trope continues to be useful. Anon., *The Plotting Cards Reviv'd; or, The New Game at Forty One* (London, 1681), a political pamphlet in the form of song lyrics, analogizes that England is playing, once again, a game of cards, but a "preposterous" one (verse 4), where Kings and Queens as well as diamonds and hearts are devalued, while the "basest" (verse 6) cards, like the black ones and the deuces and treys are "now *esteem'd / Prime* ones to win the *Day*" (verse 6).

97. Examples of decks of all of these (in various states of production) are

held by the British Museum, and descriptions can be found in Willshire, *Descriptive Catalogue*.

98. The edition was printed on four large engraved sheets, three of which are held by the Royal Geographical Society, but they were meant to be cut and mounted, and the British Museum holds several cut packs. Geography decks like these take advantage of the fact that cards are an excellent medium for presenting detailed visual material.

99. *Geographical Cards* (London: F. H. van Hove, 1675); Willshire, *Descriptive Catalogue*, 236, sect. E. 178a.

100. One of the information cards in the deck invites us to read for symbolism, maintaining that the association of a suit with a part of the world is "not without some Reason or Analogy." P. du Val, "Les Tables de géographie réduites en un jeu de cartes," in *A Collection of Maps of the World by P. du Val. Engraved by L. Cordier, J. F. D. Lapointe, J. Lhulier, N. Michu, J. Somer and I. Swelinck* (1660–76).

101. *Geographical Cards* (London: F. H. van Hove, 1675), Willshire, *Descriptive Catalogue*, 237, sect. E. 178. The deck presents an interesting visual echo with another English set c. 1661, which has England's reigning monarch, Queen Henrietta Maria, depicted on the American Colonies card.

102. *Geographical Cards of the World* (London: Henry Winstanley, c. 1675–6), Willshire, *Descriptive Catalogue*, 237, sect. E. 179.

103. The statements throw doubt on the claim made by the modern publishers of this deck, whose own prefatory materials claim that the cards are for "instruction to the young, rather than for serious play." Robert Morden, *Facsimile of Morden's Playing Cards* (Lympne Castle, Kent, UK: Harry Margary, 1972). Cf. Hargrave, *History of Playing Cards*, 175.

104. See Worthen, *Shakespeare and the Authority of Performance*.

105. Arthur Saul, *The Famous Game of Chesse-Play, Truely Discovered, and All Doubts Resolved; So That by Reading This Small Booke Thou Shalt Profit More Than by the Playing a Thousand Mates. An Exercise Full of Delight; Fit for Princes, or Any Person of What Qualitie Soever* (London, 1614), sig. C3v.

106. See Eales, *Chess*, 51–2, on the spread of chess.

107. Even published texts replicate this format. Gioachino Greco's release of *Royall Game of Chesse-Play*, trans. Francis Beale (London, 1656), is very straightforward in laying out key laws for gameplay, with little narrative/fictional embellishment.

108. Anon., "Commonplace Book" (Folger Library, c. 1650–70), E. a. 6.

109. Eales argues that print devalued these texts; writers could make more money by selling the manuscripts to patrons, who wanted to keep new strategies for themselves so as to improve their own playing (Eales, *Chess*, 86).

110. Arthur Saul, with Jo. Barbier, *The Famous Game of Chesse-Play. Being a Princely Exercise; Wherin the Learner May Profit More by Reading of This Small Book, Than by Playing of a Thousand Mates. Now Augmented of Many Materiall Things Formerly Wanting, and Beautified with a Three-Fold Methode, viz. of the Chesse-Men, of the Chesse-play, of the Chesse-lawes* (London, 1640). Barbier adds a third part, "The Moderatour at Chess; or, The Lawest of Chesse-play," which

operates, it would seem, as a crib sheet that a player might consult to remember basic guidelines read earlier in the book. Listed in numerical order, as with similar such documents, each law is very brief, and many return to key concepts from the first section, effectively serving as a condensed version of it.

111. Greco, *Royall Game of Chesse-Play*, dedication.

112. John Cotgrave, *Wits Interpreter, the English Parnassus; or, A Sure Guide to Those Admirable Accomplishments That Compleat Our English Gentry*, 2nd ed. (London, 1662 [1655]), 368. Although Cotgrave uses "rules" in the way we have come to understand them today—what earlier writers would have termed "laws"—he still imagines his instructional book to be of use during gameplay. He proposes a scenario where, during a particular match, questions arise about how to proceed, and his book can be consulted, in dialogue with players' "Reason."

113. Charles Cotton, *The Compleat Gamester; Instructions How to Play at Billiards, Trucks, Bowls, and Chess: Together with All Manner of Usual and Most Gentile Games Either on Cards or Dice: To Which Is Added, the Arts and Mysteries of Riding, Racing, Archery, and Cock-Fighting* (London, 1674), sig. I1v.

114. See Consalvo, *Cheating*. Boluk and LeMieux argue, in fact, that it is the metagame—essentially, the gaming of the rules—that makes videogames into games at all. While some might consider metagaming to be cheating because it involves working around the game's recognized laws, the line between cheating and fun is blurry enough that the distinction cannot hold.

115. Cram et al., eds., *Willughby's Book of Games*, 113.

116. Cleland, *Institution of a Young Noble Man*, 227. This is the same logic found in early modern "coney-catching" pamphlets, but I'd argue that it serves a very different purpose in the history of gaming, where cheating, while an ethical problem, is also crucial to game development.

117. Randle Holme, *The Academy of Armory; or, A Storehouse of Armory and Blazon* [1688], ed. Isaac Herbert Jeayes, vol. 2 (London: Roxburghe Club, 1905), 71-74, 74.

118. Cram et al., eds., *Willughby's Book of Games*, 114.

119. Cardano, "Book on Games of Chance," 211.

120. Ibid., 210.

121. Gilbert Walker, *Mihil Mumchance, His Discoverie of the Art of Cheating in False Dyce Play, and Other Unlawfull Games: With a Discourse of the Figging Craft* (London, 1597), sig. E1v. The Folger catalog notes say this is essentially a reprint of *A Manifest Detection of the Moste Vyle and Detestable Use of Diceplay, and Other Practises Lyke the Same* (c. 1555), which has been attributed (dubiously) to Gilbert Walker.

122. Ibid., sig. A4v.

123. Cotton, *Compleat Gamester*, sig. A7v.

124. Walker, *Mihil Mumchance*, sig. C4v.

125. Cardano, "Book on Games of Chance," 190.

126. Eales, *Chess*, 56, 83, 87.

127. Damiano, *Pleasaunt and Wittie Playe*, 3.

128. On Vida's theatrical retelling of the tale, see Mario A. di Cesare, "Introduction," in *The Game of Chess: Marco Girolamo Vida's "Scacchia ludus," with Eng-*

lish Verse Translation and the Texts of the Three Earlier Versions, ed. Mario A. di Cesare (Nieuwkoop, The Netherlands: De Graaf, 1975), 9–35, at 33.

129. Mark N. Taylor, "How Did the Queen Go Mad?," in *Chess in the Middle Ages and Early Modern Age: A Fundamental Thought Paradigm of the Premodern World*, ed. Daniel E. O'Sullivan (Berlin: Walter de Gruyter, 2012), 169–83.

130. This idea is articulated in one of the earliest defining works for performance studies: Judith Butler, "Performative Acts and Gender Constitution: An Essay in Phenomenology and Feminist Theory," *Theatre Journal* 40.4 (1988): 519–31.

131. "Plays become meaningful in the theatre through the disciplined application of conventionalized practices—acting, directing, scenography—that transform writing into something with performative force: performance behavior." W. B. Worthen, *Shakespeare and the Force of Modern Performance* (Cambridge: Cambridge University Press, 1998), 9.

132. Ibid., 13.

133. Eales, *Chess*, 97.

134. In Diana Taylor, *The Archive and the Repertoire: Performing Cultural Memory in the Americas* (Durham, NC: Duke University Press, 2003), performance studies scholar Taylor presents the archive and the repertoire as containing two different forms of knowledge—the archive as a space of static texts, the repertoire as a space of moving bodies—but other scholars in performance studies have explored the ways the archive is itself shaped by bodily performances. For instance, Barbara Hodgdon views the archive of material objects associated with past theatrical performances—costumes, promptbooks, programs, photographs—as "gestures toward a future reenactment." Barbara Hodgdon, *Shakespeare, Performance, and the Archive* (New York: Routledge, 2016), 11.

135. Hodgdon articulates this method powerfully when she presents herself not only as an archaeologist, trying to unearth these traces for what they once meant, but also as a performer who inhabits traces of performance in the archive: "As I attempt to discern performance's 'walking shadows,' its subjects and subjectivities, I work toward a performative re-wrighting, re-imagining, replaying, the force of performance processes" (11).

136. John Hall, *Horae vacivae; or, Essays: Some Occasionall Considerations* (London, 1646), quoted in David Parlett, *Oxford Guide to Card Games*, 55.

137. Frances E. Dolan, *True Relations: Reading, Literature, and Evidence in Seventeenth-Century England* (Philadelphia: University of Pennsylvania Press, 2013).

138. Bruce R. Smith, "Getting Back to the Library, Getting Back to the Body," in *Shakespeare and the Digital World: Redefining Scholarship and Practice*, ed. Christie Carson and Peter Kirwan (Cambridge: Cambridge University Press, 2014), 24–32. See also Smith, *Phenomenal Shakespeare*.

CHAPTER 2

1: Although critics of the play often mention the card game as among Heywood's most theatrically interesting scenes, few say much about it, and those who do are interested in its emphasis on domestic detail or in its intriguing use of double-entendres. Keith Sturgess, ed. *Three Elizabethan Domestic Tragedies: Arden of Faversham, A Yorkshire Tragedy, A Woman Killed with Kindness* (Harmondsworth, Middlesex, UK: Penguin, 1985) calls this scene "a masterpiece of sustained metaphor" (45). The most extensive commentary on the scene's use of double-entendres is Thomas Moisan, "Framing with Kindness: The Transgressive Theatre of *A Woman Killed with Kindness*," in *Essays on Transgressive Readings: Reading over the Lines,* ed. Georgia Johnston (Lewiston, NY: Edwin Mellen Press, 1997): 171–84.

2. Pearce, *Interactive Book*, esp. 422–3.

3. Salen and Zimmerman, *Rules of Play*. On cards see David Parlett, *A Dictionary of Card Games* (Oxford: Oxford University Press, 1992).

4. Genevieve Love, "Performance Criticism without Performance: The Study of Non-Shakespearean Drama," in *New Directions in Renaissance Drama and Performance Studies,* ed. Sarah Werner (New York: Palgrave Macmillan, 2010), 131–46, examines "the theatrical energy of . . . unseen moments," exploring the way another of Heywood's plays, *A Mayden-head Well Lost*, constructs what cannot be seen as a "site of theatrical desire" (145, 143). Preiss, "Interiority," describes the early modern commercial theater's success as predicated on convincing audiences that theater offered "something just beyond the range of perception" (60).

5. Sofer, *Dark Matter*, 62.

6. For discussion of how Goffman's experience in casinos informed his work on social theory, see Jeffrey J. Sallaz, "Introduction: Dealing with Globalization," in *The Labor of Luck: Casino Capitalism in the United States and South Africa* (Berkeley and Los Angeles: University of California Press, 2009).

7. Goffman explores these ideas throughout his work, but the classic essay is "Where the Action Is" in Erving Goffman, *Interaction Ritual: Essays on Face-to-Face Behavior* (New York: Pantheon Books, 1967). See also Erving Goffman, *Strategic Interaction* (Philadelphia: University of Pennsylvania Press, 1969).

8. At the same time, Goffman, "Where the Action Is," reminds us that the success of any one participant in the game is unpredictable, for if personal relationships are information games requiring strategy, no one can be expected to play well every time (even the most skilled players lose occasionally), and, we might add, not everyone will agree on what constitutes cheating. Indeed, the card games dramatized in both *Gammer* and *A Woman Killed with Kindness* are plagued by cheating, which turns out to be more the norm than the exception in early modern representations of card play.

9. Alan Bray, *The Friend* (Chicago: University of Chicago Press, 2003); Laurie Shannon, *Sovereign Amity: Figures of Friendship in Shakespearean Contexts* (Chicago: Chicago University Press, 2002); Jeffrey Masten, *Textual Intercourse: Collaboration, Authorship, and Sexualities in Renaissance Drama* (Cambridge: Cambridge University Press, 1997). The classic study is Lauren J. Mills, *One Soul in Bodies Twain: Friendship in Tudor Literature and Stuart Drama* (Bloomington, IN: Principia Press, 1937). Bray argues that this model was not a sixteenth-century reinvention but a "device for negotiating the equivocal demands of friendship that had been the hallmark of churchmen since the eleventh century" (68).

10. Goffman argues, in fact, that although all theater audiences "actively collaborate in sustaining this playful unknowingness . . . [t]hose who have already read or seen the play carry this cooperativeness one step further; they put themselves as much as possible back into a state of ignorance." Erving Goffman, *Frame Analysis: An Essay on the Organization of Experience* (Cambridge, MA: Harvard University Press, 1974), 136.

11. On Tudor plays as structured by and productive of epistemological crises, see Joel B. Altman, *The Tudor Play of Mind: Rhetorical Inquiry and the Development of Elizabethan Drama* (Berkeley: University of California Press, 1978). I explore a similar theatrical spirit of inquiry not in terms of the rhetorical arts, but in relation to the practice of gaming. For discussion of how less deliberate forms of recollection shape playgoing (and playmaking) competency, see Gina Bloom, Anston Bosman, and William N. West, "Ophelia's Intertheatricality; or, How Performance Is History," *Theatre Journal* 65 (2013): 165–82.

12. The play's allusions to card play have yet to be addressed by critics, with the exception of J. W. Robinson, "The Art and Meaning of *Gammer Gurton's Needle,*" *Renaissance Drama* 14 (1983): 45–77, who suggests that the depiction of villagers playing cards, an illegal recreation, illustrates yet another way the villagers fall into vice, needing moral correction. I complicate that view herein. My citations below are drawn from Mr. S., *Gammer Gurton's Needle*, 2nd ed., ed. Charles Whitworth (New York: W. W. Norton, 1997).

13. Robinson, "Art and Meaning."

14. On the play as farce, see Whitworth's introduction to his edition of *Gammer Gurton's Needle*; and B. J. Whiting, "Diccon's French Cousin," *Studies in Philology* 42.1 (1945): 31–40. For a discussion of early criticism dismissive of the play's comedy and a more complex discussion of its humor, see R. W. Ingram, "*Gammer Gurton's Needle*: Comedy Not Quite of the Lowest Order?," *Studies in English Literature, 1500–1900* 7.2 (1967): 257–68.

15. Among the lessons critics have identified are the following: the uncertainties of circumstantial evidence, discussed in Hutson, *Invention of Suspicion,* and in David M. Bergeron, "The Education of Rafe in Lyly's *Gallathea,*" *Studies in English Literature, 1500–1900* 23.2 (1983): 197–206; the foolishness of becoming fixated on insignificant matters, in Robinson, "Art and Meaning"; that logic is only one, and not the most important, of humanist goals, discussed in Kent Cartwright, *Theatre and Humanism: English Drama in the Sixteenth Century* (Cambridge: Cambridge University Press, 1999); and that students, though distant from their mothers, cannot escape relationships of dependency, discussed in Wendy Wall, *Staging Domesticity: Household Work and English Identity in Early Modern Drama* (Cambridge: Cambridge University Press, 2002) and Gail Kern Paster, *The Body Embarrassed: Drama and the Disciplines of Shame in Early Modern England* (Ithaca, NY: Cornell University Press, 1993).

16. On the play as epitomizing humanist education, see Bergeron, "Education of Rafe"; and Cartwright, *Theatre and Humanism*. On the play as mocking humanist education, see Wall, *Staging Domesticity*; and Douglas Duncan, "*Gammer Gurton's Needle* and the Concept of Humanist Parody," *Studies in English Literature, 1500–1900* 27.2 (1987): 177–96.

17. Wall, *Staging Domesticity*, esp. 24.

18. On how the classical model of friendship was taken up by women, see Valerie Traub, *The Renaissance of Lesbianism in Early Modern England* (Cambridge: Cambridge University Press, 2002).

19. Michel de Montaigne, *The Essays of Michael Lord of Montaigne, . . . The First Booke, Volume 2*, trans. John Florio (London: J. M. Dent, 1897), 7.

20. For a discussion of how dismissals of cross-gender and cross-class friendship reveal the homoerotics of ideal male friendship, see Masten, *Textual Intercourse*, esp. chap. 2.

21. See Robinson, "Art and Meaning."

22. As Whitworth observes in the introduction to his edition (xiii), the play regularly uses offstage action in this way.

23. Richard Southern, *The Staging of Plays before Shakespeare* (London: Faber & Faber, 1973). See also Whitworth's edition, xxiii.

24. Hutson's *Invention of Suspicion* briefly discusses the play in the context of "intrigue plots" that ask readers and audiences to perform "detective work," work she argues approximates the forensic models being articulated by mid- to late sixteenth-century legal bodies (156). Hutson's argument about the play and more generally about how sixteenth-century dramatists used "revelation—a change in the contours of knowledge—to produce a sense of the contingencies of knowing" (290) dovetails nicely with my argument about drama as a game of imperfect information.

25. See Wall, *Staging Domesticity*; Paster, *Body Embarrassed*; N. Lindsay McFadyen, "What Was Really Lost in *Gammer Gurton's Needle*," *Renaissance Papers* (1982): 9–13.

26. John Brand and Sir Henry Ellise, *Observations on Popular Antiquities, Chiefly Illustrating the Origin of our Vulgar Customs, Ceremonies and Superstitions*, vol. 2 (London: F.C. & J. Rivington, 1873), 435.

27. Many editors miss this reference in part because they render *thong* as *throng*, even though the edit does not make sense syntactically. Unless otherwise noted, all references to Shakespeare's plays are taken from *The Norton Shakespeare*, 2nd ed., ed. Stephen Greenblatt (New York: W. W. Norton, 1997).

28. I agree here with Carol Thomas Neely, *Distracted Subjects: Madness and Gender in Shakespeare and Early Modern Culture* (Ithaca: Cornell University Press, 2004), who argues that Diccon, rather than being in cahoots with the audience in mocking the play's low characters, in fact, turns the tables on the audience. He "makes everyone he encounters eat shit" (32).

29. On the pains and pleasures of the schoolroom's disciplinary mechanisms, see Wall, *Staging Domesticity*, chap. 2; and Alan Stewart, *Close Readers: Humanism and Sodomy in Early Modern England* (Princeton, NJ: Princeton University Press, 1997),

30. Walker, *Mihil Mumchance*, sig. C4v.

31. We do not have clear evidence of the time of year *Gammer* was first performed, but according to G. C. Moore Smith, *College Plays Performed in the University of Cambridge* (Cambridge: Cambridge University Press, 1923), great numbers of plays were performed at Cambridge during the Christmas season. For instance, at Trinity in 1560, it was mandated that five plays be given during the twelve days of Christmas (21). By 1621 there is a decree on the

books at Corpus Christi College confining English plays to the Christmas holidays (42).

32. Benham, *Playing Cards*, 26. The statute was introduced under pressure from parties interested in the promotion of archery. Hargrave, *History of Playing Cards*, 169, cites a similar earlier edict of 1495.

33. James Bass Mullinger, *The University of Cambridge*, vol. 1 (Cambridge: University Press, 1873), 39.

34. Curtis Perry, "Commodity and Commonwealth in *Gammer Gurton's Needle*," *Studies in English Literature, 1500–1900* 42.2 (2002): 217–34. Perry doesn't discuss cards explicitly, but they are precisely the kind of trivial, leisure-based commodity items about which reformers complained.

35. Fletcher, "Old Playing Cards."

36. Benham, *Playing Cards*, 26.

37. Keith L. Sprunger, "Ames, William (1576–1633)," in *Oxford Dictionary of National Biography* (Oxford: Oxford University Press, 2004–9). Interestingly, Ames goes on many years later to publish a defense of games involving wagering as long as they don't lead to fighting or blaspheming of God, and as long as no one involved invokes superstitious entities such as stars, spirits, or fortune. William Ames, *Conscience with the Power and Cases Thereof* (London, 1639). See further discussion of Ames in Wood, "Seventeenth Century English Casuists."

38. This is the argument made by Robinson, "Art and Meaning."

39. After Latimer had given his first sermon on the cards, Buckenham gave a sermon in response that used the metaphor of dice play to refute Latimer: Buckenham urged the good Christian to throw fours and fives to refute Latimer (fours being the four doctors of the church, and fives the five passages Latimer quotes). Latimer did not back down and delivered his second sermon on the cards in response. See the introduction to Hugh Latimer, "Sermons on the Card and Other Discourses," ed. Henry Morley (Project Gutenberg, 2005). Available at http://www.gutenberg.org/files/2458/2458.txt (accessed 3 November 2017). All subsequent citations are from this edition. For Foxe, see *John Foxe's The Act and Monuments Online*, "Queene Mary. M. Latimers replie to a bald Sermon of a Frier in Cambridge." Available at https://www.johnfoxe.org/index.php?realm=text&edition=1583&pageid=1758&gototype=modern (accessed 3 November 2017).

40. See Bray, *Friend*, 24–5, 84–5.

41. Latimer, "Sermons," second.

42. See Robinson, "Art and Meaning."

43. Robert Hornback, "'Holy Crap!': Scatalogical Iconoclasm in Tudor Evangelical Comedy," in *Thunder at a Playhouse: Essaying Shakespeare and the Early Modern Stage*, ed. Peter Kanelos and Matt Kozusko (Selinsgrove: Susquehanna University Press, 2010), 67–86.

44. Hoffmann, *Playing Card*, 40.

45. Laura A. Smoller, "Playing Cards and Popular Culture in Sixteenth-Century Nuremberg," *Sixteenth Century Journal* 17.2 (1986): 183–214, at 188–9.

46. Some religio-moral attacks on cards include Balmford, *Short and Plaine Dialogue*; Fenner, *Short and Profitable Treatise*; Rice, *Invective against Vices*; Bird, *Friendlie Communication*. A humorous dedicatory verse in Gayton, *Chartæ*

Scriptæ, a royalist treatise, mocks such criticism of card play, which, the verse suggests, prevents religious zealots from recognizing that cards can, in fact, teach spiritual lessons:

> The Cards are *hallow'd* now, all but the name.
> Here are *Religious Kings* and *Queens*, we may
> Worke out *Salvation*, while we seeme to *Play*.
> Blest Reformation! see how Grace gets in
> By th'very meanes which did intice to sin.
> Now may in godly sort the *Zealous* mate
> *Deale* with a Brother yet *Communicate*.
> They that forbad th'Prophaner *Ace* and *Duce*,
> Should they see these, they would command their *Use*.
> Virtue thus Conquers Vice by an unknowne way,
> And *Satan's* beaten now at his owne *Play*.
> What good may wee not hope for, when we heare,
> A *Sermon* Preach'd by Nicholas Benie're?

The card analogy is used even more extensively in royalist satire. For instance, see Anon., *The Bloody Game at Cards* [London], c. 1642.

47. Thomas Heywood, *A Woman Killed with Kindness*, ed. Brian Scobie, with introduction by Frances E. Dolan, New Mermaids (London: Methuen Drama, 2012). Further citations appear in my text.

48. Cotton, *Compleat Gamester*, 118–19.

49. On "knave" as the male equivalent of whore or "quean," see Rebecca Ann Bach, *Shakespeare and Renaissance Literature Before Heterosexuality* (New York: Palgrave Macmillan, 2007), 74.

50. The precise nature of Anne's role in the scheme is left ambiguous, though she would be essential to Wendoll's foul play. In modern-day bridge, of which Vide Ruff was a precursor, the person to the right of the dealer often shuffles and the one to the left cuts the deck. This deters the dealer, who has the most control of the cards, from cheating. If early moderns followed this practice, then Wendoll shuffles, working covertly with Anne, who cuts the deck to benefit his hand. Francis Willughby's seventeenth-century manuscript of games has the dealer in charge of shuffling and assigns the task of cutting cards to the person who last dealt a round and is sitting to the dealer's right hand. See Cram et al., eds., *Willughby's Book of Games*, 134. If that is the case, then Wendoll isn't directly involved in "setting" the cards, which would only increase Anne's culpability in the cheating scheme.

51. We can assume the seating plan based on the game actions. Wendoll and Anne are paired against Frankford and Cranwell. Since Frankford deals and Anne cuts, presumably Anne is to the left of Frankford and Wendoll is to his right. Willughby writes, "the generall custome is to goe round from the left hand [of the dealer]. And the reason is because hee that sits next on the left hand of the dealer has his right hand readie to receive the cards from him" when it is time to cut the deck (Cram et al., eds., *Willughby's Book of Games*, 132–3).

52. If we take the definition of rub to mean "to take all the cards of one suit," then Anne would have to have played a lower-valued heart. This would not

change the outcome of the game in any significant way, though, since her heart is still lower than Wendoll's. See "rub, v.2," *OED Online*, June 2017 (Oxford University Press), http://www.oed.com/view/Entry/168278?rskey=Qoam1o&result=5 (accessed 9 January 2018).

53. For instance, David Cook, "*A Woman Killed with Kindness:* An Unshakespearian Tragedy," *English Studies* 45.5 (1964): 353–72, at 359.

54. Such a reading of Anne counters longstanding critical views of her as a passive victim of Wendoll's seduction and would support readings of her later starvation and willed suicide as subversive acts. On starvation as evidence of Anne's agency, see Reina Green, "Open Ears, Appetite, and Adultery in *A Woman Killed with Kindness*," *English Studies in Canada* 31.4 (2005): 53–74; Theresia de Vroom, "Female Heroism in Heywood's Tragic Farce of Adultery: *A Woman Killed with Kindness*," in *The Female Tragic Hero in English Renaissance Drama*, ed. Naomi Conn Liebler (New York: Palgrave, 2002), 119–40; and Christopher Frey and Leanore Lieblein, "'My Breasts Sear'd': The Self-Starved Female Body and *A Woman Killed with Kindness*," *Early Theatre* 7.1 (2004): 45–66.

55. On Wendoll as villain, see, for example, Michael McClintock, "Grief, Theater and Society in Thomas Heywood's *A Woman Killed with Kindness*," in *Speaking Grief in English Literary Culture: Shakespeare to Milton*, ed. Margo Swiss and David A. Kent (Pittsburgh: Duquesne University Press, 2002), 98–118. The opposition case has also been made: that Wendoll is a passionate victim of love, a contrast with the cold, unemotional Frankford. For instance, see Cook, "Unshakespearian Tragedy." Other critics who present Wendoll as not fully to blame for his actions include Herbert R. Coursen Jr., "The Subplot of *A Woman Killed with Kindness*," *English Language Notes* 2.3 (1965): 180–5; Leanore Lieblein, "The Context of Murder in English Domestic Plays, 1590–1610," *Studies in English Literature, 1500–1900* 23.2 (1983): 181–96; Nancy A. Gutierrez, "The Irresolution of Melodrama: The Meaning of Adultery in *A Woman Killed with Kindness*," *Exemplaria* 1.1 (1989): 265–91; and Laura G. Bromley, "Domestic Conduct in *A Woman Killed with Kindness*," *Studies in English Literature, 1500–1900* 26.2 (1986): 259–76, who writes that Wendoll "is not extraordinarily wicked, but the kind of man who might well mislead an honorable, well-intentioned gentleman like Frankford. He is a man who will not control his passions . . . and so he is a threat to the social order" (272).

56. We might be reminded here of Margreta de Grazia's argument about the early modern soliloquy as a moment of sharing rather than eavesdropping. Though we are tempted to think that we are gaining some insight into the character's "real" thoughts and feelings, the soliloquy is a performance of intimacy, and in fact *produces* a sense of depth of character. Margreta de Grazia, "The Motive for Interiority: Shakespeare's *Sonnets* and *Hamlet*," *Style* 23.3 (1989): 430–44. Preiss, "Interiority," also considers inscrutability as a marker of that attribute, as does Hutson in her discussion of how forensic rhetoric produced a sense of character depth in late sixteenth-century English drama (*Invention of Suspicion*, esp. chap. 5).

57. Katharine Eisaman Maus, "Horns of Dilemma: Jealousy, Gender and Spectatorship in English Renaissance Drama," *English Language History* 54.3 (1987): 561–83.

58. Subha Mukherji, *Law and Representation in Early Modern Drama* (Cambridge: Cambridge University Press, 2006) also considers the play's use of a theatrical idiom to contemplate problems of evidence; but she, like Maus and others, focuses on the offstage scene of adultery that Frankford, but not the audience, witnesses.

59. Rebecca Ann Bach, "The Homosocial Imaginary of *A Woman Killed with Kindness*," *Textual Practice* 12.3 (1998): 503–24. Other critics who argue that the play emphasizes Frankford's relationship to Wendoll (and male bonds more generally) over his relationship to his wife include Louis B. Wright, "The Male-Friendship Cult in Thomas Heywood's Plays," *Modern Language Notes* 42.8 (1927): 510–14; Bromley, "Domestic Conduct"; Orlin, *Private Matters*, chap. 3; Lyn L. Bennett, "The Homosocial Economics of *A Woman Killed with Kindness*," *Renaissance and Reformation* 24.2 (2000): 35–61; and Lisa Hopkins, "Maternity in *A Woman Killed with Kindness*," in *Performing Maternity in Early Modern England*, ed. Kathryn M. Montcrief and Kathryn R. McPherson (Aldershot, UK: Ashgate, 2007), 73–84.

60. Others have shown, of course, that the rhetoric of perfect affinity was less an expression of ideal friendship than a subtle way of negotiating friendship's practical imperfections and material challenges. See Bray, *Friend*, and also Stewart, *Close Readers*, who explores how sixteenth-century humanists negotiated their way into higher status by claiming the "moral highground of the Ciceronian *amicus*" (125), all the while consolidating their power through traditional patriarchal means, by marrying into established families.

61. Cicero, *De amitia*, in *"De amicitia," to Which Is Added "Scipio's Dream" and Cicero, "De senectute,"* trans. Andrew P. Peabody (Boston: Little, Brown, 1884), 68. Available at http://archive.fo/20160422122603/ancienthistory.about.com/library/bl/bl_text_cic_friendship.htm, sect. 26 (accessed 23 October 2017). I have cited Peabody's translation because it captures well the game reference from the Latin: "Quid autem turpius quam *illudi*?" (my emphasis). The Latin original can be found in Cicero, *De senectute, De amicitia, De divinatione*, trans. William Armistead Falconer (Cambridge, MA: Harvard University Press, 1923), 205. Available at https://www.loebclassics.com/view/marcus_tullius_cicero-de_amicitia/1923/pb_LCL154.205.xml (accessed 23 October 2017).

62. Daneau, *True and Christian Friendshippe*, sigs. A4v–A5r.

63. Ibid., sig. A7r.

64. Montaigne, 13.

65. Francis Bacon, *Bacon's Essays, with Annotations by Richard Whately and Notes and a Glossarial Index, by Franklin Fiske Heard* (Boston: Lee & Shepard, 1868; reprint, Making of America [online], University of Michigan Library, 2005), 281. Available at https://quod.lib.umich.edu/m/moa/ABV4738.0001.001/331?rgn=full+text;view=image (accessed 29 December 2017).

66. My argument corresponds somewhat with Tom MacFaul, *Male Friendship in Shakespeare and His Contemporaries* (Cambridge: Cambridge University Press, 2007): that early modern dramas, though they may take up the humanist rhetoric of friendship as a relationship among equals, do so only to critique that model, suggesting instead that friendships involve the recognition of the other's difference from the self. Though he does not discuss *A Woman Killed with*

Kindness in any detail, MacFaul convincingly shows how other plays treat the humanist discourse of parity with suspicion, dramatizing the way the bonds of friendship flourish not in spite of but because of a gulf between two men. Like MacFaul's, my argument also expands on Lorna Hutson, *The Usurer's Daughter: Male Friendship and Fictions of Women in Sixteenth-Century England* (London: Routledge, 1994), who contends that the humanist topos of like-minded friendship is a pretext for teaching men the instrumentality of effective speech. Although I wouldn't go as far as Hutson to suggest that literary representations of male friendship are less *about* friendship than they are about a "humanist reading programme" (3), her ideas about the "textualization of friendship" (78) shed useful light on the development and demise of the relationship between Wendoll and Frankford. I suggest that their friendship is precipitated through an act of sharing information and engaging in what Hutson characterizes as a "knowledge transaction" (78). Orlin, *Private Matters*, anticipates these arguments to some degree in her reading of *A Woman Killed with Kindness*, which argues that the play critiques classical ideals of male friendship, presenting it as plagued by a "psychology of distrust and resentment" (165). While I agree that the play queries Ciceronian ideals of friendship, I see it less as demonstrating how the classical ideal of friendship fails to survive in a changing social and economic world than as detailing the logical repercussions of this model of friendship. Rather than a critique of classical-humanist idealistic friendship, the play is an exposé of its practical exigencies.

67. Goffman, *Interaction Ritual*, 167–8. We might interpret "favorable" less literally here—friends also bond when sharing flaws about themselves. On the face of it, this may not seem like favorable information, but it is favorable insofar as it can demonstrate lovable imperfections.

68. My understanding of Goffman's perspectives on the ludic structure of social interaction has been shaped by Lori J. Ducharme and Gary Alan Fine, "No Escaping Obligation: Erving Goffman on the Demands and Constraints of Play," in *The Play of Self*, ed. Ronald Bogue and Mihai I. Spariosu (Albany: SUNY Press, 1994), 89–111.

69. My thanks to Fran Dolan for helping me work out this point.

70. Orlin, *Private Matters*, makes a similar claim, observing that the "ruthless subtext of the card game" (166) is evidence of the ways male friendship is "relentlessly contestatory" (165). I would add that this ruthlessness is not confined only to the game's "subtext" but is functionally explicit in any card game.

71. Salen and Zimmerman, *Rules of Play*, 256. I discuss the limitations of this "magic circle" view of gaming in my Introduction. The hawking match evinces those limitations, for its participants do not abide by the rules of play.

72. Wendoll fervently argues that Charles's hawk was outfitted improperly: its "Milan bells" are not weighted the same and are not tuned correctly (one ought to be slightly higher in pitch than the other) and this "spoils the mounting" of the bird (11.18–19).

73. My reading of the substance of this debate is indebted to Scobie's glosses.

74. On the centrality of cheating in the history of videogames, see Consalvo, *Cheating*.

75. Julian Dibbell, "Mutilated Furries, Flying Phalluses: Put the Blame on

Griefers, the Sociopaths of the Virtual World," *Wired Magazine* 16.2 (2008): 90–100. Available at https://www.wired.com/2008/01/mf-goons/ (accessed 3 November 2017). For a fascinating discussion of how gamers have responded to griefer attacks, see Colin Milburn, "Atoms and Avatars: Virtual Worlds as Massively-Multiplayer Laboratories," *Spontaneous Generations* 2.1 (2008): 63–89.

76. Boluk and LeMieux, *Metagaming*.

77. Gregory Bateson, "A Theory of Play and Fantasy," in *Steps to an Ecology of Mind* (New York: Ballatine, 1972), 177–93.

78. My thanks to Susan Kaiser for suggesting this interpretation.

79. Rice, *Invective against Vices*, sig. B4r.

80. Cotton, *Compleat Gamester*, 115. Cotgrave, *Wits Interpreter*, recognizes that some false play is done by mistake and seems to accept that since intentions are hard to judge, one is better of handling problems in a matter-of-fact way: "If the Dealer give the other more Cards then his due, whether it be through a mistake, or otherwise, with a purpose of foul play, it is in the choice of the elder hand whether he shall deal again or no: or whether it shall be played out" (362).

81. Cotton, *Compleat Gamester*, 117.

82. On the harshness of Anne's punishment, see Jennifer Panek, "Punishing Adultery in *A Woman Killed with Kindness*," *Studies in English Literature, 1500–1900* 34.2 (1994): 357–78.

83. See Bach, "Homosocial Imaginary."

84. Salen and Zimmerman note that, in games, "imperfect information invites treachery, trickery, and deception and can be used as a design element in games meant to inspire mistrust among players" (*Rules of Play*, 205). A good example is poker, where part of the pleasure and challenge of the game is figuring out whether one's opponent is lying about how good his or her hand is.

85. Geertz, "Deep Play," 450.

86. Geertz's work resonates with much interesting work in early modern studies on the phenomenology of theatergoing as well as on male friendship. Rich studies of emotion have deepened our understanding of audience response at the same time as they have undergirded important work on the passionate and often homoerotic undertones of male friendship. Useful work on early modern emotion includes Gail Kern Paster, *Humoring the Body: Emotions and the Shakespearean Stage* (Chicago: Chicago University Press, 2004) and Gail Paster, Katherine Rowe, and Mary Floyd-Wilson, eds., *Reading the Early Modern Passions: Essays in the Cultural History of Emotion* (Philadelphia: University of Pennsylvania Press, 2004). The significance of affect to the study of male friendship and sexuality is well summarized in David M. Halperin, "Introduction: Among Men—History, Sexuality, and the Return of Affect," in *Love, Sex, Intimacy, and Friendship between Men, 1550–1800*, ed. Katherine O'Donnell and Michael O'Rourke (New York: Palgrave, 2003), 1–11, and elucidated in many of the essays in that volume.

87. The play was performed by Worcester's Men in 1603, during the brief time when the company was staging plays at the Rose Theatre.

88. Preiss, "Interiority," 59.

89. Thomas Kavanagh's work on French gambling addresses a similar point.

He argues that gamblers enter into an imaginative world, not a state of perfect knowledge: "To gamble is to enter a realm where one wagers not on the cold certainties of what we know but on the blood-warm premonitions of that about which we can never be certain." Kavanagh, *Dice, Cards, Wheels*, 23.

90. Alexander Balloch Grosart, ed. *The Dr. Farmer Chetham Ms: Being a Commonplace-book in the Chetham Library, Manchester*, 2 vols. (Manchester: Chetham Society and Charles Simms, 1873), 1:104.

CHAPTER 3

1. For the sake of simplicity and clarity for modern readers, I refer to "tables" as "backgammon" throughout this chapter. Although modern backgammon derives originally from ancient Roman and Islamic "race games" and was an adaptation of various forms of the game played throughout Europe and England (as *todad tablas* in Spain, *toutes tables* in France, *tavole reale* in Italy, and as Irish in England), it came to England at the turn of the seventeenth century. See Murray, *Board-Games Other than Chess*, esp. chap. 6. We cannot know for sure what form of tables is being played in *Arden*, but if backgammon was just coming into vogue, we may surmise that the theater would have capitalized on the freshest game fashions.

2. Viviana Comensoli, *"Household Business": Domestic Plays of Early Modern England* (Toronto: University of Toronto Press, 1996), esp. 87, mistakes this as a game of cards. Sources that refer to this as a dice game include Frank Whigham, *Seizures of the Will in Early Modern English Drama* (Cambridge: Cambridge University Press, 1996), 116; and Tom Lockwood, "Introduction," in Anon., *Arden of Faversham*, 2nd ed., ed. Martin White, New Mermaids (London: A & C Black, 2007), ix.

3. A useful primary source for the early modern rules of backgammon and other table games is Cram et al., eds., *Willughby's Book of Games*. See also Murray, *Board-Games Other than Chess*, esp. 119-29.

4. Salen and Zimmerman, *Rules of Play*. On cards, see Parlett, *Dictionary of Card Games*.

5. The sketch of the Swan Theatre appears in Aernout van Buchel (Arnoldus Buchelius), *Adversaria* (Utrecht, University Library, Ms. 842, 7 E 3; c. 1592–1621), fol. 132r, and is purportedly copied from a 1596 drawing by Johan de Witt, who claims to have attended a play at the Swan while in London.

6. In a letter dated 21 August 1624, John Chamberlain explains that he had to miss a play because he was not prepared to arrive more than an hour early to find a seat: "for we must have ben there before one a clocke at farthest to find any roome." Quoted in Andrew Gurr, *Playgoing in Shakespeare's London*, 2nd ed. (Cambridge: Cambridge University Press, 1996), 245, no. 141.

7. Quoted in ibid., 214, no. 6.

8. For discussion of these terms in the context of theater proxemics, see Keir Elam, *The Semiotics of Theatre and Drama*, 2nd ed. (London: Routledge, 2002), esp. 58.

9. Bristol, "Theater and Popular Culture," maintains that the professional

theater "conferred at least a temporary social equality on all consumers of the same product." In exchange for "alienation from direct participation in the creative process," he argues, consumers received a "higher standard of performance" as well as a sense of being "socially undifferentiated" from other consumers (248). Everyone was paying for the same thing.

10. Such structures of sociospatial difference may have been more advertising than actuality. Dekker's *Lanthorne and Candlelight* mocks gentlemen theatergoers who presume the galleries were socially exclusive: "Pay thy two-pence to a *Player*, in his gallerie maist thou sitte by a harlot." Quoted in Andrew Gurr and Karoline Szatek, "Women and Crowds at the Theater," *Medieval and Renaissance Drama in England* 21 (2008): 157–69, at 157. The theater was merely a microcosm of emergent social trends in England, where status could be bought.

11. Gurr, *Playgoing*, 24.

12. Ibid., 22.

13. On theater as creating community, see Gay McAuley, *Space in Performance: Making Meaning in the Theatre* (Ann Arbor: University of Michigan Press, 2000); and Bruce McConachie, "Using Cognitive Science to Understand Spatiality and Community in the Theater," *Contemporary Theatre Review* 12.3 (2002): 97–114.

14. Michel de Certeau, *The Practice of Everyday Life* [vol. 1], trans. Steven Rendall (Berkeley: University of California Press, 1988), 92. De Certeau was writing of the World Trade Center.

15. Ibid., 117–18. De Certeau's argument about maps and scopic dominance has become almost commonplace in the scholarly discourse on cartography. In addition to the sources in the subsequent note, see Christian Jacob, *The Sovereign Map: Theoretical Approaches in Cartography Through History*, ed. Edward H. Dahl, trans. Tom Conley (Chicago: University of Chicago Press, 2006); and Michel Foucault, "Questions on Geography," in *Power/Knowledge: Selected Interviews and Other Writings*, ed. Colin Gordon, tran. Colin Gordon et al., 63–77 (New York: Pantheon, 1980).

16. See John Gillies, *Shakespeare and the Geography of Difference* (Cambridge: Cambridge University Press, 1994); Philip Armstrong, "Spheres of Influence: Cartography and the Gaze in Shakespearean Tragedy and History," *Shakespeare Studies* 23 (1995): 39–70; Henry S. Turner, *The English Renaissance Stage: Geometry, Poetics, and the Practical Spatial Arts 1580–1630* (Oxford: Oxford University Press, 2006), esp. chap. 5. On maps and early modern drama, see Valerie Traub, "The Nature of Norms in Early Modern England: Anatomy, Cartography, *King Lear*," *South Central Review* 26.1–2 (2009): 42–81; Rhonda Lemke Sanford, *Maps and Memory in Early Modern England: A Sense of Place* (New York: Palgrave, 2002), esp. chaps. 3 and 5; Henry S. Turner, "Literature and Mapping in Early Modern England, 1520–1688," in *Cartography in the Renaissance, Part I*, ed. David Woodward (Chicago: University of Chicago Press, 2007), 412–26; Garrett A. Sullivan Jr., *The Drama of Landscape: Land, Property, and Social Relations on the Early Modern Stage* (Stanford, CA: Stanford University Press, 1998); Richard Helgerson, *Adulterous Alliances: Home, State, and History in Early Modern European Drama and Painting* (Chicago: University of Chicago Press, 2003).

17. P. D. A. Harvey, "Board Games and Early Cartography" (paper pre-

sented at the International Conference on the History of Cartography, New-berry Library, Chicago, 25 June 1993). My thanks to Robert W. Karrow at the Newberry Library for giving me a copy of this unpublished talk and to Harvey for granting me permission to quote from it.

18. Parlett, *Oxford History of Board Games*, 99.

19. This and other map games are discussed in R. V. Tooley, *Geographical Oddities; or, Curious, Ingenious, and Imaginary Maps and Miscellaneous Plates Published in Atlases* (London: Map Collectors' Circle, 1963).

20. De Certeau, 106, 92.

21. Ibid., 106.

22. I am thus extending to board games and theater the important argument Valerie Traub has made about maps in her "History in the Present Tense: Feminist Theories, Spatialized Epistemologies, and Early Modern Embodiment," in *Mapping Gendered Routes and Spaces in the Early Modern World*, ed. Merry E. Weiser-Hanks (Burlington, VT: Ashgate, 2015), 15–53.

23. "board, n.," I.1.c, *OED Online*, June 2017 (Oxford University Press), http://www.oed.com/view/Entry/20731?rskey=m4qAw3&result=1&isAdvanced=false (accessed 30 December 2017).

24. On topos study as a method for media archaeology, see Huhtamo, "Dismantling the Fairy Engine."

25. See Sullivan, *Drama of Landscape*, esp. 42-43.

26. Ibid., 54.

27. Michael Neill, "'This Gentle Gentleman': Social Change and the Language of Status in *Arden of Faversham*," *Medieval and Renaissance Drama in England* 10 (1998): 73–97.

28. Anon, *Arden of Faversham*, ed. White; scene and line numbers are given parenthetically in the text.

29. In this, the murderers are like the writers of early modern urban guidebooks and surveys, as they are described in Karen Newman, *Cultural Capitals: Early Modern London and Paris* (Princeton, NJ: Princeton University Press, 2009). As Newman argues, these writers' peripatetic walks are invested in the "kind of scopic cogito" found in aerial maps (28).

30. Kathleen M. Kirby, "Re: Mapping Subjectivity: Cartographic Vision and the Limits of Politics," in *BodySpace: Destabilizing Geographies of Gender and Sexuality*, ed. Nancy Duncan (New York: Routledge, 1996), 45–55, maintains that cartography separates the mapper from the environment so as to enable him (and, for Kirby, the mapper is male) to "occupy a secure and superior position in relation to it, without it affecting him in return"; for "[t]o actually be *in* the surroundings, incapable of separating one's self from them in a larger objective representation, is to be lost," an experience of significant discomfort to those who wish to dominate their surroundings (48; her emphasis). While I am wary of the gender binary at the heart of Kirby's and other feminist geographers' claims—occupying a position of spatial superiority is not necessarily or inherently masculine—I find their efforts to consider the gender issues at stake in sociospatial management valuable.

31. We might also consider Mosby in this grouping, although I have not included an extended discussion of him in this essay because his social position

is somewhat different from that of Greene, Black Will, and Shakebag. Mosby does turn to murder to advance his social position, but he also, like Arden, pursues more "civilized" routes: he romances Alice, who is his social superior, and he actively pursues the patronage of Lord Clifford. Notably, Mosby's murder plots involve less physical engagement than do the other murderers' plots. He maintains an even greater distance from his target and doesn't get his hands dirty, as it were, until the final backgammon scene. If, as I argue below, murder is like gameplay—necessitating physical interaction between players and the "men" on the boards—then it is especially significant that Mosby can bring about Arden's death only by engaging in an actual board game with his target.

32. Neill takes to task feminist scholars of *Arden* for "reducing the tragedy to a two-dimensional fable of patriarchal orthodoxy" ("'This Gentle Gentleman,'" 75) when they foreground Alice Arden's transgressions (adultery and the attempted murder of her husband) to argue that the play is predominantly a critique of the institution of marriage. Although Neill is right to call our attention to the crucial role of social status in this play—crucial for making sense of the murderous acts of Greene, Black Will, and Shakebag, social climbers all—his portrayal of social status as working independently from gender is problematic. For a related argument, which criticizes feminist approaches to the play on similar grounds, see David Attwell, "Property, Status, and the Subject in a Middle-Class Tragedy: *Arden of Faversham*," *English Literary Renaissance* 21.3 (1991): 328–48.

33. Helgerson argues that "Arden's appropriation of the abbey lands in Faversham finds its counterpart in Mosby's appropriation of Alice Arden's body" (*Adulterous Alliances*, 28).

34. Shepard, *Meanings of Manhood*, esp. 26.

35. Ibid., 248–9.

36. In using the term "masculinity" instead of Shepard's "manhood," I make room for analysis of those women who, because of their higher status and sometimes their more advanced age or particular social circumstances (e.g., widowhood), subscribed to codes of patriarchal masculinity in an attempt to usurp patriarchal roles and privileges, acting even as heads of households. Alice, who questions Arden's right to "govern me that am to rule myself" (10.84), may serve as one such example, though I do not have space to discuss her and other such female characters here.

37. Upon Arden's death, Greene will ostensibly reclaim his lands (which belong to Arden for the "term of Master Arden's life"; 1.467), and Black Will and Shakebag will reap great financial and, they believe, social rewards.

38. That the murderers might be models of masculinity *because* of their turn to violence chafes against the ways some critics have approached them. For instance, David Attwell argues that the murder plots and their failures are evidence of the play's call "for a central form of control by means of the institutions of bourgeois civil society" ("Property, Status, and the Subject," 348). But as Frances E. Dolan points out, the play also invites its audiences to root for the murderers; see Frances E. Dolan, "The Subordinate('s) Plot: Petty Treason and the Forms of Domestic Rebellion," *Shakespeare Quarterly* 43.3 (1992): 317–40. (A revised version appears in Frances E. Dolan, *Dangerous Familiars: Representa-*

tions of Domestic Crime in England, 1550–1700 [Ithaca, NY: Cornell University Press, 1994], 59–88.) Murder may be outside of lawful patriarchal society, but it is also a viable option for men who are structurally disempowered by a patriarchal system.

39. De Certeau, 106.

40. Murray, *Board-Games Other than Chess*, 120.

41. My reading of Arden complements that of Dolan in *Dangerous Familiars*, which argues that Arden is less of an agent in the play than in other accounts of the crime and yet remains central as the target of the murderers' plot. There has been some disagreement among critics about whether Arden's life is preserved by luck or by Providence. On the argument for Providence, see Comensoli, *"Household Business."* Alexander Leggatt, *"Arden of Faversham," Shakespeare Survey: An Annual Survey of Shakespearian Study and Production* 36 (1983): 121–33, argues that the play keeps its audience guessing on this point. It's worth noting that the question of luck versus Providence is debated with great stakes in many treatises on gaming in the early modern period.

42. By which he means the governing official of a legitimate livery company. See Anon., *Arden of Faversham*, ed. White, 34 n. 105.

43. On the significance of social climbing in the play, see Whigham, *Seizures of the Will, esp. chap. 2*; Attwell, "Property, Status, and the Subject"; Neill, "'This Gentle Gentleman'"; and Helgerson, *Adulterous Alliances, esp. chap. 1*.

44. Michael does as he is instructed and tells the murderers that he will leave the door to Arden's home unlocked that evening so they can find Arden in his bedchamber. It is notable that when asked for a place for the murder, Michael answers not with a map of the house but with what de Certeau calls a "tour" (*Practice of Everyday Life*, 118–22): "No sooner shall ye enter through the latch, / Over the threshold to the inner court, / But on your left hand shall you see the stairs / That leads directly to my master's chamber" (3.173–6). Of course, this plan fails, and in retrospect Michael's *tour* of Arden's house works subversively in the ways de Certeau describes: because Michael has narrated through a story how Black Will can find Arden's bedroom, Black Will has no bird's-eye *map* of the house. When he finds the doors locked, his plans are foiled entirely; he cannot even begin to contemplate another way to get into the bedroom—he has no idea where it is except by way of Michael's tour.

45. Anon., *Arden of Faversham*, ed. White, 54 n. 18.

46. De Certeau, *Practice of Everyday Life*, 92.

47. Ibid., 93.

48. Ibid.

49. M. L. Wine, ed. *The Tragedy of Master Arden of Faversham* (London: Methuen, 1973), 161, 155.

50. The illustration is also (as here) printed facing sideways on the page, which some have called an awkward positioning because it seems to demand that the reader turn the book in order to see the image from the "correct" perspective. But if the illustration functions as a representation of the phenomenology of gameplay, then its positioning on the page is actually ingenious: it puts readers on the side of the game board facing Mosby so that they inhabit the playing perspective of Arden.

51. In theater, as in board games, interaction could be intense even if it was not obviously physical. Cognitive science research on board games has found that players produce mental maps of a game board, imagining different playing scenarios even when they are not physically manipulating pieces. See Pertti Saariluoma, *Chess Players' Thinking: A Cognitive Psychological Approach* (London: Routledge, 1995). In fact, this dynamic helps explain why board games can be engaging spectator sports, as they were in the early modern period and remain in some cultural contexts today. Such research on board games supports findings by scholars of embodied cognition and theater who argue for spectatorship as an active, indeed physically interactive, engagement, even when spectators do not make explicit physical contact with actors or the stage. See, for example, Susan Leigh Foster, "Movement's Contagion: The Kinesthetic Impact of Performance," in *The Cambridge Companion to Performance Studies*, ed. Tracy C. Davis (Cambridge: Cambridge University Press, 2008), 46–59; Bruce McConachie, *Engaging Audiences: A Cognitive Approach to Spectating in the Theatre* (New York: Palgrave Macmillan, 2008); Mary Thomas Crane, "What Was Performance?," *Criticism* 43.2 (2001): 169–87; and Amy Cook, "Wrinkles, Wormholes, and *Hamlet*: The Wooster Group's *Hamlet* as a Challenge to Periodicity," *TDR: The Drama Review* 53.4 (2009): 104–19.

52. Catherine Richardson, *Domestic Life and Domestic Tragedy in Early Modern England: The Material Life of the Household* (Manchester: Manchester University Press, 2006), esp. 106. Marissa Greenberg also observes the play's obsessive staging of places as part of her interesting argument that domestic tragedy more generally maps London, offering playgoers the fantasy of an "imageable" and thus safer city. See Marissa Greenberg, "Signs of the Crimes: Topography, Murder, and Early Modern Domestic Tragedy," *Genre* 40.1–2 (2007): 1–29.

53. The main difference between Irish and backgammon is that the latter game allows players who cast doubles on the dice to play out the doubles, resulting in a faster game. For example, a player who casts double aces would move a total of four points (spaces) instead of two, as in Irish.

54. Cram et al., eds., *Willughby's Book of Games*, 124–5.

55. Notably, Arden describes himself as eluding place when he offers Anne promises of his constancy: "That time nor place nor persons alter me" (10.30).

56. Excerpted in the Appendix to Anon., *Arden of Faversham*, ed. White, 119.

57. On patriarchal authority as existing in a state of perpetual contest, see Dolan, *Dangerous Familiars*, esp. 57, which observes that only when the Arden household is empty can the conflict end.

58. Marianne Brish Evett, "Introduction," in Evett, ed., *Henry Porter's Two Angry Women*, 1–84, esp. 34–59. Mary Bly, "Bawdy Puns and Lustful Virgins: The Legacy of Juliet's Desire in Comedies of the Early 1600s," *Shakespeare Survey: An Annual Survey of Shakespearian Study and Production* 49 (1996): 97–109.

59. The husband's failure to play vicariously compromises the theater audience's ability to follow the game as well. Overlooking the game board, the husbands have the capacity to be objective informants about what is happening on the board and to report that to spectators who want to play along; but they fail to do so.

60. Jeremy Taylor, William Perkins, and William Ames maintain that the real

danger of gaming is men's loss of control over their passions when they lose. Thus even these conservative moralists sanction tables provided the player does not wager more than he can comfortably be prepared to lose in the course of recreation. For a short summary of these arguments, see Wood, "Seventeenth Century English Casuists."

61. Evett, ed., *Henry Porter's Two Angry Women*, 1.124n.

62. As Evett points out (*Henry Porter's Two Angry Women*, 80-81), the quarrel is problematic because the women are not the appropriate mediators of questions of adultery. Mr. Goursey ought to handle the situation, defending his wife if the accusations are false, and, we might add, punishing her if they are true. In much the way *Arden* (at least initially) blames its eponymous character for failing to handle his wife's infidelity effectively, *Two Angry Women* (at least initially) blames Mr. Goursey for failing to speak up for his wife's fidelity.

63. Bateson, "Theory of Play and Fantasy."

64. On the possibility that theater audiences wagered on the action in a play, see Hedrick, "Real Entertainment."

65. See Lopez, *Theatrical Convention*, for a discussion of the theatricality of darkness scenes. He argues that scenes where characters are supposed to be invisible to each other (but are visible to the audience) "deliberately strain the imaginative resources of the audience" who must be continually reminded that the stage is supposed to be dark. Thus the plays resort to "sudden, unexpectedly silly . . . use of the physical space of the stage[,] [e]mphasizing, even flaunting, the visible in scenes whose actions and consequences are predicated on invisibility" (106). A key example in *Arden* is Shakebag's slapstick stage business of falling into a ditch; in *Two Angry Women*, Coomes, too, stumbles into a ditch.

66. When Francis will not reprimand the Boy, his servant, for impertinence to Coomes, Coomes remarks, "Why then, 'tis a fine world, when boys keep boys and know not how to use them" (8.336–7). He not only calls Francis that most derogatory of insults for men, "boy," but in questioning Francis's capacity to handle his servants appropriately, he challenges Francis's own aspirations toward patriarchal masculinity. What is more, when Francis objects to being called a "boy" and threatens to strike Coomes, the outraged Coomes compares himself to the family's real patriarch: "Strike me? Alas, he were better strike his father" (8.340).

67. Gina Bloom, "Manly Drunkenness: Binge Drinking as Disciplined Play," in *Masculinity and the Metropolis of Vice, 1550–1650*, ed. Amanda Bailey and Roze Hentschell (New York: Palgrave Macmillan, 2010), 21–44. See also Patricia Fumerton, "Not Home: Alehouses, Ballads, and the Vagrant Husband in Early Modern England," *Journal of Medieval and Early Modern Studies* 32.3 (2002): 493–518.

68. When Francis loses his temper with his servants, a frequent occurrence in the play, Phillip advises his friend to control his emotions: "O fie, Frank, fie! / Nay, nay, your reason hath no justice now" (2.68–69) and, when Francis fights with Coomes, "Stay, Frank. This pitch of frenzy will defile thee. / Meddle not with it; thy unreprovéd valor / Should be high-minded" (8.346–48). Phillip is also the voice of reason and authority in his interventions into the feud between his parents. Phillip doesn't simply align with his father, insisting to his mother

that his father does indeed love her, but he passes judgment on the marriage: "He loves ye but too well, I swear, / Unless ye knew much better how to use him" (3.249–50).

69. Just before Phillip arrives, Francis declares that he is "too young to marry" (6.15) and that "[t]he shape of marriage / Which I do see in others seems so severe / I dare not put my youngling liberty / Under the awe of that instruction" (6.24–27).

70. Mr. Goursey tries to convince his son to pursue the marriage by delivering a patriarch's advice, quoting his own father's speech to him on the importance of matrimony, but Francis simply turns in response to Phillip: "Phillip, what should I say?" (6.54).

71. For an interesting discussion of this in relation to *King Lear*'s Dover cliff episode, see Turner, *English Renaissance Stage*, 166–9. Turner argues that Gloucester's blindness may prevent him from perceiving the "place" of Dover cliff but enables him to perceive "space" in a way the seeing Edgar, and most modern readers of the play, cannot (169). See also Henry S. Turner, "*King Lear* Without: The Heath," *Renaissance Drama* 28 (1997): 161–93, esp. 184. *Two Angry Women*'s more extended dramatization of blindness—and particularly its representation of blindness as a temporary state—makes possible a similar commentary on theatergoing as a spatial practice that can, but does not always or conclusively, become regimented and regulated by strategies of placement.

72. On blind and blindfolded players of videogames, see Boluk and LeMieux, *Metagaming*, chap. 3.

73. The only way for a woman to win at the game of wooing is, the play intimates, by cheating. At one point when Mistress Goursey tries to convince Francis to give up Mall, she imagines herself in a game with Mall: "let me win thee from her, / And I will gild my blessing, gentle son, / With store of angels. I would not have thee / Check thy good fortune by this cozening choice" (8.278–81). The assumption here is that Francis needs to be won back by his mother, for he has already played a game with Mall, who has cheated to win him. In one sense Mistress Goursey is right about Mall's foul play: Mall consigns herself to marriage not to satisfy Phillip, her father, or Francis, but to satisfy herself. She explains that this is the only way for a virtuous maid to experience the pleasures of sex.

74. "goose, v.," in *Online Etymology Dictionary*, https://www.etymonline.com/word/goose (accessed 31 December 2017).

75. John Lydgate, "The Debate of the Horse, Goose, and Sheep," *The Minor Poems of John Lydgate*, part 2: *Secular Poems*, ed. Henry Noble MacCracken, 539–65 (London: Oxford University Press, for Early English Text Society, 1934). Available at https://archive.org/stream/TheMinorPoemsOfJohnLydgate2/The_Minor_Poems_of_John_Lydgate_2#page/n174/mode/1up/search/goose (accessed 25 October 2017).

76. John Taylor, *Taylor's Goose* (London, 1621).

77. Lydgate, l. 28; Taylor, *Taylor's Goose*, sigs. D4r, D1r–D1v.

78. Parlett, *Oxford History of Board Games*, 98, observes that versions of this game can be traced to the late sixteenth century: There is a German board en-

graved on stone dated 1589, with geese replaced by the figure of Fortuna, and there is a surviving French example from 1601 (Lyon). The first English version we know of is John Wolfe's "The newe and most pleasant Game of the Goose," registered at Stationers' Hall in 1597. A seventeenth-century description of the game can be found in Holme, *Academy of Armory*, 68. See also Parlett, 95.

79. The extent of the role of fiction or narrative in videogames is still a subject of debate in game studies today, with "ludologists" arguing that even in games with a strong fictional component, players ultimately look beyond the fiction, finding pleasure in the algorithms that structure the game. The varying perspectives on this debate can be found in Noah Wardrip-Fruin and Pat Harrigan, eds., *First Person: New Media as Story, Performance, and Game* (Cambridge, MA: MIT Press, 2004). From a ludologist perspective a player's experience of Game of the Goose is the same whether the spaces are marked with geese, cars, or numbers.

80. Other French versions include *Jeu de France* (Paris, 1674), where each space is a small map of a region of France; and *Le Jeu des princes de l'Europe* (1670), where each space is a small map of a European country.

81. Alexander R. Galloway, *Gaming: Essays on Algorithmic Culture* (Minneapolis: University of Minnesota Press, 2006), esp. 3–5, quotes at 2, 3.

82. Simon Penny, "Representation, Enaction, and the Ethics of Simulation," in *First Person*, ed. Wardrip-Fruin and Harrigan, 73–84, at 83.

83. Diana Gromala, "Response" (to Stuart Moulthrop, "From Work to Play: Molecular Cultures in the Time of Deadly Games," 56–69), in *First Person*, ed. Wardrip-Fruin and Harrigan, 56–60, at 57.

84. Milburn, "Atoms and Avatars"; Milburn, *Mondo Nano*.

85. One of the few game studies scholars who has explored the relation of theater to ludic interaction is Gonzalo Frasca, but he insists that the analogy works only if we abandon classical theater and turn to modern theater experiments, particularly to Brazilian playwright Augusto Boal and his Brechtian "Theater of the Oppressed." Gonzalo Frasca, "Videogames of the Oppressed: Critical Thinking, Education, Tolerance and Other Trivial Issues," in *First Person*, ed. Wardrip-Fruin and Harrigan, 85–94.

86. Laurel, *Computers as Theatre*, esp. 15.

87. On how this embodied interactivity has been theorized in the history of modern dance performance, see Foster, "Movement's Contagion."

88. Smith, *Phenomenal Shakespeare*, esp. 147, 133.

89. Herbert Berry, "The Stage and Boxes at Blackfriars," *Studies in Philology* 63.2 (1966): 163–86.

90. Bernard Beckerman, *Dynamics of Drama: Theory and Methods of Analysis* (New York: Alfred A. Knopf, 1970), esp. 9-10 and 130, maintains that some degree of physical distance from the stage is essential for viewing pleasure and understanding, presumably making it impossible for theater patrons close to the stage or on it to follow the play.

91. Quoted in Gurr, *Playgoing*, 28 and 249, no. 164.

92. Berry, "Stage and Boxes," 165.

93. This appears to have been a practice. In another legal case, Sir Richard

Cholmley had purchased a stool on the Blackfriars stage for a performance in 1603, but when he stood up between the scenes "to refresh himself," another gallant took his seat, which led to a duel. Quoted in Gurr, *Playgoing*, 199.

94. Quoted in Gurr, *Playgoing*, 44.

CHAPTER 4

1. Other early modern plays that use chess in interesting ways, beyond the plays discussed below, are George Chapman's *Bussy D'Ambois*, *Sir Giles Goosecap*, and *Byron's Tragedy*; and John Fletcher and Philip Massinger's *The Spanish Curate*.

2. For instance, Elyot, *Boke Named the Governour*, bk. 1, sect. 26, claims that chess sharpens the mind of young princes, male and female alike. Indeed, chess was part of Roger Ascham's curriculum for the young Elizabeth I, who continued to enjoy the game throughout her life.

3. Critics tend to be in agreement about *The Tempest*'s links to its Jacobean political context, with some even arguing that Prospero is a figure for King James I. On *The Tempest* as tightly connected to James I and/or Jacobean politics, see David M. Bergeron, *Royal Family, Royal Lovers: King James of England and Scotland* (Columbia: University of Missouri Press, 1991); David Scott Kastan, "'The Duke of Milan / And His Brave Son': Old Histories and New in *The Tempest*," in *Shakespeare's Romances*, ed. Alison Thorne (Basingstoke, UK: Palgrave, 2003), 226–44; Robin Headlam Wells, *Shakespeare on Masculinity* (Cambridge: Cambridge University Press, 2000); Kim F. Hall, *Things of Darkness: Economies of Race and Gender in Early Modern England* (Ithaca, NY: Cornell University Press, 1995); Heather Campbell, "Bringing Forth Wonders: Temporal and Divine Power in *The Tempest*," in *The Witness of Times: Manifestations of Ideology in Seventeenth Century England*, ed. Katherine Z. Zeller and Gerald J. Schiffhorst (Pittsburgh: Duquesne University Press, 1993), 69–89; Melissa E. Sanchez, "Seduction and Service in *The Tempest*," *Studies in Philology* 105.1 (2008): 50–82; Lorie Jerrell Leininger, "The Miranda Trap: Sexism and Racism in Shakespeare's *Tempest*," in *The Woman's Part: Feminist Criticism of Shakespeare*, ed. Carolyn Ruth Swift Lenz, Gayle Greene, and Carol Thomas Neely (Urbana: University of Illinois Press, 1980), 285–94; Paul Siegel, "Historical Ironies in *The Tempest*," *Shakespeare-Jahrbuch* 119 (1983): 104–11. See also note 41 below.

4. On the culminating chess game in *The Tempest* between Prospero's daughter and her betrothed as emblematic of a peace between Prospero and his former enemies, see Gary Schmidgall, "The Discovery at Chess in *The Tempest*," *English Language Notes* 23.4 (1986): 11–16; Bryan Loughrey and Neil Taylor, "Ferdinand and Miranda at Chess," *Shakespeare Survey: An Annual Survey of Shakespearian Study and Production* 35 (1982): 113–18. Although Stephen Orgel is suspicious of efforts to read the play as tied in some special way to the Jacobean court simply because of its performances there in 1611 and 1613, he is no less convinced than others of the play's connections to the politics of dynastic marriage in the early modern period. See his introduction to William Shakespeare, *The Tempest*, ed. Stephen Orgel (Oxford: Clarendon Press, 1987), esp. 1–4.

5. Citations throughout are from Thomas Middleton, *A Game at Chess*, ed. T. H. Howard-Hill (Manchester: Manchester University Press, 1993).

6. The enactment of chess onstage can be compared to the Civil War reenactments describe in Rebecca Schneider, *Performing Remains: Art and War in Times of Theatrical Reenactment* (London: Routledge, 2011). Schneider argues that these reenactments initiate "an intense, embodied inquiry into temporal repetition, temporal recurrence" (2) that can "loosen the *habit* of linear time" (19; her emphasis). She goes on to argue for the body as a living archive, capable of storing and transmitting information across time, thereby participating in and producing history while imitating it. I'd argue that the (re)production of history is like the staging of chess, not merely mimetic but hypertheatrical. If, as the credo of performance studies puts it, all behavior is citational, or, as Richard Schechner describes it (e.g., in *Performance Theory*, 324), "twice-behaved"— then, as Schneider writes, "the explicit *twiceness* of reenactment trips the otherwise daily condition of repetition into reflexive hyper-drive" (14; her emphasis), making "restored behavior . . . available for recognition" (10).

7. Although chess had traditionally been a game for the elite, it was increasingly available to a range of players in the early modern period—in part because new rules that made for faster play turned it into a wagering game, and in part because the printing press supported the publication of texts that taught chess rules and strategies. An English example of the latter is G. B., *Ludus Scacchiae: Chesse-Play. A Game, Both Pleasant, Wittie, and Politicke* (London, 1597). On the development of "new chess" in the period, see Murray, *History of Chess*, esp. chap. 11.

8. Schneider's work, although it does not engage the logic of gamification explicitly, underscores the ways historiography, whether official/scholarly or unofficial/popular, is always already gamified. Historiography is a practice of reiteration—the re-citing of facts/discoveries that have sedimented over time to create the view of the past that we take as history. I suggest that in using embodied knowledge of gameplay to research the "explicit *twiceness*" (see note 6) of early modern stagings of games, the scholar engages in a kind of explicit *thriceness*, the aim of which is to reveal the way all theater history is played, and might be played differently.

9. This is the Brechtian spectator theorized elegantly in Elin Diamond, *Unmaking Mimesis: Essays on Feminism and Theatre* (London and New York: Routledge, 1997), esp. chap. 2.

10. Walter Benjamin, "On the Concept of History," in *Walter Benjamin: Selected Writings, Vol. 4: 1938–1940*, ed. Howard Eiland and Michael W. Jennings (Cambridge, MA: Belknap Press of Harvard University Press, 2006), 389–400, at 389. (His "angel of history" appears at 392.) Further citations appear in my text.

11. On games as systems of information, see Pearce, *Interactive Book*, esp. 422–3; and Salen and Zimmerman, *Rules of Play*, esp. 202-11.

12. Florio, *Florio's Second Frutes*, 77.

13. Diego Rasskin-Gutman, *Chess Metaphors: Artificial Intelligence and the Human Mind*, trans. Deborah Klosky (Cambridge, MA: MIT Press, 2009).

14. This extensive research is well summarized and also taken up in Saariluoma, *Chess Players' Thinking*. The polytemporal structure of memory has been

discussed widely in cognitive science, whose findings have been applied to early modern drama and performance. See, for example, Evelyn B. Tribble and John Sutton, "Minds In and Out of Time: Memory, Embodied Skill, Anachronism, and Performance," *Textual Practice* 26.4 (2012): 587–607.

15. These attributes of chess, as I discuss further below, resonate startlingly well with the definition of performance offered in Daniel Sack, *After Live: Possibility, Potentiality, and the Future of Performance* (Ann Arbor: University of Michigan Press, 2015), affirming my argument about the overlaps between chess and theatrical plays.

16. The classic study is Hubert L. Dreyfus, *What Computers Still Can't Do: A Critique of Artificial Reason* (Cambridge, MA: MIT Press, 1972), though Dreyfus's arguments have been challenged, not only by AI researchers, but also by other philosophers. See, for example, Evan Selinger, "Chess-Playing Computers and Embodied Grandmasters: In What Ways Does the Difference Matter," in *Philosophy Looks at Chess*, ed. Benjamin Hale (Chicago: Open Court, 2008), 65–87; Andy Miah, "A Deep Blue Grasshopper: Playing Games with Artificial Intelligence," in ibid., 13–23; and John Hartmann, "Garry Kasparov Is a Cyborg; or, What ChessBase Teaches Us about Technology," in ibid., 39–64.

17. Cotton, *The Compleat Gamester*, 77.

18. By contrast, in a game of cards, the evidence of cheating remains after the false card has been played; nicked cards must be prepared in advance of the match and can be deciphered well after it concludes.

19. See the entry for "lightning chess" in David Hooper and Kenneth Whyld, *The Oxford Companion to Chess*, 2nd ed. (Oxford: Oxford University Press, 1996), 226. The entry "timing of moves" explains that in the nineteenth century, there was enough concern about overly long pauses between moves in regular chess matches that the clock was also used to constrain players, who had to perform a certain number of moves within a specified amount of time (422–3).

20. Greco, *Royall Game of Chesse-Play*, 15.

21. Such technology was used to decipher whether in a famous 1994 match between Garry Kasparov and Judit Polgár, Kasparov had violated the touch-move rule and then gone on to win; slow playback revealed that Kasparov had touched a piece for a quarter of a second before letting go, but in part because Polgár did not raise questions about Kasparov's cheating during the game, the game's outcome was left to stand.

22. For a history of cheating in videogames, see Consalvo, *Cheating*.

23. Dibbell, "Mutilated Furries, Flying Phalluses." On how gamers have responded to griefer attacks, see Milburn, "Atoms and Avatars."

24. Bateson, "Theory of Play and Fantasy," 191–3.

25. William Shakespeare, *The Tempest*, ed. Virginia Mason Vaughan and Alden T. Vaughan (London: Arden Shakespeare, 2000), 5.1.172–177.

26. By contrast, Eric C. Brown, "'Like Men at Chess': Time and Control in *The Tempest*," *Shakespeare Yearbook* 10 (1999): 481–9, argues that the chess game ushers in a shift from the "temporal blending" seen throughout the play toward a more conventional temporality, such that "the future may proceed unimpeded" (486).

27. Prospero's subjection of others has been discussed at length by postcolo-

nialist and feminist scholars. See, for example, Janet Adelman, *Suffocating Mothers: Fantasies of Maternal Origin in Shakespeare's Plays, "Hamlet" to "The Tempest"* (New York: Routledge, 1992); Coppélia Kahn, "The Providential Tempest and the Shakespearean Family," in *Representing Shakespeare: New Psychoanalytic Essays*, ed. Murray M. Schwartz and Coppélia Kahn (Baltimore: Johns Hopkins University Press, 1980), 217–43; Leininger, "Miranda Trap"; Thomas Cartelli, "Prospero in Africa: *The Tempest* as Colonialist Text and Pretext," in *Shakespeare Reproduced: The Text in History and Ideology*, ed. Jean E. Howard and Marion F. O'Connor (New York and London: Methuen, 1987), 99–115; Francis Barker and Peter Hulme, "Nymphs and Reapers Heavily Vanish: the Discursive Con-texts of *The Tempest*," in *Alternative Shakespeares*, 2nd ed., ed. John Drakakis (London and New York: Methuen, 2002 [1985]), 194–208; Paul Brown, "'This Thing of Darkness I Acknowledge Mine': *The Tempest* and the Discourse of Colonialism," in *Political Shakespeare: New Essays in Cultural Materialism*, ed. Jonathan Dollimore and Alan Sinfeld (Manchester: Manchester University Press, 1985), 48–71; Jessica Slights, "Rape and the Romanticization of Shakespeare's Miranda," *Studies in English Literature, 1500–1900* 41.2 (2001): 357–79; Ania Loomba, *Gender, Race, Renaissance Drama* (Manchester: Manchester University Press, 1989); Sanchez, "Seduction and Service."

28. Michael Neill writes, "A restoration of the past is found necessary to the full discovery and possession of a 'brave new world.'" Michael Neill, *Putting History to the Question: Power, Politics, and Society in English Renaissance Drama* (New York: Columbia University Press, 2000), 391.

29. Orgel cites this as evidence that Prospero does not renounce power at the end of the play, as many claim he does. Shakespeare, *Tempest*, ed. Orgel, esp. 54-5.

30. Art historian Patricia Simons examines early modern paintings of lovers playing chess and notes, interestingly, that these were sometimes uses to adorn the bedrooms of newlyweds. See Patricia Simons, "(Check)Mating the Grand Masters: The Gendered, Sexualized Politics of Chess in Renaissance Italy," *Oxford Art Journal* 16.1 (1993): 59–74.

31. Suzanne Gossett, "'I'll Look to Like': Arranged Marriages in Shakespeare's Plays," in *Sexuality and Politics in Renaissance Drama*, ed. Carole Levin and Karen Robertson (Lewiston, NY: Edwin Mellen Press, 1991), 57–74, notes that there was a growing consensus in the period that arranged marriages were inferior to companionate marriages, creating a problem in the case of noble marriages, where important political issues were often at stake. She compellingly argues that Shakespeare resolves this problem by making it seem that female characters entering dynastic marriages, such as Miranda, actually desire them. But if we accept the argument about marriage in Dolan, *Marriage and Violence*, then *The Tempest*'s dynastic union could be seen to lay bare the problematic structures of all marriages, whether desired/companionate or not.

32. The precise location for the staging of this scene is conjectural but difficult to dispute in light of theater historians' research on stage architecture, which concludes that between the two doors on most stages was some sort of central opening that was used for "within" or "discovery" scenes, such as this one. Andrew Gurr and Mariko Ichikawa, *Staging in Shakespeare's Theatres* (Ox-

ford: Oxford University Press, 2000), 156. See also the entry for "discover" in Alan C. Dessen and Leslie Thompson, *A Dictionary of Stage Directions in English Drama, 1580–1642* (Cambridge: Cambridge University Press, 2001), 70. Bruce R. Smith convincingly maintains that although there is no explicit mention of a curtain, this scene has so much in common with other scenes of "discovery" that it invariably takes place in the stage's central discovery space, which tended to be covered with a cloth hanging of some sort. Bruce R. Smith, *The Key of Green: Passion and Perception in Renaissance Culture* (Chicago: University of Chicago Press, 2009), 240.

33. See also Gina Bloom, "Games," in *Early Modern Theatricality*, ed. Henry S. Turner (Oxford: Oxford University Press, 2013), 189–211.

34. This view is widely accepted. See, for example, Deborah Willis, "Shakespeare's *The Tempest* and the Discourse of Colonialism," *Studies in English Literature* 29.2 (1989): 277–89; Kastan, "'Duke of Milan'"; and Hall, *Things of Darkness*, who argues that while the play criticizes Alonso's arranged marriage between Claribel and an African outsider, it celebrates Prospero's match: Prospero "prospers" because he does not "open the sex/gender system to non-European outsiders" (149). An exception is Sanchez, "Seduction and Service."

35. In the form of chess played by Shakespeare's audiences—the same form played today—pawns that reach the other side of the board can be promoted, usually to queen. Shakespeare was not the first to twist this game strategy into a narrative about marriage. Marco Girolamo Vida's early sixteenth-century Italian narrative poem, an English free rendering of which appears in G. B., *Ludus scacchiae*, describes the pawns as "waiting maides." One of these pawns "hopes by valor to obtaine / the marriage of the King" (sig. D3r), and when she reaches the other end of the board, the King "takes her to his loving wife, / which was her whole desire" (sig. D3v).

36. Dolan's *Marriage and Violence* shows that conflict and competition are the logical consequence of early modern ideologies of marriage, which explains why marriages in drama tend to end in loss for one partner.

37. Melissa Sanchez's analysis of *The Tempest* in "Seduction and Service" similarly underscores its questioning of dynastic marriage, but locates that critique in the problematic of affection in hierarchical political marriages.

38. James I, *Basilikon Dōron*, 125.

39. Kastan interestingly points out that the play's use of dynastic marriage to solve political conflicts "is vulnerable, if only to irony" ("'Duke of Milan,'" 240) because it accomplishes what Alonso attempted in the first place: "the dissolution of Milanese sovereignty into Neapolitan dynastic rule" (241). But if dynastic marriage is as fraught as I've suggested, then the play raises doubts about Alonso's political strategy. Can anyone be sure that Miranda's identity as a ruler will be completely subsumed by her husband's?

40. Feminist scholars theorizing the "future anterior" would point us toward such a view of historical irony. See for example, Diane Elam, *Feminism and Deconstruction: Ms. en abyme* (New York: Routledge, 1994).

41. Virtually all criticism on the play has been concerned with unpacking the play's political allegory (and determining how oppositional its politics are), even to the point of working out which chess piece characters stood for which

historical figures. Examples include Caroline Bicks, "Staging the Jesuitess in *A Game at Chess," Studies in English Literature, 1500–1900* 49.2 (2009): 463–84; Martin Butler, "William Prynne and the Allegory of Middleton's *Game at Chess," Notes and Queries* 30.2 (1983): 153–4; Thomas Cogswell, "Thomas Middleton and the Court, 1624: *A Game at Chess* in Context," *Huntington Library Quarterly* 47.4 (1984): 273–88; Margot Heinemann, *Puritanism and Theatre: Thomas Middleton and Opposition Drama under the Early Stuarts* (Cambridge: Cambridge University Press, 1980); Jerzy Limon, *Dangerous Matter: English Drama and Politics in 1623/24* (Cambridge: Cambridge University Press, 2010). For overviews of critical debates about the play's relationship to its historical moment, see Richard Dutton, "Thomas Middleton's *A Game at Chess*: A Case Study," in *The Cambridge History of British Theatre*, vol. 1: *Origins to 1660*, ed. Jane Milling and Peter Thomson (Cambridge: Cambridge University Press, 2004), 424–38; James Hogg, "An Ephemeral Hit: Thomas Middleton's *A Game at Chess*," in *Jacobean Drama as Social Criticism*, ed. James Hogg (Lewiston, NY: Edwin Mellen Press, 1995); Jane Sherman, "The Pawns' Allegory in Middleton's *A Game at Chess*," *Review of English Studies* 29.114 (1978): 147–59; and John Robert Moore, "The Contemporary Significance of Middleton's *Game at Chesse*," *PMLA* 50.3 (1935): 761–8, who also addresses the contemporary significance of chess—a game, he argues, that was especially popular at the Spanish court and among Roman Catholic clergy. The most nuanced reading of the play's relationship to contemporaneous politics is Thomas Postlewait, "Theater Events and Their Political Contexts: A Problem in the Writing of Theater History," in *Critical Theory and Performance: Revised and Enlarged Edition*, ed. Janelle G. Reinelt and Joseph R. Roach (Ann Arbor: University of Michigan Press, 2007), 198–222, which, arguing that "politics" is more complex than prior criticism has assumed, provides an exhaustive list of political factors that could have shaped production and reception of the play.

42. See Sack, *After Live*, esp. chap. 4, for a trenchant analysis of how spectators experience potentiality in theatrical performance. See also Rebecca Bushnell, *Tragic Time in Drama, Film, and Videogames: The Future in the Instant* (London: Palgrave Macmillan, 2016) on how new media and experimental theater can produce this sense of "looping" time even through the genre of tragedy, whose narratives traditionally produce a highly linear sense of time.

43. Paul Yachnin, "*A Game at Chess* and Chess Allegory," *Studies in English Literature, 1500–1900* 22.2 (1982): 317–30, offers the most extreme positions. He maintains that the piece-characters' failure to follow chess rules precisely demonstrates that Middleton had little interest in or even knowledge of the game as such, appealing to it only for its rich analogic potential. He and other critics that address the chess setting thus focus only on the game's symbolic meaning. For instance, critics discuss chess as a noble game or a game that lends itself to political meaning, especially in a monarchic context, because of the royal and aristocratic names for the pieces. For instance, Richard A. Davies and Alan R. Young, "'Strange Cunning' in Thomas Middleton's *A Game at Chess," University of Toronto Quarterly* 45.3 (1976): 236–45, calls attention to chess as a noble game that instills virtue—which, Davies and Young argue, is a source of irony in Middleton's play. See also T. H. Howard-Hill, *Middleton's "Vulgar Pasquin": Essays on "A Game at Chess"* (Newark: University of Delaware Press), 71. Whatever

their differences concerning the play's meaning, critics overwhelmingly concur with Howard-Hill's conclusion that "the spectator's understanding should be prompted by the play rather than by his or her knowledge of chess" and that "spectators were not invited to play chess mentally as they watched. Chess is used not so much as a device to control the play's action as a sustained metaphor through which the allegory was elaborated." See Middleton, *Game at Chess*, ed. Howard-Hill, 36. An exception is Swapan Chakravorty, *Society and Politics in the Plays of Thomas Middleton* (Oxford and New York: Clarendon Press, 1996), esp. chap. 8.

44. My interpretation of *A Game at Chess* thus links three arenas of investigation that other readers have tended to disarticulate: chess, theatrical performance, and political history. For instance, Howard-Hill, *Middleton's "Vulgar Pasquin"* and his introduction to his Revels edition of *A Game at Chess* invigorate interest in the play's theatricality by insisting that the play is neither a historical political allegory nor a play that takes its chess setting seriously. The "conventions of chess and the addition of topical color," he writes, "were secondary concerns" within Middleton's scheme to write a morality play (*Middleton's "Vulgar Pasquin,"* 35). Gary Taylor, one of the very few critics to explore the performative implications of Middleton's chess setting, nevertheless arrives at much the same conclusion as Howard-Hill, in this case disarticulating political history from both theatrical performance and chess. See Gary Taylor, "Introduction to *A Game at Chesse*: An Early Form," in *Thomas Middleton: The Collected Works*, ed. Gary Taylor and John Lavagnino (Oxford: Clarendon Press, 2007), 1773–1779, at 1775. Taylor argues that the chess setting is more pronounced in an earlier published edition of the play, which was meant for readers; subject to censorship, this version had to veil its political historical meaning, and it used chess as "layer" or "alienation device" to do so. He goes on to argue that the play's political meaning becomes more clear in performance because characters are associated there with actors, costumes, and other visual cues that enable audiences to look *past* their identity as chess pieces and see more directly their political relevance. For Taylor chess is a layer that can be opaque or transparent, but it is always one step removed from the play's actual political work.

45. An exception is Chakravorty, *Society and Politics*, who similarly proposes that there are important overlaps among politics, chess, and theater, and maintains that pretense is essential to successful performance in all three activities (see esp. 191). But I would question whether pretense is the most fundamental of their commonalities. If Middleton sets up politics, games, and theater as analogous activities in order to emphasize pretense, then why does he use chess as opposed to a game like cards, which, as a game of imperfect information, is so much better suited to plots about deception? What does pretense mean in a game like chess, a game of perfect information in which cheating is so difficult? Although I follow Chakravorty in suggesting that it is the similarities between chess and theater that enable Middleton to offer his political critique, my focus on the specificity of chess as a game—the phenomenology of chess play, and the particular competencies chess develops and requires of its players and spectators—locates and defines the politics of *A Game at Chess* differently. To dissemble in a game of chess is not simply to cheat, but to cheat *time*.

46. For instance, see Gary Taylor, "Introduction to *A Game at Chesse:* A Later Form," in *Thomas Middleton: The Collected Works,* eds. Gary Taylor and John Lavagnino (Oxford: Clarendon Press, 2007), 1825–1828, esp. 1827.

47. Jenny Adams argues that whereas medieval authors used chess to "model an ideal civic order based on contractual obligation and exchange" (*Power Play,* 2), as the period went on, and there was a rise in trades and professions combined with a greater emphasis on individual autonomy, authors ceased using chess as an allegory for political organization. Interestingly, Adams treats *A Game at Chess* as an exception to this rule, claiming that it harkens back to medieval precedents in its allegorical presentation of chess. As I see it, though, the play very much confirms Adams's overall argument about what happens to chess in the early modern period.

48. Edmund Husserl, *On the Phenomenology of the Consciousness of Internal Time (1893–1917),* trans. John Barnett Brough (Dordrecht: Kluwer Academic, 1991), esp. sect. 1.

49. Once could say that the Black Jesting Pawn effectively disrupts what Elizabeth Freeman has called the "chrononormativity" of labor systems that use "time to organize individual human bodies toward maximum productivity." See Elizabeth Freeman, *Time Binds: Queer Temporalities, Queer Histories* (Durham, NC: Duke University Press, 2010), 3.

50. "behindhand, adv. (and adj.)," 2, 4. OED Online, June 2017 (Oxford University Press), http://www.oed.com/view/Entry/17228?redirectedFrom=behind hand (accessed 10 January 2018).

51. Ibid., 3.

52. On Gary Taylor's redating of the play's composition, see Susan Wiseman's introduction to *The Nice Valour; or, The Passionate Madman* in *Middleton: Collected Works,* ed. Taylor and Lavagnino, 1679–1683 at 1679–80.

53. James Bromley, *Intimacy and Sexuality in the Age of Shakespeare* (Cambridge: Cambridge University Press, 2012), 92–107, demonstrates that masochism in *The Nice Valour* operates as an alternative form of sexuality that undermines the social and gender hierarchies of the court and, indeed, of the play as a whole, which attempts unsuccessfully to displace masochistic male relations in favor of conventional heterosexual marriage. But, as Bromley convincingly shows, the end does not crown all, and the socially destabilizing pleasures of masochism, which partly stem from its theatricality, leave their mark on the theater audience.

54. Richard Dutton, *Licensing, Censorship, and Authorship in Early Modern England: Buggeswords* (Houndmills, Basingstoke, UK and New York: Palgrave, 2000) provides an array of potential reasons the scene may have been cut from the play's official published version, among them that, as a clown scene, it was explicitly for performance and unnecessary to print beyond that context. Taylor argues that the published version of the play, in which the scene does not appear, was primarily for readers and not for performance. He also maintains that this passage, along with the other three that were cut, were removed so as "to eliminate unnecessary elaborations that might detract from the clarity of the play's very complicated action." See Gary Taylor, "Introduction to [Apparatus for] A Game at Chess: A Later Form" in Gary Taylor and John Lavagnino, eds.,

Thomas Middleton and Early Modern Textual Culture: A Companion to the Collected Works (Oxford: Clarendon Press, 2007), 912–91, at 914. We cannot know for sure whether this scene was performed, though we do know that Middleton originally imagined its inclusion. And if the scene was, in fact, deleted from some performances, then, in the context of my argument, such a deletion curtailed the play's political impact and its audience's political agency.

55. She is saved again only because she turns out to be collateral in the Black Queen's Pawn's true plot to take revenge on the corrupt Black Bishop's Pawn. The Black Queen's Pawn tricks the Black Bishop's Pawn into having sex with her by substituting herself for the White Queen's Pawn in his bed.

56. Margreta de Grazia, "Teleology, Delay, and the 'Old Mole'," *Shakespeare Quarterly* 50.3 (1999): 251–67, at 251.

57. As de Grazia describes it, Derrida's time is "punctuated by Benjaminian 'blasts' through the temporal continuum. Broken as it is, time does not lead into the future; rather it opens up spaces of access to the future, what Derrida terms 'the space of Deconstruction'" (265). This "perforated temporality is complemented by a new construal of delay" (265), which does not halt but catalyzes true revolution.

58. For a sophisticated reading of this scene, see Bicks, "Staging the Jesuitess," which argues that the Black Queen's Pawn, like her real-life counterpart—the historical English Jesuitess Mary Ward—teaches the White Queen's Pawn how to harness the power of theatricality.

59. For instance, Espen Aarseth, "Genre Trouble: Narrativism and the Art of Simulation," in *First Person*, ed. Wardrip-Fruin and Harrigan, 45–55, defines games as comprised of rules, gameplay, and a material/semiotic system, and he argues that the latter is the most "coincidental" (48).

60. Amandine Mussou, "Playing with Memory: The Chessboard as a Mnemonic Tool in Medieval Didactic Literature," in *Chess in the Middle Ages and Early Modern Age: A Fundamental Thought Paradigm of the Premodern World*, ed. Daniel E. O'Sullivan (Berlin: Walter de Gruyter, 2012), 187–97. Mussou points out that in some cases, such as *Les Eschez amoureux*, the text's reader is required "to cooperate with the author and to replay the game so as to reach the meaning of the poem" (196).

61. This difference explains why Mussou's argument about *Les Eschez amoureux*, though invested in phenomenologies of gameplay, reaches a very different conclusion than I do about how chess functions and what lessons it teaches. Mussou argues that the poem's chess setting "forces a linear approach" (196) to reading, imposing a grid that forestalls individual, silent, and thus more discontinuous forms of reading. I have shown that Middleton's use of chess achieves precisely the opposite effect with respect to theater spectatorship.

62. De Certeau, *Practice of Everyday Life*, 106.

63. In the case of chess, Mark N. Taylor's recent archival work on the game's medieval history ("How Did the Queen Go Mad?") has shown that the queen's expanded movements and other changes that defined the "new chess" evolved slowly over the late Middle Ages, not in one fell swoop.

64. For an overview and critique of how scholars have read the relations between drama and history, see Dolan, *True Relations*, which makes a related argument about drama as a patchwork of fragments that audiences—in the

early modern period and in critical discourse today—stitch together. The assumption that each performance is an "event" that occurs in a specific and thus ephemeral moment is so widespread that it is taken for granted even in scholarship that recognizes the polytemporality of theater. See, for instance, Matthew D. Wagner, *Shakespeare, Theatre, and Time* (New York: Routledge, 2011); Brian Walsh, "'Unkind Division': The Double Absence of Performing History in 1 Henry VI," *Shakespeare Quarterly* 55.2 (2004): 119–47; and Tribble and Sutton, "Minds In and Out of Time," 601.

65. Bloom, Bosman, and West, "Ophelia's Intertheatricality." The concept of the "intertheatrical" has been explored by a number of scholars, including Jonathan Gil Harris, *Untimely Matter in the Time of Shakespeare* (Philadelphia: University of Pennsylvania Press, 2008); William N. West, "Replaying Early Modern Performances," in *New Directions in Renaissance Drama and Performance Studies*, ed. Sarah Werner (New York: Palgrave Macmillan, 2010), 30–50; Anston Bosman, "Renaissance Intertheater and the Staging of Nobody," *English Language History* 71.3 (2004): 559–85; and Jacky Bratton, *New Readings in Theatre History* (Cambridge: Cambridge University Press, 2003).

66. Bloom et al., "Ophelia's Intertheatricality," 167.

67. Sack, *After Live.*

68. Shakespeare explores more obscurely the link between chess and doomed marriage in many of his plays. He puns often on mating as a move in chess and a marital coupling. The noun *mate* could mean marital coupling as early as the sixteenth century, but notably, a third definition of *mate*, which chess historians claim to be the etymology of the chess term "check mate" or "*mate*," is the adjective "mat," meaning helpless—the king (in Persian, a term close to *check*) is made helpless (*mated*) by another piece on the board. The noun and adjective forms of *mate* may have different etymologies, but Shakespeare's pun on "mate" brings them into a fascinating convergence that supports Dolan's argument in *Marriage and Violence*: to be mated or married to someone may mean to be rendered helpless. Whether or not every audience member heard echoes of chess when Shakespeare invokes mating in his plays, the resonance is there and is certainly prominent in a play like *The Tempest.*

69. This is the approach of Jeffrey A. Netto, "Intertextuality and the Chess Motif: Shakespeare, Middleton, Greenaway," in *Shakespeare, Italy, and Intertextuality*, ed. Michele Marrapodi (Manchester: Manchester University Press, 2004), 216–26.

70. They exist, to borrow terminology from performance studies theorist Diana Taylor, in "repertoires," not just in archives. Taylor, *Archive and the Repertoire. See also* Chapter 1, note 134.

71. Some postmodern forms of theater, such as promenade (where audiences are free to move about the performance space), would allow audiences effectively to "zoom in" on the action. Portable binoculars, not available when these plays were first performed, would allow for this to some extent as well.

72. The only essay I have found that considers how their experience with chess is reflected in their ideas is Freddie Rokem, "Dramaturgies of Exile: Brecht and Benjamin 'Playing' Chess and Go," *Theatre Research International* 37.1 (2012): 5–19, which focuses on the spatial, but not temporal, aspects of chess play.

73. They would have been in close proximity for a total of about eleven months between 1933 and 1940, when Benjamin intermittently visited Brecht in Denmark, sometimes for extended stretches of time; see Erdmut Wizisla, *Walter Benjamin and Bertolt Brecht: The Story of a Friendship*, trans. Christine Shuttleworth (New Haven: Yale University Press, 2009), 55.

74. Quoted in ibid., 59.

75. Benjamin, "On the Concept of History," 395, 393.

76. Wendy Brown, *Edgework: Critical Essays on Knowledge and Politics* (Princeton, NJ: Princeton University Press, 2005), 12.

77. Ibid.

78. Schneider, *Performing Remains*; Taylor, *Archive and the Repertoire*

79. Sutton, "Batting, Habit and Memory," analyzing batters in the game of cricket, explains that whereas personal memory comprises recollections of "unique, irreversible moments," habit memory "can only derive from long, repeated training, from routines and practices, from many related experiences rather than one" — a process that, like the intertheatricality I discuss above, may be "consciously inaccessible and verbally inarticulable" (765–6). This does not mean that the so-called enskilled body must be completely disarticulated from the mind. In fact, Sutton's main argument is that that game players can improve their skill level by allowing conscious, even if not verbally articulated, thoughts or personal memories to shape their bodily habits.

80. Ibid., 765. McConachie, *Engaging Audiences,* makes a similar point when he calls for "cognitive audience histories" (190). That call is partly answered by scholarship that uses findings from modern cognitive science to understand performance, such as Amy Cook, *Shakespearean Neuroplay: Reinvigorating the Study of Dramatic Texts and Performance Through Cognitive Science* (New York: Palgrave Macmillan, 2010). That said, neither Cook nor McConachie is able to show that cognitive science offers a more useful set of critical tools than phenomenology. To the contrary, their analyses of spectatorship are a "near fit" (McConachie, 46) with phenomenological accounts such as those of Stanton Garner, Bert O. States, and Bruce R. Smith.

81. I am drawing here on Evelyn Tribble's application to theater of the concept of "enskillment" — a term introduced by anthropologist Tim Ingold to describe how individuals learn skills through their embodied engagement in a particular environment. See Evelyn B. Tribble, *Cognition in the Globe: Attention and Memory in Shakespeare's Theatre* (New York: Palgrave Macmillan, 2011), esp. chap. 3. See also Tribble and Sutton, "Minds In and Out of Time"; Crane, "What Was Performance?" These scholars of embodied cognition have focused primary on the enskillment of actors/performers, but the concept, I am suggesting, is useful for understanding theater spectators as well.

82. Adams, *Power Play,* 160.

EPILOGUE

1. For sample titles, see Introduction, note 7.

2. The term "mimetic interface game" is introduced in Juul, *Casual Revolution,* esp. chap. 5, who offers a useful definition than includes these variables.

3. Ibid., 103.

4. Microsoft recorded the show and broadcast it later on select cable stations, including MTV and Nickelodeon. The show can now be seen on *YouTube* as "Kinect—E3 2010—Cirque Du Soleil Event" in three parts, the first of which is available at https://www.youtube.com/watch?v=vS2_3cBjQIU (accessed 20 August 2016).

5. A useful overview of these techniques can be found in Machon, *Immersive Theatres*.

6. Milburn, *Mondo Nano*, esp. chap. 0011 [*sic*].

7. Steven E. Jones and George K. Thiruvathukal, *Codename Revolution: The Nintendo Wii Platform* (Cambridge, MA: MIT Press, 2012).

8. Ibid., 164.

9. "Cirque Helps Launch 'Project Natal,'" https://www.richasi.com/Cirque/Treasure/bigtop22a.htm (accessed 30 October 2017), sect. "The Big Reveal." (This site includes links to all three parts of the E3 2010 video.)

10. The videos of gameplay were clearly prerecorded, as many people at and after the event noted. But clearly the aim was to show how the human body would ideally work as a controller.

11. See, e.g., the 2011 advertisement for Xbox 360, https://www.youtube.com/watch?v=QjjkqBLRALo and for Xbox 360 Adventures games https://www.youtube.com/watch?v=iK_UlfO42sc (accessed 20 August 2016).

12. For instance, see 0:57 of Part III on YouTube.

13. Miller, *Playing Along*, 15.

14. Ibid., 125.

15. Ibid., 151.

16. Ibid., 137.

17. *Play the Knave* runs on a platform called Mekanimator, which was created by UC Davis graduate students Evan Buswell and Nicholas Toothman, with the help of computer scientist Michael Neff. I am the project director, and Colin Milburn is the project manager. Created in Unity, a game engine developed by Unity Technologies, Mekanimator seamlessly integrates the Microsoft Kinect camera with a universal scene-staging system. Although *Play the Knave* is Mekanimator's first application, the platform has other uses and, when completed, will be available as open-source software. *Play the Knave* was accepted for distribution by Steam Greenlight (see http://steamcommunity.com/sharedfiles/filedetails/?id=874426069&searchtext=Play+the+Knave [accessed 23 December 2017]) and will be released separately as a fully functional software application. Our work has been funded by various academic institutions and nonprofit agencies (see Acknowledgments), not by Microsoft.

18. For more images of gameplay, visit http://playtheknave.org. In the current version, players choose between two script levels, full and abridged. The abridged script still uses Shakespeare's original language but eliminates some of the more complicated imagery and unfamiliar diction so as to suit users newer to Shakespeare. Like karaoke, the words appear in segments of one to three lines at most. Players have some control over the pacing of the lines, choosing from three different speeds: fast, medium, or slow. The current version includes four theater stages and several dozen avatars representing differ-

ent historical eras (ancient, Elizabethan, modern) as well as fantasy/science fiction settings.

19. See Gina Bloom, "Videogame Shakespeare: Enskilling Audiences through Theater-Making Games," *Shakespeare Studies* 43 (2015): 114–27; Gina Bloom et al., "'A Whole Theatre of Others': Amateur Acting and Immersive Spectatorship in the Digital Shakespeare Game *Play the Knave*," in special issue on "#Bard," ed. Douglas Lanier, *Shakespeare Quarterly* 67.4 (2016): 408–30.

20. PhD student Sawyer Kemp spearheaded the research at Stratford, doing a month of fieldwork there to investigate how users and audiences responded to the game. Initial findings from Stratford and other installations are elucidated in Bloom et al., "'Whole Theatre of Others.'" Since 2015, I have curated over two dozen installations. Among the longer-running were the Gallaudet University "First Folio! Tour" exhibit on Shakespeare in deaf culture, 6–30 October 2016; and the exhibit "Shakespeare in Deaf History," at the Dyer Arts Center, National Technical Institute for the Deaf, Rochester, NY, 27 January–4 March 2017. Other major installations include those at the Utah Shakespeare Festival, Cedar City, UT, 2–3 October 2015; and "Shakespeare 400 Chicago," Evanston, IL, 28 April 2016. *Play the Knave* was also mounted at several academic conferences, including the Shakespeare Association of America meetings in Vancouver, BC, Canada, 1–4 April 2015 and Atlanta, GA, 6–9 April 2017; and the American Shakespeare Center's Eighth Blackfriars Theatre Conference, Staunton, VT, 30–1 October 2015. Currently under way is a program I co-developed with UCD undergraduate Amanda Shores to bring *Play the Knave* into K–12 schools and study its pedagogical impact.

21. I am grateful to Sawyer Kemp for first observing these spectator activities at early installations of *Play the Knave*. Kemp's thoughtful comments on these installations helped me think about how to integrate *Play the Knave* into this book.

22. Games such as *Proteus, The Stanley Parable,* and *The Plan* encourage players to appreciate interesting images and sounds or think about philosophical concepts much more so than to win or to succeed at a particular task better than others.

23. The "glitch" is in the eye of the beholder, explains Michael Bettencourt, *Glitch Art in Theory and Practice: Critical Failures and Post-Digital Aesthetics* (New York: Routledge, 2017). Although our tendency is to blame our software or hardware for failing to comply with user will, in fact glitches are not signs of computer malfunction. The computer is continuing to function according to its protocols, but "with a set of instructions that are aberrant" (106). The glitch emerges because the user experiences a "disrupt[ion of] those semiotic protocols that produce meaning" (105).

24. Multiple cameras and more sophisticated, costly equipment are used in motion capture theater experiments discussed in Matt Delbridge, *Motion Capture in Performance: An Introduction* (Houndmills, Basingstoke, UK: Palgrave Macmillan, 2015). See also the skin deformation system for motion capture developed by Sang Il Park and Jessica K. Hodgins, demonstrated and described at http://graphics.cs.cmu.edu/projects/muscle/ (accessed 12 January 2018). In our system, skeletal quality is further constrained by the recognizer's training data

set and the depth image, which can suffer from poor sensor placement and the performer's bodily orientation. I am grateful to Nicholas Toothman and Michael Neff for helping me understand these technical details.

25. Matthew Causey, "The Screen Test of the Double: The Uncanny Performer in the Space of Technology," *Theatre Journal* 51.4 (1999): 383–94; Susan Kozel, *Closer: Performance, Technologies, Phenomenology* (Cambridge, MA: MIT Press, 2007). See also Jennifer Parker-Starbuck, *Cyborg Theatre: Corporeal/Technological Intersections in Multimedia Performance* (New York: Palgrave Macmillan, 2014); Gabriella Giannachi and Nick Kaye, *Performing Presence: Between the Live and the Simulated* (Manchester, UK: Manchester University Press, 2011); Sue-Ellen Case, *Performing Science and the Virtual* (New York: Routledge, 2007), esp. chap. 4; Sita Popat, "Missing in Action: Embodied Experience and Virtual Reality," *Theatre Journal* 68.3 (2016): 357–78; Broadhurst and Machon, eds., *Performance and Technology*; Bay-Cheng et al., *Performance and Media*; Salter, *Entangled*.

26. Bloom, "Videogame Shakespeare."

27. Mark Wilson, "Exclusive: Microsoft Has Stopped Manufacturing the Kinect," *Co.Design* (25 October 2017), https://www.fastcodesign.com/90147868/exclusive-microsoft-has-stopped-manufacturing-the-kinect (accessed 3 January 2018).

28. Adi Robertson, "Replacing VR and AR with 'Mixed Reality' is Good For Microsoft but Bad for the Rest of Us," *The Verge* (12 May 2017), https://www.theverge.com/2017/5/12/15625972/microsoft-build-windows-mixed-reality-hololens-vr-confusing (accessed 3 January 2018).

29. Mark B. N. Hansen, *New Philosophy for New Media* (Cambridge, MA: MIT Press, 2004), esp. chap. 1. See also Popat, "Missing in Action," who counters Josephine Machon's argument that immersive theater shows people's desire "for real-world, interpersonal communication in physical space, in direct rebellion against the disembodied, distancing effect of VR"; in fact, Popat maintains, "VR environments can enable us to relocate ourselves as embodied beings rather than distancing us from our bodies" (359).

Works Cited

Aarseth, Espen. "Genre Trouble: Narrativism and the Art of Simulation." In *First Person: New Media as Story, Performance, and Game*, edited by Noah Wardrip-Fruin and Pat Harrigan, 45–55. Cambridge, MA: MIT Press, 2004.

Aarseth, Espen. "Playing Research: Methodological Approaches to Game Analysis." Paper presented at the Game Approaches / Spil-veje: Papers for spilforskning.dk Conference, 28–9 August 2003.

Adams, Jenny. *Power Play: The Literature and Politics of Chess in the Late Middle Ages*. Philadelphia: University of Pennsylvania Press, 2006.

Adelman, Janet. *Suffocating Mothers: Fantasies of Maternal Origin in Shakespeare's Plays, "Hamlet" to "The Tempest."* New York: Routledge, 1992.

Agnew, Jean-Christophe. *Worlds Apart: The Market and the Theater in Anglo-American Thought, 1550–1750*. Cambridge: Cambridge University Press, 1986.

Altman, Joel B. *The Tudor Play of Mind: Rhetorical Inquiry and the Development of Elizabethan Drama*. Berkeley: University of California Press, 1978.

Ames, William. *Conscience with the Power and Cases Thereof*. London, 1639.

Anon. *Arden of Faversham*. 2nd ed. Edited by Martin White. London: A & C Black, 2007.

Anon. *The Bloody Game at Cards*. [London], c. 1642.

Anon. *The Boke of the New Cardys*. London, 1530.

Anon. "Commonplace Book." Folger Library, E.a.6, ca. 1650–70.

Anon. *Geographical Cards*. London: F. H. van Hove, 1675.

Anon. *Geographical Cards of the World*. London: Henry Winstanley, c. 1675–6.

Anon. *The Plotting Cards Reviv'd; or, The New Game at Forty One*. London, 1681.

Arcangeli, Alessandro. *Recreation in the Renaissance: Attitudes toward Leisure and Pastimes in European Culture, c. 1425–1675*. New York: Palgrave Macmillan, 2003.

Armstrong, Philip. "Spheres of Influence: Cartography and the Gaze in Shakespearean Tragedy and History." *Shakespeare Studies* 23 (1995): 39–70.

Ascham, Roger. *Toxophilus*. Edited by Peter E. Medine. Medieval and Renaissance Texts and Studies 244. Tempe: Arizona Center for Medieval and Renaissance Studies, 2002 [1545].

Attwell, David. "Property, Status, and the Subject in a Middle-Class Tragedy: *Arden of Faversham*." *English Literary Renaissance* 21, no. 3 (1991): 328–48.

Bach, Rebecca Ann. "The Homosocial Imaginary of *A Woman Killed with Kindness*." *Textual Practice* 12, no. 3 (1998): 503–24.

Bach, Rebecca Ann. *Shakespeare and Renaissance Literature before Heterosexuality.* New York: Palgrave Macmillan, 2007.

Bacon, Francis. *Bacon's Essays, with Annotations by Richard Whately and Notes and a Glossarial Index, by Franklin Fiske Heard.* Boston: Lee & Shepard, 1868. Reprint, Making of America [online], University of Michigan Library, 2005. http://name.umdl.umich.edu/ABV4738.0001.001.

Balmford, James. *A Short and Plaine Dialogue Concerning the Unlawfulnes of Playing at Cards or Tables, or Any Other Game Consisting in Chance.* London, 1593.

Barber, C. L. *Shakespeare's Festive Comedies.* Princeton, NJ: Princeton University Press, 1959.

Barker, Francis, and Peter Hulme. "Nymphs and Reapers Heavily Vanish: The Discursive Con-Texts of *The Tempest.*" In *Alternative Shakespeares,* 2nd ed., edited by John Drakakis, 194–208. London and New York: Methuen, 2002 [1985].

Bateson, Gregory. "A Theory of Play and Fantasy." In *Steps to an Ecology of Mind,* 177–93. New York: Ballatine, 1972.

Bay-Cheng, Sarah, Jennifer Parker-Starbuck, and David Z. Saltz. *Performance and Media: Taxonomies for a Changing Field.* Ann Arbor: University of Michigan Press, 2015.

Beckerman, Bernard. *Dynamics of Drama: Theory and Methods of Analysis.* New York: Alfred A. Knopf, 1970.

Bell, R. C. *Board and Table Games from Many Civilizations.* London: Oxford University Press, 1960.

Benham, W. Gurney. *Playing Cards: History of the Pack and Explanations of Its Many Secrets.* London: Ward, Lock & Co., 1931.

Benjamin, Walter. "On the Concept of History." In *Walter Benjamin: Selected Writings,* Vol. 4: *1938–1940,* edited by Howard Eiland and Michael W. Jennings. Cambridge, MA: Belknap Press of Harvard University Press, 2006.

Bennett, Lyn L. "The Homosocial Economics of *A Woman Killed with Kindness.*" *Renaissance and Reformation* 24, no. 2 (2000): 35–61.

Bennett, Susan. *Theatre Audiences: A Theory of Production and Reception.* New York: Routledge, 1990.

Bergeron, David M. "The Education of Rafe in Lyly's *Gallathea.*" *Studies in English Literature, 1500–1900* 23, no. 2 (1983): 197–206.

Bergeron, David M. *Royal Family, Royal Lovers: King James of England and Scotland.* Columbia: University of Missouri Press, 1991.

Berry, Edward. *Shakespeare and the Hunt: A Cultural and Social Study.* Cambridge: Cambridge University Press, 2001.

Berry, Herbert. "The Stage and Boxes at Blackfriars." *Studies in Philology* 63, no. 2 (1966): 163–86.

Berry, Ralph. *Shakespeare and the Awareness of the Audience.* London: Macmillan, 1985.

Bicks, Caroline. "Staging the Jesuitess in *A Game at Chess.*" *Studies in English Literature, 1500–1900* 49, no. 2 (2009): 463–84.

Bird, Samuel. *A Friendlie Communication or Dialogue between Paule and Demas Wherein Is Disputed How We Are to Use the Pleasures of This Life.* London, 1580.

Bishop, Tom. "Shakespeare's Theater Games." *Journal of Medieval and Early Modern Studies* 40, no. 1 (2010): 65–88.

Bloom, Gina. "Games." In *Early Modern Theatricality*, edited by Henry S. Turner, 189–211. Oxford Twenty-First Century Approaches to Literature. Oxford: Oxford University Press, 2013.

Bloom, Gina. "The Historicist as Gamer." In *Shakespeare in Our Time: A Shakespeare Association of America Collection*, edited by Dympna Callaghan and Suzanne Gossett, 223–8. The Arden Shakespeare. London: Bloomsbury, 2016.

Bloom, Gina. "Manly Drunkenness: Binge Drinking as Disciplined Play." In *Masculinity and the Metropolis of Vice, 1550–1650*, edited by Amanda Bailey and Roze Hentschell, 21–44. Early Modern Cultural Studies, 1500–1700. New York: Palgrave Macmillan, 2010.

Bloom, Gina. "Videogame Shakespeare: Enskilling Audiences through Theater-Making Games." *Shakespeare Studies* 43 (2015): 114–27.

Bloom, Gina. *Voice in Motion: Staging Gender, Shaping Sound in Early Modern England*. Material Texts. Philadelphia: University of Pennsylvania Press, 2007.

Bloom, Gina, Anston Bosman, and William N. West. "Ophelia's Intertheatricality; or, How Performance Is History." *Theatre Journal* 65 (2013): 165–82.

Bloom, Gina, Sawyer Kemp, Nicholas Toothman, and Evan Buswell. "'A Whole Theatre of Others': Amateur Acting and Immersive Spectatorship in the Digital Shakespeare Game *Play the Knave*." Special issue on "#Bard," ed. Douglas Lanier, *Shakespeare Quarterly* 67, no. 4 (2016): 408–30.

Bly, Mary. "Bawdy Puns and Lustful Virgins: The Legacy of Juliet's Desire in Comedies of the Early 1600s." *Shakespeare Survey* 49 (1996): 97–109.

Boluk, Stephanie, and Patrick LeMieux. *Metagaming: Playing, Competing, Spectating, Cheating, Trading, Making, and Breaking Videogames*. Minneapolis: University of Minnesota Press, 2017.

Bosman, Anston. "Renaissance Intertheater and the Staging of Nobody." *English Language History* 71, no. 3 (2004): 559–85.

Bownde, Nicholas. *Sabbathum Veteris et Noui Testamenti; or, The True Doctrine of the Sabbath*. London, 1606.

Brand, John, and Sir Henry Ellis. *Observations on Popular Antiquities, Chiefly Illustrating the Origin of Our Vulgar Customs, Ceremonies and Superstitions*. London: F. C. & J. Rivington, 1873.

Brathwaite, Richard. *Whimzies; or, A New Cast of Characters*. London, 1631.

Bratton, Jacky. *New Readings in Theatre History*. Cambridge: Cambridge University Press, 2003.

Bray, Alan. *The Friend*. Chicago: University of Chicago Press, 2003.

Breton, Nicholas. *The Workes of a Young Wyt*. London, 1577.

Bristol, Michael D. *Big-Time Shakespeare*. London: Routledge, 1996.

Bristol, Michael D. "Shamelessness in Arden: Early Modern Theater and the Obsolescence of Popular Theatricality." In *Print, Manuscript, Performance: The Changing Relations of the Media in Early Modern England*, edited by Arthur F. Marotti and Michael D. Bristol, 279–306. Columbus: Ohio State University Press, 2000.

Bristol, Michael D. "Theater and Popular Culture." In *A New History of Early English Drama*, edited by John D. Cox and David Scott Kastan, 231–48. New York: Columbia University Press, 1997.

Broadhurst, Susan, and Josephine Machon, eds. *Performance and Technology: Practices of Virtual Embodiment and Interactivity.* New York: Palgrave Macmillan, 2011 [2006].

Bromley, James. *Intimacy and Sexuality in the Age of Shakespeare.* Cambridge: Cambridge University Press, 2012.

Bromley, Laura G. "Domestic Conduct in *A Woman Killed with Kindness.*" *Studies in English Literature, 1500–1900* 26, no. 2 (1986): 259–76.

Brown, Eric C. "'Like Men at Chess': Time and Control in *The Tempest.*" *Shakespeare Yearbook* 10 (1999): 481–9.

Brown, Paul. "'This Thing of Darkness I Acknowledge Mine': *The Tempest* and the Discourse of Colonialism." In *Political Shakespeare: New Essays in Cultural Materialism,* edited by Jonathan Dollimore and Alan Sinfeld, 48–71. Manchester: Manchester University Press, 1985.

Brown, Wendy. *Edgework: Critical Essays on Knowledge and Politics.* Princeton, NJ: Princeton University Press, 2005.

Bruster, Douglas. *Drama and Market in the Age of Shakespeare.* Cambridge: Cambridge University Press, 1992.

Burton, Robert. *Anatomy of Melancholy.* 5th ed. Oxford, 1638 [1621].

Bushnell, Rebecca. *Tragic Time in Drama, Film, and Videogames: The Future in the Instant.* Palgrave Pivot. London: Palgrave Macmillan, 2016.

Butler, Judith. "Performative Acts and Gender Constitution: An Essay in Phenomenology and Feminist Theory." *Theatre Journal* 40, no. 4 (1988): 519–31.

Butler, Martin. "William Prynne and the Allegory of Middleton's *Game at Chess.*" *Notes and Queries* 30, no. 2 (1983): 153–4.

Caillois, Roger. *Man, Play and Games.* Translated by Meyer Barash. Urbana: University of Illinois Press, 2001 [1961].

Campbell, Heather. "Bringing Forth Wonders: Temporal and Divine Power in *The Tempest.*" In *The Witness of Times: Manifestations of Ideology in Seventeenth Century England,* edited by Katherine Z. Zeller and Gerald J. Schiffhorst, 69–89. Pittsburgh: Duquesne University Press, 1993.

Cardano, Gerolamo. "The Book on Games of Chance." Translated by Sydney Henry Gould. In Øystein Ore, *Cardano: The Gambling Scholar,* 181–242. Princeton, NJ: Princeton University Press, 1953.

Carson, Christie. "Democratising the Audience?" In *Shakespeare's Globe: A Theatrical Experiment,* edited by Christie Carson and Farah Karim-Cooper, 115–26. Cambridge: Cambridge University Press, 2008.

Carson, Christie. "Technology as a Bridge to Audience Participation?" In *Performance and Technology: Practices of Virtual Embodiment and Interactivity,* edited by Susan Broadhurst and Josephine Machon, 181–93. New York: Palgrave Macmillan, 2011 [2006].

Cartelli, Thomas. "Prospero in Africa: *The Tempest* as Colonialist Text and Pretext." In *Shakespeare Reproduced: The Text in History and Ideology,* edited by Jean E. Howard and Marion F. O'Connor, 99–115. New York and London: Methuen, 1987.

Cartwright, Kent. *Theatre and Humanism: English Drama in the Sixteenth Century.* Cambridge: Cambridge University Press, 1999.

Cartwright, William. *The Game at Chesse: A Metaphoricall Discourse Shewing the Present Estate of This Kingdome. London,* 1643.

Case, Sue-Ellen. *Performing Science and the Virtual*. New York: Routledge, 2007.

Causey, Matthew. "The Screen Test of the Double: The Uncanny Performer in the Space of Technology." *Theatre Journal* 51, no. 4 (1999): 383–94.

Cessolis, Jacobus de. *The Game and Playe of Chesse*. Translated by William Caxton. London, 1474.

Chakravorty, Swapan. *Society and Politics in the Plays of Thomas Middleton*. Oxford and New York: Clarendon Press, 1996.

Charles I, King. *The Kings Majesties Declaration to His Subjects Concerning Lawfull Sports to Be Used*. London, 1633 [1618].

Chatto, William Andrew. *Facts and Speculations on the Origin and History of Playing Cards*. London: John Russell Smith, 1848.

Cicero. *"De amicitia," to Which Is Added "Scipio's Dream" and Cicero, "De senectute."* Translated by Andrew P. Peabody. Boston: Little, Brown, 1884. Available at http://archive.fo/20160422122603/ancienthistory.about.com/library/bl/bl_text_cic_friendship.htm (accessed 23 October 2017).

Cicero. *De senectute, De amicitia, De divinatione*. Translated by William Armistead Falconer. Loeb Classical Library 154. Cambridge, MA: Harvard University Press, 1923. Available at https://www.loebclassics.com/view/marcus_tullius_cicero-de_amicitia/1923/pb_LCL154.205.xml (accessed 23 October 2017).

Cleland, James. *Hērō-paideia; or, The Institution of a Young Noble Man*. Oxford, 1607.

Clopper, Lawrence M. *Drama, Play, and Game: English Festive Culture in the Medieval and Early Modern Period*. Chicago: University of Chicago Press, 2001.

Cogswell, Thomas. "Thomas Middleton and the Court, 1624: *A Game at Chess* in Context." *Huntington Library Quarterly* 47, no. 4 (1984): 273–88.

Comensoli, Viviana. *"Household Business": Domestic Plays of Early Modern England*. Toronto: University of Toronto Press, 1996.

Consalvo, Mia. *Cheating: Gaining Advantage in Videogames*. Cambridge, MA: MIT Press, 2007.

Cook, Amy. *Shakespearean Neuroplay: Reinvigorating the Study of Dramatic Texts and Performance through Cognitive Science*. New York: Palgrave Macmillan, 2010.

Cook, Amy. "Wrinkles, Wormholes, and *Hamlet*: The Wooster Group's *Hamlet* as a Challenge to Periodicity." *TDR: The Drama Review* 53, no. 4 (2009): 104–19.

Cook, David. *"A Woman Killed with Kindness:* An Unshakespearian Tragedy." *English Studies* 45, no. 5 (1964): 353–72.

Cotgrave, John. *Wits Interpreter, the English Parnassus; or, A Sure Guide to Those Admirable Accomplishments That Compleat Our English Gentry*. 2nd ed. London, 1662 [1st ed., 1655].

Cotton, Charles. *The Compleat Gamester; Instructions How to Play at Billiards, Trucks, Bowls, and Chess: Together with All Manner of Usual and Most Gentile Games Either on Cards or Dice: To Which Is Added, the Arts and Mysteries of Riding, Racing, Archery, and Cock-Fighting*. London, 1674.

Coursen, Herbert R., Jr. "The Subplot of *A Woman Killed with Kindness*." *English Language Notes* 2, no. 3 (1965): 180–5.

Cram, David, Jeffrey L. Forgeng, and Dorothy Johnston, eds. *Francis Willugh-*

by's *Book of Games: A Seventeenth-Century Treatise on Sports, Games and Pastimes*. Burlington, VT: Ashgate, 2003.

Crane, Mary Thomas. "What Was Performance?" *Criticism* 43, no. 2 (2001): 169–87.

Crimsal, Richard. *John Hadlands Advice; or, A Warning for All Young Men That Have Meanes Advising Them to Forsake Lewd Company Cards, Dice, and Queanes, to the Tune of the Bonny Bonny Broome*. London, 1635.

Damiano da Odemia, Pedro. *The Pleasaunt and Wittie Playe of the Cheasts Renewed with Instructions Both to Learne It Easely, and to Play It Well*. Translated by William Ward. London, 1562.

Daneau, Lambert. *True and Christian Friendshippe . . .* Together Also with a Right Excellent Invectiue of the Same Author, Against the Wicked Exercise of Diceplay, and other Prophane Gaming. Translated by Thomas Newton. London, 1586.

Davies, Richard A., and Alan R. Young. "'Strange Cunning' in Thomas Middleton's *A Game at Chess*." *University of Toronto Quarterly* 45, no. 3 (1976): 236–45.

Dawson, Anthony B., and Paul Yachnin, *The Culture of Playgoing in Shakespeare's England: A Collaborative Debate*. Cambridge: Cambridge University Press, 2001.

de Certeau, Michel. *The Practice of Everyday Life* [vol. 1]. Translated by Steven Rendall. Berkeley: University of California Press, 1988 [1984].

de Grazia, Margreta. "The Motive for Interiority: Shakespeare's *Sonnets* and *Hamlet*." *Style* 23, no. 3 (1989): 430–44.

de Grazia, Margreta. "Teleology, Delay, and the 'Old Mole.'" *Shakespeare Quarterly* 50, no. 3 (1999): 251–67.

de Vroom, Theresia. "Female Heroism in Heywood's Tragic Farce of Adultery: *A Woman Killed with Kindness*." In *The Female Tragic Hero in English Renaissance Drama*, edited by Naomi Conn Liebler, 119–40. New York: Palgrave, 2002.

Delbridge, Matt. *Motion Capture in Performance: An Introduction*. Palgrave Pivot. Houndmills, Basingstoke, UK: Palgrave Macmillan, 2015.

Dessen, Alan C., and Leslie Thompson. *A Dictionary of Stage Directions in English Drama, 1580–1642*. Cambridge: Cambridge University Press, 2001.

Deutermann, Allison. *Listening for Theatrical Form in Early Modern England*. Edinburgh Critical Studies in Renaissance Culture. Edinburgh: Edinburgh University Press, 2016.

di Cesare, Mario A. "Introduction." In *The Game of Chess: Marco Girolamo Vida's "Scacchia ludus," with English Verse Translation and the Texts of the Three Earlier Versions*, edited by Mario A. di Cesare, 9–35. Nieuwkoop, The Netherlands: De Graaf, 1975.

Diamond, Elin. *Unmaking Mimesis: Essays on Feminism and Theatre*. London and New York: Routledge, 1997.

Dibbell, Julian. "Mutilated Furries, Flying Phalluses: Put the Blame on Griefers, the Sociopaths of the Virtual World." *Wired Magazine* 16, no. 2 (2008): 90–100. Available online at https://www.wired.com/2008/01/mf-goons/ (accessed 16 October 2017).

Dixon, Steve. *Digital Performance: A History of New Media in Theater, Dance, Performance Art, and Installation.* Cambridge, MA: MIT Press, 2007.

Dolan, Frances E. *Dangerous Familiars: Representations of Domestic Crime in England, 1550–1700.* Ithaca, NY: Cornell University Press, 1994.

Dolan, Frances E. *Marriage and Violence: The Early Modern Legacy.* Philadelphia: University of Pennsylvania Press, 2008.

Dolan, Frances E. "The Subordinate('s) Plot: Petty Treason and the Forms of Domestic Rebellion." *Shakespeare Quarterly* 43, no. 3 (1992): 317–40.

Dolan, Frances E. *True Relations: Reading, Literature, and Evidence in Seventeenth-Century England.* Philadelphia: University of Pennsylvania Press, 2013.

Downe, John. *Certaine Treatises of the Late Reverend and Learned Divine, Mr John Downe . . . Published at the Instance of His Friends.* Oxford, 1633.

Dreyfus, Hubert L. *What Computers Still Can't Do: A Critique of Artificial Reason.* Cambridge, MA: MIT Press, 1972.

du Val, P. "Les Tables de géographie réduites en un jeu ee cartes." In *A Collection of Maps of the World by P. du Val. Engraved by L. Cordier, J. F. D. Lapointe, J. Lhulier, N. Michu, J. Somer and I. Swelinck.* [Paris], 1660–76.

Ducharme, Lori J., and Gary Alan Fine. "No Escaping Obligation: Erving Goffman on the Demands and Constraints of Play." In *The Play of Self*, edited by Ronald Bogue and Mihai I. Spariosu, 89–111. Albany: SUNY Press, 1994.

Duncan, Douglas. "*Gammer Gurton's Needle* and the Concept of Humanist Parody." *Studies in English Literature, 1500–1900* 27, no. 2 (1987): 177–96.

Dutton, Richard. *Licensing, Censorship, and Authorship in Early Modern England: Buggeswords.* Houndmills, Basingstoke, UK and New York: Palgrave, 2000.

Dutton, Richard. "Thomas Middleton's *A Game at Chess*: A Case Study." In *The Cambridge History of British Theatre*, vol. 1: *Origins to 1660*, edited by Jane Milling and Peter Thomson, 424–38. Cambridge: Cambridge University Press, 2004.

Eales, Richard. *Chess: The History of a Game.* Glasgow: Hardinge Simpole, 2002 [1985].

Elam, Diane. *Feminism and Deconstruction: Ms. en abyme.* New York: Routledge, 1994.

Elam, Keir. *The Semiotics of Theatre and Drama.* 2nd ed. New Accents. London: Routledge, 2002.

Elyot, Thomas. *The Boke Named the Governour.* London, 1537.

England and Wales, Parliament of. *Committee Appointed by Parliament for the Navy and Customes Upon the Humble Complaints of Severall Poore Cardmakers of London.* London, 1643.

Evett, Marianne Brish, ed. *Henry Porter's Two Angry Women of Abington: A Critical Edition.* New York: Garland, 1980.

Falocco, Joe. *Reimagining Shakespeare's Playhouse: Early Modern Staging Conventions in the Twentieth Century.* Cambridge: D. S. Brewer, 2010.

Farber, Matthew. "Games in Education: Teacher Takeaways," *Edutopia* (9 October 2014), http://www.edutopia.org/blog/games-in-education-teacher-takeaways-matthew-farber (accessed 11 October 2015).

Faret, Nicolas. *The Honest Man; or, The Art to Please in Court.* Translated by Edward Grimeston: London, 1632.

Fenner, Dudley. *A Short and Profitable Treatise of Lawfull and Unlawfull Recreations, and of the Right Use and Abuse of Those That Are Lawfull.* London, 1590.

Finkenzeller, Roswin, Wilhelm Ziehr, and Emil M. Bührer. *Chess: A Celebration of 2,000 Years.* New York: Arcade/Little, Brown, 1990.

Fischer-Lichte, Erika. *The Transformative Power of Performance: A New Aesthetics.* Translated by Saskya Iris Jain. London: Routledge, 2008.

Fletcher, Walter Morley. "On Some Old Playing Cards Found in Trinity College." *Proceedings of the Cambridge Antiquarian Society* 11, no. 3 (1907): 454–64.

Floreale, Alba. *Game and Gaming Metaphor: Proteus and the Gamester Masks in Seventeenth-Century Conduct Books and the Comedy of Manners.* Biblioteca di Cultura. Rome: Bulzoni, 2004.

Florio, John. *Florio's Second Frutes.* London, 1591.

Ford, John R. "Changeable Taffeta: Re-Dressing the Bears in *Twelfth Night.*" In *Inside Shakespeare: Essays on the Blackfriars Stage,* edited by Paul Menzer, 174–91. Selinsgrove, PA: Susquehana University Press, 2006.

Foster, Susan Leigh. "Movement's Contagion: The Kinesthetic Impact of Performance." In *The Cambridge Companion to Performance Studies,* edited by Tracy C. Davis, 46–59. Cambridge: Cambridge University Press, 2008.

Foucault, Michel. "Questions on Geography." In *Power/Knowledge: Selected Interviews and Other Writings,* edited by Colin Gordon, translated by Colin Gordon et al., 63–77. New York: Pantheon, 1980.

Frasca, Gonzalo. "Videogames of the Oppressed: Critical Thinking, Education, Tolerance and Other Trivial Issues." In *First Person: New Media as Story, Performance, and Game,* edited by Noah Wardrip-Fruin and Pat Harrigan, 85–94. Cambridge, MA: MIT Press, 2004.

Freeman, Elizabeth. *Time Binds: Queer Temporalities, Queer Histories.* Durham, NC: Duke University Press, 2010.

Frey, Christopher, and Leanore Lieblein. "'My Breasts Sear'd': The Self-Starved Female Body and *A Woman Killed with Kindness.*" *Early Theatre* 7, no. 1 (2004): 45–66.

Fumerton, Patricia. "Not Home: Alehouses, Ballads, and the Vagrant Husband in Early Modern England." *Journal of Medieval and Early Modern Studies* 32, no. 3 (2002): 493–518.

G. B. *Ludus Scacchiae: Chesse-Play. A Game, Both Pleasant, Wittie, and Politicke . . . Translated out of the Italian into the English Tongue.* London, 1597.

Galloway, Alexander R. *Gaming: Essays on Algorithmic Culture.* Minneapolis: University of Minnesota Press, 2006.

Garner, Stanton B., Jr. *Bodied Spaces: Phenomenology and Performance in Contemporary Drama.* Ithaca, NY: Cornell University Press, 1994.

Gataker, Thomas. *A Just Defence of Certaine Passages in a Former Treatise Concerning the Nature and Use of Lots.* London, 1619.

Gayton, Edward. *Chartæ Scriptæ; or, A New Game at Cards Call'd Play by the Booke.* London, 1645.

Geertz, Clifford. "Deep Play: Notes on the Balinese Cockfight." In *The Interpretation of Cultures.* New York: Basic Books, 1972.

Giannachi, Gabriella, and Nick Kaye. *Performing Presence: Between the Live and the Simulated*. Manchester, UK: Manchester University Press, 2011.

Gillies, John. *Shakespeare and the Geography of Difference*. Cambridge Studies in Literature and Culture. Cambridge: Cambridge University Press, 1994.

Gitelman, Lisa. *Always Already New: Media, History, and the Data of Culture*. Cambridge, MA: MIT Press, 2006.

Gitelman, Lisa, and Geoffrey B. Pingree, eds. *New Media, 1740–1915*. Cambridge, MA: MIT Press, 2003.

Goffman, Erving. *Frame Analysis: An Essay on the Organization of Experience*. Cambridge, MA: Harvard University Press, 1974.

Goffman, Erving. *Interaction Ritual: Essays on Face-to-Face Behavior*. New York: Pantheon Books, 1967.

Goffman, Erving. *Strategic Interaction*. Philadelphia: University of Pennsylvania Press, 1969.

Goggin, Joyce. "A History of Otherness: Tarot and Playing Cards from Early Modern Europe," *Journal for the Academic Study of Magic* 1, no. 1 (2003): 45–74.

Gossett, Suzanne. "'I'll Look to Like': Arranged Marriages in Shakespeare's Plays." In *Sexuality and Politics in Renaissance Drama*, edited by Carole Levin and Karen Robertson, 57–74. Studies in Renaissance Literature. Lewiston, NY: Edwin Mellen Press, 1991.

Greco, Gioachino (Il Calabrese). *The Royall Game of Chesse-Play*. Translated by Francis Beale. London, 1656.

Green, Reina. "Open Ears, Appetite, and Adultery in *A Woman Killed with Kindness*." *English Studies in Canada* 31, no. 4 (2005): 53–74.

Greenberg, Marissa. "Signs of the Crimes: Topography, Murder, and Early Modern Domestic Tragedy." *Genre* 40, nos. 1–2 (2007): 1–29.

Gromala, Diana. "Response" (to Stuart Moulthrop, "From Work to Play: Molecular Cultures in the Time of Deadly Games," 56–69). In *First Person: New Media as Story, Performance, and Game*, edited by Noah Wardrip-Fruin and Pat Harrigan, 56–60. Cambridge, MA: MIT Press, 2004.

Grosart, Alexander Balloch, ed. *The Dr. Farmer Chetham Ms: Being a Commonplace-Book in the Chetham Library, Manchester*. 2 vols. Manchester: Chetham Society and Charles Simms, 1873.

Gurr, Andrew. "Bears and Players: Philip Henslowe's Double Acts." *Shakespeare Bulletin* 22, no. 4 (2004): 31–41

Gurr, Andrew. *Playgoing in Shakespeare's London*. 2nd ed. Cambridge: Cambridge University Press, 1996.

Gurr, Andrew, and Mariko Ichikawa. *Staging in Shakespeare's Theatres*. Oxford Shakespeare Topics. Oxford: Oxford University Press, 2000.

Gurr, Andrew, and Karoline Szatek. "Women and Crowds at the Theater." *Medieval and Renaissance Drama in England* 21 (2008): 157–69.

Gutierrez, Nancy A. "The Irresolution of Melodrama: The Meaning of Adultery in *A Woman Killed with Kindness*." *Exemplaria* 1, no. 1 (1989): 265–91.

Hall, Kim F. *Things of Darkness: Economies of Race and Gender in Early Modern England*. Ithaca, NY: Cornell University Press, 1995.

Halperin, David M. "Introduction: Among Men—History, Sexuality, and the Return of Affect." In *Love, Sex, Intimacy, and Friendship between Men, 1550–1800*, edited by Katherine O'Donnell and Michael O'Rourke, 1–11. New York: Palgrave, 2003.

Hansen, Mark B. N. *New Philosophy for New Media*. Cambridge, MA: MIT Press, 2004.

Hargrave, Catherine Perry. *A History of Playing Cards and a Bibliography of Cards and Gaming*. Reprint ed. New York: Dover, 1966 [1930].

Harris, Jonathan Gil. *Untimely Matter in the Time of Shakespeare*. Philadelphia: University of Pennsylvania Press, 2008.

Hartmann, John. "Garry Kasparov Is a Cyborg; or, What Chessbase Teaches Us about Technology." In *Philosophy Looks at Chess*, edited by Benjamin Hale, 39–64. Chicago: Open Court, 2008.

Harvey, P. D. A. "Board Games and Early Cartography." Paper presented at the International Conference on the History of Cartography, Newberry Library, Chicago, 25 June 1993.

Hedrick, Donald. "Real Entertainment: Sportification, Coercion, and Carceral Theater." In *Thunder at a Playhouse: Essaying Shakespeare and the Early Modern Stage*, edited by Peter Kanelos and Matt Kozusko, 50–66. Selinsgrove, PA: Susquehanna University Press, 2010.

Heinemann, Margot. *Puritanism and Theatre: Thomas Middleton and Opposition Drama under the Early Stuarts*. Cambridge: Cambridge University Press, 1980.

Helgerson, Richard. *Adulterous Alliances: Home, State, and History in Early Modern European Drama and Painting*. Chicago: University of Chicago Press, 2003.

Heylyn, Peter. *The History of the Sabbath*. London, 1636.

Heywood, Thomas. *A Woman Killed with Kindness*. Edited by Brian Scobie. New Mermaids. London: Methuen Drama, 2012.

Hobgood, Allison P. *Passionate Playgoing in Early Modern England*. Cambridge: Cambridge University Press, 2014.

Hodgdon, Barbara. *Shakespeare, Performance, and the Archive*. New York: Routledge, 2016.

Hoffmann, Detlef. *The Playing Card: An Illustrated History*. Translated by C. S. V. Salt, with Sylvia Mann. Greenwich, CT: New York Graphic Society Ltd., 1973.

Hogg, James. "An Ephemeral Hit: Thomas Middleton's *A Game at Chess*." In *Jacobean Drama as Social Criticism*, edited by James Hogg, 285–318. Salzburg University Studies. Lewiston, NY: Edwin Mellen Press, 1995.

Holme, Randle. *The Academy of Armory; or, A Storehouse of Armory and Blazon*. [1688]. Edited by Isaac Herbert Jeayes. Vol. 2. London: Roxburghe Club, 1905.

Hooper, David, and Kenneth Whyld. *The Oxford Companion to Chess*. 2nd ed. Oxford: Oxford University Press, 1996.

Hopkins, Lisa. "Maternity in *A Woman Killed with Kindness*." In *Performing Maternity in Early Modern England*, edited by Kathryn M. Montcrief and Kathryn R. McPherson, 73–84. Aldershot, UK: Ashgate, 2007.

Hornback, Robert. "'Holy Crap!': Scatalogical Iconoclasm in Tudor Evangelical Comedy." In *Thunder at a Playhouse: Essaying Shakespeare and the Early Modern Stage*, edited by Peter Kanelos and Matt Kozusko, 67–86. Selinsgrove, PA: Susquehanna University Press, 2010.

Howard, Jean E. *Shakespeare's Art of Orchestration: Stage Technique and Audience Response*. Urbana: University of Illinois Press, 1984.

Howard-Hill, T. H. *Middleton's "Vulgar Pasquin": Essays on "A Game at Chess."* Newark: University of Delaware Press, 1995.

Huhtamo, Erkki. "Dismantling the Fairy Engine: Media Archaeology as Topos Study." In *Media Archaeology: Approaches, Applications, and Implications*, edited by Erkki Huhtamo and Jussi Parikka, 27–47. Berkeley: University of California Press, 2011.

Huhtamo, Erkki. *Illusions in Motion: Media Archaeology of the Moving Panorama and Related Spectacles*. Cambridge, MA: MIT Press, 2013.

Huizinga, Johan. *Homo Ludens: A Study of the Play-Element in Culture*. Boston: Beacon Press, 1950.

Huntemann, Nina B., and Matthew Thomas Payne, eds. *Joystick Soldiers: The Politics of Play in Military Video Games*. New York: Routledge, 2010.

Husserl, Edmund. *On the Phenomenology of the Consciousness of Internal Time (1893–1917)*. Translated by John Barnett Brough. Dordrecht: Kluwer Academic, 1991.

Hutson, Lorna. *The Invention of Suspicion: Law and Mimesis in Shakespeare and Renaissance Drama*. Oxford: Oxford University Press, 2007.

Hutson, Lorna. *The Usurer's Daughter: Male Friendship and Fictions of Women in Sixteenth-Century England*. London: Routledge, 1994.

Ingram, R. W. "*Gammer Gurton's Needle*: Comedy Not Quite of the Lowest Order?" *Studies in English Literature, 1500–1900* 7, no. 2 (1967): 257–68.

Jacob, Christian. *The Sovereign Map: Theoretical Approaches in Cartography through History*. Edited by Edward H. Dahl. Translated by Tom Conley. Chicago: University of Chicago Press, 2006.

James I, King. *Basilikon Dōron; or, His Majesties Instructions to His Dearest Sonne, Henry the Prince*. London, 1603.

James I, King. . . . *Makers of Playing Cards within Our Realme of England*. London, 1615.

Jones, Steven E., and George K. Thiruvathukal. *Codename Revolution: The Nintendo Wii Platform*. Cambridge, MA: MIT Press, 2012.

Juul, Jesper. *A Casual Revolution: Reinventing Video Games and Their Players*. Cambridge, MA: MIT Press, 2010.

Kahn, Coppélia. "The Providential Tempest and the Shakespearean Family." In *Representing Shakespeare: New Psychoanalytic Essays*, edited by Murray M. Schwartz and Coppélia Kahn, 217–43. Baltimore: Johns Hopkins University Press, 1980.

Kastan, David Scott. "'The Duke of Milan / and His Brave Son': Old Histories and New in *The Tempest*." In *Shakespeare's Romances*, edited by Alison Thorne, 226–44. New Casebooks. Basingstoke, UK: Palgrave, 2003.

Kavanagh, Thomas M. *Dice, Cards, Wheels: A Different History of French Culture*. Philadelphia: University of Pennsylvania Press, 2005.

Kirby, Kathleen M. "Re: Mapping Subjectivity: Cartographic Vision and the Limits of Politics." In *BodySpace: Destabilizing Geographies of Gender and Sexuality*, edited by Nancy Duncan, 45–55. New York: Routledge, 1996.

Kittler, Friedrich A. *Discourse Networks 1800/1900*. Translated by Michael Metteer, with Chris Cullens. Stanford, CA: Stanford University Press, 1990 [1985].

Kittler, Friedrich A. *Gramophone, Film, Typewriter*. Translated by Geoffrey Winthrop-Young and Michael Wutz. Stanford, CA: Stanford University Press, 1999.

Kolve, V. A. *The Play Called "Corpus Christi."* Stanford, CA: Stanford University Press, 1966.

Kozel, Susan. *Closer: Performance, Technologies, Phenomenology*. Leonardo Book Series. Cambridge, MA: MIT Press, 2007.

Laroque, François. *Shakespeare's Festive World: Elizabethan Seasonal Entertainment and the Professional Stage*. Translated by Janet Lloyd. Cambridge: Cambridge University Press, 1991 [1988].

Latimer, Hugh. *Sermons on the Card and Other Discourses*. Edited by Henry Morley. Project Gutenberg [eBook no. 2458], 2005 [1883], http://www.gutenberg.org/files/2458/2458.txt.

Laurel, Brenda. *Computers as Theatre*. Reading, MA: Addison–Wesley, 1993.

Leggatt, Alexander. "*Arden of Faversham*." *Shakespeare Survey* 36 (1983): 121–33.

Leininger, Lorie Jerrell. "The Miranda Trap: Sexism and Racism in Shakespeare's *Tempest*." In *The Woman's Part: Feminist Criticism of Shakespeare*, edited by Carolyn Ruth Swift Lenz, Gayle Greene, and Carol Thomas Neely, 285–94. Urbana: University of Illinois Press, 1980.

Lieblein, Leanore. "The Context of Murder in English Domestic Plays, 1590–1610." *Studies in English Literature, 1500–1900* 23, no. 2 (1983): 181–96.

Liebler, Naomi Conn. *Shakespeare's Festive Tragedy: The Ritual Foundations of Genre*. New York: Routledge, 1995.

Limon, Jerzy. *Dangerous Matter: English Drama and Politics in 1623/24*. Cambridge: Cambridge University Press, 2010.

Lin, Erika T. "Popular Festivity and the Early Modern Stage: The Case of *George a Greene*." *Theatre Journal* 61, no. 2 (2009): 271–97.

Lockwood, Tom. "Introduction." In *Arden of Faversham*, 2nd ed., edited by Martin White, vii–xxxi. London: A & C Black, 2007.

Loomba, Ania. *Gender, Race, Renaissance Drama*. Manchester: Manchester University Press, 1989.

Lopez, Jeremy. *Theatrical Convention and Audience Response in Early Modern Drama*. Cambridge: Cambridge University Press, 2003.

Loughrey, Bryan, and Neil Taylor. "Ferdinand and Miranda at Chess." *Shakespeare Survey* 35 (1982): 113–18.

Love, Genevieve. "Performance Criticism without Performance: The Study of Non-Shakespearean Drama." In *New Directions in Renaissance Drama and Performance Studies*, edited by Sarah Werner, 131–46. New York: Palgrave Macmillan, 2010.

Low, Jennifer A. *Manhood and the Duel: Masculinity in Early Modern Drama and Culture*. New York: Palgrave Macmillan, 2003.

Lydgate, John. "The Debate of the Horse, Goose, and Sheep." *The Minor Poems of John Lydgate,* part 2: *Secular Poems,* edited by Henry Noble MacCracken, 539–65. London: Oxford University Press, for Early English Text Society. Available at https://archive.org/stream/TheMinorPoemsOfJohnLydgate2/ The_Minor_Poems_of_John_Lydgate_2#page/n174/mode/1up/search/ goose (accessed 25 October 2017).

MacFaul, Tom. *Male Friendship in Shakespeare and His Contemporaries.* Cambridge: Cambridge University Press, 2007.

Machon, Josephine. *Immersive Theatres: Intimacy and Immediacy in Contemporary Performance.* Basingstoke, UK: Palgrave Macmillan, 2013.

Marcus, Leah S. *The Politics of Mirth: Jonson, Herrick, Milton, Marvell and the Defense of Old Holiday Pastimes.* Chicago: University of Chicago Press, 1986.

Margolin, Jean-Claude, and Diana Wormuth. "Mathias Ringmann's *Grammatica figurata; or, Grammar as a Card Game.*" *Yale French Studies* 47 (1972): 33–46.

Marshall, Cynthia. "Wrestling as Play and Game in *As You Like It.*" *Studies in English Literature, 1500–1900* 33, no. 2 (1993): 265–87.

Masten, Jeffrey. *Textual Intercourse: Collaboration, Authorship, and Sexualities in Renaissance Drama.* Cambridge Studies in Renaissance Literature and Culture. Cambridge: Cambridge University Press, 1997.

Maus, Katharine Eisaman. "Horns of Dilemma: Jealousy, Gender and Spectatorship in English Renaissance Drama." *English Language History* 54, no. 3 (1987): 561–83.

McAuley, Gay. *Space in Performance: Making Meaning in the Theatre.* Theatre: Theory/Text/Performance. Ann Arbor: University of Michigan Press, 2000.

McClintock, Michael. "Grief, Theater and Society in Thomas Heywood's *A Woman Killed with Kindness.*" In *Speaking Grief in English Literary Culture: Shakespeare to Milton,* edited by Margo Swiss and David A. Kent, 98–118. Pittsburgh: Duquesne University Press, 2002.

McConachie, Bruce. *Engaging Audiences: A Cognitive Approach to Spectating in the Theatre.* Cognitive Studies in Literature and Performance. New York: Palgrave Macmillan, 2008.

McConachie, Bruce. "Using Cognitive Science to Understand Spatiality and Community in the Theater." *Contemporary Theatre Review* 12, no. 3 (2002): 97–114.

McCullen, Joseph T., Jr. "The Use of Parlor and Tavern Games in Elizabethan and Early Stuart Drama." *Modern Language Quarterly* 14, no. 1 (1953): 7–14.

McFadyen, N. Lindsay. "What Was Really Lost in *Gammer Gurton's Needle.*" *Renaissance Papers* (1982): 9–13.

Menzer, Paul. "The Actor's Inhibition: Early Modern Acting and the Rhetoric of Restraint." *Renaissance Drama* 35 (2006): 83–111.

Menzer, Paul. "Crowd Control." In *Imagining the Audience in Early Modern Drama, 1558–1642,* edited by Jennifer A. Low and Nova Myhill, 19–36. New York: Palgrave Macmillan, 2011.

Miah, Andy. "A Deep Blue Grasshopper: Playing Games with Artificial Intelligence." In *Philosophy Looks at Chess,* edited by Benjamin Hale, 13–23. Chicago: Open Court, 2008.

Middleton, Thomas. *A Game at Chess,* edited by T. H. Howard-Hill. The Revels Plays. Manchester: Manchester University Press, 1993.

Milburn, Colin. "Atoms and Avatars: Virtual Worlds as Massively-Multiplayer Laboratories." *Spontaneous Generations* 2, no. 1 (2008): 63–89.

Milburn, Colin. *Mondo Nano: Fun and Games in the World of Digital Matter*. Durham, NC: Duke University Press, 2015.

Miller, Kiri. *Playing Along: Digital Games, YouTube, and Virtual Performance*. Oxford Music/Media. New York and Oxford: Oxford University Press, 2012.

Mills, Lauren J. *One Soul in Bodies Twain: Friendship in Tudor Literature and Stuart Drama*. Bloomington, IN: Principia Press, 1937.

Moisan, Thomas. "Framing with Kindness: The Transgressive Theatre of *A Woman Killed with Kindness*." In *Essays on Transgressive Readings: Reading over the Lines*, edited by Georgia Johnston, 171–84. Lewiston, NY: Edwin Mellen Press, 1997.

Montaigne, Michel de. *The Essays of Michael Lord of Montaigne, . . . The First Booke, Volume 2*. Translated by John Florio. London: J. M. Dent, 1897.

Montrose, Louis A. "'Sport by Sport O'erthrown': *Love's Labour's Lost* and the Politics of Play." *Texas Studies in Literature and Language* 18, no. 4 (1977): 528–52.

Moore, John Robert. "The Contemporary Significance of Middleton's *Game at Chesse*." *PMLA* 50, no. 3 (1935): 761–8.

Morden, Robert. *Facsimile of Morden's Playing Cards*. Lympne Castle, Kent, UK: Harry Margary, 1972.

Moxon, Joseph. *The Use of the Astronomical Playing-Cards Teaching Any Ordinary Capacity by Them*. London, 1676.

Mukherji, Subha. *Law and Representation in Early Modern Drama*. Cambridge: Cambridge University Press, 2006.

Mullaney, Steven. *The Place of the Stage: License, Play, and Power in Renaissance England*. Chicago: University of Chicago Press, 1988.

Mullinger, James Bass. *The University of Cambridge*. Vol. 1 (of 3). Cambridge: University Press, 1873.

Murray, H. J. R. *A History of Board-Games Other than Chess*. Oxford: Clarendon Press, 1951.

Murray, H. J. R. *A History of Chess*. Reprint ed. London: Oxford at the Clarendon Press, 1962 [1913].

Murray, Janet H. *Hamlet on the Holodeck: The Future of Narrative in Cyberspace*. 2nd printing. Cambridge, MA: MIT Press, 1999.

Mussou, Amandine. "Playing with Memory: The Chessboard as a Mnemonic Tool in Medieval Didactic Literature." In *Chess in the Middle Ages and Early Modern Age: A Fundamental Thought Paradigm of the Premodern World*, edited by Daniel E. O'Sullivan, 187–97. Berlin: Walter de Gruyter, 2012.

Myhill, Nova. "Taking the Stage: Spectators as Spectacle in the Caroline Private Theaters." In *Imagining the Audience in Early Modern Drama, 1558–1642*, edited by Jennifer A. Low and Nova Myhill, 37–54. New York: Palgrave Macmillan, 2011.

Nardo, Anna K. *The Ludic Self in Seventeenth-Century English Literature*. Albany: SUNY Press, 1991.

Neely, Carol Thomas. *Distracted Subjects: Madness and Gender in Shakespeare and Early Modern Culture*. Ithaca, NY: Cornell University Press, 2004.

Neill, Michael. *Putting History to the Question: Power, Politics, and Society in English Renaissance Drama*. New York: Columbia University Press, 2000.

Neill, Michael. "'This Gentle Gentleman': Social Change and the Language of Status in *Arden of Faversham*." *Medieval and Renaissance Drama in England* 10 (1998): 73–97.

Netto, Jeffrey A. "Intertextuality and the Chess Motif: Shakespeare, Middleton, Greenaway." In *Shakespeare, Italy, and Intertextuality*, edited by Michele Marrapodi, 216–26. Manchester: Manchester University Press, 2004.

Neville, Henry. *Shuffling, Cutting, and Dealing in a Game at Picquet*. [London,], 1659.

Newman, Karen. *Cultural Capitals: Early Modern London and Paris*. Princeton, NJ: Princeton University Press, 2009.

Northbrooke, John. *A Treatise Wherein Dicing, Dauncing, Vaine Playes or Enterluds with Other Idle Pastimes &c. Commonly Used on the Sabboth Day, Are Reproved*. London, 1577.

Novy, Marianne L. "Patriarchy and Play in *The Taming of the Shrew*." *English Literary Renaissance* 9, no. 2 (1979): 264–80.

Olson, Glending. "Plays as Play: A Medieval Ethical Theory of Performance and the Intellectual Context of the *Tretise of Miraclis Pleyinge*." *Viator: Medieval and Renaissance Studies* 26 (1995): 195–221.

Orlin, Lena Cowen. *Private Matters and Public Culture in Post-Reformation England*. Ithaca, NY: Cornell University Press, 1994.

The Oxford English Dictionary. Online ed. Oxford: Oxford University Press.

Panek, Jennifer. "Punishing Adultery in *A Woman Killed with Kindness*." *Studies in English Literature, 1500–1900* 34, no. 2 (1994): 357–78.

Parikka, Jussi. *A Geology of Media*. Electronic Mediations. Minneapolis: University of Minnesota Press, 2015.

Parikka, Jussi. *What Is Media Archaeology?* Cambridge: Polity Press, 2012.

Parker-Starbuck, Jennifer. *Cyborg Theatre: Corporeal/Technological Intersections in Multimedia Performance*. Performance Interventions. New York: Palgrave Macmillan, 2014.

Parlett, David. *A Dictionary of Card Games*. Oxford: Oxford University Press, 1992.

Parlett, David. *The Oxford Guide to Card Games*. Oxford: Oxford University Press, 1990.

Parlett, David. *The Oxford History of Board Games*. Oxford: Oxford University Press, 1999.

Paster, Gail Kern. *The Body Embarrassed: Drama and the Disciplines of Shame in Early Modern England*. Ithaca, NY: Cornell University Press, 1993.

Paster, Gail Kern. *Humoring the Body: Emotions and the Shakespearean Stage*. Chicago: Chicago University Press, 2004.

Paster, Gail, Katherine Rowe, and Mary Floyd-Wilson, eds. *Reading the Early Modern Passions: Essays in the Cultural History of Emotion*. Philadelphia: University of Pennsylvania Press, 2004.

Pearce, Celia. *The Interactive Book: A Guide to the Interactive Revolution*. Indianapolis: Macmillan Technical, 1997.

Penny, Simon. "Representation, Enaction, and the Ethics of Simulation." In

First Person: New Media as Story, Performance, and Game, edited by Noah Wardrip-Fruin and Pat Harrigan, 73–84. Cambridge, MA: MIT Press, 2004.

Perry, Curtis. "Commodity and Commonwealth in *Gammer Gurton's Needle*." *Studies in English Literature, 1500–1900* 42, no. 2 (2002): 217–34.

Philpot, John. *A Prospective-Glasse for Gamesters; or, A Short Treatise against Gaming*. London, 1646.

Popat, Sita. "Missing in Action: Embodied Experience and Virtual Reality." *Theatre Journal* 68, no. 3 (2016): 357–78.

Postlewait, Thomas. "Theater Events and Their Political Contexts: A Problem in the Writing of Theater History." In *Critical Theory and Performance: Revised and Enlarged Edition*, edited by Janelle G. Reinelt and Joseph R. Roach, 198–222. Ann Arbor: University of Michigan Press, 2007.

Preiss, Richard. *Clowning and Authorship in Early Modern Theatre*. Cambridge: Cambridge University Press, 2014.

Preiss, Richard. "Interiority." In *Early Modern Theatricality*, edited by Henry S. Turner, 47–70. Oxford Twenty-First Century Approaches to Literature. Oxford: Oxford University Press, 2013.

Prynne, William, with Henry Burton. *The Lord's Day, the Sabbath Day*. London, 1636.

Rackin, Phyllis. "The Role of Audience in Shakespeare's *Richard II*." *Shakespeare Quarterly* 36, no. 3 (1985): 262–81.

Rancière, Jacques. *The Emancipated Spectator*. Translated by Gregory Elliott. London: Verso, 2011.

Rasskin-Gutman, Diego. *Chess Metaphors: Artificial Intelligence and the Human Mind*. Translated by Deborah Klosky. Cambridge, MA: MIT Press, 2009.

Rice, Richard. *An Invective against Vices, Taken for Vertue*. London, 1581.

Richardson, Catherine. *Domestic Life and Domestic Tragedy in Early Modern England: The Material Life of the Household*. Manchester: Manchester University Press, 2006.

Robertson, Adi. "Replacing VR and AR with 'Mixed Reality' is Good For Microsoft but Bad for the Rest of Us," The Verge (12 May 2017), https://www.theverge.com/2017/5/12/15625972/microsoft-build-windows-mixed-reality-hololens-vr-confusing (accessed 3 January 2018).

Robinson, J. W. "The Art and Meaning of *Gammer Gurton's Needle*." *Renaissance Drama* 14 (1983): 45–77.

Rokem, Freddie. "Dramaturgies of Exile: Brecht and Benjamin 'Playing' Chess and Go." *Theatre Research International* 37, no. 1 (2012): 5–19.

Rumbold, Kate. "From 'Access' to 'Creativity': Shakespeare Institutions, New Media, and the Language of Cultural Value." *Shakespeare Quarterly* 61, no. 3 (2010): 313–36.

S., Mr. *Gammer Gurton's Needle*. 2nd ed. Edited by Charles Whitworth. New Mermaids. New York: W. W. Norton, 1997.

Saariluoma, Pertti. *Chess Players' Thinking: A Cognitive Psychological Approach*. London: Routledge, 1995.

Sack, Daniel. *After Live: Possibility, Potentiality, and the Future of Performance*. Ann Arbor: University of Michigan Press, 2015.

Salen, Katie, and Eric Zimmerman. *Rules of Play: Game Design Fundamentals.* Cambridge, MA: MIT Press, 2004.

Sallaz, Jeffrey J. *The Labor of Luck: Casino Capitalism in the United States and South Africa.* Berkeley and Los Angeles: University of California Press, 2009.

Salter, Chris. *Entangled: Technology and the Transformation of Performance.* Cambridge, MA: MIT Press, 2010.

Sanchez, Melissa E. "Seduction and Service in *The Tempest.*" *Studies in Philology* 105, no. 1 (2008): 50–82.

Sanford, Rhonda Lemke. *Maps and Memory in Early Modern England: A Sense of Place.* New York: Palgrave, 2002.

Saul, Arthur. *The Famous Game of Chesse-Play, Truely Discovered, and All Doubts Resolved; So That by Reading This Small Booke Thou Shalt Profit More Than by the Playing a Thousand Mates. An Exercise Full of Delight; Fit for Princes, or Any Person of What Qualitie Soever.* London, 1614.

Saul, Arthur, with Jo. Barbier. *The Famous Game of Chesse-Play. Being a Princely Exercise; Wherin the Learner May Profit More by Reading of This Small Book, Then by Playing of a Thousand Mates. Now Augmented of Many Materiall Things Formerly Wanting, and Beautified with a Three-Fold Methode, Viz. Of the Chesse-Men, of the Chesse-Play, of the Chesse-Lawes.* London, 1640.

Schechner, Richard. *Performance Theory.* Revised ed. Routledge Classics. London: Routledge, 2003.

Schmidgall, Gary. "The Discovery at Chess in *The Tempest.*" *English Language Notes* 23, no. 4 (1986): 11–16.

Schneider, Rebecca. *Performing Remains: Art and War in Times of Theatrical Reenactment.* London: Routledge, 2011.

Scott-Warren, Jason. "When Theaters Were Bear-Gardens; or, What's at Stake in the Comedy of Humors." *Shakespeare Quarterly* 54, no. 1 (2003): 63–82.

Selinger, Evan. "Chess-Playing Computers and Embodied Grandmasters: In What Ways Does the Difference Matter." In *Philosophy Looks at Chess,* edited by Benjamin Hale, 65–87. Chicago: Open Court, 2008.

Semenza, Gregory M. Colón. *Sport, Politics, and Literature in the English Renaissance.* Newark: University of Delaware Press, 2003.

Shakespeare, William. *The Norton Shakespeare,* 2nd ed. Edited by Stephen Greenblatt. New York: W. W. Norton, 1997.

Shakespeare, William. *The Tempest.* Edited by Stephen Orgel. The Oxford Shakespeare. Oxford: Clarendon Press, 1987.

Shakespeare, William. *The Tempest.* Edited by Virginia Mason Vaughan and Alden T. Vaughan. London: Arden Shakespeare, 2000.

Shannon, Laurie. *Sovereign Amity: Figures of Friendship in Shakespearean Contexts.* Chicago: Chicago University Press, 2002.

Shepard, Alexandra. *Meanings of Manhood in Early Modern England.* Oxford: Oxford University Press, 2003.

Sherman, Jane. "The Pawns' Allegory in Middleton's *A Game at Chess.*" *Review of English Studies* 29, no. 114 (1978): 147–59.

Siegel, Paul. "Historical Ironies in *The Tempest.*" *Shakespeare-Jahrbuch* 119 (1983): 104–11.

Simons, Patricia. "(Check)Mating the Grand Masters: The Gendered, Sexualized Politics of Chess in Renaissance Italy." *Oxford Art Journal* 16, no. 1 (1993): 59–74.

Skura, Meredith Anne. *Shakespeare the Actor and the Purposes of Playing*. Chicago: Chicago University Press, 1993.

Slights, Jessica. "Rape and the Romanticization of Shakespeare's Miranda." *Studies in English Literature, 1500–1900* 41, no. 2 (2001): 357–79.

Smith, Bruce R. "Getting Back to the Library, Getting Back to the Body." In *Shakespeare and the Digital World: Redefining Scholarship and Practice*, edited by Christie Carson and Peter Kirwan, 24–32. Cambridge: Cambridge University Press, 2014.

Smith, Bruce R. *The Key of Green: Passion and Perception in Renaissance Culture*. Chicago: University of Chicago Press, 2009.

Smith, Bruce R. *Phenomenal Shakespeare*. Blackwell Manifestos. Chichester, UK: Wiley–Blackwell, 2010.

Smith, G. C. Moore. *College Plays Performed in the University of Cambridge*. Cambridge: Cambridge University Press, 1923.

Smoller, Laura A. "Playing Cards and Popular Culture in Sixteenth-Century Nuremberg." *Sixteenth Century Journal* 17, no. 2 (1986): 183–214.

Sofer, Andrew. *Dark Matter: Invisibility in Drama, Theater, and Performance*. Theatre: Theory/Text/Performance. Ann Arbor: University of Michigan Press, 2013.

Solem, Delmar E. "Some Elizabethan Game Scenes." *Educational Theatre Journal* 6, no. 1 (1954): 15–21.

Southern, Richard. *The Staging of Plays before Shakespeare*. London: Faber & Faber, 1973.

Sprunger, Keith L. "Ames, William (1576–1633)." In *Oxford Dictionary of National Biography*. Oxford: Oxford University Press, 2004–9.

Stern, Tiffany. "Taking Part: Actors and Audience on the Stage at Blackfriars." In *Inside Shakespeare: Essays on the Blackfriars Stage*, edited by Paul Menzer, 35–53. Selinsgrove, PA: Susquehanna University Press, 2006.

Stephens, Frederick G., and E. Hawkins, comps. *Catalogue of Prints and Drawings in the British Museum, Division 1: Political and Personal Satires*, vol. 1. (1320–1689). London: Chiswick Press, 1870.

Stewart, Alan. *Close Readers: Humanism and Sodomy in Early Modern England*. Princeton, NJ: Princeton University Press, 1997.

Stubbes, Phillip. *The Anatomie of Abuses*. London, 1583.

Sturgess, Keith, ed. *Three Elizabethan Domestic Tragedies: Arden of Faversham, A Yorkshire Tragedy, A Woman Killed with Kindness*. Harmondsworth, Middlesex, UK: Penguin, 1985.

Suits, Bernard. *The Grasshopper: Games, Life, and Utopia*. Toronto: University of Toronto Press, 1978.

Sullivan, Garrett A., Jr. *The Drama of Landscape: Land, Property, and Social Relations on the Early Modern Stage*. Stanford, CA: Stanford University Press, 1998.

Sutton, John. "Batting, Habit and Memory: The Embodied Mind and the Nature of Skill." *Sport in Society: Cultures, Commerce, Media, Politics* 10, no. 5 (2007): 763–86.

Taffin, Jean. *The Amendment of Life*. London, 1595.

Taylor, Diana. *The Archive and the Repertoire: Performing Cultural Memory in the Americas*. Durham, NC: Duke University Press, 2003.

Taylor, E. S. *The History of Playing Cards, with Anecdotes of Their Use in Conjuring, Fortune-Telling, and Card-Sharping*. Rutland, VT: Charles E. Tuttle, 1973.

Taylor, Gary. "Introduction to *A Game at Chesse:* An Early Form." In *Thomas Middleton: The Collected Works*, edited by Gary Taylor and John Lavagnino, 1773–1779. Oxford: Clarendon Press, 2007.

Taylor, Gary. "Introduction to *A Game at Chesse:* A Later Form," in *Thomas Middleton: The Collected Works*, edited by Gary Taylor and John Lavagnino, 1825–1828. Oxford: Clarendon Press, 2007.

Taylor, Gary. "Introduction to [Apparatus for] *A Game at Chesse:* A Later Form." In *Thomas Middleton and Early Modern Textual Culture: A Companion to the Collected Works*, edited by Gary Taylor and John Lavagnino, 912-915. Oxford: Clarendon Press, 2007.

Taylor, John. *Taylor's Goose*. London, 1621.

Taylor, Mark N. "How Did the Queen Go Mad?" In *Chess in the Middle Ages and Early Modern Age: A Fundamental Thought Paradigm of the Premodern World*, edited by Daniel E. O'Sullivan, 169–83. Berlin: Walter de Gruyter, 2012.

Tooley, R. V. *Geographical Oddities; or, Curious, Ingenious, and Imaginary Maps and Miscellaneous Plates Published in Atlases*. London: Map Collectors' Circle, 1963.

Traub, Valerie. "History in the Present Tense: Feminist Theories, Spatialized Epistemologies, and Early Modern Embodiment." In *Mapping Gendered Routes and Spaces in the Early Modern World*, edited by Merry E. Weiser-Hanks, 15–53. Burlington, VT: Ashgate, 2015.

Traub, Valerie. "The Nature of Norms in Early Modern England: Anatomy, Cartography, *King Lear*." *South Central Review* 26, no. 1–2 (2009): 42–81.

Traub, Valerie. *The Renaissance of Lesbianism in Early Modern England*. Cambridge Studies in Renaissance Literature and Culture. Cambridge: Cambridge University Press, 2002.

Tribble, Evelyn B. *Cognition in the Globe: Attention and Memory in Shakespeare's Theatre*. New York: Palgrave Macmillan, 2011.

Tribble, Evelyn B., and John Sutton. "Minds in and out of Time: Memory, Embodied Skill, Anachronism, and Performance." *Textual Practice* 26, no. 4 (2012): 587–607.

Turner, Henry S. *The English Renaissance Stage: Geometry, Poetics, and the Practical Spatial Arts 1580–1630*. Oxford: Oxford University Press, 2006.

Turner, Henry S. "*King Lear* Without: The Heath." *Renaissance Drama* 28 (1997): 161–93.

Turner, Henry S. "Literature and Mapping in Early Modern England, 1520–1688." In *Cartography in the Renaissance, Part I*, edited by David Woodward, 412–26. Chicago: University of Chicago Press, 2007.

von Hilgers, Philipp. *War Games: A History of War on Paper*. Translated by Ross Benjamin. Cambridge, MA: MIT Press, 2012.

Wagner, Matthew D. *Shakespeare, Theatre, and Time*. New York: Routledge, 2011.

Walker, Gilbert. *Mihil Mumchance, His Discoverie of the Art of Cheating in False*

Dyce Play, and Other Unlawfull Games: With a Discourse of the Figging Craft. London, 1597.

Wall, Wendy. *Staging Domesticity: Household Work and English Identity in Early Modern Drama.* Cambridge Studies in Renaissance Literature and Culture. Cambridge: Cambridge University Press, 2002.

Walsh, Brian. "'Unkind Division': The Double Absence of Performing History in 1 Henry VI." *Shakespeare Quarterly* 55, no. 2 (2004): 119–47.

Wardrip-Fruin, Noah, and Pat Harrigan, eds. *First Person: New Media as Story, Performance, and Game.* Cambridge, MA: MIT Press, 2004.

Weimann, Robert. *Author's Pen and Actor's Voice: Playing and Writing in Shakespeare's Theatre,* edited by Helen Higbee and William West. Cambridge Studies in Renaissance Literature and Culture. Cambridge: Cambridge University Press, 2000.

Weimann, Robert. *Shakespeare and the Popular Tradition in the Theater: Studies in the Social Dimension of Dramatic Form and Function,* edited by Robert Schwartz. Baltimore: Johns Hopkins University Press, 1978.

Wells, Robin Headlam. *Shakespeare on Masculinity.* Cambridge: Cambridge University Press, 2000.

West, William N. "Replaying Early Modern Performances." In *New Directions in Renaissance Drama and Performance Studies,* edited by Sarah Werner, 30–50. New York: Palgrave Macmillan, 2010.

Whigham, Frank. *Seizures of the Will in Early Modern English Drama.* Cambridge Studies in Renaissance Literature and Culture. Cambridge: Cambridge University Press, 1996.

White, Gareth. *Audience Participation in Theatre: Aesthetics of the Invitation.* New York: Palgrave Macmillan, 2013.

Whiting, B. J. "Diccon's French Cousin." *Studies in Philology* 42, no. 1 (1945): 31–40.

Whitney, Charles. *Early Responses to Renaissance Drama.* Cambridge: Cambridge University Press, 2006.

W[ilcox], T[homas]. *A Glasse for Gamesters: And Namelie for Suche as Delight in Cards & Dise.* London, 1581.

Willis, Deborah. "Shakespeare's *The Tempest* and the Discourse of Colonialism." *Studies in English Literature* 29, no. 2 (1989): 277–89.

Willshire, William Hughes. *A Descriptive Catalogue of Playing and Other Cards in the British Museum.* London: Trustees of the British Museum, 1876.

Wilson, Mark. "Exclusive: Microsoft Has Stopped Manufacturing the Kinect," *Co.Design* (25 October 2017), https://www.fastcodesign.com/90147868/exclusive-microsoft-has-stopped-manufacturing-the-kinect (accessed 3 January 2018).

Wine, M. L., ed. *The Tragedy of Master Arden of Faversham.* The Revels Plays. London: Methuen, 1973.

Wiseman, Susan. "Introduction" to Thomas Middleton, *The Nice Valour; or, The Passionate Madman,* edited by Gary Taylor. In *Thomas Middleton: The Collected Works,* edited by Gary Taylor and John Lavagnino, 1679–83. Manchester: Manchester University Press, 1993.

Wither, George. *Prosopopoeia Britannicus: Britan's Genius, or Good-Angel, Person-*

ated; Reasoning and Advising, Touching the Games Now Playing, and the Adventures Now at Hazard in These Islands. London, 1648.

Wizisla, Erdmut. *Walter Benjamin and Bertolt Brecht: The Story of a Friendship*. Translated by Christine Shuttleworth. New Haven: Yale University Press, 2009 [2004].

Wood, Thomas. "The Seventeenth Century English Casuists on Betting and Gambling." *Church Quarterly Review* 149, no. 248 (1950): 159–74.

Woodbridge, Linda. "'He Beats Thee 'Gainst the Odds': Gambling, Risk Management, and *Antony and Cleopatra*." In *Antony and Cleopatra: New Critical Essays*, edited by Sara Munson Deats, 193–211. New York: Routledge, 2004.

Worthen, W. B. "Interactive, Immersive, Original Shakespeare," *Shakespeare Bulletin*, special issue on "Shakespeare and Performance Studies: A Dialogue," eds. Susan Bennett and Gina Bloom, 35, no. 3 (2017): 407–24.

Worthen, W. B. *Shakespeare and the Authority of Performance*. Cambridge: Cambridge University Press, 1997.

Worthen, W. B. *Shakespeare and the Force of Modern Performance*. Cambridge: Cambridge University Press, 1998.

Worthen, W. B. *Shakespeare Performance Studies*. Cambridge: Cambridge University Press, 2014.

Wright, Louis B. "The Male-Friendship Cult in Thomas Heywood's Plays." *Modern Language Notes* 42, no. 8 (1927): 510–14.

Yachnin, Paul. "*A Game at Chess* and Chess Allegory." *Studies in English Literature, 1500–1900* 22, no. 2 (1982): 317–30.

Yachnin, Paul. *Stage-Wrights: Shakespeare, Jonson, Middleton, and the Making of Theatrical Value*. Philadelphia: University of Pennsylvania Press, 1997.

Zielinski, Siegfried. *Deep Time of the Media: Toward an Archaeology of Hearing and Seeing by Technical Means*. Translated by Gloria Custance. Cambridge, MA: MIT Press, 2006.

Zimmerman, Eric. "Play as Research: The Interactive Design Process." Final Draft, 8 July 2003, http://static1.squarespace.com/static/579b8aa26b8f5b8f49605c96/t/59921253cd39c3da5bd27a6f/1502745178453/Iterative_Design.pdf (accessed 18 October 2017).

Index